12943754

 **W9-BBF-660**

WITHDRAWN
NDSU

NORTH DAKOTA
STATE UNIVERSITY

NOV 10 1986

LIBRARY

Guide to Popular
U.S. Government Publications

Guide to
Popular U.S.
Government Publications

Compiled by
LeRoy C. Schwarzkopf

Libraries Unlimited, Inc.

Littleton, Colorado   1986

Copyright © 1986 Libraries Unlimited, Inc.
All Rights Reserved
Printed in the United States of America

No part of this publication may be reproduced, stored in a retrieval system, or transmitted, in any form or by any means, electronic, mechanical, photocopying, recording, or otherwise, without the prior written permission of the publisher.

LIBRARIES UNLIMITED, INC.
P.O. Box 263
Littleton, Colorado 80160-0263

Library of Congress Cataloging-in-Publication Data

Schwarzkopf, LeRoy C.
    Guide to popular U.S. government publications.

    Includes indexes.
    1. United States--Government publications--
Bibliography.   I. Title.
Z1223.Z7S34   1986   [J83]   015.73'053   85-28444
ISBN 0-87287-452-4

Libraries Unlimited books are bound with Type II nonwoven material that meets and exceeds National Association of State Textbook Administrators' Type II nonwoven material specifications Class A through E.

Table of Contents

Introduction

Guide to Popular U.S. Government Publications is a complete revision of the second edition in this series, *New Guide to Popular Government Publications* (Libraries Unlimited, 1978) compiled by Walter L. Newsome. The first edition compiled by L. C. Pohle was titled *A Guide to Popular Government Publications for Libraries and Home Reference* (Libraries Unlimited, 1972). The title has been changed to reflect the fact that this is a guide to publications issued by the United States government, as was indeed the case in the two earlier editions. The primary selection criteria for the approximately twenty-nine hundred titles in this edition remain currency or long-term popular interest.

This compilation primarily includes publications which have been issued since June 1978, which was the approximate cutoff date for the previous edition. Publications issued before that date are included, but only if they are still in print and for sale by the Superintendent of Documents. The purpose and format of this edition remain similar to those of the 1978 edition. In general, the same topics have been used for the organization of this volume; however, some topics have been deleted, and others have been added due to political, social, and technological developments and the publishing activity of federal agencies. A major change in topical arrangement has involved establishing as separate main topics a number of subjects which appeared as subtopics in the earlier edition. For example, in the earlier edition "Children" appeared as a subtopic of "Family Living," "Foods" as a subtopic of "Home Management," and "Gardening" as a subtopic of "Agriculture." In this edition all these subjects appear as main topics.

Entries are again arranged alphabetically by titles under main topics and subtopics, and include information on date of publication, pagination, illustrations, stock number, price, and Superintendent of Documents (SuDocs) classification number. However, the following additional information appears in the citations, where appropriate and available: issuing agency, series, and publication number; and the presence of charts, maps, or tables is specifically indicated. The following two appendices have been deleted: "Popular Government Publications in Reprint: A Guide to Selected Commercial Editions" and "Directory of Agencies Distributing Listed Publications Not Sold by GPO." "Selected Guides to Government Audiovisual Resources" has been moved to the regular listing as a main topic.

In the previous edition the issuing agency was indicated only for non-GPO publications by cross-references to the second deleted appendix mentioned above. However, it was indirectly referenced by the SuDocs classification number. Knowledge of the issuing agency is important and valuable for several reasons. As a general rule, personal authors are not significant in government publishing and bibliography, and they have not been included in the citation. The issuing agency, therefore, may be the only source from which to obtain the publication or to obtain a free copy. For the address of an agency, the reader should consult *The United States Government Manual* (entry 1554). In addition, the issuing agency provides a clue both to the treatment accorded the subject of the publication and to the degree of authoritativeness. It also provides a clue as to which agencies have a responsibility for, or an interest in, publishing materials on the topic and are thus a source for seeking additional information on a particular topic, or later edition.

The purpose of this volume remains to point out some of the more interesting and useful inexpensive publications that are sold by the Government Printing Office (GPO), or that may in some cases be available free from the issuing agency or from the Consumer Information Center. At the same time, it is hoped that anyone not familiar with U.S. government publications as sources of information on almost any conceivable subject will gain some insight into the wide variety of materials available. The reader should first consult the table of contents for broad subjects which may be of interest. References to more specific subjects will be found in the subject and title indexes.

With regard to selection criteria, two problems had to be addressed. What is a "popular" government publication, and among the large number of "popular" government publications issued each year, which deserve listing in this guide? A number of subjective judgments have been made by the compiler: A "popular" government publication is generally one devoted to a topic of broad interest to a large segment of the general public. Furthermore, the treatment of the subject in that publication is geared to the general reader, rather than to the professional or technician. Thus, one will find in this volume a number of publications on food and nutrition, gardening, health care, and recreation. The compiler has also included titles which he believes the general public should be interested in or have knowledge of.

The basis for selection were those U.S. government publications distributed to federal depository libraries in paper format. The compiler was for many years the depository librarian at a regional depository which is required by law to receive all publications distributed by the Government Printing Office under the program. Every depository shipping list from 1 July 1978 was screened for eligible titles. For earlier titles which are still in print and sold by the Superintendent of Documents, all current Subject Bibliographies as well as the *GPO Sales Publications Reference File (PRF)* were screened. Approximately twenty thousand titles in paper format are distributed each year to depository libraries.

Several significant developments since 1978 have affected the types and number of government publications and their availability. Certainly it should be mentioned that the day of the nickel and dime (or even quarter) government publication has long since passed. A major reason is, of course, inflation, but a significant contribution resulted from the establishment of the United States Postal Service in 1971 which forced the GPO to pay full postage cost for its sales publications operation. Previously, the GPO reimbursed the Post Office Department for only a fraction of the true costs and the remaining costs were subsidized. As a result the average cost of U.S. government publications quickly doubled and tripled in the early 1970s. The appropriations committees of Congress meanwhile forced the GPO to make the sales program self-supporting, where formerly any deficits had been subsidized. The GPO also adopted a policy of establishing a minimum price for a publication, which rose from $1.00 in the mid 1970s to $2.50 in the early 1980s. Thus the hardest hit were the former nickel and dime thin pamphlets (many ten pages or less) which became grossly overpriced. The GPO also made frequent changes to its pricing structure—always higher—and repriced not only newly issued publications but also those already in stock. Thus, with prices "subject to change" one could not be sure of the exact price of the publication at the time of ordering.

Some of these excesses were corrected by the GPO under Public Printer Danford L. Sawyer, Jr. (1981-1984). In April 1983 he endorsed the recommendations of a task force which he appointed to develop improved methods of pricing and distribution. Most of the recommendations were implemented 1 October 1983. Among the more significant policy changes was that paper copy publications would be available for sale over an eighteen-month period, and once priced and in inventory would keep their original price until sold. However, subscriptions for serials and loose-leaf services may be repriced each year. The other recommendation which particularly affected "popular" publications in a positive manner dealt with pricing of small publications. The minimum price was eliminated, and more consideration was given to the size of a publication in establishing its price. An example of this policy is the reduction in price for single copies of *Background Notes* from $2.00 to $1.00 each. However, another policy established by Sawyer instigated a reduction in the number of titles available for sale by the GPO. Sawyer significantly raised the criterion for the minimum amount of expected sales before a title would be accepted for the sales publications program. This reduced the average number of active titles in the GPO sales inventory from approximately twenty thousand to approximately sixteen thousand. He also reduced the average number of copies per title entered into the inventory with the result a title may go out of print sooner. Sawyer also attempted unsuccessfully to close most of the GPO bookstores. On the other hand, Sawyer established a marketing section to promote the sale of government publications, and under his tenure was begun the publication of *U.S. Government Books* (entry 1733), a quarterly annotated, illustrated listing of new and in-print popular publications, and *New Books* (entry 1731), a bimonthly listing of all new titles added to the sales publications program.

The policies of the Reagan administration have had a significant effect on government publications. On 20 April 1981, President Reagan directed federal agencies to "eliminate wasteful spending on government periodicals, pamphlets, and audiovisual products." This policy was implemented by Office of Management and Budget *Bulletin* 81-16. The effects of this economy move were felt in several ways. First, the number of titles produced by government agencies was reduced. Secondly, the number of printed copies of a single title was reduced. This reduction was usually made in the amount distributed free to the general public automatically or upon request. Probably the hardest hit was the Department of Agriculture (USDA) with its extensive catalog of Home and Garden Bulletins and other series of consumer-oriented publications. Not only was the number of new titles and revisions reduced, but also abolished was the previous USDA generous policy of distributing free publications.

In addition to such economy measures, the Reagan administration is attempting to reduce the number of publications through its implementation of the Paperwork Reduction Act of 1980. On 15 March 1985, the Office of Management and Budget published in the *Federal Register* (pp. 10734-47) for comment a draft circular, "Management of Information Resources." It sets forth a policy which would severely limit publication and dissemination of information, would place primary reliance on the private sector, and would count on users' fees to recover costs.

I should like to acknowledge the support and assistance of the following librarians and officials who made available to me the collections of U.S. government publications under their jurisdiction: Mark Scully, director, Library Programs Service, and Parker Covington, chief, Depository Distribution Service, Government Printing Office; Agnes Ferruso, chief, Government Publications Section, Serial and Government Publications Division, Library of Congress; and Lola Warren, head, Government Documents and Maps Room, University of Maryland Libraries.

Getting the Most from This Guide

Readers will gain more from this guide by understanding the items in the citations for each numbered entry, and how and why some modifications of standard cataloging and bibliographical practices have been made. A complete citation contains these items in the following order: title, number of volumes or parts, issuing agency, imprint statement, collation statement, series statement, publication number, stock number (S/N) and price for GPO sales publications, and Superintendent of Documents (SuDocs) Classification number.

Title. The full title as found on the title page (or cover) of the publication is normally presented. Subtitles found on the title page are also entered. This is the title used in normal cataloging practice, and found in official as well as commercial catalogs. The title index contains references to both main titles and subtitles. The title is the first item in the citation except in the case of two subtopics ("Federal Agencies: History, Organization, Service" and "Government Property: Purchase and Sales") and the Appendix ("Publications Catalogs"). In these cases the issuing agency is used as the first item in the citation, followed by the title.

Issuing Agency. The issuing agency is normally the corporate author which not only prepared, but also published the title. Normally, the bureau or comparable unit within an executive department which issued the title is listed, and not the executive department itself, and not other intermediate or lower-level units in the organizational hierarchy. For example, the National Cancer Institute (NCI) is indicated as the issuing agency; and not included in the citation are the Department of Health and Human Services, Public Health Service, and National Institutes of Health of which NCI is a subordinate agency. The reader may obtain clues as to those other agencies in the government hierarchy by interpreting the SuDocs Classification number. The direct form, which is usually the official form, is used for the agency name rather than the inverted form which is the practice in the *Monthly Catalog of U.S. Government Publications*: i.e., "Bureau of the Census" is used rather than "Census Bureau." Names of personal authors have not been entered.

Imprint Statement. In normal cataloging practice, the imprint statement usually includes the place of publication, publisher, and date of publication. The imprint statement in this volume consists only of the date of publication—indicating revised ("Rev.") and reprinted ("repr.") publications. For most U.S. government publications available to the public, the place of publication is Washington, D.C. (or its Maryland and Virginia suburbs). The publisher is normally the issuing agency—though in general cataloging practice the Government Printing Office is usually listed as publisher despite the fact that it is, in reality, the printer, not the publisher.

In normal cataloging practice only the year of publication is listed. This volume lists the month as well as the year when the month is indicated on the title page. This serves to more positively identify a publication, particularly a revision, and serves better to indicate the timeliness of a publication. Many government titles are frequently revised, some several times within the same year. If the title page contains an edition statement, that is listed here. If this statement indicates that the publication is a revision, there is an excellent chance the title may be revised again. Revisions through June 1985 are listed.

In lieu of the year of publication, the imprint may contain a statement of issuing frequency for periodicals (i.e., weekly, monthly, quarterly, etc.). In the case of serials issued at less frequent intervals, (i.e., annually, biennially, etc.) the latest edition published is presented and the issuing frequency is indicated as the first statement in the annotation.

Collation Statement. In normal cataloging practice, the collation statement usually includes the number of pages and the presence of illustrations. The number of pages for entries in this volume includes the pages in the main text with arabic numbers, plus the pages in the introductory material with small roman numerals, as well as uniquely numbered appendix pages. The number of pages for a periodical title is the average number of pages per issue over the last two years.

Usually the abbreviation "ill." is used broadly to include all types of illustrations. In this volume, the abbreviation "ill." is used in the narrow sense to include only photographs, portraits, sketches, and drawings, and not to designate charts, maps, and tables—their existence is specifically designated.

Also found in the collation may be a statement that the publication is a "folder" in which case the number of pages indicates the number of panels or folded sections on which text and/or illustrations appear.

Series Statement and Publication Number. This volume has added information on series and publication number where pertinent. This provides additional information to identify the publication more precisely, particularly if one is requesting a copy from an issuing agency. The *Monthly Catalog* also provides indexes by series and publication numbers.

Stock Number and Price. The stock number (S/N) and price are provided for publications which were in print and sold by the Superintendent of Documents as of May 1985. The amount is the domestic price for a single paper copy unless indicated otherwise, such as for "cloth" (i.e., bound volume with cloth cover), or "microfiche." In the case of periodicals and subscription (loose-leaf) services sold by the GPO, the price for an annual subscription is shown as well as the price for a single copy if available. Also shown is the order symbol for periodicals and subscription services, which the GPO prefers on orders since orders for single copy publications are handled separately from those for periodicals and subscription services. If a price is listed without a stock number, the publication is sold by the issuing agency and order information is provided in the annotation for that entry.

Superintendent of Documents Classification Number. The Superintendent of Documents (SuDocs) Classification number not only provides a standard, nationally recognized filing and identification number, its shorthand notation also provides information on the issuing agency, the publication series, and the issue number for serials. The normal SuDocs Classification number consists of three elements: the author symbol, the series symbol, and the book number. The author symbol is the combination of letter(s) and number(s) which appear before the first period, followed by the series symbol. The book number appears to right of the colon which separates it from the series symbol. For example in the SuDocs number **L2.3:2223**, the author symbol is **L2** (Bureau of Labor Statistics, a subordinate unit of the Department of Labor); the series symbol is **.3** (bulletin); and the book number is **2223** (bulletin 2223). A book number of **15/3** would indicate volume 15, issue 3 of a periodical. The combination of the author and series symbols (which appears before the colon) is called the *class stem*. A complete list of current class stems of publications series will be found in the quarterly *List of Classes of United States Government Publications Available for Selection by Depository Libraries* (entry 1729), which is now available as a subscription sales item from the GPO.

The *Monthly Catalog* is arranged in SuDocs Classification number order. Many commercial publications and services on U.S. government documents include the SuDocs number in their citations. Most depository libraries (as well as other libraries with extensive collections) keep many, or most of their U.S. government publications in a separate collection and file them by SuDocs Classification number.

Annotations. The brief annotations include several items which are uniformly entered, as appropriate. A statement on the frequency of serials published semiannually or at greater intervals is found at the beginning of the annotation. At the end of the annotation is indicated the existence of bibliographies, lists of references, footnote references, and indexes. The annotations are descriptive, rather than evaluative. The titles (and subtitles), of course, also provide information as to the contents or value of the title. For additional clues as to the extent, type, or authoritativeness of the treatment of a subject, readers should note the number of pages, the series in which the material is published, and the issuing agency or author.

Acquiring and Using U.S. Government Publications

For readers interested in acquiring their own copy of U.S. government publications, the main source is the Government Printing Office, either through mail order or from a GPO bookstore. Other acquisition sources are the issuing agencies and the Consumer Information Center. For readers interested in using publications, the main source is the depository library system which is discussed on pages xxvi-xxvii.

As noted previously, approximately twenty thousand titles are distributed annually in paper copy format to depository libraries, and an additional twenty-five thousand titles or more are distributed annually in microfiche format to depository libraries. However, only a small fraction of these titles, approximately 10 percent of the titles distributed in paper format, are made available for sale to the public by the Superintendent of Documents. As noted above, under former Public Printer Danford L. Sawyer, Jr., policies were established to increase the minimum sales criterion for a title to be included thereby decreasing the number of titles added to the sales program. However, GPO has under consideration a plan to make available for sale in microfiche copy, or "blowback" (i.e., photocopy) any publication for which GPO has either obtained a master microfiche from the issuing agency or has produced a master microfiche for the depository library or international exchange programs. At present some GPO publications are distributed to depository libraries only in microfiche format (e.g., congressional bills and resolutions), or are available in both paper and microfiche format (e.g., congressional hearings and prints). However, readers should not expect prices for these reproduced copies to be the same (or in the same range) as those for the original or similar printed paper copies. The cost will probably be much higher and similar to the pricing of National Technical Information Service-furnished paper copy publications.

Most publications sold by the GPO are sold through mail order. The following information is offered to provide the best service and the quickest response time. Whenever possible use GPO preprinted mail-order forms. These will be found in GPO catalogs including the *Monthly Catalog, New Books,* and *U.S. Government Books,* in Subject Bibliographies, and in GPO sales flyers. They contain spaces for all essential order information, and usually afford the purchaser space to fill in a shipping label which saves the GPO time in processing.

Orders should be sent to Superintendent of Documents, U.S. Government Printing Office, Washington, DC 20402. For each publication ordered (whether on preprinted form or separate letter) include the STOCK NUMBER, TITLE, and PRICE. In case of multiple copies of the name title, include the number of copies, unit price, and total price. Full payment should accompany the order, either by money order or by personal check drawn on a bank located in the United States, Canada, or United States possessions and made payable to "Superintendent of Documents." Do not send cash or postage stamps. However, purchases may now be made by either VISA or MasterCard credit cards. Include the credit card number, expiration date (month/year), and name as listed on the credit card. Credit card purchases may also be placed by telephone to any GPO bookstore or to the order desk in Washington, D.C. Volume purchasers should consider establishing a GPO Deposit Account. With the exception of certain publications and subscriptions, a discount of 25 percent is allowed on orders of one hundred or more copies of a single title mailed to one address. A discount of 25 percent is also applicable on orders from book dealers, for orders of any quantity, mailed to the dealer's business address.

Subscriptions to government periodicals and subscription services (i.e., those listed in *Price List 36*) should be submitted on a separate order form or letter from orders for regular publications. For subscription orders, use the order symbol in lieu of the stock number. Subscriptions are processed in a different manner than regular publications, and mixing the two will only delay the orders.

For international customers, mailing regulations require special handling for orders mailed to addresses outside the United States or its possessions (except of course to U.S. military addresses) for which the GPO charges an additional 25 percent of the domestic price. Advance payment is required by one of the methods indicated above. Foreign checks and foreign currency will not be accepted. The GPO will accept remittance by UNESCO coupons or by International Postal Money Order made payable to the Superintendent of Documents. All orders must be submitted in English. Orders will be sent by surface mail unless otherwise requested and GPO contacted in advance for the total cost of the order.

In order to check on availability and current price consult the *GPO Sales Publications Reference File* (entry 1728) which is distributed to most depository libraries on a bimonthly basis. GPO bookstores also have a copy of the *PRF* which they receive on a more timely basis. The most current information is available from the Superintendent of Documents Order and Inquiry Desk, telephone (202) 783-3238. However, this is not a toll-free number, and purchasers must pay for their own calls.

Purchases may also be made from the 24 GPO bookstores which are located in the following cities: Atlanta; Birmingham; Boston; Chicago; Cleveland; Columbus, Ohio; Dallas; Denver; Detroit; Houston; Jacksonville;

Kansas City, Missouri; Los Angeles; Milwaukee; New York; Philadelphia; Pittsburgh; Pueblo, Colorado; San Francisco; Seattle; and Washington, D.C. (four stores). Most of these are located in federal buildings. However, stores in the following cities are now located in commercial shopping centers: Birmingham, Houston, Kansas City, Los Angeles, and Pueblo. The GPO plans to shift more bookstores out of difficult-to-find federal building locations into more accessible commercial shopping centers. The bookstores do not stock all of the GPO's approximately sixteen thousand in-print titles, but do carry the more popular titles. A list of bookstores will be found in GPO catalogs, including the *Monthly Catalog*, *Price List 36*, and *U.S. Government Books*.

Another major source of popular government publications is the Consumer Information Center, Pueblo, Colorado, which is operated by the Government Printing Office for the General Services Administration. It was established by an executive order in 1970 to help federal agencies promote and distribute useful consumer information to the public. It issues an annotated quarterly catalog, *Consumer Information Catalog*, (entry 1717) which lists free and inexpensive publications. Previously most of the publications distributed by the center were free. However, as a result of the economy moves mentioned above, the trend has shifted to more sales publications. For example, the spring 1985 catalog listed 129 sales publications (priced from $0.50 to $7.00) and 89 free publications. However, an order of two or more free titles (one copy each) requires remittance of $1.00 for postage and handling charges, with a limit of twenty-five titles per order. Forty-three of the sales publications are priced at $0.50 under a recently established GPO program to provide a more reasonable price for small pamphlets. Entries are arranged alphabetically by title under such topics as "Careers and Education," "Food," "Health," and "Gardening," and include many titles listed in this volume. Readers may wish to consult the latest edition of the *Consumer Information Catalog* to determine if they can obtain a free copy from this source. The catalog does not contain SuDocs Classification numbers. Each publication has a unique order number which is not permanent, and may change with subsequent editions of the catalog. Otherwise the sales titles are part of the GPO sales programs, and are priced at the same amount as indicated herein. However, the titles priced at $0.50 are part of a special GPO sales program, and are available only from the Consumer Information Center.

The issuing agencies are the primary source for free publications; for GPO publications (i.e., those printed at GPO facilities, or under contract to the GPO) which are not part of the sales program; and for so-called non-GPO publications which are not printed by, or contracted by, GPO but are printed either in-house by agency printing facilities or under contract to the agencies. Until the late 1970s it was often possible to obtain free from the issuing agency a U.S. government publication which the Superintendent of Documents sold. However, as a general rule, that is no longer true. Indeed due to recent economy measures in government printing and publishing it is more difficult to obtain non-GPO publications and nonsales publications since agencies have generally reduced the number of copies printed of a specific title. Issuing agencies are still a primary, and often the only source, but it has become more important than ever to obtain early knowledge of the existence of a title, and submit a request before the stock is depleted. The policy on free distribution also differs widely among agencies. In the past the Department of Agriculture was one of the most liberal; now it is one of the most tightfisted. Congressional publications are still distributed free, but quantities are more limited so early requests are important. For hearings and committee prints, send requests to the appropriate committee. For bills and resolutions, and numbered reports and documents, send requests to the Document Room of the House or Senate, as appropriate. Within the National Institutes of Health, the National Cancer Institute offers a number of free pamphlets (and few are included in the GPO sales programs), while most of the other institutes depend on the GPO sales program for dissemination to the public.

FEDERAL DEPOSITORY LIBRARIES

As mentioned above, the main source for people who want to use U.S. government publications is the nearly fourteen hundred federal depository libraries located throughout the United States and its outlying territories. The depository library system had its origins in legislation in the Thirteenth Congress (1813) which authorized public distribution of certain congressional publications to selected classes of institutions. The system as presently organized had its origin in legislation in 1857 and 1858 which established the principle of congressional designation of libraries by representatives and senators. Major codifications and/or revisions to the system were accomplished by the General Printing Act of 1895 and the Depository Library Act of 1962.

Under present law, each of the 495 congressional districts is authorized to have two designated depository libraries, plus each state is authorized four at-large designations (two per each senator). In addition, special designations may be awarded to the following classes of libraries: state libraries (one per state), state highest appellate court libraries (one per state), land grant college libraries, libraries of accredited law schools, U.S. military academy libraries, and federal libraries of executive departments and independent agencies and their major subordinate bureaus. There are two major types of depositories: selective and regional. Each state is authorized to have a maximum of two regional libraries. However, some states have only one, and six have none and are not served by a regional of an adjoining state. The regional libraries must receive all publications distributed by the GPO, and retain them permanently (with some exceptions). Each regional must also provide to the selective depository libraries within its area interlibrary loan, assistance in disposal of unwanted publications, and reference. The selectives may choose as many, or as few of the approximately five thousand publications series (items) available under the program as they wish. These series are listed in the quarterly *List of Classes of United States Government Publications Available for Selection by Depository Libraries* (entry 1729). Selectives may discard these publications after five years with the permission of their regional depository.

A list of depository libraries will be found in the annual Joint Committee on Printing directory, *Government Depository Libraries: The Present Law Governing Designated Depository Libraries*, in varying issues of the *Monthly Catalog*, and in a booklet issued by the Office of the Public Printer, *Federal Depository Libraries [as of May 1983]* (S/N 021-606-00002-2). The booklet is free from the Superintendent of Documents. Many copies of the booklet have been distributed to public libraries, large and small, throughout the country as part of the advertising campaign to promote the depository library program. This campaign has received support from the Advertising Council and includes public service announcements on television and radio.

The library depository program is a cooperative program between libraries and the federal government. The libraries receive the publications free. However, they are required by law to maintain the collections and to make them "available for the free use of the general public." Although there are depository libraries in most of the congressional districts, limitations on use of the program result from the fact that approximately two-thirds of the libraries are college and university libraries, and slightly less than one-fourth are public libraries. Most depositories are selectives, and the smaller libraries may receive only a small number of the series available. However, as indicated above, selective depositories may obtain publications on interlibrary loan from their regional depository. In view of the depository library program advertising campaign, most public libraries should now be able to readily provide information to readers on the location of the nearest depository library. Many public libraries, which are not depository libraries, also purchase (or otherwise obtain) many of the titles mentioned in this volume since they find U.S. government publications to be an authoritative and inexpensive source of information on a variety of subjects of interest to their readers.

Guide to Abbreviations

Some common government abbreviations, acronyms, and initialisms used in titles, series, and annotations in this guide.

AC	Advisory Circular (Federal Aviation Administration)
ADM	Alcohol, Drug Abuse, and Mental Health Administration
AEC	Atomic Energy Commission
AEF	American Expeditionary Force (World War I)
AFDC	Aid to Families with Dependent Children
AFM	Air Force Manual
AFP	Air Force Pamphlet
AR	Army Regulation
ATF	Bureau of Alcohol, Tobacco, and Firearms
AU	Air University
BLM	Bureau of Land Management
BLS	Bureau of Labor Statistics
BUPERS	Bureau of Naval Personnel
CAB	Civil Aeronautics Board
CB	Citizens' Band [radio]
CBO	Congressional Budget Office
CDC	Centers for Disease Control
CG	Coast Guard
CHAMPUS	Civilian Health and Medical Program for the Uniformed Services
CIA	Central Intelligence Agency
COMDINST	Commandant's Instruction (Coast Guard)
CPSC	Consumer Product Safety Commission
CRS	Congressional Research Service
CSA	Community Services Administration
ct	Cutter [number]

DA	Department of the Army
DFSS	Department and Foreign Service Series (Department of State)
DHEW	Department of Health, Education and Welfare
DHHS	Department of Health and Human Services
DoD	Department of Defense
DOE	Department of Energy
DoS	Department of State
DOT	Department of Transportation
EIA	Energy Information Administration
EP	Educational Publication (NASA)
EP	Engineer Pamphlet (Army Corps of Engineers)
EPA	Environmental Protection Agency
FAA	Federal Aviation Administration
FBI	Federal Bureau of Investigation
FCC	Federal Communications Commission
FDA	Food and Drug Administration
FEC	Federal Election Commission
FM	Field Manual (Army)
FNS	Food and Nutrition Service
FTC	Federal Trade Commission
FY	Fiscal Year
GAO	General Accounting Office
GPO	Government Printing Office
GSA	General Services Administration
H	House of Representatives (Congress)
HCFA	Health Care Financing Administration
HRA	Health Resources Administration
HRSA	Health Resources and Services Administration
HSA	Health Services Administration
HUD	Department of Housing and Urban Development
IB	Information Bulletin (Veterans Administration)
IRS	Internal Revenue Service
JCS	Joint Chiefs of Staff
JCP	Joint Committee on Printing (Congress)
JPL	Jet Propulsion Laboratory (NASA)
MCO	Marine Corps Order
MIL-STD	Military Standard
MTMC	Military Traffic Management Command
NACA	National Advisory Committee for Aeronautics
NASA	National Aeronautics and Space Administration
NATO	North Atlantic Treaty Organization

NAVAIR	Naval Air Systems Command
NAVEDTRA	Naval Education and Training Command
NAVSEA	Naval Sea Systems Command
NAVSO	Office, Chief of Naval Operations
NCES	National Center for Education Statistics
NCI	National Cancer Institute
NCIC	National Cartographic Information Center
NCJ	National Criminal Justice
NEH	National Endowment for the Humanities
NF	NASA Facts [series]
NIH	National Institutes of Health
NIOSH	National Institute for Occupational Safety and Health
NMFS	National Marine Fisheries Service
NOAA	National Oceanic and Atmospheric Administration
NSB	National Science Board
NSF	National Science Foundation
NTIA	National Telecommunications and Information Administration
NTIS	National Technical Information Service
OASI	Old Age and Survivors Insurance
OHDS	Office of Human Development Services
OMB	Office of Management and Budget
OPM	Office of Personnel Management
OSHA	Occupational Safety and Health Administration
OTA	Office of Technology Assessment (Congress)
PA	Program Aid (Department of Agriculture)
PRF	GPO Sales Publications Reference File
repr.	Reprinted
Rev.	Revised
ROTC	Reserve Officers Training Corps
S	Senate (Congress)
SB	Subject Bibliography (GPO)
SBA	Small Business Administration
SBD	Savings Bonds Division (Treasury Department)
SEC	Securities and Exchange Commission
SIC	Standard Industrial Classification
S/N	Stock Number
SP	Special Publication (NASA)
S.prt.	Senate [Committee] Print
SSI	Supplementary Security Income
SuDocs	Superintendent of Documents
Title IX	Educational Amendments of 1972 (prohibits sex discrimination in education)
TM	Technical Manual (Army)
TM	Technical Memorandum

UN	United Nations
UNESCO	United Nations Educational, Scientific, and Cultural Organization
USA	United States Army
USAF	United States Air Force
USDA	United States Department of Agriculture
USGS	United States Geological Survey
USN	United States Navy
VA	Veterans Administration

Accidents, Accident Prevention, and Safety

GENERAL

1. **CPSC Guide to Electrical Safety**. Consumer Product Safety Commission. 1983. 13p. ill. **Y3.C76/3:8El2**.
    Discusses precautions against accidental electrocution and shock as well as electrically caused fires and safer user of household electric appliances.

2. **For Kid's Sake: Think Toy Safety . . . by Knowing the Nine Toy Dangers**. Consumer Product Safety Commission. July 1984. folder, 8p. **Y3.C76/3:2K54/7**.
    Discusses hazards from toys due to sharp edges, small parts, loud noise, cords and strings, sharp points, and propelled objects.

3. **A Guide to Teaching Poison Prevention in Kindergartens and Primary Grades**. Consumer Product Safety Commission. 1976. 66p. ill. S/N 052-003-00257-4. $4.75. **Y3.C76/3:8P75/2**.
    Includes suggested classroom activities, games, and trips for teaching poison prevention in kindergarten and primary grades.

4. **Hazards of Children's Products: Safety Sampler**. Consumer Product Safety Commission. 1979. 15p. ill. S/N 052-011-00221-6. $3.00. **Y3.C76/3:2Sa1**.
    Includes a checklist of general safety hints and discusses infant falls, baby furniture, toys, electrical toys and children's products, toy chests, baby rattles, tricycles, and misuse of consumer products.

5. **A Holiday Safety Guide**. Consumer Product Safety Commission. July 1980. 12p. ill. **Y3.C76/3:8H71**.
    Provides safety precautions for Christmas trees, lights, and ornaments; fireplaces; and extension cords and wall outlets.

1

6. **"It's No Accident": A Consumer Product Safety Commission Education Curriculum Resource Guide for Teachers of Grades 3 through 6**. Consumer Product Safety Commission. 1984. 117p. ill. **Y3.C76/3:8Ac2**.

Includes eight basic units: basic safety concepts; home fire safety; playground safety; bicycle, roller skate, and skateboard safety; poison prevention; toy safety; holiday safety; and electrical safety. References.

7. **Merry Christmas with Safety**. Consumer Product Safety Commission. Rev. 1983. 6p. ill. **Y3.C76/3:2M55/983**.

Provides safety precautions for Christmas trees, artificial snow, lights, candles, trimmings, fires, and paper.

8. **The Perils of PIP, Preventive Poisoning**. Consumer Product Safety Commission. 1978. 16p. ill. S/N 052-011-00176-7. $2.75. **Y3.C76/3:2P66**.

A cartoon comic book featuring PIP, the magic safety elephant with lessons on how to prevent poisoning from common household products.

9. **Sprocket Man**. Consumer Product Safety Commission. 1978. 28p. ill. S/N 052-011-00174-1. $3.00. **Y3.C76/3:2Sp8**.

A cartoon comic book featuring Sprocket Man with tips on operating a bicycle safely. Bibliography.

10. **A Toy and Sports Equipment Safety Guide**. Consumer Product Safety Commission. July 1980. 25p. ill. S/N 052-011-00229-1. $2.25. **Y3.C76/3:8T66/2**.

Describes safety problems and precautions in using electrically operated toys, bicycles, tricycles, minibikes and minicycles, roller skates and ice skates, skate boards, and sleds.

11. **Young Children and Accidents in the Home**. Children's Bureau. 1974 (repr. 1979). 28p. ill. DHEW Publication No. (OHDS) 74-30034. S/N 017-091-00191-1. $4.25. **HE1.452:Ac2**.

Describes the major causes of accidents to young children and contains suggestions on how to learn safety habits. Includes a checklist by age groups of accident-causing situations to avoid, and a pullout first aid poster.

See also entries 73, 83, 174, 185, 238, 242, 369, 443, 708, 731, 733, 1104, 1106, 1373, 1374, 1535.

See also "Disaster Preparedness and Emergency Management" (entries 562-569).

For additional publications on this topic, see Subject Bibliography **SB-229, Accidents and Accident Prevention**.

OCCUPATIONAL SAFETY AND HEALTH

12. **Asbestos Exposure: What It Means, What to Do**. National Cancer Institute. September 1983. 11p. NIH Publication No. 83-1594. **HE20.3152:As1/2**.

Discusses health risks from exposure to asbestos dust, particularly in the workplace.

13. **Hazardous Materials Storage and Handling Pocketbook**. Defense Logistics Agency. April 1984. 98p. ill. S/N 008-007-03262-3. $9.50. **D7.6/4:H33/2**.

Provides precautions for the handling and storage of hazardous materials such as chemicals, explosives, and radioactive materials. Includes first aid measures in case of an accident.

14. **Noise Control: A Guide for Workers and Employers**. Occupational Safety and Health Administration. 1980. 119p. ill. OSHA 3048. **L35.8:N69/2**.

Discusses effects of noise on human health, some keywords and concepts in noise control, specific principles of noise control, and particular techniques for controlling noise in the workplace.

15. **Protecting People at Work: A Reader in Occupational Safety and Health**. Department of Labor. 1980. 361p. ill. S/N 029-015-00055-4. $9.00. **L1.2:P94/5**.

A collection of twenty-five essays presenting the historical dimensions of the problem of occupational safety and health and elements of the solution; efforts by the federal government and national nongovernmental efforts; and five case studies. References.

16. **Respiratory Protection: A Guide for the Employee**. National Institute for Occupational Safety and Health. October 1978. 36p. ill. NIOSH Publication No. 78-1938. S/N 017-033-00327-1. $4.25. **HE20.7108:R31/3**.

Describes different types of masks and respiratory protection devices, and how to use and maintain them in the workplace.

See also entries 636, 709-7, 1041, 1307, 1393.

For additional publications on this topic see Subject Bibliography **SB-213, Occupational Safety and Health**.

Aeronautics and Space Sciences

GENERAL

17. **Aeronautics and Space Report of the President, 1983 Activities**. National Aeronautics and Space Administration. 1984. 107p. ill., tables. **NAS1.52:983**.

Issued annually. Provides separate sections for summaries and highlights of aeronautics and space activities during the year in the National Aeronautics and Space Administration and in thirteen other federal agencies.

18. **Aerospace Bibliography**. 7th ed. National Aeronautics and Space Administration. 1982. 140p. EP-48. S/N 033-000-00866-0. $6.00. **NAS1.19:48/4**.

An annotated and graded list of books and reference materials published between 1971 and 1980 dealing with aerospace subjects.

19. **Bibliography of Space Books and Articles from Non-Aerospace Journals, 1957-1977**. National Aeronautics and Space Administration. 1979. 258p. HHR-51. **NAS1.9/2:Sp1/957-77**.

Entries are grouped under fourteen topics and are arranged alphabetically by author.

20. **The Literature of Aeronautics, Astronautics, and Air Power**. Office of Air Force History. 1984. 77p. USAF Warrior Studies. S/N 008-070-00523-9. $2.50. **D301.96:L71**.

A bibliographical essay which provides a guide to significant books and articles related to aeronautics, astronautics, and air power from antiquity to 1982. Index.

21. **Managing NASA in the Apollo Era**. National Aeronautics and Space Administration. 1982. 343p. charts, tables. NASA SP-4102. S/N 033-000-00844-9. $10.00. **NAS1.21:4102**.

This official history describes the organization and management of the National Aeronautics and Space Administration from its establishment in 1958 until 1969. Footnote references. Index.

22. **NASA Activities**. National Aeronautics and Space Administration. Monthly. approx. 20p. ill. S/N 733-001-00000-3. Symbol NACT. $23.00 per yr. Single copy $2.00. **NAS1.46:vol/no**.

This periodical contains news items of NASA activities which are of interest to the general public. Departments include lists of launches to date, with pictorial highlights of recent launches; Another Dividend from Air and Space, which highlights contributions of NASA research to the public sector; and news items produced by NASA for radio and TV programming.

23. **NASA 1958-1983: Remembered Images**. National Aeronautics and Space Administration. 1983. 136p. ill. EP-200. S/N 033-000-00901-1. $22.00. **NAS1.19:200**.

This fully illustrated color book takes a look at highlights of NASA's twenty-five-year history including the space shuttle, the Apollo program, the moon walk, the Apollo-Soyuz venture, the Voyager and Mariner missions, and the Spacelab.

24. **NASA: The First 25 Years, 1958-1983; A Resource for Teachers**. National Aeronautics and Space Administration. 1983. 132p. ill. EP-182. S/N 033-000-00909-7. $8.00. **NAS1.19:182**.

Provides a reference guide to significant NASA programs and accomplishments during its first twenty-five years, and numerous suggestions for classroom projects. References.

25. **National Aeronautics and Space Administration: Twenty-Fifth Anniversary, 1958-1983**. National Aeronautics and Space Administration. 1983. 13p. ill. NASA Facts 200. S/N 033-000-00879-1. $2.75. **NAS1.2:An7**.

A pictorial chronology of NASA beginning with the launching of Explorer 1 and continuing through the flight of space shuttle Challenger.

26. **Orders of Magnitude: A History of NACA and NASA, 1915-1980**. National Aeronautics and Space Administration. Rev. 1981. 117p. ill. NASA History Series. NASA SP-4403. S/N 033-000-00834-1. $4.75. **NAS1.21:4403/2**.

Presents a brief history of the National Advisory Committee for Aeronautics (NACA) and its successor, the National Aeronautics and Space Administration (NASA) spanning the period from World War I (1915) to the eve of the space shuttle in 1980. This is a revision of a popular history prepared for the American Revolution Bicentennial. Bibliography. Index.

27. **Spinoff, 1984**. National Aeronautics and Space Administration. 1984. 126p. ill. S/N 033-000-00920-8. $4.75. **NAS1.1/4:984**.

Issued annually. This report describes spinoffs of NASA technology to the private and public sectors in such areas as health and medicine, public safety, computer technology, and environmental protection.

See also entries 710, 711.

AERONAUTICS AND AVIATION

28. **Air Navigation**. Department of the Air Force. Rev. March 1983. 359p. ill. AFM 51-40. NAVAIR 00-80V-49. S/N 008-070-00494-1. $6.00. **D301.7:51-40/6**.

This manual provides information on all phases of air navigation. It explains how to measure, map, and chart the earth and how to use basic navigation instruments to solve basic problems of dead reckoning. Many special navigation techniques are also covered in detail.

29. **Directory of FAA Certificated Aviation Maintenance Technical Schools**. Federal Aviation Administration. Rev. October 1983. 5p. AC 147-2X. S/N 050-007-00665-9. $1.00. **TD4.8/5:147-2X**.

This directory lists alphabetically by state the aviation maintenance technician schools which have been certificated by the Federal Aviation Administration.

30. **FAA General Aviation News: A DOT/FAA Flight Operations Safety Publication**. Federal Aviation Administration. Bimonthly. 16p. ill. S/N 750-002-00000-5. Symbol FAN. $13.00 per yr. Single copy $2.50. **TD4.9:vol/no**.

This periodical includes articles and news items of interest to operators of small private planes, including helicopters, balloons, gliders, antique, sport and experimental aircraft. provides updates on major rule changes and proposals, as well as refresher information on flight rules, maintenance, airworthiness, avionics, accident analysis, and related aviation safety topics.

31. **List of Certificated Pilot Schools**. Federal Aviation Administration. Rev. July 1983. 50p. AC 140-2R. S/N 050-007-00664-1. $2.00. **TD4.8/5:140-2R**.

This directory lists the names and addresses of pilot schools that are certificated by the Federal Aviation Administration. It also contains a list of certificated aircraft dispatcher and flight engineer courses.

32. **Pilot's Handbook of Aeronautical Knowledge**. Federal Aviation Administration. Rev. 1980. 269p. ill. S/N 050-011-00077-1. $10.00. **TD4.408:P64/5/980**.

Contains essential information for training and guiding pilots. Topics include principles of flight, airplanes and engines, flight instruments, airplane performance, weather, navigation, and flight information publications. References.

33. **Student Pilot Guide**. Federal Aviation Administration. Rev. 1979. 36p. AC 61-12J. S/N 050-007-00476-1. $4.25. **TD4.8/5:61-12J**.

Presents general procedures for obtaining student and private pilot certificates, and gives information about the private pilot written test and flight test including sample test questions.

34. **Written Test Guide: Private Pilot Question Book**. Federal Aviation Administration. 1984. 144p. ill. FAA-T-8080-1. S/N 050-007-00648-9. $5.00. **TD4.32/21:1**.

Contains over nine hundred multichoice questions on topics applicable to the written test for private pilot applicants. An appendix provides a general reference for each question.

See also entries 324, 406, 412, 525, 709-4, 1062-24, 1694, 1695.

AIR TRANSPORTATION

35. **The Cutting Air Crash: Case Study in Early Federal Aviation Policy.** 2d ed. Federal Aviation Administration. 1984. 104p. ill. S/N 050-007-00677-2. $4.00. **TD4.2:C85**.

Discusses the airliner accident in Missouri on 6 May 1935 in which five people were killed, including Senator Bronson M. Cutting (R.-N.Mex.) and its effect on federal aviation policy during the early days of President Franklin D. Roosevelt's New Deal. Footnote references. Bibliography. Index.

36. **DOT Guide to CAB Sunset.** Department of Transportation. January 1985. 65p. charts. **TD1.8:Su7**.

Describes where airline economic regulatory functions which were formerly administered by the Civil Aeronautics Board (CAB) have been integrated into various offices and agencies of the Department of Transportation (DOT), rather than being consolidated as previously. CAB was abolished on December 31, 1984.

37. **FAA Statistical Handbook of Aviation, Calendar Year 1983.** Federal Aviation Administration. 1984. 202p. tables. S/N 050 007 00685-3. $7.00. **TD4.20:983**.

Issued annually. This report presents statistical information pertaining to the Federal Aviation Administration, the national airspace system, airports, U.S. civil air carrier fleet and operating data, air personnel, general aviation aircraft, aircraft accidents, and aeronautical manufacture and foreign trade.

38. **Safe, Separated, and Soaring: A History of Federal Civil Aviation Policy, 1961-1972.** Federal Aviation Administration. 1980. 427p. ill. FAA History Series. S/N 050-007-00566-1. $8.00. **TD4.2:Sa1/8/961-72/paper**.

Traces the history of the federal government's role in the promotion and regulation of civil aviation during the administrations of presidents Kennedy, Johnson, and Nixon. Footnote references. Index.

39. **Takeoff at Mid-Century: Federal Civil Aviation Policy in the Eisenhower Years, 1953-1961.** Federal Aviation Administration. 1976 (repr. 1984). 360p. ill. FAA History Series. S/N 050-007-00355-2. $12.00. **TD4.2:T13/953-61**.

Third in a series of histories tracing the federal government's role in the promotion and regulation of civil aviation since 1926. Significant events during the Eisenhower years which are covered are the passage of the Federal Aviation Act of 1958 and the creation of the independent Federal Aviation Agency. Footnote references. Index.

40. **Turbulence Aloft: The Civil Aeronautics Administration amid War and Rumors of Wars, 1938-1953.** Federal Aviation Administration. 1979. 353p. ill. FAA History Series. S/N 050-007-00496-6. $11.00, cloth. **TD4.2:T84/2/938-53**.

Discusses the role of the Civil Aeronautics Administration created by the Civil Aeronautics Act of 1938 through a stormy independence (1938-1940), the war years (1941-1945), and the Truman administration (1945-1953). Footnote references. Index.

See also entry 898.

ASTRONOMY

41.   **The Comet Halley Handbook: An Observer's Guide**. 2d ed. National Aeronautics and Space Administration. Jet Propulsion Laboratory. Rev. June 1983. 52p. charts, tables. JPL Publication No. 400-91. S/N 033-000-00892-9. $4.75. **NAS1.12/7:400-91/2**.

   Provides background information on the orbit of Comet Halley, and its expected physical behavior and observing conditions during 1985 and 1986. Also includes an ephemeris for Comet Halley at one day intervals from 8 August 1984 to 4 May 1987.

42.   **International Halley Watch Amateur Observer's Manual for Scientific Comet Studies**. 2 pts. National Aeronautics and Space Administration. Jet Propulsion Laboratory. March 1983. JPL Publication No. 83-16. Pt. 1. **Methods**. 76p. ill., tables. S/N 033-000-00888-1. $4.50. Pt. 2. **Ephemeris and Star Charts**. 80p. ill., tables. S/N 033-000-00889-9. $4.50. **NAS1.12/7:83-16/pt.1,2**.

   Part 1 provides detailed instructions for observation projects in six areas of study which are valuable to the International Halley Watch. Part 2 includes an ephemeris for Comet Halley for the period 1985-1987 and star charts showing its position from November 1985 through May 1986. Bibliography.

43.   **Stars in Your Eyes: A Guide to the Northern Skies**. Army Corps of Engineers. 1981. 23p. ill. S/N 008-022-00155-7. $1.50. **D103.2:St2**.

   Tells how to locate ten constellations which are visible in the northern skies during the summer. Introduces the myths and legends that have been woven around these constellations.

   For additional publications on this topic see Subject Bibliography **SB-115, Astronomy and Astrophysics**.

SPACE EXPLORATION

44.   **Aboard the Space Shuttle**. National Aeronautics and Space Administration. 1980. 32p. ill. EP-169. S/N 033-000-00806-6. $2.75. **NAS1.19:169**.

   A popular account of life aboard the space shuttle. Describes the clothes worn, how the launch feels, weightlessness, food, sleep, exercise, and personal hygiene.

45.   **Apollo Expeditions to the Moon**. National Aeronautics and Space Administration. 1975. 313p. ill. NASA SP-350. S/N 033-000-00630-6. $13.00, cloth. **NAS1.21:350**.

   A comprehensive history of the fifteen-year Apollo space program to place a man on the moon and return him safely. Written by eighteen key members of the Apollo team. Footnote references. Index.

46.   **Apollo Soyuz**. National Aeronautics and Space Administration. 1976. 131p. ill. EP-109. S/N 033-000-00652-7. $4.75. **NAS1.19:109**.

   A popular account of the Apollo Soyuz Test Project in which U.S. Apollo and Soviet Soyuz spacecraft docked together in space 17-21 July 1975.

47. **Astronauts and Cosmonauts Biographical and Statistical Data. [Revised March 31, 1983].** Congress. House. Committee on Science and Technology. Rev. April 1983. 340p. ill., tables. Committee print, 98th Congress, 1st session. Serial J. S/N 052-070-05856-1. $6.00. **Y4.Sci2:98/J.**

Contains photographs and brief biographies of all present and former U.S. astronauts from the NASA, X-15, X-20, Dyna-Soar, and Manned Orbiting Laboratory programs. It contains similar information for known Soviet cosmonauts, and "spacenauts" from other countries.

48. **Chariots of Apollo: A History of Manned Lunar Spacecraft.** National Aeronautics and Space Administration. 1979. 556p. ill. NASA History Series. NASA SP-4205. S/N 033-000-00768-0. $12.00. **NAS1.21:4205.**

Begins with the establishment of NASA in 1958 and definition of the manned space flight program for Project Mercury. Ends with Apollo 11 when the program achieved its purpose of landing a man on the moon in July 1969. Emphasizes the spacecraft, i.e., command and service modules, and lunar modules. Footnote references. Bibliography. Index.

49. **Civilian Space Stations and the U.S. Future in Space.** Congress. Office of Technology Assessment. 1984. 234p. ill., charts, maps. OTA-STI-241. S/N 052-003-00969-2. $7.50. **Y3.T22/2:2C49/2.**

Examines the range of technology and technical issues surrounding the selection and acquisition of space stations, as well as the broad policy issues. Footnote references. Index.

50. **Living and Working in Space: A History of Skylab.** National Aeronautics and Space Administration. 1983. 462p. ill. NASA History Series. NASA SP-4208. S/N 033-000-00847-3. $20.00, cloth. **NAS1.21:4208.**

Comprehensive history of the Skylab program. Traces the beginnings from the program's inception in 1963 (as Apollo) to its demise in 1983. Describes development, preparations, and missions. Footnote references. Index.

51. **Moonport: A History of Apollo Launch Facilities and Operations.** National Aeronautics and Space Administration. 1978. 636p. ill. NASA Historical Series. NASA SP-4204. S/N 033-000-00740-0. $13.00. **NAS1.21:4204.**

A detailed history of the Apollo launch facilities and operations at the John F. Kennedy Space Center, Cape Canaveral, Florida. Footnote references. Index.

52. **On Mars: Exploration of the Red Planet, 1958-1978.** National Aeronautics and Space Administration. 1984. 551p. ill., charts, tables. NASA History Series. NASA SP-4212. S/N 033-000-00869-4. $20.00. **NAS1.21:4212.**

Describes NASA's program to explore the planet Mars, including the Mariner spacecraft and the Voyager Orbiter and Voyager Lander programs. Footnote references. Bibliography. Index.

53. **Pioneer Venus.** National Aeronautics and Space Administration. 1983. 262p. ill. NASA SP-461. S/N 033-000-00873-2. $11.00. **NAS1.21:461.**

Describes the Pioneer Venus mission, knowledge and understanding of Venus as a planet, and the Venus environment that it revealed.

54. **Prelude to the Space Age: The Rocket Societies, 1924-1940**. National Air and Space Museum. 1983. 222p. ill. S/N 047-000-00380-6. $6.50. **SI9.2:Sp1**.

Records the significant contributions of rocket societies in Germany, Austria, Russia, United States, and Great Britain during the 1920s and 1930s toward the development of rockets and interplanetary space travel. Footnote references. Index.

55. **Space Activities of the United States, Soviet Union, and Other Launching Countries/Organizations, 1957-1982**. Congress. House. Committee on Science and Technology. April 1983. 148p. tables. Committee print, 98th Congress, 1st session. Serial F. **Y4.Sci2:98/F**.

Includes lists of space flight launches and other data and descriptive information on space activities of the United States and Soviet Union. Discusses space activities of China, European Space Agency, India, and Japan.

56. **Space Station: The Next Logical Step**. National Aeronautics and Space Administration. 1984. 51p. ill. EP-213. S/N 033-000-00932-1. $3.00. **NAS1.19:213**.

Discusses NASA plans and proposals for an operating space station.

57. **Spacelab: An International Short-Stay Orbiting Laboratory**. National Aeronautics and Space Administration. 1983. 82p. ill. EP-165. S/N 033-000-00895-3. $7.00. **NAS1.19:165**.

Well-illustrated popular account of what Spacelab is, what it does, how it came to be, and what its users expect from it.

58. **Stages to Saturn: A Technological History of the Apollo/Saturn Launch Vehicles**. National Aeronautics and Space Administration. 1980. 531p. ill. NASA History Series. NASA SP-4206. S/N 033-000-00794-9. $12.00. **NAS1.21:4206**.

Presents a topical description of the Saturn launch vehicle program which as Saturn I (1961-1965), Saturn 1B (1966-1975), and Saturn V (1967-1973) successfully launched thirty-two missions, including eleven Apollo missions. Footnote references. Index.

59. **This New Ocean: A History of Project Mercury**. National Aeronautics and Space Administration. 1966 (repr. 1978). 681p. ill. NASA Historical Series. NASA SP-4201. S/N 033-000-00244-1. $13.00. **NAS1.21:4201**.

Describes the origin, preparation, and nature of the first U.S. achievements in manned space flight. Footnote references. Index.

60. **Viking: The Exploration of Mars**. National Aeronautics and Space Administration. 1984. 56p. ill. EP-208. S/N 033-000-00915-1. $4.50. **NAS1.19:208**.

Includes numerous photographs of Mars from the Viking Orbiter mission which landed on the planet in 1976 and continued to transmit pictures until 1982.

61. **The Voyager Flights to Jupiter and Saturn**. National Aeronautics and Space Administration. 1982. 60p. ill. EP-191. S/N 033-000-00854-6. $5.50. **NAS1.19:191**.

Includes pictures sent by Voyager 1 and 2 spacecraft which were launched in September 1977 and traced the orbit of Jupiter March-July 1979 and of Saturn November 1980-August 1981.

62.   **Voyages to Saturn**. National Aeronautics and Space Administration. 1982. 236p. ill. NASA SP-451. S/N 033-000-00842-2. $9.50. **NAS1.21:451**.

A colorfully illustrated account of Pioneer and Voyager spacecraft missions to Saturn, 1973-1981. Describes what new information was learned about this second largest plant in our system. Glossary. Bibliography. Index.

See also entry 1261.

For additional publications on this topic see Subject Bibliography **SB-297, Space, Rockets, and Satellites.**

Aging and Problems
of the Elderly

63. **Accidental Hypothermia: A Winter Hazard for the Old**. National Institute on Aging. Rev. October 1980. 12p. NIH Publication No. 81-1464. **HE20.3852:H99/980**.
Discusses the symptoms, diagnosis, prevention, and treatment of hypothermia and why the aged are more susceptible.

64. **Aging**. Administration on Aging. Bimonthly. 48p. ill. S/N 717-003-00000-4. Symbol AGING. $15.00 per yr. Single copy $2.75. **HE23.3110:no**.
This periodical contains articles of general interest on the aging process and problems of the elderly. Departments provide news items of national, state, and community activities of interest to the aged; book reviews; and "The Numbers Game" with current statistics.

65. **America in Transition: An Aging Society**. Bureau of the Census. September 1983. 32p. charts, tables. Current Population Reports, Series P-23, No. 128. S/N 003-001-91543-0. $3.50. **C3.186:P-23/128**.
Presents a statistical profile of the elderly population of the United States covering the following topics: numerical growth, income and poverty, health status, social and other characteristics. References.

66. **Chartbook on Aging**. White House Conference on the Aging, 1981. 1981. 141p. charts. **Y3.W58/4:2C38**.
Organized under the following topics: overview, employment, income, health, family, physical environment, and continued social and economic involvement in the community.

67. **Consumer Frauds and Elderly Persons: A Growing Problem**. Congress. Senate. Special Committee on the Aging. 1983. 75p. Committee Print, 98th Congress, 1st session. S.Prt. 98-12. S/N 052-070-05823-4. $4.50. **Y4.Ag4:S.prt.98-12**.
Discusses the ten most harmful frauds against the elderly, and provides advice on combating them. Appendices include directories of government and private organizations that may provide help.

68. **Crime Prevention Handbook for Senior Citizens**. Law Enforcement Assistance Administration. June 1977. 55p. ill. S/N 027-000-00589-6. $2.50. **J1.8/2:Se5**.

Provides advice for senior citizens on how to reduce the odds of being the victim of a burglary, a robbery or larcency, or a fraud. Bibliography.

69. **Deadly Cold: Health Hazards due to Cold Weather**. Congress. House. Select Committee on Aging. February 1984. 65p. tables. Committee Publication No. 98-414. **Y4.Ag4/2:H34/21**.

Discusses the scope of cold weather hazards which particularly affect the elderly, analyzes federal and nonfederal efforts to reduce mortality, and suggests reform measures.

70. **Demographic and Socioeconomic Aspects of Aging in the United States**. Bureau of the Census. August 1984. 159p. charts, tables. Current Population Reports, Series P-23, No. 138. S/N 003-001-91555-3. $5.50. **C3.186:P-23/138**.

Brings together and analyzes data on selected topics related to the demographic and socioeconomic aspects of aging, and to the demographic and socioeconomic character-istics of old people in the United States.

71. **Directory of State and Area Agencies on Aging**. 4th ed. Congress. House. Select Committee on Aging. March 1985. 149p. maps, tables. Committee Publication No. 99-490. **Y4.Ag4/2:Ag4/9/985**.

Lists state offices on aging, and area agencies on aging established by some states to serve specific communities. Includes state and/or area maps showing the area covered by each agency.

72. **Drug Taking among the Elderly**. National Institute of Mental Health. 1982. 25p. tables. DHHS Publication No. (ADM) 83-1229. S/N 017-024-01154-1. $3.25. **HE20.8217/3:El2**.

Presents information on the significance of psychoactive drug use by the elderly; the extent to which the elderly use psychoactive drugs, alcohol, and tobacco; and a larger exploration of drug use and health issues.

73. **80 Do's and 50 Don'ts for Your Safety: A Practical Guide for Eldercare**. Veterans Administration. 1984. 16p. ill. **VA1.10:Sa1**.

Presents tips for preventing accidents inside and outside the home.

74. **Food Guide for Older Folks**. Agricultural Research Service. Rev. August 1984. 19p. ill. Home and Garden Bulletin 17. S/N 001-000-03321-2. $3.25. **A1.77:17/11**.

Provides advice for older folks on selecting, buying, and preparing food. Includes recipes that can be prepared with a minimum of kitchen equipment.

75. **A Guide to Medical Self-Care and Self-Help Groups for the Elderly**. National Institute on Aging. August 1980. 28p. ill. NIH Publication No. 80-1687. S/N 017-062-00132-4. $3.50. **HE20.3858:M46**.

Provides advice on taking care of oneself, and information on national self-help groups for the elderly. References.

76. **A Guide to Planning Your Retirement Finances**. Congress. House. Select Committee on Aging. Rev. December 1982. 37p. tables. Committee Publication No. 97-354. S/N 052-070-05784-0. $4.25. **Y4.Ag4/2:R31/10/982**.

Provides answers to basic questions for prospective retirees regarding retirement income, investment instruments, benefits for federal employees, private pensions, planning and estates, and more.

77. **Health Promotion for Older Persons: A Selected Annotated Bibliography**. Administration on Aging. September 1984. 42p. DHHS Publication No. (OHDS) 84-20819. **HE23.3011:H34**.

Organized under the following topics: health promotion, exercise and fitness, nutrition, mental health, injury control, drug management, and certain health conditions associated with old age.

78. **Heat Stress and Older Americans: Problems and Solutions**. Congress. Senate. Special Committee on Aging. July 1984. 19p. maps. Committee Print 98th Congress, 1st Session. S.Print 98-76. **Y4.Ag4:S.prt.98-76**.

Discusses the danger of hot weather for older people, how to prevent stroke, and how to plan for heat waves.

79. **How to Select a Nursing Home**. Health Care Financing Administration. Rev. 1980 (repr. 1985). 63p. ill. HCFA Publication No. 80-30043. S/N 017-062-00123-5. $4.75. **HE22.208:N93/980**.

Provides general background to help assess needs and to understand what one sees and hears during inspection visits, step-by-step procedures to quantitatively evaluate each home visited, and a checklist to compare different nursing homes.

80. **Income of the Population 55 and Over, 1982**. Social Security Administration. 1984. 106p. tables. S/N 017-070-00407-5. $4.50. **HE3.75:982**.

Issued biennially. This report focuses on the major sources, and combination of sources of income for persons aged fifty-five and over, and the amount received from each source. Labor force participation of seniors is also measured in detail.

81. **Maintenance of Family Ties of Long-Term Care Patients: Theory and Guide to Practice**. National Institute of Mental Health. 1977. 126p. DHEW Publication No. (ADM) 77-400. S/N 017-024-00637-8. $6.00. **HE20.8108:F21**.

Discusses the importance of maintaining ties between the elderly in institutions and their families. Provides suggestions to staff on how to preserve and strengthen family ties. Footnote references. Bibliography.

82. **Profiles of Older People**. General Accounting Office. 1981. 24p. ill., charts, tables. S/N 020-000-00208-5. $2.75. **GA1.2:P94/5**.

A statistical profile of older people in Cleveland, Ohio, which includes comparisons with older people in selected counties in Kentucky and Oregon where similar surveys were conducted. Bibliography.

83. **Safety for Older Consumers: Home Safety Checklist**. Consumer Product Safety Commission. January 1985. 29p. ill. **Y3.C76/3:2Sa1/4**.

A checklist for safety hazards in all parts of the home.

84. **Self-Care and Self-Help Groups for the Elderly: A Directory**. National Institute on Aging. 1984. 128p. NIH Publication No. 84-738. S/N 017-062-00134-1. $4.25. **HE20.3852:El2**.

Lists a broad variety of national organizations that deal specifically with the elderly, or have programs that relate to older persons, their families, and health professionals. Index.

85. **Sodium: Facts for Older Citizens**. Food and Drug Administration. May 1983. 11p. DHHS Publication No. (FDA) 83-2169. **HE20.4002:So1**.

Discusses what sodium is, what it does, where it is found, and how to watch the amount you need since studies show that most Americans take in more sodium than they need.

86. **Treasure Hunt**. National Institute on Aging. March 1980. 31p. ill. NIH Publication No. 80-1403. S/N 017-062-00120-1. $4.75. **HE20.3852:T71**.

A story book to enlighten children on the active daily lives of the elderly, and on special ways in which some older people try to deal with prejudice against the elderly.

87. **Turning Home Equity into Income for Older Homeowners**. Congress. Senate. Special Committee on Aging. July 1984. 19p. S.Print 98-216. **Y4.Ag4:S.prt.98-216**.

Describes home equity conversion programs which are designed to help home-rich and cash-poor homeowners unlock the value of their home and convert it into income.

88. **You and Your Medicines: Guidelines for Older Americans**. Congress. Senate. Special Committee on Aging. June 1983. 16p. S.Print 98-66. **Y4.Ag4:S.prt.98-66**.

Provides advice for the elderly on the proper use of prescription and nonprescription drugs.

See also entries 506-12, 931, 932, 989, 1045, 1312, 1314, 1315, 1506, 1508, 1644, 1655.

See also "Medicare and Medical Insurance" (entries 1046-1051), "Military Retirement and Survivors Benefits" (entries 1658-1663), and "Social Security" (entries 1481-1501).

For additional publications on this topic see Subject Bibliography **SB-039, Aging**.

Agriculture and Farming

89. **Agricultural Outlook**. Economic Research Service. Monthly, except January/February (combined). approx. 48p. ill., charts, tables. S/N 701-003-00000-4. Symbol ARGO. $29.00 per yr. No single copies sold. **A93.10/2:no**.

This periodical consists primarily of brief news items, usually with statistics to provide updates and analyses of developments affecting the outlook for the U.S. food and fiber economy. It highlights major interrelated developments in farming, input industries, and produce marketing, and discusses potential impact on U.S. agriculture and the consumer.

90. **Agricultural Statistics, 1984**. Department of Agriculture. 1984. 567p. tables. S/N 001-000-04437-1. $12.00. **A1.47:984**.

Issued annually. This statistical compilation is designed to meet diverse needs for a reliable reference source on agricultural production, supplies, consumption, facilities, costs, and returns. Index.

91. **Beekeeping for Beginners**. Department of Agriculture. Rev. June 1979. 12p. ill. Home and Garden Bulletin 158. S/N 001-000-03936-9. $1.75. **A1.77:158/5**.

Provides basic information for the beginner to get started in keeping honey bees.

92. **Beekeeping in the United States**. Department of Agriculture. Rev. October 1980. 201p. ill., maps, tables. Agriculture Handbook 335. S/N 001-000-04137-1. $7.50. **A1.76:335/980**.

Provides information on the life history of the honey bee, bee behavior, breeding and gestation of honey bees, managing colonies for high honey yield and crop pollination, diseases and pests of honey bees, and effects of pesticides on honey bee mortality.

93. **Extension Review**. Extension Service. Quarterly. approx. 40p. ill. S/N 701-018-00000-1. Symbol ESR. $14.00 per yr. Single copy $3.75. **A43.7:vol/no**.

This periodical includes reports and feature articles on agriculture extension programs, including 4-H clubs, homemakers, community and rural development, and volunteer efforts. Articles are prepared primarily by extension specialists in state extension service agencies.

94. **Face of Rural America**. Department of Agriculture. 1976. 284p. ill. Yearbook of Agriculture 1976. S/N 001-000-03521-5. $16.00. **A1.10:976**.

A photobook of American farming, farm families, and country living as it was during the Bicentennial Year. Unlike previous yearbooks, this volume has no articles but only short captions to accompany the mostly black-and-white photographs.

95. **Factbook of United States Agriculture, 1985**. Department of Agriculture. Rev. 1984. 135p. tables. Miscellaneous Publication 1063. S/N 001-000-04432-0. $4.00. **A1.38:1063/10**.

This chart book is intended as a handy reference source on the main trends in American agriculture. Data are grouped under five topics: farm production, income, and value; the farming operation; food marketing; agricultural services; and the rural environment.

96. **Farmline**. Economic Research Service. Monthly, except January/February (combined). approx. 18p. ill., charts, tables. S/N 701 021 00000 2. Symbol FRMLIN. $18.00 per yr. Single copy $2.00. **A93.33/2:vol/no**.

This periodical is intended for a general agricultural audience. Using statistical data, articles report and analyze trends in farm production, foreign trade, commodity prices, land use and values, farm finances, rural population and employment, productivity, policy, and related subjects.

97. **Food from Farm to Table**. Department of Agriculture. 1982. 412p. ill. Yearbook of Agriculture 1982. S/N 001-000-04298-0. $12.00, cloth. **A1.10:982**.

Essays contributed by Department of Agriculture specialists are grouped into three major sections: changing economics of agriculture; farm marketing and a new environment; and food buying—making decisions.

98. **Getting Started in Farming on a Small Scale**. Department of Agriculture. Rev. April 1982. 43p. Agriculture Information Bulletin 451. S/N 001-000-04259-9. $3.25. **A1.75:451/2**.

Explores ways of getting into farming on a small scale and raises questions about financing, farm selection, planning, training, and crop selection.

99. **Glossary of Some Terms Commonly Used in the Futures Trading Industry**. Commodity Futures Trading Commission. Rev. November 1979. 30p. **Y3.C73/5: 2G51/979**.

This dictionary of terms has been compiled from generally accepted trade sources.

100. **Handbook of Agricultural Charts, 1984**. Department of Agriculture. December 1984. 88p. charts. Agriculture Handbook 637. S/N 001-019-00368-5. $3.75. **A1.76:637**.

100-A. **Handbook of Agricultural Charts, 1984: Enlargements**. 1985. 272p. charts. Agricultural Handbook 637. S/N 001-019-00371-5. $7.50. **A1.76: 637/enl**.

Issued annually. The charts present agriculture-related data for the latest year available, as well as historical data. Charts are grouped under the following topics: the farm, population and rural developments, the consumer, food and nutrition, U.S. trade and world production, and commodity trends. The *Enlargements* volume contains full-page enlargements of the 272 charts in the main volume. Index.

101. **Living on a Few Acres**. Department of Agriculture. 1978. 472p. ill., tables. Yearbook of Agriculture 1978. S/N 001-000-03809-5. $13.00, cloth. **A1.10:978**.

Intended as a practical guide for part-time farmers who do not intend to gain their principal income from the land. Its fifty-three articles discuss pros and cons of farm life, suggest ways to find and improve a farm, and describe crops that are best suited for small farms. References. Index.

102. **People on the Farm: Growing Vegetables**. Department of Agriculture. March 1982. 32p. ill. **A1.2:V52/5**.

Provides case studies of six farm families who grow tomatoes, lettuce, peas, potatoes, pepper, and other commercial vegetables.

103. **People Who Follow the Crops**. Commission on Civil Rights. Rev. June 1978. 80p. ill. **CR1.2:P39/2/978**.

A photobook which describes the plight of migrant farm workers, especially child laborers in Colorado and North Dakota.

104. **Pesticides and Honey Bees**. Agricultural Research Service. Rev. October 1981. 7p. Leaflet 563. **A1.35:563/3**.

Discusses precautions on the use of pesticides which should be observed by farmers to protect honey bee colonies.

105. **Pork: Slaughtering, Cutting, Preserving, and Cooking on the Farm**. Department of Agriculture. Rev. November 1983. 62p. ill. Farmers' Bulletin 2265. **A1.9:2265/3**.

Provides detailed instructions on slaughtering, skinning, cutting, preserving, and cooking hogs on the farm.

106. **Raising Geese**. Extension Service. Rev. April 1983. 16p. ill. Farmers' Bulletin 2251. S/N 001-000-04356-1. $2.50. **A1.9:2251/4**.

Describes nine breeds of geese. Provides advice on raising geese, and marketing the poultry and feathers.

107. **Sludge: Recyling for Agricultural Use**. Environmental Protection Agency. October 1982. 16p. ill. EPA-430/9-82-008. **EP2.2:Sl7/2**.

Provides examples of how communities are using sludge for agricultural applications. Sludge is the residue of materials removed from sewage during wastewater treatment.

108. **That We May Eat**. Department of Agriculture. 1975. 401p. ill. Yearbook of Agriculture 1975. S/N 001-000-03471-5. $9.00. **A1.10:975**.

Its thirty-seven articles commemorate the centennial of state agricultural experiment stations. Articles concern such varied topics as plant diseases, soil research, raising cattle and crops, scientific advances that will improve our home life, and predictions about the future of agriculture.

109.   **Viticulture Areas**. Bureau of Alcohol, Tobacco and Firearms. October 1983. 43p. maps. **T70.2:V83**.

Presents maps and descriptions of forty approved viticulture areas in the United States, twenty-six of which are in California. The name of an approved viticulture area may be used as an appellation of origin in wine labeling and advertising.

110.   **Will There Be Enough Food?** Department of Agriculture. 1981. 343p. ill. Yearbook of Agriculture 1981. S/N 001-000-04257-2. $7.00, cloth. **A1.10:981**.

Its thirty articles tell how U.S. food production fills our domestic need for food and provides millions of jobs, as well as helping ease hunger throughout the world. They also question whether farmers and the American agricultural system can continue to do the job. References. Index.

See also entries 449, 506-7, 547-3, 1152, 1154, 1399, 1413, 1423, 1429, 1671.

For additional publications on this topic see Subject Bibliographies **SB-031, Agricultural Year Books** and **SB-161, Farms and Farming**.

Alcohol and Drug Abuse

GENERAL

111.   **National Directory of Drug Abuse and Alcoholism Treatment and Prevention Programs**. National Institute on Drug Abuse. September 1982. 312p. DHHS Publication No. (ADM) 83-321. S/N 017-024-01159-2. $6.50. **HE20.8302:D84**.

Lists approximately seventy-five hundred federal, state, local, and privately funded agencies responsible for the administration or provision of alcoholism or drug abuse services.

ALCOHOL ABUSE AND ALCOHOLISM

112.   **Alcohol and Health: Fifth Special Report to the U.S. Congress from the Secretary of Health and Human Services**. National Institute on Alcoholism and Alcohol Abuse. December 1983. 159p. charts, tables. DHHS Publication No. (ADM) 84-1291. S/N 017-024-01199-1. $5.00. **HE20.8313:5**.

Topics covered include epidemiology of alcohol abuse and alcoholism, genetics and alcoholism, psychobiological effects of alcohol, consequences of alcoholism, effects of alcohol on pregnancy, adverse social consequences of alcoholism, treatment, and prevention. References. Index.

113.   **Alcohol and Your Unborn Baby**. National Institute on Alcoholism and Alcohol Abuse. 1978. 14p. ill. DHHS Publication No. (ADM) 81-521. S/N 017-024-00721-8. $2.75. **HE20.8302:Al1/10**.

Emphasizes the dangers to unborn children from alcohol use by the mother.

114.   **Drinking Etiquette: For Those Who Drink and Those Who Don't**. National Institute on Alcoholism and Alcohol Abuse. January 1976. 13p. ill. DHEW Publication No. (ADM) 79-305. S/N 017-024-00497-9. $2.00. **HE20.8302:D83/3**.

This colorful booklet helps set general guidelines of conduct for host or hostess as well as guests regarding serving and consumption of alcoholic drinks.

115. **Facing Up to Alcoholism**. National Institute on Alcoholism and Alcohol Abuse. 1978. 11p. ill. DHEW Publication No. (ADM) 78-568. S/N 017-024-00751-0. $2.50. **HE20.8302:Al1/11**.

Summarizes the nature, symptoms, and treatment of alcoholism.

116. **Facts about Alcohol and Alcoholism**. National Institute on Alcoholism and Alcohol Abuse. Rev. 1980. 53p. DHHS Publication No. (ADM) 80-31. S/N 017-024-01028-6. $4.50. **HE20.8302:F11/980**.

Discusses the following topics: alcoholic beverages, alcohol and its effects, problem drinking and alcoholism, origins of alcoholism, overcoming alcoholism, and preventing alcohol problems. References.

117. **Here's to Your Health: Alcohol Facts for Women**. National Institute on Alcoholism and Alcohol Abuse. 1981. 7p. DHHS Publication No. (ADM) 81-1169. **HE20.8302:H34/3**.

Discusses dangers of alcohol use by women.

118. **How Much Do You Know about Drinking and Driving? A Self Evaluation for Teenagers**. National Highway Traffic Safety Administration. July 1983. 16p. DOT HS 806 429. **TD8.2:D83/50**.

Consists of eight topics each with five graded responses that provide a score on an "attitude danger scale." Also includes sixteen questions which test your knowledge of drinking and driving.

119. **How to Save Lives and Reduce Injuries: A Citizen Activist Guide to Effectively Fight Drunk Driving**. National Highway Traffic Safety Administration. November 1982. 139p. ill. DOT HS 806 250. **TD8.8:L75**.

Designed to educate victims and concerned citizens on the methods they can use effectively to get drunk drivers off the roads in large enough numbers to reduce alcohol-related accidents.

120. **Is Beer a Four Letter Word? An Alcohol Abuse Prevention Program Idea Book**. National Institute on Alcoholism and Alcohol Abuse. Rev. 1978. 58p. ill. DHEW Publication No. (ADM) 78-725. S/N 017-024-00800-1. $5.50. **HE20.8302: B39/980**.

Contains project ideas, materials, suggestions, and alcohol education concepts from many sources to interest young people in alcohol-related issues that affect them and to encourage them to start projects.

121. **Play It Smart: Facts for Teenagers about Drinking**. National Institute on Alcoholism and Alcohol Abuse. 1981. 8p. ill. DHHS Publication No. (ADM) 81-1170. **HE20.8302:Sm2**.

Provides answers to some common questions that teenagers ask about drinking alcoholic beverages.

122. **Presidential Commission on Drunk Driving: Final Report**. Presidential Commission on Drunk Driving. November 1983. 49p. **Pr40.8:D84/In8/final**.

Includes recommendations of the commission related to public awareness and education, alcoholic beverage regulations, systems support, enforcement, prosecution, adjudication, licensing administration, and education.

See also entry 184.

For additional publications on this topic see Subject Bibliography **SB-175, Alcoholism**.

DRUG ABUSE

123. **Adolescent Peer Pressure: Theory, Correlates, and Program Implications for Drug Abuse Prevention**. National Institute on Drug Abuse. 1981 (repr. 1984). 120p. charts. DHHS Publication No. (ADM) 84-1152. S/N 017-024-01110-0. $4.00. **HE20.8202:Ad7**.
Examines the concept of peer pressure among youth and focuses on constructive ways of channeling peer pressure to control drug use. References.

124. **Catching On: A Drug Information Booklet**. National Institute on Drug Abuse. 1981. 24p. ill. DHHS Publication No. (ADM) 81-764. S/N 017-024-01054-5. $2.75. **HE20.8202:C28/evaluation**.
This comic book was developed as a source of drug information for young people. Includes puzzles and games.

125. **Controlled Substances: Use, Abuse, and Effects**. Drug Enforcement Administration. 1984. 4p. ill., table. **J24.2:C76**.
Contains table listing common narcotics, depressants, stimulants, hallucinogens, and cannabis with information on medical uses, physical and psychological dependence, tolerance, duration, effects, and withdrawal syndrome.

126. **Deciding about Drugs: A Woman's Choice**. National Institute on Drug Abuse. 1979. 28p. ill. DHEW Publication No. (ADM) 80-820. S/N 017-024-00867-2. $3.50. **HE20.8202:W84**.
Discusses the use of drugs, when they may be helpful in dealing with stress, and when using drugs may only add to the problem. References.

127. **Drug Abuse from the Family Perspective: Coping Is a Family Affair**. National Institute on Drug Abuse. 1980. 149p. DHHS Publication No. (ADM) 80-910. S/N 017-024-00999-7. $5.50. **HE20.8202:F21**.
A collection of twelve commissioned papers which emphasize the significance of family factors in understanding and controlling drug-abusing behavior among youth. References. Bibliography.

128. **Drug Abuse Prevention and Your Family**. National Institute on Drug Abuse. Rev. 1980. 22p. ill. DHHS Publication No. (ADM) 81-584. **HE20.8202:D84/5/980**.
Provides information on the effects of many commonly used drugs and how you and your family can become active and effective drug abuse preventors. Bibliography.

129. **Drug Abuse Prevention for You and Your Friends**. National Institute on Drug Abuse. Rev. 1980. 22p. ill. DHHS Publication No. (ADM) 81-583. **HE20.8202: P92/4/980**.
Discusses drug abuse prevention as it applies to teenagers and summarizes basic information on commonly abused drugs. Bibliography.

130. **Drugs and American High School Students, 1975-1983**. National Institute on Drug Abuse. 1984. 492p. charts, tables. **HE20.8202:D84/975-83**.

Fourth in a series of detailed reports on the prevalence of drug use among high school seniors, and trends since 1975. Contains separate chapters with detailed data on eleven drugs. Also presents data on attitudes and beliefs about drugs, and perceptions of the social milieu.

131. **Drugs of Abuse**. Drug Enforcement Administration. 1980. 39p. ill. S/N 027-004-00031-8. $4.50. **J24.3/2a:D84**.

Contains information on the Controlled Substances Act and describes drugs of abuse, including narcotics, depressants, stimulants, hallucinogens, and cannabis.

132. **For Kids Only: What You Should Know about Marijuana**. National Institute on Drug Abuse. Rev. 1982. 12p. ill. DHHS Publication No. 82-986. S/N 017-024-01142-8. $2.00. **HE20.8202:M33/3/982**.

Explains what marijuana is, what causes the high, what hashish is, what burnout and dependence are, and the effects of marijuana on the mind and body.

133. **For Parents Only: What You Need to Know about Marijuana**. National Institute on Drug Abuse. Rev. 1984. 30p. ill. DHHS Publication No. (ADM) 84-909. S/N 017-024-01203-3. $1.50. **HE20.8202:M33/984**.

Contains the latest scientifically accepted information on the effects of marijuana and provides advice to parents on how to deal with possible use by their children. Glossary. References.

134. **The Global Legal Framework for Narcotics and Prohibitive Substances**. Department of State. June 1979. 86p. tables. **S1.2:N16/2**.

Presents data on the legal status and penalties for illegal possession, trafficking, cultivation and production of cannabis, coca leaf, opium poppy, and their derivatives and other prohibitive substances in foreign countries. Also provides information on criminal procedures in foreign countries.

135. **Highlights from Drugs and American High School Students, 1975-1983**. National Institute on Drug Abuse. 1984. 141p. charts, tables. DHHS Publication No. (ADM) 84-1317. S/N 017-024-01208-4. $4.00. **HE20.8202:D84/23/975-83/high**.

Seventh in an annual series of reports. Discusses current prevalence of drug use among American high school seniors and trends since 1975. Also reports data on grade of first use, trends in use at earlier grade levels, intensity of drug use, and attitudes and beliefs concerning various types of drug use.

136. **It Starts with People: Experiences in Drug Abuse Prevention**. National Institute on Drug Abuse. 1978. 78p. DHEW Publication No. (ADM) 78-590. S/N 017-024-00747-1. $5.00. **HE20.8202:P39**.

Intended for parents, teachers, and others who want to be involved with youth, this book tells what you can do to help young people grow up without drugs. Includes case studies of successful programs. References.

137. **Let's Talk about Drug Abuse: Some Questions and Answers**. National Institute on Drug Abuse. 1979. 45p. ill. DHEW Publication No. (ADM) 78-706. **HE20.8202: T14/981**.

Presents many of the questions about drugs and drug taking that concern adults and young people, and provides answers. References.

138. **Marijuana and Health: Ninth Report to the U.S. Congress from the Secretary of Health and Human Services**. National Institute on Drug Abuse. 1982. 32p. DHHS Publication No. (ADM) 82-1216. S/N 017-024-01148-7. $3.50. **HE20.8210:982**.

Issued annually. Presents highlights on recent research or trends regarding the health consequences of marijuana use.

139. **1984 National Strategy for Prevention of Drug Abuse and Drug Trafficking**. Drug Abuse Policy Office. 1984. 129p. charts. S/N 041-012-00004-8. $4.25. **PrEx24.2:St8/984**.

Discusses the Reagan administration's five-stage strategy to reduce the availability of illicit drugs and to reduce the adverse effects of drug abuse to the individual and society.

140. **Parents, Peers, and Pot**. National Institute on Drug Abuse. 1979. 106p. DHEW Publication No. (ADM) 80-812. S/N 017-024-00941-5. $5.00. **HE20.8202:P21/2**.

Describes the drug culture among youths nine to fourteen years old, and discusses what parents can do to prevent or stop children from using drugs, and how parents can work with the school and community to create a drug-free environment. References. Bibliography.

141. **Parents, Peers, and Pot II—Parents in Action**. National Institute on Drug Abuse. 1983. 171p. DHHS Publication No. (ADM) 83-1290. S/N 017-024-01174-6. $4.50. **HE20.8202:P21/5**.

Presents case studies from nine states of the development of individual parents and parent groups acting with the school and community as a major force against drug use by youth. Footnote references.

142. **Parents: What You Can Do about Drug Abuse**. National Institute on Drug Abuse. 1983. 8p. ill. DHHS Publication No. (ADM) 83-1267. S/N 017-024-01164-9. $14.00 per 100 copies. No single copies sold. **HE20.8202:P21/4**.

Brief advice to parents on how to help their children resist drug abuse, how to get medical help, and how to work with other parents and groups. References.

143. **Saying No: Drug Abuse Prevention Ideas for the Classroom**. National Institute on Drug Abuse. 1980. 27p. DHHS Publication No. (ADM) 80-916. S/N 017-024-01009-0. $3.50. **HE20.8202:P92/6**.

Provides suggestions for elementary and high school teachers for class projects in art, science, social sciences, and physical education courses on the theme of saying no to drug use. References.

144. **Soozie and Katy: We're Teaming Up for Your Good Health**. Drug Enforcement Administration. 1984. 30p. ill. S/N 027-004-00036-9. $1.25. **J24.2:So6/2**.

This study guide is intended to promote home and classroom discussion of medicine, and use and misuse of drugs. Designed for very young children.

145. **Teens in Action: Creating a Drug-free Future for America's Youth.** National Institute on Drug Abuse. 1985. 47p. ill. DHHS Publication No. (ADM) 85-1376. S/N 017-024-01225-4. $2.00. **HE20.8202:T22/2.**

Describes the problems, challenges, successes, and hopes that fifteen teenagers across the country have experienced in trying to cope with and succeed in an environment that often promotes drug use.

146. **This Side Up: Making Decisions about Drugs.** National Institute on Drug Abuse. Rev. 1980. 64p. ill. DHHS Publication No. (ADM) 80-420. **HE20.8202: T34/980.**

Designed as an entertaining source of information for teenagers who are faced with decisions about drugs. Contains cartoons, games, and puzzles.

See also entries 72, 88.

For additional publications on this topic see Subject Bibliography **SB-163, Drug Education.**

Archives, Genealogical
and Vital Records

147. **Age Search Information**. Bureau of the Census. Rev. 1981. 51p. ill. S/N 003-024-02923-5. $5.00. **C3.6/2:Ag3/981**.

Describes retrieval of personal data about individuals from Census Bureau records to satisfy requirements for birth certificates when information is unavailable elsewhere. Describes genealogical sources and references for information not in census materials.

148. **Genealogical Records in the National Archives**. National Archives and Records Service. Rev. 1983. 16p. General Information Leaflet No. 5. **GS4.22:5/5**.

Briefly describes those federal records in the custody of the National Archives which are most useful for genealogical research. This includes census schedules, land records, naturalization records, ship passenger lists, and military personnel records.

149. **Getting Started: Beginning Your Genealogical Research in the National Archives**. National Archives and Records Service. 1983. 23p. ill. **GS1.2:G28/6**.

Intended for the novice at genealogical research. Provides information on use of census records, military service and pension records, passenger arrival and naturalization records, and land records.

150. **Guide to the National Archives of the United States**. National Archives and Records Service. 1974. 909p. S/N 022-003-00908-6. $21.00. **GS4.6/2:N21**.

Lists all official records of the U.S. government received by the National Archives as of 30 June 1970 with the exception of presidential papers. Includes inclusive years, number of items, description of holdings, and record group number. Arranged by major executive departments, then by subordinate agencies.

151. **List of Record Groups of the National Archives and Records Service**. National Archives and Records Service. July 1984. 77p. **GS4.19:984**.

Record groups are arranged in three lists: alphabetically by keyword, by National Archives operating unit which has custody, and by record group number. Includes information on cubic feet/meters for typical paper collections. Provides notes on cartographic, audiovisual, and machine-readable records, and on other special holdings.

152. **Listing of Personnel for State Vital and Health Statistics Offices**. National Center for Health Statistics. April 1983. 65p. **HE20.6202:P43**.

Lists the name, title, address, and telephone number for each state of key personnel in the state health department who are responsible for vital statistics. Also lists registrars and statisticians in the federal and provincial offices of Canada.

153. **Military Service Records in the National Archives of the United States**. National Archives and Records Service. Rev. 1977. 15p. General Information Leaflet No. 7. **GS4.22:7/2**.

Briefly describes military service records which are open to the public for genealogical or other research seventy-five years after completion of such service. These records are housed in facilities in Washington, D.C.; Suitland, Maryland; and St. Louis, Missouri.

154. **Where to Write for Vital Records: Births, Deaths, Marriages and Divorces**. National Center for Health Statistics. Rev. August 1984. 18p. DHHS Publication No. (PHS) 84-1142. S/N 017-022-00847-5. $1.50. **HE20.6202:V83/984**.

Lists the name and address of state vital statistics offices from which to obtain copies of birth, death, marriage, and divorce records. The cost of copying, if known, is provided. Alternate sources of records, and inclusive dates of records are also provided.

See also entries 547-2, 1327.

Arts and Humanities

GENERAL

155. **Arts Review**. National Endowment for the Arts. Quarterly. approx. 36p. ill. S/N 736-001-00000-4. Symbol TCP. $10.00 per yr. Single copy $3.50. **NF2.13:vol/no**.

This periodical contains articles of general interest on the arts, primarily the performing arts. Has frequent interview articles with famous artists and performers, and a list of grant deadlines.

156. **Humanities**. National Endowment for the Humanities. Bimonthly. approx. 30p. ill. S/N 736-002-00000-1. Symbol NR. $14.00 per yr. Single copy $2.50. **NF3.11:vol/no**.

This periodical uses a newspaper tabloid format. Primarily contains articles on a broad range of topics by outstanding authors and humanities scholars. Departments include complete listing of recent NEH grants by discipline, news of NEH-supported projects, news of programs, changes in guidelines, and a calendar of deadlines for grant applications. Annual bibliography lists books published which were assisted by NEH grants.

See also entries 305, 1313.

ART

157. **Art in the United States Capitol**. Congress. 1978. 466p. ill. House Document 94-660. S/N 052-071-00546-3. $20.00, cloth. **X94-2:H.doc.660**.

Includes reproductions of portraits, paintings, busts, statues, reliefs, frescoes and murals, exterior sculpture, and miscellaneous works of art in the U.S. Capitol building, Washington, D.C.

158. **Freer Gallery of Art**. Smithsonian Institution. 1983. 31p. ill. **SI7.2:F87/3**.

Discusses the building, the collections, and founder Charles Lang Freer of the Freer Gallery of Art, Washington, D.C.

159. **Matting and Hinging of Works of Art on Paper**. Library of Congress. 1980. 39p. ill. S/N 030-000-00134-6. $4.75. **LC1.2:Ar7**.

Contains detailed illustrated instructions for four procedures of hinging works of art on mats for preservation purposes. Includes lists of supplies and suppliers. Glossary. References.

160. **National Collection of Fine Arts, Smithsonian Institution**. National Collection of Fine Arts. Rev. 1978. 40p. S/N 047-003-00061-0. $6.00. **SI6.2:N21/978**.

Provides a history of the national collection of art, which was first established as the National Gallery of Art in 1906 and renamed the National Collection of Fine Arts. References.

161. **National Portrait Gallery Permanent Collection Illustrated Checklist**. National Portrait Gallery. Rev. 1982. 320p. ill. **SI11.2:C41/982**.

Includes reproductions of individual and group portraits in the permanent collections of the National Portrait Gallery. Entries include brief information about the subject, the artist, and the work.

162. **Perspectives on John Philip Sousa**. Library of Congress. 1983. 144p. ill. S/N 030-001-00103-2. $17.00, cloth. **LC12.2:So8/2**.

This compilation of seven essays is designed to provide some perspectives on John Philip Sousa (1854-1932), the composer of "Stars and Stripes Forever" as an important figure in our nation's social as well as musical development.

163. **U.S. Army Art Collection**. Army Center of Military History. June 1984. 9p. ill. **D114.2:Ar7**.

Provides a brief description of the Army Art Collection and the army traveling exhibition program.

For additional publications on this topic see Subject Bibliography **SB-107, Art and Artists**.

LITERATURE

164. **The Best of Children's Books, 1964-1978**. Library of Congress. 1980. 95p. S/N 030-001-00093-1. $5.50. **LC1.12/2:C43/5/964-78**.

An annotated list of children's books published between 1964 and 1978, arranged by topic. Entries include price, publisher, and suggested grade levels.

165. **Books in Our Future: A Report from the Librarian of Congress to the Congress**. Congress. Joint Committee on the Library. 1984. 50p. S.Print 98-231. S/N 052-070-05978-8. $2.50. **Y4.L61/2:B64**.

This report on the changing role of the book in the future was directed by a 1983 congressional resolution. It draws on interviews with authors, publishers, booksellers, computer experts, librarians, scientists, educators, and scholars.

166. **Children and Poetry: A Selective, Annotated Bibliography**. 2d ed. Library of Congress. 1979. 96p. ill. S/N 030-000-00099-4. $5.50. **LC1.12/2:P75/979**.

Lists both rhymes and more serious poetry and provides a guide to the best children's poetry available today. In many cases excerpts of poetry have been included.

167. **Children's Book, 1984**. Library of Congress. 1985. 20p. S/N 030-001-00111-3. $1.00. **LC2.11:984**.

Issued annually. This annotated catalog lists titles selected for literary merit, usefulness, and enjoyment which are suitable for preschool through junior high school age children. Entries include price and age group suitability.

168. **The Openhearted Audience: Ten Authors Talk about Writing for Children**. Library of Congress. 1980. 206p. ill. S/N 030-001-00089-3. $13.00, cloth. **LC1.2:Op2**.

A collection of ten lectures presented at the Library of Congress between 1966 and 1978 in which the authors talk about their experiences in writing books for children. References.

See also entries 379, 903, 904, 905, 906, 907, 908, 1061-15, 1312.

For additional publications on this topic see Subject Bibliography **SB-142, Poetry and Literature**.

STYLE MANUALS AND WRITING

169. **Guide for Air Force Writing**. Department of the Air Force. November 1973 (repr. 1979). 231p. AFP 13-2. S/N 008-070-00330-9. $6.00. **D301.35:13-2**.

The first part describes the basic principles of writing, and the second part discusses the application of those principles. Index.

170. **A Style Guide for CBO: About Writing and Word Usage**. Congressional Budget Office. 1984. 100p. **Y10.8:C76**.

This style manual was developed for authors of CBO publications, but it has general application to all prose writers.

171. **The Tongue and Quill: Communicating to Manage in Tomorrow's Air Force**. Air University. Rev. July 1982. 204p. ill. AU-22. S/N 008-070-00484-4. $6.00. **D301.26/6:T61/982**.

An introductory manual for developing verbal and written skills.

172. **United States Government Printing Office Style Manual**. Government Printing Office. Rev. 1984. 488p. ill. S/N 021-000-00120-1. $11.00, paper. S/N 021-000-00121-0. $15.00, cloth. **GP1.23/4:St9/984**.

A standardization manual designed to achieve uniform word and type treatment in government printing and publishing. It answers many questions about style and good usage, capitalization, preferred spelling, abbreviations, compound words, numerals, and many other topics. References.

173.   **Word Division: Supplement to Government Printing Office Style Manual**.
Government Printing Office. Rev. 1984. 218p. S/N 021-000-00123-6. $2.25.
GP1.23/4:St9/984/supp.

Serves as a quick reference guide for finding correct word divisions and as a
spelling and pronunciation guide. Also contains rules for word breaks and line endings.

See also entry 491.

Automobiles and Highways

AUTOMOBILE OPERATION AND MAINTENANCE

174. **The Automobile Safety Belt Fact Book**. National Highway Traffic Safety Administration. Rev. May 1982. 21p. ill. DOT HS 802 157. **TD8.2:Au8/982**.
Provides some hard and very persuasive facts about the protection offered by use of fastened safety belts during motor vehicle accidents.

175. **Back-Yard Mechanic, Vols. 1-3**. Department of the Air Force. 1976-1981. 226p. ill. S/N 008-070-00475-5. $7.00. **D301.72/a:M46/v.1-3**.
Specially priced set of the three volumes listed below which are sold separately. Contains articles from *Driver: The Traffic Safety Magazine for the Military Driver* (entry 178).

175-1. **Back-Yard Mechanic. Vol. 1**. 1976 (repr. 1981). 57p. ill. S/N 008-070-00374-1. $2.50. **D301.72/a:M46/v.1**.
Takes willing but inexperienced mechanics through an oil change, lube job, transmission check, and installation of brake pads.

175-2. **Back-Yard Mechanic. Vol. 2**. 1978. 75p. ill. S/N 008-070-00406-2. $3.00. **D301.72/a:M46/v.2**.
Discusses ignition systems and spark plugs and guides you through a tuneup, brake lining job, brake system flushing, power brake check, carburetor cleaning, air conditioner check, oil change, and front-end lube job.

175-3. **Back-Yard Mechanic. Vol. 3**. 1981. 92p. ill. S/N 008-070-00463-1. $3.00. **D301.72/a:M46/v.3**.
Covers such vital areas as the electrical system, automotive body work, basic dent removal, painting, tuning for mileage, how to make your car last forever, and more.

176.   **Cost of Owning and Operating Automobiles and Vans, 1984.** Federal Highway Administration. Rev. May 1984. 20p. tables. HHP-41. **TD2.60:984.**

Traces the following types of vehicles in personal use and their costs through a twelve-year lifetime of 120,000 miles using recent data: large size, intermediate, compact, and subcompact automobiles; and passenger vans.

177.   **Driver License Administration Requirements and Fees: Status as of January 1, 1984.** Federal Highway Administration. Rev. 1984. 50p. charts, tables. HHP-41/3. **TD2.61:984.**

Presents a wide variety of information on requirements and restrictions of individual states on the licensing of motor vehicle drivers.

178.   **Driver: The Traffic Safety Magazine for the Military Driver.** Department of the Air Force. Monthly. 32p. ill. S/N 708-022-00000-4. Symbol AFDM. $22.00 per yr. Single copy $2.00. **D301.72:vol/no.**

This periodical has articles on safely operating civilian vehicles, motorcycles, and bicycles under all types of conditions. Departments include The Backyard Mechanic (tips on automobile maintenance); Timely Topics (news items); and True Accidents (brief accounts of actual off-post accidents by Air Force personnel).

179.   **55 MPH Fact Book.** National Highway Traffic Safety Administration. Rev. November 1979. 54p. charts, tables. DOT HS 804 979. **TD8.2:F11/979.**

Contains data on compliance, enforcement, fatality rate, fuel economy, and safety benefits of the fifty-five miles per hour national speed limit established in 1974.

180.   **Legal Impediments to Ridesharing Agreements.** Federal Highway Administration. December 1979. 67p. tables. S/N 050-001-00164-1. $4.75. **TD2.2:R43/4.**

Identifies and analyzes state laws that impede ridesharing agreements under the following topics: common or contract motor carrier laws, insurance laws, state vehicle codes, state fair labor standards acts, state income tax laws, and restrictions on government-owned vehicles.

181.   **License Plates, 1985.** Federal Highway Administration. 1985. folder, 8p. ill., tables. S/N 050-001-00288-4. $3.75. **TD2.63:985.**

Issued annually. A colorful folder showing automobile license plates from the fifty states, District of Columbia, territories, Canadian provinces, and armed forces. Also shows D.C. presidential inaugural plates from 1933 and diplomatic license plates. Tables provide detailed information.

182.   **A Primer on Auto Emission Systems for Home Mechanics.** Environmental Protection Agency. November 1977. 110p. ill. EPA-450/3-77-043. S/N 055-003-00090-4. $5.50. **EP1.2:Au8/9.**

Tells why automobile emission control systems are needed, how various systems work, how to check for proper operation, and how to correct malfunctions.

183.   **Simple Self Service.** Department of the Air Force. 1983. 6p. ill. S/N 008-070-00507-7. $1.00. **D301.72/a:Se6.**

Reprint from *Driver* (entry 178). Describes simple checks that an owner can perform to prolong the life of a car.

184. **State Laws on Early License Revocation for Driving While under the Influence**. National Highway Traffic Safety Administration. February 1984. 98p. tables. DOT HS 806 481. **TD8.2:L61/4**.

Contains state-by-state description of laws on early license revocation for drunk driving, comparison of state laws by topic, and the text of a model state law. Footnote references.

185. **Study of Methods for Increasing Safety Belt Use**. National Highway Traffic Safety Administration. 1981. 65p. DOT HS 805 556. S/N 050-003-00400-6. $5.00. **TD8.2:Sa1/36**.

Summarizes techniques that have been or could be used to induce people to wear safety belts. References.

186. **The Three-Part Gasoline Engine Tuneup**. Department of the Air Force. 1983. 18p. ill. S/N 008-070-00506-9. $1.50. **D301.72/a:T83**.

Reprint from *Driver* (entry 178). Takes you through a step-by-step complete tuneup, explaining what to do in clear layperson's terms.

187. **Vehicle Theft Prevention and Strategies**. National Institute of Justice. 1984. 127p. S/N 027-000-01196-9. $4.75. **J28.23:V53**.

Describes the following prevention strategies: identification of vehicles and parts, control of vehicle titling and registration, and claims practices by insurance companies to discourage theft.

See also entries 118, 119, 122, 527.

HIGHWAYS

188. **America's Highways, 1776-1976: A History of the Federal-Aid Program**. Federal Highway Administration. 1977. 558p. ill. S/N 050-001-00123-3. $22.00, cloth. **TD2.2:Am3/3/776-976**.

Published to commemorate the American Revolution Bicentennial. Part 1 contains a history of highways from colonial times to the present. Part 2 discusses several areas of federal responsibilities for highway construction and maintenance. Footnote references. Index.

189. **Auto in the City: An Examination of Techniques Mayors Can Use to Reduce Traffic in Downtown Areas**. Department of Transportation. October 1980. 61p. ill., charts, tables. DOT-P-30-80-35. **TD1.20/6:30-80-35**.

Discusses selected strategies for coping with automobiles in downtown areas from capital projects such as transit malls to traffic and parking management programs. Footnote references.

190. **Highway Statistics, 1983**. Federal Highway Administration. 1984. 189p. tables. S/N 050-001-00286-8. $5.50. **TD2.23:983**.

Issued annually. Presents statistics of general interest on motor fuel, motor vehicles, driver licensing, highway-user taxation, state highway financing and mileage, and federal aid to highways.

191. **The Interstate Highway System: Issues and Options.** Congressional Budget Office. June 1982. 116p. charts, maps, tables. S/N 050-070-05741-6. $5.50. **Y10.2:H53**.

Analyzes current problems and suggests alternative solutions for the interstate highway system: the increasing cost of completing the remaining 5 percent, the projected decline in the financing base, and the increasing cost of repairs.

192. **Motorists Information Services.** Federal Highway Administration. 1980. 36p. ill. FHWA-TS-80-201. **TD2.30/4:80-201**.

An illustrated description of good signage and facilities that some states have found to deliver motorists information services. Provides historical background on highways and information services. Bibliography.

193. **Our Nation's Highways: Selected Facts and Figures.** Federal Highway Administration. 1983. 23p. ill., charts, tables. HHP-41/4. **TD2.2:H53/29**.

A chart book with data about the U.S. highway system and its condition, number of vehicles, number of licensed drivers, motor fuel use, and highway financing.

194. **The Status of the Nation's Highways: Conditions and Performance.** Congress. House. Committee on Public Works and Transportation. July 1983. 171p. charts, tables. Committee Print, 98th Congress, 1st Session. Serial 98-14. **Y4.P96/11:98-14**.

Includes the seventh biennial report by the secretary of transportation on the nation's highway needs. References.

195. **United States Road Symbol Signs.** Federal Highway Administration. 1979. folder, 8p. ill. S/N 050-000-00152-1. $2.25. **TD2.59/2:R53**.

Gives examples of different kinds of symbol signs showing significant colors and shapes. Includes examples of warning, regulatory, guide, services, construction, and recreation signs and state highway route markers for each state.

See also entries 308, 901.

Birds and Wildlife

BIRDS

196. **Discovering Birding in the National Forests**. Forest Service. Rev. December 1980. folder, 8p. ill. PA 1216. **A1.68:1216/2**.
Intended to encourage you to try bird watching in the national forests and grasslands.

197. **Fifty Birds of Town and City**. Fish and Wildlife Service. 1973 (repr. 1978). 50p. ill. S/N 024-010-00382-1. $7.50. **I49.2:B53/4**.
Describes fifty birds commonly seen in American cities, their characteristics and feeding habits.

198. **Homes for Birds**. Fish and Wildlife Service. Rev. 1979. 22p. ill., tables. Conservation Bulletin 14. S/N 024-010-00525-4. $2.50. **I1.72:14/3**.
Reviews specific nesting requirements for various species of song birds, describes principles of bird house design, and contains plans and instructions for bird house construction and placement. References.

199. **Invite Birds to Your Home: Conservation Plantings for the Northwest**. Soil Conservation Service. July 1975 (repr. 1980). 20p. ill. PA 1094. S/N 001-000-03307-7. $1.00. **A1.68:1094**.
Includes illustrations of familiar birds of the Northwest, and the plants that attract birds seeking food.

200. **Invite Birds to Your Home: Conservation Plantings for the Southeast**. Soil Conservation Service. Rev. October 1981. 16p. ill. PA 1093. **A1.68:1093/2**.
Describes plants preferred as sources of food by southeastern birds. Also discusses other ways of attracting birds.

201.   **Migration of Birds**. Fish and Wildlife Service. Rev. 1979. 119p. ill., charts, maps. Circular 16. S/N 024-010-00484-3. $6.00. **I49.4:16/2**.

Discusses techniques for studying migration of birds, when and where birds migrate, influence of weather and topography, perils of migration, and routes and patterns of migration. Bibliography.

See also entry 1436.

For additional publications on this topic see Subject Bibliography **SB-177, Birds**.

WILDLIFE

202.   **Discovering Fire Island: The Young Naturalist's Guide to the World of the Barrier Beach**. National Park Service. 1978. 95p. ill. S/N 024-005-00723-7. $5.50. **I29.9/2:F51/2**.

Describes and illustrates the ecology and wildlife of Fire Island, New York.

203.   **Everglades Wildguide**. National Park Service. 1972 (repr. 1979). 105p. ill., maps. Natural History Series. S/N 024-005-00497-1. $6.50. **I29.62:Ev2**.

Describes the natural interactions that support the diverse plant and wildlife communities in the Florida Everglades. Glossary. References.

204.   **Whales, Dolphins, and Porpoises of the Eastern North Pacific and Adjacent Arctic Waters: A Guide to Their Identification**. National Marine Fisheries Service. 1982. 249p. ill. Circular 444. S/N 024-020-00154-8. $6.50. **C55.13:NMFS CIRC 444**.

This profusely illustrated field guide is designed to permit observers to identify whales, dolphins, and porpoises in the eastern North Pacific including the Gulf of California, Hawaii, and western Arctic of North America. Animals are grouped by similarities in appearance.

205.   **Whales, Dolphins, and Porpoises of the Western North Atlantic: A Guide to Their Identification**. National Marine Fisheries Service. 1976 (repr. 1983). 180p. ill., maps. Circular 396. S/N 024-020-00119-0. $7.00. **C55.13:NMFS CIRC 396**.

For description see entry 204. Covers the western North Atlantic, including the Caribbean, Gulf of Mexico, and coastal waters.

206.   **Yellowstone Wildlife**. National Park Service. 1972 (repr. 1977). 32p. ill., maps. S/N 024-005-00474-2. $4.00. **I29.2:Y3/2**.

Serves as a guide to finding, observing, and photographing some of the more noticeable, interesting, and rare species of wildlife in Yellowstone National Park.

For additional publications on this topic see Subject Bibliographies **SB-116, Wildlife Management** and **SB-209, Fish and Marine Life**.

ENDANGERED SPECIES

207. **Endangered Means There's Still Time**. Fish and Wildlife Service. January 1981. 32p. ill. S/N 024-010-00526-2. $3.75. **I49.2:En2/12**.
Describes the federal program to preserve endangered species of plants and animals.

208. **Endangered Species: The Road to Recovery**. Fish and Wildlife Service. Rev. 1981. 11p. ill. **I49.2:En2/5/981**.
Discusses various recovery methods, such as habitat protection, manipulation, or cleanup to save endangered species.

HUNTING AND FISHING

209. **Angler's Guide to the U.S. Atlantic Coast: Fish, Fishing Grounds and Fishing Facilities**. 8 sections. National Marine Fisheries Service. 1974-1977. ill., maps. **C55.308/An4/sec.1-8**.
This series of guides provides anglers with detailed information on fishing the Atlantic Coast from Maine to Florida. Included are the following types of information: identification and habits of, and methods of catching almost all game fish occurring along the Atlantic Coast; maps showing fishing grounds; where to write for more information; state fishing regulations; and information on boating facilities. Glossary.

209-1.   . . . **Section 1. Passamaquoddy Bay, Maine to Cape Cod**. 1974. 15p. S/N 003-020-00068-1. $9.00.

209-2.   . . . **Section 2. Nantucket Shoals to Long Island Sound**. 1974. 15p. S/N 003-020-00070-3. $9.00.

209-3.   . . . **Section 3. Block Island to Cape May, New Jersey**. 1974. 20p. S/N 003-020-00071-1. $9.00.

209-4.   . . . **Section 4. Delaware Bay to False Cape, Virginia**. 1974. 17p. S/N 003-020-00072-0. $9.00.

209-5.   . . . **Section 5. Chesapeake Bay**. 1976. 17p. S/N 003-020-00096-7. $9.00.

209-6.   . . . **Section 6. False Cape, Virginia to Altahama Sound, Georgia**. 1976. 21p. S/N 003-020-00097-5. $9.00.

209-7.   . . . **Section 7. Altahama Sound, Georgia to Fort Pierce Inlet, Florida**. 1976. 21p. S/N 003-020-00098-3. $9.00.

209-8.   . . . **Section 8. St. Lucie, Florida to the Dry Tortugas**. 1976. 25p. S/N 003-020-00099-1. $9.50.

210. **Angler's Guide to the United States Pacific Coast: Marine Fish, Fishing Grounds, and Facilities**. November 1977. 144p. ill., maps. S/N 003-020-00113-1. $8.50. **C55.308:An4/2**.
Covers the marine and estuarine waters along the coasts of Alaska, Washington, Oregon, California, Hawaii, American Somoa, and Guam. Describes 237 types of game fishes, and forty fishing areas with nautical charts included. References. Index.

211. **Duck Stamp Data**. Fish and Wildlife Service. 1981. looseleaf, 53p. ill. S/N 924-001-00000-3. Symbol DUSD. $12.00 (includes basic service plus annual supplements for indeterminate period). Supplements available at $2.00 each. **I49.93:934-81**.

Duck stamps have been issued for each hunting season since 1934-1935. Separate page for each season has black-and-white drawing of the art, basic information on the artist, and philatelic background on each stamp.

212. **The "Duck Stamp" Story**. Fish and Wildlife Service. Rev. 1984. folder, 6p. ill. **I49.2:D85/4/984**.

Describes the program begun in 1934 which requires adult waterfowl hunters to buy and carry a Migratory Bird Hunting and Conservation Stamp, commonly known as a Duck Stamp.

213. **1980 National Survey of Fishing, Hunting, and Wildlife-associated Recreation**. Fish and Wildlife Service. November 1982. 156p. ill., charts, tables. S/N 024-010-00639-1. $7.00. **I49.2:H92/2/980**.

Sixth in a series of surveys conducted at five-year intervals since 1955. Presents statistical data on fishing, hunting, and wildlife associated recreation during 1980. The 1980 survey provided expanded data on wildlife observation, photography, and feeding.

214. **Summary of Federal Hunting Regulations, 1983-84**. Fish and Wildlife Service. Rev. 1983. 9p. tables. **I29.24/2:983-84**.

Contains a summary of major federal regulations which pertain to hunters of doves, pigeons, ducks, cranes, and other selected migratory birds.

215. **Waterfowl Hunters: Know the Black Duck**. Fish and Wildlife Service. 1984. folder, 6p. ill. **I49.2:W29/21**.

Intended to aid federal and state efforts to protect the black duck. Provides colored illustrations of black ducks and mallards which highlight their differences for identification purposes.

See also entries 233, 1177-5.

Birth Control

216. **Birth Control Info for Teens: Can You Picture Birth Control for Teens?** Bureau of Community Health Services. 1980. 9p. ill. DHHS Publication No. (HSA) 81-5618. **HE20.5102:B53**.
Discusses foam as one method of birth control for females.

217. **Birth Control Info for Teens: Have You Solved the Body Puzzle?** Bureau of Community Health Services. 1980. 11p. ill. DHHS Publication No. (HSA) 81-5620. **HE20.5102:B53/2**.
Uses a crossword puzzle to help answer questions about fertility and conception.

218. **Birth Control Info for Teens: Here's the Word on Birth Control for Teens**. Bureau of Community Health Services. 1980. 17p. ill. DHHS Publication No. (HSA) 81-5616. **HE20.5102:B53/4**.
Uses a puzzle to discuss eight methods of birth control: withdrawal, jellies, inserts, foam, condoms, cream, natural planning, and saying no.

219. **Birth Control Info for Teens: Maybe You Need to Take Another Look**. Bureau of Community Health Services. 1980. 11p. ill. DHHS Publication No. (HSA) 81-5617. **HE20.5102:B53/3**.
Discusses use of condoms as a method of birth control.

220. **Birth Control Info for Teens: You'd Be Amazed at How Many Teens Say "No."** Bureau of Community Health Services. 1980. 7p. ill. DHHS Publication No. (HSA) 81-5660. **HE20.5102:N66**.
Includes checklist of questions which highlight possible consequences of teenage sex.

221. **Changes and Choices: Your Children and Sex**. Bureau of Community Health Services. 1980. 16p. ill. **HE20.5102:C36**.
Provides advice to parents on how to explain sex to their teenage children.

222. **Changes: Sex and You**. Bureau of Community Health Service. 1980. 16p. ill. DHHS Publication No. (HSA) 80-5648. **HE20.5102:C36/2**.

Discusses changes that occur to boys and girls during puberty. Glossary.

223. **Choices: You and Sex**. Bureau of Community Health Services. 1980. 16p. ill. DHHS Publication No. (HSA) 80-5649. **HE20.5102:C45/2**.

Discusses choices that teenagers must make about sex, including birth control methods.

224. **Contraception: A Self-Instructional Booklet to Aid in the Understanding of Contraception**. Bureau of Community Health Services. Rev. 1980. 30p. ill. DHHS Publication No. (HSA) 80-5659. **HE20.5102:C76/3/980**.

Describes six methods of contraception: oral contraceptives, intrauterine devices, diaphragm (and contraceptive creams or jellies), foam, condoms, and "natural" methods.

225. **Facts about Oral Contraceptives**. National Institute of Child Health and Human Development. 1984. 19p. **HE20.3352:Or1**.

Discusses some of the risks associated with the use of oral contraceptives.

226. **Many Teens Are Saying "No."** Bureau of Community Health Services. 1981. 9p. DHHS Publication No. (HSA) 81-5640. **HE20.5102:N66/2**.

Discusses making decisions about sex.

227. **Teenage Pregnancy: Everybody's Problem**. Bureau of Community Health Service. 1977. 11p. DHEW Publication No. (HSA) 77-5619. S/N 017-026-00063-1. $2.00. **HE20.5102:P91/3**.

Briefly discusses the risks and consequences of teenage pregnancy, outlines the alternatives, and provides advice on facing the problem.

228. **Understanding Female Sterilization**. Bureau of Community Health Services. 1976 (repr. 1982). 13p. ill. DHHS Publication No. (HSA) 82-5625. S/N 017-001-00443-0. $37.00 per 100 copies. No single copies sold. **HE20.5102:St4**.

A self-instructional booklet to aid in understanding female sterilization. Describes the tubal sterilization operation.

229. **Your Sterilization Operation: Information for Men**. Public Health Service. 1978. 11p. ill. DHEW Publication (OS) 79-50062. S/N 017-001-00406-5. $2.00. **HE20.8:St4**.

Describes different types of sterilization operations, their discomforts and their risks.

230. **Your Sterilization Operation: Information for Women**. Public Health Service. 1978. 11p. ill. DHEW Publication No. (OS) 79-50061. S/N 017-001-00405-7. $2.25. **HE20.8:St4/2**.

Discusses four types of tubal ligations and other methods of birth control.

See also entry 804.

For additional publications on this topic see Subject Bibliography **SB-292, Family Planning**.

Boating, Diving, and Water Safety

231. **Boating Safety Manual (State Edition)**. Coast Guard. October 1984. 506p. ill. COMDINST M16750.5A. **TD5.8:B63/16**.

Intended for state law enforcement agencies to promote and coordinate uniform boating safety and law enforcement. Provides information for them to assist boaters in complying with the law and operating boats safely.

232. **Boating Statistics, 1983**. Coast Guard. June 1984. 33p. charts, tables. COMDINST 16754.1E. **TD5.11:983**.

Issued annually. Presents data on accidents involving numbered boats and boats used for recreation, and on boating safety activities of the Coast Guard during the year.

233. **Boating Tips for Sportsmen**. Coast Guard. 1980. 13p. ill. **TD5.2:B63/6**.

Provides safety precautions for hunters and fishermen using small boats, including survival in cold water. References.

234. **How to Use Your VHF Marine Radio: FCC Rules for Recreational Boaters**. Federal Communications Commission. Rev. 1981. 30p. ill. S/N 004-000-00386-1. $3.75. **CC1.7:83/subpart CC**.

A question and answer booklet outlining FCC rules for recreational boaters who have VHF (very high frequency) marine radios in their boat.

235. **Navigate Safely**. National Oceanic and Atmospheric Administration. 1973. 12p. ill. NOAA/PA-73028. S/N 003-017-00168-7. $1.75. **C55.2:N22**.

Discusses nautical charts and other helpful navigation publications and information which are available from NOAA. Includes list of safety hints for the navigator.

236. **Navigation Rules: International-Inland**. Coast Guard. Rev. December 1983. 217p. ill. COMDINST M16672.2A. S/N 050-012-00205-3. $6.00. **TD5.6:In8/983**.

Contains the unified Inland Navigation Rules which became effective in 1983. Also includes the International Regulations for Preventing Collisions at Sea.

237.   **NOAA Diving Manual: Diving for Science and Technology**. 2d ed. National Oceanic and Atmospheric Administration. Rev. December 1979. 545p. ill., charts, tables. S/N 003-017-00468-6. $17.00. **C55.8:D64/979**.

Provides the scuba diver with information needed for safe and efficient diving and for carrying out useful scientific investigations. Primarily addresses diving at depths of less than 250 feet. References. Index.

238.   **A Pocket Guide to Cold Water Survival**. Coast Guard. Rev. October 1980. 21p. ill. COMDINST M3131.5. S/N 050-012-00175-8. $3.50. **TD5.8:C67/980**.

Examines the hazards of cold water exposure to shipwreck victims, and provides advice on proven methods of countering the death-dealing effects of such exposure.

239.   **Recreational Boating in the Continental United States in 1973 and 1976: The Nationwide Boating Survey**. Coast Guard. March 1978. 281p. maps, tables. CG-B 003-78. S/N 050-012-00144-8. $8.00. **TD5.11/2:003-78**.

Provides estimates of the number of pleasure boats and their characteristics, safety and communications aboard the boats, household and operator characteristics, and use of Coast Guard services in 1976. Makes comparisons with the 1973 survey.

240.   **The Skipper's Course**. Coast Guard. Rev. December 1979. 86p. ill. S/N 050-012-00159-6. $5.50. To be revised 1985. S/N 050-012-00211-8. **TD5.2:Sk3/979**.

Self-instructional course in boating safety, illustrated with nautical signs, charts, and cartoon drawings.

241.   **United States Diving Manual**. 2 vols. Naval Sea Systems Command. ill., charts, tables. **D211.6/2:D64/v.1,2**.

241-1.   . . . **Vol. 1. Air Diving**. 1985. 329p. NAVSEA-0994-LP-001-9010. S/N 008-046-00110-3. $21.00.

Contains sections on the history of diving, underwater physiology, scuba diving, and diving emergencies. Index.

241-2.   . . . **Vol. 2. Mixed-Gas Diving**. 1981. 240p. NAVSEA 0994-LP-001-9020. S/N 008-046-00103-1. $12.00.

Contains chapters on mixed-gas diving theory and operations planning, mixed-gas and underwater breathing apparatuses, surface-supplied mixed-gas diving operations, deep sea diving systems, and more. Index.

242.   **Water Safety**. Army Corps of Engineers. 1982. 8p. ill. S/N 008-022-00162-0. $2.25. **D103.2:W29/14**.

This booklet for children on water safety includes word games, puzzles, and a picture to color.

243.   **Your Safe Boating Should Include a CME**. Coast Guard. 1983. 4p. AUX 204. **TD5.2:B63/7**.

Describes the Coast Guard Auxiliary Courtesy Marine Examination (CME) which is a free check of your boat's equipment covering federal and state requirements plus additional standards recommend by the CG Auxiliary.

See also entry 706.

Budgeting for the Family

244. **Family Food Budgeting for Good Meals and Good Nutrition**. Home Nutrition Information Service. Rev. December 1981. 15p. tables. Home and Garden Bulletin 94. **A1.77:94/8**.

Presents family food plans at four levels of costs. These plans are guides for estimating food needs and food costs for families.

245. **Guide to Budgeting for the Family**. Agricultural Research Service. Rev. March 1976. 14p. tables. Home and Garden Bulletin 108. S/N 001-000-03514-2. $2.50. **A1.77:108/4**.

Provides brief advice on making and carrying out a family budget, and on using consumer credit.

246. **Guide to Budgeting for the Young Couple**. Agricultural Research Service. Rev. October 1981. 15p. tables. Home and Garden Bulletin 98. S/N 001-000-04262-9. $1.00. **A1.77:98/8**.

Provides brief advice on making and following a budget plan, and on using consumer credit.

247. **Impact of Household Size and Income on Food Spending Patterns**. Economics and Statistics Service. Rev. May 1981. 21p. tables. USDA Technical Bulletin 1650. S/N 001-000-04233-5. $3.00. **A1.36:1650/2**.

Describes the statistical spending relationships which allow policy makers to anticipate what can happen to family food spending behavior when income and household size change.

Business, Economics, and Industry

GENERAL

248. BCD Handbook of Cyclical Indicators: A Supplement to the Business Conditions Digest. 2d ed. Bureau of Economic Analysis. 1984. 195p. tables. S/N 003-010-00127-5. $5.50. **C59.9/3:In2/984.**

Part 1 has a brief description of the three hundred economic time series in *Business Conditions Digest* (entry 249). Part 2 provides historical data for BCD series 1947-1982, both monthly and quarterly.

249. Business Conditions Digest. Bureau of Economic Analysis. Monthly. 116p. charts, tables. S/N 703-012-00000-1. Symbol BCD. $44.00 per yr. Single copy $4.00. **C59.9:vol/no.**

This periodical provides charts and tables on nearly five hundred cyclical economic indicators grouped under the following topics: national income and product; prices, wages, and productivity; labor force, employment, and unemployment; government activities; U.S. international transactions; and international comparisons.

250. Business Statistics Data Finder. Bureau of the Census. Rev. 1984. 19p. tables. **C3.163/6:B96/984.**

Provides brief descriptions of reports from the Current Business Reports series and the Economic Censuses which are published by the Census Bureau.

251. Business Statistics, 1982: A Supplement to the Survey of Current Business. 23d ed. Bureau of Economic Analysis. November 1983. 228p. tables. S/N 003-010-00124-1. $8.00. **C59.11/3:982.**

Issued biennially. Presents the historical data and methodical notes for approximately twenty-one hundred series that appear in the monthly *Survey of Current Business* (entry 260). Monthly data for 1979-1982 and annual data for 1961-1982 are provided for approximately nineteen-hundred series from the "S" (or "blue") pages of the *Survey*. Index.

252. **Directory of Companies Required to File Annual Reports with the Securities and Exchange Commission**. Securities and Exchange Commission. July 1984. 461p. S/N 046-000-00131-1. $12.00. **SE1.27:984**.

Issued annually. Contains an alphabetical listing and industry classification listings of the over nine thousand companies required to file annual reports with the SEC as of 30 April 1983.

253. **Economic Indicators**. Council of Economic Advisors. Monthly. 38p. charts, tables. S/N 752-004-00000-5. Symbol ECIN. $27.00 per yr. Single copy $2.50. **Y4.Ec7:Ec7/yr-no**.

This periodical provides data on current economic indicators under the following topics: total output, income, and spending; employment, unemployment, and wages; production and business activity; prices; money, credit, and security markets; federal finance; and international statistics.

254. **Economic Report of the President, Transmitted to Congress together with the Annual Report of the Council of Economic Advisors, 1985**. President. February 1985. 360p. charts, tables. S/N 040-000-00481-5. $8.00. **Pr40.9:985**.

Issued annually. The major portion of this document is the "Annual Report of Council of Economic Advisors." It contains an analysis and review of economic events and trends during the past year, and projections for the current year. Includes a number of tables with current and historic economic data.

255. **Guide to the 1982 Economic Censuses and Related Statistics**. Bureau of the Census. May 1984. 78p. ill., maps. **C3.6/2:Ec7/2**.

Includes descriptions and representative tables from the various censuses which comprise the quinquennial economic censuses (retail trade, wholesale trade, services, manufacturers, mineral industries, enterprise statistics, and minority and women-owned business).

256. **Industrial Statistics Data Finder**. Bureau of the Census. Rev. 1982. 35p. tables. **C3.163/6:In2/982**.

Provides brief descriptions of statistical series published by the Census Bureau including *Current Industrial Reports*, *Census of Manufactures*, *Census of Mineral Industries*, and other miscellaneous statistical reports.

257. **Marketer's Guide to Discretionary Income**. Bureau of the Census. 1983. 51p. charts, tables. **C3.6/2:M34**.

Discretionary income is the excess income available to families after taxes have been paid and all necessary expenditures made. Includes data for households by selected socioeconomic characteristics.

258. **National Income and Product Accounts of the United States, 1929-1976: Statistical Tables; A Supplement to the Survey of Current Business**. Bureau of Economic Analysis. September 1981. 446p. tables. S/N 003-010-00101-1. $10.00. **C59.11/4:In2/929-76**.

Presents detailed tables showing revised national income and product accounts for 1929-1976. Most annual series begin with 1929, and most quarterly and monthly series begin with 1946.

259. **Standard Industrial Classification Manual, 1972**. Office of Management and Budget. 1972 (repr. 1983). 649p. tables. S/N 041-001-00066-6. $15.00, cloth. **PrEx2.6/2:In27/972**.

> 259-A. **. . . 1977 Supplement**. 1978 (repr. 1983). 15p. tables. S/N 003-005-00176-0. $2.75. **PrEx2.6/2:In27/977/supp**.
> Defines industries in accordance with the composition and structure of the economy and covers the entire field of economic activity. Industries are systematically grouped, and assigned SIC code numbers.

260. **Survey of Current Business**. Bureau of Economic Analysis. Monthly. approx. 100p. charts, tables. S/N 703-036-00000-7. Symbol SCUB. $30.00 per yr. Single copy $4.75. **C59.11:yr/no**.
This periodical contains two parts: "The Business Situation" or "white pages" contains articles, usually with statistics that discuss and analyze various aspects of the current business situation. "Current Statistics" or the "blue pages" is divided into two section: the "General" section provides current statistics on a wide variety of topics; and the "Industry" section provides current statistics for thirteen broad industry groups.

261. **U.S. Industrial Outlook, 1985: Prospects for Over 350 Industries**. International Trade Administration. January 1985. 693p. ill., charts, tables. S/N 003-008-00195-5. $15.00. **C62.17:985**.
Issued annually. Contains an overview of the current status for over 350 manufacturing and service industries based on data from the previous year; outlook for the current year; and projections for the next five years. Index.

See also entries 547-9, 547-10, 547-11, 547-12, 547-15, 547-19.

BANKING, FINANCE, AND INVESTMENT

262. **Daily Treasury Statement: Cash and Debt Operations of the United States Treasury**. Department of the Treasury. Daily (except weekends and holidays). 2p. tables. S/N 748-003-00000-2. Symbol DTS. $110.00 per yr. No single copies sold. **T1.5:date**.
This periodical contains current data on cash, deposits, and withdrawals; public debt transactions and debt subject to the statutory limit; federal tax deposit system activities; and tax and loan note accounts by depository category.

263. **50 Questions and Answers on U.S. Savings Bonds**. Department of the Treasury. 1983. 12p. ill. SBD-1552. **T66.2:B64/64**.
Provides answers to commonly asked questions about the purchase of savings bonds, redemptions and exchange, taxes, and final maturity.

264. **FLSIC=Safety**. Federal Home Loan Bank Board. Rev. 1982. 9p. S/N 012-000-00033-2. $2.50. **FHL1.2:F31/4/982**.
Briefly explains why savings insured with the Federal Savings and Loan Insurance Corporation (FSLIC) equals safety.

265.   **A Guide to Individual Retirement Accounts (IRA's)**. Congress. Senate. Special Committee on Aging. December 1981. 14p. Committee Print, 97th Congress, 1st Session. S/N 052-070-05666-5. $2.00. **Y4.Ag4:R31/10**.

Provides a general introduction to IRAs and discusses the various savings and investment vehicles available.

266.   **Guide to the Monthly Treasury Statement of Receipts and Outlays of the United States Government**. Bureau of Government Financial Operations. May 1983. 47p. **T63.119:T71**.

Presents a step-by-step look at each table of the *Monthly Treasury Statement* and provides glossary explanations for terms as they are used in the tables and schedules. Also provides historical background on the statement.

267.   **High Interest U.S. Savings Bonds: Here's What You'll Want to Know**. Department of the Treasury. 1984. folder, 5p. tables. SBD-1737. **T66.2:Sa9/10**.

Since November 1982 U.S. savings bonds began earning market-based interest, computed every six months. This pamphlet describes denominations, savings plans, and how interest and redemption values are computed.

268.   **Members of the Federal Home Loan Bank Board, 1984**. Federal Home Loan Bank Board. March 1985. 81p. **FHL1.31:984**.

Lists thrift institutions insured by the Federal Savings and Loan Insurance Corporation (FSLIC), Federal Home Loan Bank Board member-insured savings and loan associations, non-FSLIC-insured savings banks, insurance company members, and regulated savings and loan holding companies.

269.   **National Credit Union Directory, 1985**. National Credit Union Administration. May 1985. 340p. tables. **NCU1.16:985**.

Lists approximately sixteen thousand federally insured credit unions arranged alphabetically by state, then by name. Following information is provided for each: name, address, number of members, number of shares, loans, and code to indicate asset size.

270.   **A Reference Guide to Banking and Finance**. 2d rev. ed. Congress. House. Committee on Banking, Finance, and Urban Affairs. Rev. March 1983. 111p. Committee Print 98-1. S/N 052-070-05839-1. $4.75. **Y4.B22/1:B22/27/983**.

Part 1 contains a glossary of selected economic and financial terms and organizations. Part 2 contains summaries of significant federal laws related to banking, housing, and securities. References.

271.   **Savings and Home Financing Source Book, 1983**. Federal Home Loan Bank Board. July 1984. 76p. tables. **FHL1.11:983**.

Issued annually. Presents current and historical financial data on federal home loan banks, savings and loan associations, and housing mortgage markets.

272.   **Tables of Redemption Values for $50 Series EE and $25 Series E Savings Bonds from Redemption Month July 1985 through Redemption Month December 1985**. Bureau of the Public Debt. July 1985. 7p. tables. **T63.209/5-2:985-2**.

Issued semiannually. Lists redemption values of bonds issued since May 1941.

273. **Tables of Redemption Values for United States Savings Bonds Series E for All Months from July 1985 through December 1985**. Bureau of the Public Debt. June 1985. 46p. tables. S/N 748-006-00000-1. Symbol TRVB. $10.00 per yr. (subscription includes publication described in entry 274). Single copy $1.25. **T63.209/6:985-2**.

Issued semiannually. Lists redemption values and interest earned for Series E bonds in denominations of $10, $25, $50, $100, $200, $500, and $1,000 issued from May 1941 through June 1980.

274. **Tables of Redemption Values for United Savings Bonds Series EE for All Months from July 1985 through December 1985**. Bureau of the Public Debt. June 1985. 14p. tables. S/N 748-006-00000-1. Symbol TRVB. $10.00 per yr. (subscription includes publication described in entry 273). Single copy $1.25. **T63.209/7:985-2**.

Issued semiannually. Lists redemption values and interest earned for Series EE bonds issued since January 1980 for denominations of $50, $75, $100, $200, $500, $1,000, $5,000, and $10,000.

275. **Tables of Redemption Values for United States Savings Notes for All Months from July 1985 through December 1985**. Bureau of the Public Debt. 1985. 14p. tables. **T63.210:985-2**.

Issued semiannually. Lists redemption values and interest earned for United States savings notes issued from May 1967 through October 1970 in denominations of $25, $50, $75, and $100.

276. **Treasury Bulletin**. Department of the Treasury. Quarterly. approx. 120p. charts, tables. S/N 748-007-00000-8. Symbol TRBU. $20.00 per yr. Single copy $5.50. **T1.3:yr/no**.

This periodical presents detailed statistical data on Treasury Department operations including financing operations, budget receipts and expenditures, debt operations, cash income and outflow, internal revenue collections, capital movements, yields of long-term bonds, ownership of federal securities, and international statistics.

277. **Your Insured Funds**. National Credit Union Administration. October 1984. 12p. tables. **NCU1.2:In7/2**.

Discusses the operation and coverage of the National Credit Union Share Insurance Fund which insures federal credit unions.

See also entries 76, 99, 447, 457, 473, 475, 498, 1112.

For additional publications on this topic see Subject Bibliographies **SB-128, Banks and Banking** and **SB-295, Securities and Investments**.

INTERNATIONAL TRADE

278. **Basic Guide to Exporting**. International Trade Administration. November 1981. 140p. ill., maps, tables. S/N 003-009-00349-1. $6.50. **C61.8:Ex7/3**.

Uses a step-by-step approach in discussing what is really needed to establish a profitable export trade. Intended for small and medium-sized firms.

279. **Business America: The Magazine of International Trade**. International Trade Administration. Biweekly. approx. 44p. ill. S/N 703-011-00000-4. Symbol CRTD. $57.00 per yr. Single copy $2.50. **C61.18:vol/no.**

This periodical is designed to provide American exporters with timely information on opportunities for trade and methods of doing business in foreign countries. Departments include: Calendar for World Traders (briefings and seminars for exporters and investors); Foreign Market Briefs; Worldwide Business Opportunities (trade promotion events); and Business Outlook Abroad.

280. **The Export Trading Company Guidebook**. International Trade Administration. Rev. March 1984. 186p. charts, tables. S/N 003-009-00364-4. $4.75. **C61.8:Ex7/4/984-2**.

Intended to assist small and medium-sized businesses which are considering starting or expanding their export trade as encouraged by the Export Trading Company Act of 1982. Bibliography.

281. **Foreign Direct Investment in the United States: 1983 Transactions**. International Trade Administration. September 1984. 85p. charts, tables. S/N 003-009-00370-9. $3.25. **C61.25/2:983**.

Issued annually. Identifies specific foreign direct investment transactions in the United States, analyzes recent trends in such transactions, and provides data and related information on significant transactions.

282. **Guide to Foreign Trade Statistics**. Bureau of the Census. Rev. September 1983. 159p. tables. S/N 003-024-05766-2. $4.75. **C3.6/2:F76/983**.

Provides information on the format, content, and general arrangement of data in the foreign trade statistics program conducted by the Census Bureau. Includes sample pages from press releases, reports, publications, and reference materials.

283. **Importing into the United States**. Customs Service. Rev. 1984. 84p. S/N 048-002-00092-7. $3.00. **T17.17:984**.

Outlines procedures regarding customs, invoices, classification and value, and marking of goods which foreign exporters and American importers must follow when bringing commercial goods into the United States.

284. **International Direct Investment: Global Trends and the U.S. Role**. International Trade Administration. August 1984. 99p. charts, tables. S/N 003-009-00369-5. $5.50. **C61.29:984**.

Presents the first comprehensive review by the Commerce Department of global trends and the role of the United States in international direct investment.

285. **Marketing in. . . [series]**. International Trade Administration. Irregular. maps, tables. Overseas Business Reports (OBR) Series. S/N 803-007-00000-4. Symbol OBR. $26.00 per yr. (for all OBRs issued). Single copy price varies. **C61.12:yr-no.**

Volumes of the Marketing in. . . subseries of the Overseas Business Reports series are revised irregularly and generally provide the following information on selected countries: foreign trade outlook; economic trends; best export possibilities; industry trends; trade policy and regulations; distribution and sales channels; banking, credit, and monetary policy; investments; taxation; transportation, communications, and utilities; advertising and research; employment and labor; guidance for business travelers; entrance and residence requirements; and sources of economic and commercial information. Bibliography.

285-1. . . . **Algeria**. May 1982. 37p. OBR 82-07. S/N 003-000-90791-0. $4.50. **C61.12:82-07**.

285-2. . . . **Australia**. November 1984. 32p. OBR 84-10. S/N 003-000-90831-3. $1.75. **C61.12:84-10**.

285-3. . . . **Austria**. June 1982. 46p. OBR 82-08. S/N 003-000-90792-9. $4.75. **C61.12:82-08**.

285-4. . . . **Bahrain**. March 1983. 31p. OBR 82-06. S/N 003-000-90790-2. $2.50. **C61.12:82-06**.

285-5. . . . **Bangladesh**. October 1984. 23p. OBR 84-07. S/N 003-000-90828-3. $1.50. **C61.12:84-07**.

285-6. . . . **Botswana, Lesotho, and Swaziland**. May 1983. 23p. OBR 83-05. S/N 003-000-90815-1. $2.75. **C61.12:83-05**.

285-7. . . . **Cameroon**. September 1984. 20p. OBR 84-06. S/N 003-000-90827-5. $1.50. **C61.12:84-06**.

285-8. . . . **Canada**. February 1985. 33p. OBR 85-01. S/N 803-007-00001-2. $1.25. **C61.12:85-01**.

285-9. . . . **Chile**. August 1982. 35p. OBR 82-13. S/N 003-000-90797-0. $4.50. **C61.12:82-13**.

285-10. . . . **Colombia**. April 1982. 32p. OBR 82-05. S/N 003-000-90789-9. $2.50. **C61.12:82-05**.

285-11. . . . **Congo**. October 1983. 23p. OBR 83-13. S/N 003-000-90820-8. $1.50. **C61.12:83-13**.

285-12. . . . **Cyprus**. February 1982. 24p. OBR 82-03. S/N 003-000-90787-2. $2.25. **C61.12:82-03**.

285-13. . . . **Denmark**. December 1982. 32p. OBR 82-22. S/N 003-000-90806-2. $4.25. **C61.12:82-22**.

285-14. . . . **Ecuador**. February 1982. 26p. OBR 82-02. S/N 003-000-90786-4. $2.25. **C61.12:82-02**.

285-15. . . . **the Federal Republic of Germany and West Germany**. March 1985. 44p. OBR 84-14. S/N 003-000-90835-6. $2.25. **C61.12:84-14**.

285-16. . . . **France**. July 1984. 25p. OBR 84-03. S/N 003-000-90824-1. $1.50. **C61.12:84-03**.

285-17. . . . **Gabon**. June 1982. 28p. OBR 82-10. $3.50. S/N 003-000-90794-5. $3.50. **C61.12:82-10**.

285-18. . . . **Greece**. February 1983. 31p. OBR 83-01. S/N 003-000-90807-1. $3.50. **C61.12:83-01**.

285-19. . . . **Ireland.** November 1984. 26p. OBR 84-09. S/N 003-000-90830-5. $1.50. **C61.12:84-09.**

285-20. . . . **the Ivory Coast.** 1985. 32p. OBR 84-13. S/N 003-000-90834-8. $1.75. **C61.12:84-13.**

285-21. . . . **Kenya.** May 1982. 31p. OBR 82-09. S/N 003-000-90793-7. $3.75. **C61.12:82-09.**

285-22. . . . **Korea.** April 1985. 38p. OBR 85-02. S/N 803-007-00002-1. $1.50. **C61.12:85-02.**

285-23. . . . **Liberia.** August 1982. 22p. OBR 82-12. S/N 003-000-90796-1. $3.00. **C61.12:82-12.**

285-24. . . . **the Netherlands.** March 1982. 38p. OBR 82-04. S/N 003-000-90788-1. $2.75. **C61.12:82-04.**

285-25. . . . **Nigeria.** April 1983. 38p. OBR 83-03. S/N 003-000-90809-7. $3.50. **C61.12:83-03.**

285-26. . . . **Pakistan.** January 1982. 19p. OBR 82-01. S/N 003-000-90785-6. $2.25. **C61.12:82-01.**

285-27. . . . **Peru.** June 1984. 26p. OBR 84-05. S/N 003-000-90826-7. $1.50. **C61.12:84-05.**

285-28. . . . **the Philippines.** May 1983. 33p. OBR 83-06. S/N 003-000-90812-7. $3.50. **C61.12:83-06.**

285-29. . . . **South Africa.** November 1984. 29p. OBR 84-08. S/N 003-000-90829-1. $1.75. **C61.12:84-08.**

285-30. . . . **Sri Lanka.** 1984. 27p. OBR 84-12. S/N 003-000-90833-0. $1.50. **C61.12:84-12.**

285-31. . . . **Thailand.** June 1984. 24p. OBR 84-02. S/N 003-000-90823-2. $1.50. **C61.12:84-02.**

285-32. . . . **Turkey.** November 1983. 28p. OBR 83-14. S/N 003-000-90821-6. $1.50. **C61.12:83-14.**

285-33. . . . **the United Kingdom.** October 1983. 22p. OBR 83-12. S/N 003-000-90819-4. $1.50. **C61.12:83-12.**

285-34. . . . **Venezuela.** May 1985. 24p. OBR 85-03. S/N 803-007-00003-9. $1.00. **C61.12:85-03.**

285-35. . . . **Zaire.** June 1984. 19p. OBR 84-01. S/N 003-000-90822-4. $1.50. **C61.12:84-01.**

286. **Metric Laws and Practices in International Trade: A Handbook for U.S. Exporters.** International Trade Administration. February 1982. 128p. tables. **C61.8:M56.**

Provides basic information to American exporters for fifty-five countries and the European Communities on foreign laws and regulations pertaining to metric requirements for imported products. References.

287. **Services for Exporters from the U.S. Government**. Congress. House. Committee on Energy and Commerce. November 1984. 176p. Committee Print, 98th Congress, 2d Session. Serial GG. S/N 052-070-05977-0. $4.25. **Y4.En2/3:98-GG**.

The most comprehensive current directory of federal agency and department services, programs, and publications available to exporters published by the U.S. government. References.

288. **United States Foreign Trade Annual, 1975-1981**. International Trade Administration. July 1983. 34p. tables. OBR 83-07. S/N 003-000-90813-5. $2.00. **C61.12:83-07**.

Presents summary statistics on United States exports and imports for each year 1975-1981.

289. **U.S. Trade Performance in 1983 and Outlook**. International Trade Administration. June 1984. 91p. charts, tables. S/N 003-009-00367-9. $4.50. **C61.28:983**.

The first report in a planned annual series describing developments in United States merchandise trade. Analyzes the 1983 trade deficit (largest on record) and discusses its effects on the domestic economy.

290. **United States Trade with Major Trading Partners, 1974-1980**. International Trade Administration. November 1982. 47p. tables. OBR 82-20. S/N 003-000-90804-6. $4.75. **C61.12:82-20**.

Includes statistics on U.S. trade with Australia, Belgium-Luxembourg, Brazil, Canada, France, Germany, Italy, Japan, Korea, Mexico, the Netherlands, Saudi Arabia, Taiwan, the United Kingdom, and Venezuela.

291. **United States Trade with Major World Areas, 1975-1981**. International Trade Administration. October 1983. 86p. tables. OBR 83-11. S/N 003-000-90818-6. $2.75. **C61.12:83-11**.

Presents summary statistics on U.S. exports and imports 1975-1981 broken down by major world trading areas.

See also entries 547-14, 1578.

For additional publications on this topic see Subject Bibliography **SB-123, Foreign Trade and Tariffs**.

SMALL BUSINESS

292. **Cost Accounting for Small Manufacturers**. 3d ed. Small Business Administration. 1979. 190p. charts, tables. Small Business Management Series No. 9. S/N 045-000-00162-8. $6.00. **SBA1.12:9/3**.

Provides advice on setting up cost accounting procedures for small manufacturers including jobbing plants, continuous-processing plants, and producing and assembling plants. References.

293. **Credit and Collections for Small Stores**. Small Business Administration. 1980. 73p. ill. Small Business Management Series No. 43. S/N 045-000-00169-5. $5.00. **SBA1.12:43**.

Contains guidelines for a small business to determine if it is practical to offer credit to its customers.

294. **Franchise Opportunities Handbook**. International Trade Administration and Minority Business Development Agency. October 1984. 436p. S/N 003-008-00194-7. $13.50. **C61.31:984**.

Issued annually. Lists and describes the services available from approximately 1,300 equal opportunity franchisors under forty-four categories. Introductory section includes general information on franchising and advice for potential investors.

295. **Franchising in the Economy, 1983-1985**. International Trade Administration. January 1985. 199p. charts, tables. S/N 003-008-00196-3. $4.50. **C61.31/2:983-85**.

Provides data from the fourteenth annual survey of franchisors, based on information from questionnaires filled out by 1,877 franchisors representing most of the business format franchisors and establishments in the United States.

296. **Handbook of Small Business: A Survey of Small Business Programs of the Federal Government**. 5th ed. Congress. Senate. Committee on Small Business. 1984. 248p. Senate Document 98-33. S/N 052-071-00680-0. $7.00. **Y1.1/3:98-33**.

Organized by major executive departments and independent agencies. Each section contains brief background on the organization, mission, and responsibilities of the department or agency together with descriptions of its programs designed to aid small businesses.

297. **Management Audit for Small Construction Firms**. Small Business Administration. 1979. 53p. Small Business Management Series No. 40. S/N 045-000-00161-0. $2.50. **SBA1.12:40**.

Includes checklist of questions with comments for an informal audit or self-appraisal on a broad range of management practices. References.

298. **Management Audit for Small Manufacturers**. Small Business Administration. 2d ed. 1977. 44p. Small Business Management Series No. 29. S/N 045-000-00151-2. $4.25. **SBA1.12:29/2**.

A checklist of 140 questions, with comments for use as an audit or self-appraisal of all aspects of operations and management of a small manufacturing firm. References.

299. **Managing for Profits**. Small Business Administration. Rev. 1981. 164p. S/N 045-000-00206-3. $5.50. **SBA1.2:M33/11/981**.

Provides practical advice for the small businessman on production and marketing, purchasing and collections, financial management, taxation, insurance, and more. References.

300. **Managing the Small Service Firm for Growth and Profit**. Small Business Administration. 1980. 64p. charts, tables. Small Business Management Series No. 42. S/N 045-000-00165-2. $4.25. **SBA1.12:42**.

Provides advice on identifying growth opportunities, evaluating them, determining financial resources needed to exploit them, and developing a suitable marketing strategy.

301. **Purchasing Management and Inventory Control for Small Business**. Small Business Administration. 1980. 66p. charts, tables. Small Business Management Series No. 41. S/N 045-000-00167-9. $4.50. **SBA1.12:41**.

Provides advice on designing effective order systems, making the most of your purchasing dollars, successfully managing your inventory, developing sound relations with and negotiating effectively with suppliers. References.

302. **Small and Disadvantaged Business Utilization Specialists.** Department of Defense. Rev. 1983. 57p. S/N 008-000-00390-4. $4.50. **D1.2:B96/983**.

Lists the locations of the various Defense Department procurement offices and provides the names and addresses for their specialists in small and disadvantaged businesses who can assist small and minority businesses.

303. **Starting and Managing a Small Business of Your Own.** Small Business Administration. Rev. 1982. 85p. Starting and Managing Series No. 1. S/N 045-000-00212-8. $4.75. **SBA1.15:1/4**.

Provides basic advice on starting a new business, buying a going business, investing in a franchise, managing your own business, and looking into special requirements and needs. Discusses special problems of minority and women owners.

304. **The State of Small Business: A Report of the President Transmitted to the Congress.** Small Business Administration. May 1985. 467p. S/N 045-000-00223-3. $10.00. **SBA1.1/2:985**.

Issued annually. The major portion of the document is the "Annual Report on Small Business and Competition" by the Small Business Administration which discusses and illustrates with detailed statistical data highlights and trends in American small business during the year. Footnote references.

See also entries 455, 505, 506-5, 1511, 1623.

See also "Government Property: Purchase and Sales" (entries 1625-1643).

Careers and Occupations

CAREERS

305. Career Opportunities in Art Museums, Zoos, and Other Interesting Places. Employment and Training Administration. 1980. 175p. ill. Occupational and Career Information Series No. 4. S/N 029-014-00123-6. $7.00. **L37.16:4**.

Provides general background on museum activities and preparation for museum work. Includes job descriptions with the following: occupational statement; education, training, and experience requirements; helpful personal characteristics; physical demands; opportunities for employment and promotion. Bibliography.

306. Career Opportunities in the Electric Power and Gas Utilities Industries. Employment and Training Administration. 1978. 145p. ill. Occupational and Career Information Series No. 3. **L37.16:3**.

Discusses history, characteristics, employment trends, and industry projections for the electric power and gas utilities industries. Provides job descriptions. Glossary. Bibliography. Index.

307. Career Opportunities in the Hotel and Restaurant Industries. Employment and Training Administration. 1982. 144p. ill. Occupational and Career Information Series No. 5. S/N 029-014-00199-6. $5.50. **L37.16:5**.

Presents detailed job information on sixty-five occupations in the hotel and restaurant industry. References. Job title index.

308. Career Opportunities in the Trucking Industry. Employment and Training Administration. 1978. 88p. ill. Occupational and Career Information Series No. 2. **L37.16:2**.

Discusses history of trucking, types of carriers, education and training, and career development. Provides job descriptions including those for drivers, operators, mechanics, clerks, and laborers. Glossary. Bibliography. Index.

309. **Criminal Justice Careers Guidebook**. Employment and Training Administration. 1982. 183p. tables. S/N 029-014-00200-3. $7.00. **L37.8:J98**.

Presents detailed descriptions of the duties, job requirements, and career opportunities in over seventy occupations in law enforcement, the judiciary, corrections, and criminal rehabilitation. Bibliography. Job title index.

310. **Environmental Protection Careers Guidebook**. Employment and Training Administration. 1980. 228p. ill. S/N 029-014-00205-4. $7.50. **L37.8:En8**.

Provides overviews and detailed descriptions of the activities, responsibilities, and educational and training requirements of the major occupations directly concerned with environmental protection. References. Index.

311. **Exploring Careers**. Bureau of Labor Statistics. 1979. 552p. ill., tables. Bulletin 2001. S/N 029-001-02224-7. $11.00. **L2.3:2001**.

Utilizes occupational narratives, evaluative questions, activities, and career games presented in fourteen occupational clusters to build career awareness among junior high school students.

312. **Health Careers Guidebook**. 4th ed. Employment and Training Administration. 1979. 231p. ill. S/N 029-000-00343-2. $7.50. **L37.8:H34**.

Provides information on health and health-supportive occupations, education and training, licensing and certification requirements, and sources of financial aid for education and training. References. Index.

OCCUPATIONS

313. **Conversion Table of Code and Title Changes, Third to Fourth Edition, Dictionary of Occupational Titles**. Employment Service. 1979. 394p. tables. **L37.302:Oc1/conversion**.

Section 1 matches three-digit code occupational groups from the third to the fourth edition of the *Dictionary of Occupational Titles* (entry 314). Section 2 matches nine-digit occupational codes. Section 3 lists new codes and their titles in the fourth edition.

314. **Dictionary of Occupational Titles**. 4th ed. Employment and Training Administration. 1977 (repr. 1984). 1412p. S/N 029-013-00079-9. $23.00. **L37.302:Oc1**.

Provides standardized and comprehensive descriptions of job duties and related information for twenty thousand occupations which are grouped into a systemized classification structure using a nine-digit code. Glossary. Index.

314-A. . . . **Supplement**. 1982. 49p. S/N 029-014-00208-9. $4.50. **L37.2: Oc1/2/982/supp**.

Contains titles, codes, and definitions for occupations that have emerged since 1977 and for occupations that were inadvertently omitted.

315. **Guide for Occupational Explorations**. Employment and Training Administration. 1979. 721p. ill. S/N 029-013-00080-2. $12.00. **L37.8:Oc1/2**.

Organizes thousands of jobs and occupations by twelve interest groups (artistic, scientific, plants and animals, protective, mechanical, industrial, business detail, selling, accounting, humanitarian, leading, and physical performing). Provides further breakdowns into sixty-six work groups, and 348 subgroups. Index.

316. **National Survey of Professional, Administrative, Technical and Clerical Pay: March 1984**. Bureau of Labor Statistics. 1984. 97p. Bulletin 2208. S/N 029-001-02826-1. $4.00. **L2.3:2208**.

Issued annually. Summarizes annual survey of selected professional, technical, and clerical occupations in private industry. Includes occupational definitions used in the survey, and a table which compares salaries in the private sector with those in the federal government.

317. **Occupational Conversion Manual: Enlisted/Officer/Civilian**. Department of Defense. Rev. December 1982. 366p. tables. DOD 1312.1-M. **D1.6/2:Oc1/982**.

A compilation of officer and enlisted occupational specialities and civil service general schedule (GS) and wage board (WB) occupations under two complimentary systems with separate codings. Index tables provide cross-references between occupational titles and codes.

318. **Occupational Outlook Handbook, 1984-85**. Bureau of Labor Statistics. 1984. 393p. ill., tables. Bulletin 2205. S/N 029-001-02765-6. $8.50. S/N 029-001-02766-4. $10.00, cloth. **L2.3/4:984-85**.

Issued biennially. This basic reference book is a major source of information on thousands of occupations. For each occupation, it describes what workers do, the training or education needed, usual earnings, and intermediate and long-range prospects for employment. Index.

319. **Occupational Outlook Quarterly**. Bureau of Labor Statistics. Quarterly. 36p. ill., tables. S/N 729-008-00000-1. Symbol OOQ. $11.00 per yr. Single copy $3.00. **L2.70/4:vol/no**.

This periodical contains articles on new occupations, training opportunities, trends, counseling programs, and the results of new government studies. Designed to keep young people, employment planners, and counselors abreast of current occupational and employment developments.

320. **Occupational Projections and Training Data: A Statistical and Research Supplement to the 1984-85 Occupational Outlook Handbook**. Bureau of Labor Statistics. 1984. 115p. charts, tables. Bulletin 2206. S/N 029-001-02804-1. $4.00. **L2.3:2206**.

Presents an overview of the broad changes in employment that are projected for the 1982-1995 period, as well as employment projections to 1995 for over six hundred detailed occupations. References.

321. **Selected Characteristics of Occupations Defined in the Dictionary of Occupational Titles**. Employment Service. 1981. 489p. S/N 029-014-00202-0. $11.50. **L37.302:Oc1/supp**.

Provides data on training time, physical demands, and environmental conditions for a number of occupations.

For additional publications on this topic see Subject Bibliography **SB-044, Employment and Occupations**.

CIVIL SERVICE

322. **Background on the Civil Service Retirement System.** Congress. House. Committee on Post Office and Civil Service. April 1983. 43p. tables. Committee Print 98-5. **Y4.P84/10:C49/14**.

Discusses the history of the civil service retirement system, benefits and eligibility, financing the system, and comparison with other federal retirement systems. Provides data on beneficiaries. Footnote references.

323. **Current Federal Examination Announcements.** Office of Personnel Management. Quarterly. folder, 8p. AN 2279. **PM1.21:no**.

Provides a listing of competitive examination announcements which cover federal jobs throughout the United States unless noted otherwise. Lists announcement number, places to apply, and agencies hiring.

324. **Facts You Should Know about a Career as an Air Traffic Control Specialist.** Federal Aviation Administration. Rev. January 1984. 18p. **TD4.2:Ai7/23/984**.

Provides information that applicants should know about the practices and policies of the Federal Aviation Administration and a career as an air traffic control specialist prior to the initial interview at FAA.

325. **Federal Civilian Workforce Statistics: Biennial Report of Employment by Geographic Area.** Office of Personnel Management. 1984. 130p. tables. **PM1.10/3:983**.

Issued biennially. Presents U.S. government civilian employment statistics by major departments and agencies for states, counties, standard metropolitan statistical areas (SMSAs), foreign countries, and U.S. territories.

326. **Foreign Service Careers.** Department of State. Rev. June 1983. 34p. ill. Department and Foreign Service Series 249. Department of State Publication 9202. **S1.69:249/3**.

Describes careers as foreign service officers of the Department of State, Department of Commerce, and the United States Information Agency, also as foreign service specialists. Describes competitive selection process and special recruitment programs.

327. **How to Get a Job in the Federal Government.** National Institutes of Health. 1981. 34p. ill. S/N 017-040-00481-8. $4.50. **HE20.3008:J57**.

Tells how to complete federal job application forms; explains working conditions, benefits, and holidays; and lists federal job information centers. References.

328. **National Park Service Careers.** National Park Service. Rev. August 1983. 21p. ill., map. **I29.2:C18/4/983**.

Describes employment and career opportunities in the National Park Service and application and hiring procedures. Includes list of federal job information centers.

329. **Position Classification and Pay in State and Territorial Public Health Laboratories, No. 14.** Centers for Disease Control. January 1983. 71p. tables. **HE20.7413:14**.

Provides data on position classification and pay for sixteen jobs in state and territorial public health laboratories. Also includes salary data on similar jobs in hospitals, industry, and the federal government.

330. **Salary Table No. 70: Executive Branch of the Government**. Office of Personnel Management. December 1984. 29p. OPM Document 124-48-6. S/N 006-000-01305-8. $1.50. **PM1.9:70**.

Issued annually. Shows rates of pay for federal general schedule (GS) and executive service employees which became effective 1 January 1985. Detailed tables show hourly and biweekly rates for each GS grade and step to include various deductions.

331. **Working for the USA**. Office of Personnel Management. Rev. November 1982. 26p. Pamphlet BRE-37. S/N 006-000-01297-3. $3.50. **PM1.10:BRE-37/2**.

Provides answers to commonly asked questions about a federal career, including kinds of appointments, benefits, application procedures, incentive awards, leave, ratings, and more.

GETTING A JOB

332. **Getting a Job, Keeping a Job: A Guide to Employment**. National Institute on Drug Abuse. 1984. 15p. DHHS Publication No. (ADM) 84-1287. **HE20.8202:J57**.

Provides advice for former drug addicts, recovering alcoholics, methadone patients, and exoffenders on getting and keeping a job.

333. **Jobs for Which You Can Qualify If You're a High School Graduate**. Bureau of Labor Statistics. Rev. May 1980. 20p. ill. **L2.2:J57/8/980**.

Contains a list of occupations selected from the *Occupational Outlook Handbook* that are open to high school graduates, and highlights the qualifications needed for each.

334. **Jobs for Which You Can Qualify If You're Not a High School Graduate**. Bureau of Labor Statistics. Rev. May 1980. 12p. ill. S/N 029-001-02449-5. $2.50. **L2.2:J57/12/980**.

Contains a list of occupations for which a high school diploma is not required and highlights the job qualifications for each.

335. **Jobs for Which You Can Train through Apprenticeship**. Bureau of Labor Statistics. Rev. May 1980. 8p. ill. S/N 029-001-02448-7. $2.50. **L2.2:J57/10/980**.

Contains a list of occupations such as patternmaker, carpenter, and auto mechanic which often have apprenticeship programs.

336. **Jobs for Which You Probably Will Need a College Education**. Bureau of Labor Statistics. Rev. May 1980. 14p. ill. S/N 029-001-02447-9. $2.75. **L2.2:J57/9/980**.

Contains a list of occupations for which a college education is probably needed, and highlights the educational requirements for each.

337. **Jobs for Which You Probably Will Need Some College or Specialized Training**. Bureau of Labor Statistics. Rev. May 1980. 12p. ill. S/N 029-001-02450-9. $2.75. **L2.2:J57/11/980**.

Contains a list of occupations for which some college, technical, or specialized training is required or recommended.

338. **Marketing Yourself for a Second Career: A Practical Guide for Military Personnel Who Seek a Career in Civilian Life**. Department of the Army. Rev. March 1982. 37p. DA Pamphlet 600-12. **D101.22:600-12/3**.

Provides guidance for the military retiree or veteran on applying for a civilian job, and particularly on preparing a resumé and job application. References.

339. **Merchandising Your Job Talents**. Employment and Training Administration. Rev. 1983. 21p. ill. S/N 029-014-00212-7. $2.75. **L37.2:J57/983**.

Provides advice to the job seeker on self-appraisal, preparing a resumé and letter of application, sources of job information, planning your time, the job interview, testing, and after the interview.

Children, Infants, and Youth

GENERAL

340. **Child Support: A State-by-State Review**. Office of Child Support Enforcement. 1984. folder, 5p. tables. **HE24.2:K54**.

Shows the ratio of collections to total administrative costs by state for child support enforcement programs. National average is $2.93 for each $1.00 of administrative cost.

341. **Children Today**. Office of Human Development Services. Bimonthly. approx. 36p. ill. S/N 717-006-00000-3. Symbol CT. $16.00 per yr. Single copy $2.50. **HE23.1209:vol/no**.

This periodical includes articles, features, book reviews, and other news and reports about children; child development; health and welfare laws; and federal, state, and local services for children and families.

342. **Constitutional Rights of Children**. Congress. Senate. Committee on the Judiciary. 1978. 42p. Committee Print, 95th Congress, 2d Session. S/N 052-070-04797-6. $4.25. **Y4.J89/2:C43/7**.

Reviews a series of recent Supreme Court decisions defining protections that are afforded to children by the Constitution. Footnote references.

343. **Federal Programs Affecting Children**. Congress. House. Select Committee on Children, Youth and Families. 1984. 232p. Committee Print, 98th Congress, 2d Session. S/N 052-070-05892-7. $5.50. **Y4.C43/2:C43/7**.

Describes seventy-two federal programs affecting children under the following topics: income maintenance, nutrition, social services, education and training, health, housing, and tax programs.

See also entries 506-8, 563, 594, 950, 1514, 1517.

PRENATAL AND INFANT CARE

344. **Breast Feeding**. Bureau of Community Health Services. 1980. 22p. ill. DHHS Publication No. (HSA) 80-5109. S/N 017-026-00084-4. $3.25. **HE20.5108:B75**.
Provides tips on how to prepare for breast feeding before the baby is born, how to get started, how to nurse the new baby, and how to continue if you work outside the home. References.

345. **Caring about Kids: Pre-Term Babies**. National Institute of Mental Health. 1980. 14p. ill. DHHS Publication No. (ADM) 80-972. S/N 017-024-01014-6. $2.00. **HE20.8130:B11/2**.
Discusses the medical and emotional problems of having and caring for preterm babies. References.

346. **Caring about Kids: Stimulating Baby Senses**. National Institute of Mental Health. 1978. 10p. ill. DHEW Publication No. (ADM) 77-481. S/N 017-024-00752-8. $2.75. **HE20.8130:B11**.
Offers suggestions to parents on stimulating the senses of their infants.

347. **Facts about Cesarean Childbirth**. National Institute of Child Health and Human Development. 1983. 13p. ill. **HE20.3352:C33**.
Provides answers to questions frequently asked about cesarean childbirth operations and the risks to infants and mothers.

348. **Facts about Premature Birth**. National Institute of Child Health and Human Development. 1983. 9p. ill. **HE20.3352:P91/2**.
Discusses some of the risks and problems associated with premature birth of infants.

349. **Food for the Teenager during and after Pregnancy**. Bureau of Health Care Delivery and Assistance. 1982. 31p. ill. DHHS Publication No. (HRSA) 82-5106. S/N 017-026-00103-4. $4.50. **HE20.5102:T22/2**.
Provides brief information on nutrition, diet, and food for teenagers during and after pregnancy.

350. **Handbook of Postpartum and Infant Care**. Madigan Army Medical Center, Tacoma, Wash. 1983. 24p. **D104.6/2:P84**.
A handbook provided to new mothers at Madigan Army Medical Center with useful advice to help them through the postpartum period and the first year of the baby's life.

351. **Infant Care**. Administration for Children, Youth and Families. Rev. 1981. 74p. ill., charts, tables. DHHS Publication No. (OHDS) 80-30015. S/N 017-091-00228-2. $4.75. **HE23.1002:In3/981**.
This perennial government best-seller has been revised to provide the most up-to-date information on caring for your new baby.

352. **Prenatal Care**. Bureau of Health Care Delivery and Assistance. Rev. 1983. 98p. ill. DHHS Publication No. (HRSA) 83-5070. S/N 017-091-00237-1. $4.25. **HE20.9102:P91**.

Provides a wide range of information on pregnancy, prenatal care, fetal development, lifestyles, problems of pregnancy, birth, and care of the newborn infant.

353. **What Shall I Feed My Baby? A Month-by-Month Guide**. Food and Nutrition Service. 1981. 50p. ill. PA 1281. S/N 001-000-04235-1. $4.25. **A1.68:1281**.
Provides practical advice on breast feeding, preparing formula, bottle feeding, and introducing solid foods. Includes calendar pages for notes about baby's first year.

See also entries 113, 1035, 1039.

CHILDREN: FROM ONE TO TWELVE

354. **Caring about Kids: Learning While Growing, Cognitive Development**. National Institute of Mental Health. 1981. 14p. ill. DHHS Publication No. (ADM) 81-1017. S/N 017-024-01019-7. $2.75. **HE20.8130:L47**.
Describes the development of thinking abilities in young children. References.

355. **Caring about Kids: Talking to Children about Death**. National Institute of Mental Health. 1979. 16p. ill. DHEW Publication No. (ADM) 79-838. S/N 017-024-00949-1. $2.75. **HE20.8130:D34**.
Provides advice to parents and other adults on how to discuss the subject of death with children. References.

356. **Caring about Kids: When Parents Divorce**. National Institute of Mental Health. 1981. 22p. ill. DHHS Publication No. (ADM) 81-1120. S/N 017-024-01102-9. $3.25. **HE20.8130:D64**.
Discusses the emotional problems for children when their parents divorce and offers suggestions for coping with the problems.

357. **Getting Involved [series]**. Head Start Bureau. November 1981. ill. **HE23. 1112:ct**.
Provides advice to parents on how to help in the cognitive, emotional, and social development of their children.

357-1. **Your Child and Language**. 20p. DHHS Publication No. (OHDS) 81-31145. S/N 017-092-00089-8. $2.25. **HE23.1112:L26**.

357-2. **Your Child and Math**. 20p. DHHS Publication No. (OHDS) 81-31144. S/N 017-092-00081-2. $3.00. **HE23.1112:M42**.

357-3. **Your Child and Play**. 20p. DHHS Publication No. (OHDS) 81-31151. S/N 017-092-00084-7. $2.25. **HE23.1112:P69**.

357-4. **Your Child and Problem Solving**. 20p. DHHS Publication No. (OHDS) 81-31146. S/N 017-092-00085-5. $2.25. **HE23.1112:P94**.

357-5. **Your Child and Reading**. 20p. DHHS Publication No. (OHDS) 81-31148. S/N 017-092-00086-3. $2.25. **HE23.1112:R22**.

357-6. **Your Child and Science**. 20p. DHHS Publication No. (OHDS) 81-31143. S/N 017-092-00082-1. $2.25. **HE23.1112:Sci2**.

357-7. **Your Child and TV**. 16p. DHHS Publication No. (OHDS) 81-31149. S/N 017-092-00088-0. $2.00. **HE23.1112:T23**.

357-8. **Your Child and Writing**. 16p. DHHS Publication No. (OHDS) 81-31147. S/N 017-092-00080-4. $2.00. **HE23.1112:W93**.

357-9. **Your Child's Attitude toward Learning**. 20p. DHHS Publication No. (OHDS) 81-31150. S/N 017-092-00087-1. $2.25. **HE23.1112:L47**.

358. **Review of Head Start Research since 1970**. Head Start Bureau. 1983. 99p. DHHS Publication No. (OHDS) 83-31184. S/N 017-092-00092-8. $4.50. **HE23.1102:R32**.
Reviews the literature and summarizes the findings related to the impact of Head Start on the cognitive, emotional, and social development of children; on the health of children; on the families; and on communities.

359. **Your Child from 1 to 6**. Children's Bureau. Rev. 1978. 97p. ill. DHEW Publication No. (OHDS) 78-30026. S/N 017-091-00219-3. $5.00. **HE23.1202:C43**.
Provides parents with invaluable guidance in protecting a child's well-being and guiding his/her emotional, mental, and social development during the critical preschool years.

360. **Your Child from 6 to 12**. Children's Bureau. Rev. 1966 (repr. 1976). 98p. ill. DHEW Publication No. (OHDS) 76-30040. S/N 017-091-00070-1. $5.00. **HE21.110:324**.
Discusses the role of parents as family leaders, what play means in the life of a child, children and money, keeping your child healthy, guiding the child's social involvement, and more.

See also entries 996, 1022.

ADOLESCENCE AND YOUTH

361. **Adolescent in Your Home**. Children's Bureau. 1976 (repr. 1984). 27p. ill. DHEW Publication No. (OHDS) 77-30041. S/N 017-091-00202-9. $3.50. **HE1.452:Ad7**.
Examines the kinds of problems that young people and their parents usually face and tries to stimulate understanding between the members of two very different generations.

362. **Comparative Analysis of Juvenile Codes**. Office of Juvenile Justice and Delinquency Prevention. July 1980. 90p. tables. **J26.2:J98/5**.
Compares juvenile justice codes of the states. Footnote references. Bibliography.

363. **Facts about Precocious Puberty**. National Institute of Child Health and Human Development. 1983. folder, 8p. **HE20.3352:P91**.
Discusses the effects, causes, and treatment of precocious puberty. Precocious puberty is generally considered to be sexual development before age nine in girls, and age ten in boys.

364. **Facts about Youth and Delinquency: A Citizen's Guide to Juvenile Justice**. Office of Juvenile Justice and Delinquency Prevention. November 1982. 38p. NCJ-83888. **J32.8:F11**.

Provides basic information about juvenile crime and the juvenile justice system. Glossary. References.

365. **Homeless Youth: The Saga of "Pushouts" and "Throwaways" in America**. Congress. Senate. Committee on the Judiciary. December 1980. 263p. tables. Committee Print, 96th Congress, 2d Session. S/N 052-070-05481-6. $6.50. **Y4.J89/2:Y8/2**.

Examines the phenomenon of homeless youth, defines the population, describes the families these youth come from, discusses their survival tactics, examines the services available or lacking to them, and assesses their future. Footnote references. Bibliography.

366. **On the Run: A Guide to Helping Runaway Youth in Transportation Centers**. Federal Railroad Administration. 1980. 28p. ill. S/N 050-005-00032-1. $3.50. **TD3.8:R87**.

Discusses the problem of teenagers running away from home and provides profiles of successful programs based in urban bus and train stations that deal with the problem.

367. **One Friendship at a Time: Your Guide to International Youth Exchange**. President's Council for International Youth Exchange. September 1983. 61p. **Pr40.8:Y8/In8/4**.

Tells how to become an exchange student or a host family. Describes various youth exchange organizations and provides guidelines to select a suitable program and organization.

See also entries 123, 130, 135, 145, 216, 217, 218, 219, 220, 221, 222, 223, 508, 955, 974, 1470, 1473.

BABYSITTING

368. **Pocket Guide to Babysitting**. Administration for Children, Youth and Families. 1980. 68p. ill. DHHS Publication No. (OHDS) 80-30045. S/N 017-091-00236-3. $4.50. **HE23.1008:B11**.

Provides practical advice for the teenage babysitter on getting along with parents and children; and on play, feeding, dressing, and bedtime. Includes hints on first aid.

369. **The Super Sitter**. Consumer Product Safety Commission. Rev. 1983. 15p. ill. S/N 052-011-00241-1. $1.25. **Y3.C76/3:2Si8/983**.

Provides advice on safety precautions which the baby-sitter should observe.

CHILD ABUSE AND NEGLECT

370. **Child Abuse and Neglect among the Military**. Children's Bureau. August 1980. 9p. DHHS Publication No. (OHDS) 80-30275. S/N 017-092-00074-0. $2.50. **HE23.1210:M59**.

Discusses the incidence of child abuse and neglect, and programs and regulations of the military to deal with the problem. References. Bibliography.

371. **Child Abuse and Neglect: State Reporting Laws.** Children's Bureau. Rev. December 1979. 39p. tables. DHHS Publication No. (OHDS) 80-30265. **HE23.1210: St2/979.**

Surveys key elements of child abuse and neglect statutes of the fifty states and the outlying territories. Also considers statutory elements of reporting requirements, child protective services, and judicial proceedings of the fifty-five jurisdictions.

372. **Child Sexual Abuse: Incest, Assault, and Sexual Exploitation.** Children's Bureau. April 1981. 18p. DHHS Publication No. (OHDS) 81-30166. S/N 017-090-00061-5. $3.25. **HE23.1210:Se9/981.**

Provides a brief overview of recent research concerning the nature, extent, dynamics, and effects of child sexual abuse, as well as promising treatment techniques. References.

373. **Child Sexual Abuse Prevention: Tips to Parents.** Administration for Children, Youth and Families. 1984. folder, 5p. **HE23.1002:Se9.**

Provides advice on preventing, detecting, and reporting child sexual abuse, and on choosing a preschool or child care center.

374. **The Educator's Role in the Prevention and Treatment of Child Abuse and Neglect.** Children's Bureau. August 1979. 78p. DHEW Publication No. (OHDS) 79-30172. S/N 017-092-00043-0. $5.00. **HE23.1210/4:Ed8.**

Focuses on the following: why educators should be concerned, how to recognize child abuse in a classroom setting, steps to take when reporting suspected child abuse and neglect, and intervention strategies. Bibliography.

375. **Perspectives on Child Maltreatment in the Mid '80s.** Children's Bureau. 1984. 70p. tables. DHHS Publication No. (OHDS) 84-30338. S/N 017-090-00076-3. $2.75. **HE23.1210:P43.**

A collection of twenty articles dealing with the identification, prevention and treatment of the physical, emotional, and sexual abuse of children. Bibliography.

For additional publications on this topic see Subject Bibliography **SB-309, Child Abuse and Neglect.**

CHILDREN: TOYS AND PLAY

376. **Beautiful Junk.** Head Start Bureau. 1975. 12p. DHEW Publication No. (OHDS) 78-31036. S/N 017-092-00004-9. $2.50. **HE23.1102:B38.**

Consists of a list of discarded material or equipment and supplies which can be acquired at relatively low cost to supplement purchased aids for Head Start programs for preschool children.

377. **Caring about Kids: The Importance of Play.** National Institute of Mental Health. 1981. 16p. ill. DHHS Publication No. (ADM) 81-969. S/N 017-024-01020-1. $2.00. **HE20.8130:P69.**

Describes how play is a child's way of living and learning. Offers suggestions on how parents can help.

378. **Children's Play and Social Speech**. National Institute of Mental Health. 1976. 24p. DHEW Publication No. (ADM) 77-354. S/N 017-024-00593-2. $3.75. **HE20.8102:C43/7**.

Outlines findings of a research program which focuses on children's speech in spontaneous play and on the ways in which children develop communications skills. References.

379. **A Child's World As Seen in His Stories and Drawings**. National Institute of Mental Health. 1974. 131p. ill. DHEW Publication No. (ADM) 74-118. S/N 017-024-00380-8. $6.00. **HE20.8102:C43/4**.

Discusses the meanings of drawings and stories in terms of children's perceptions, interests, and abilities from grades one through five. Discusses types of books that children read. References.

380. **Toys: Fun in the Making**. Administration for Children, Youth and Families. October 1979. 30p. ill. DHEW Publication No. (OHDS) 79-30031. S/N 017-090-00052-6. $3.75. **HE23.1002:T66**.

Contains some ideas for making children's toys and games with discarded materials such as egg cartons, milk cartons, shoe boxes, and old clothes.

See also entries 2, 4, 10, 357-3, 1404.

HANDICAPPED CHILDREN

381. **Caring about Kids: Dyslexia**. National Institute of Mental Health. 1978 (repr. 1984). 9p. DHHS Publication No. (ADM) 84-616. S/N 017-024-00780-3. $2.25. **HE20.8130:D99**.

Discusses the problem of children afflicted with dyslexia which is loss of power to grasp the meaning of what has been read.

382. **Caring about Kids: Helping the Hyperactive Child**. National Institute of Mental Health. 1978 (repr. 1984). 9p. ill. DHHS Publication No. (ADM) 84-561. S/N 017-024-00779-0. $2.50. **HE20.8130:H99**.

Discusses the problem of children afflicted with the hyperkinetic behavior syndrome ("minimal brain dysfunction"), and how the parent can help.

383. **Mainstreaming Preschoolers [series]**. Head Start Bureau. 1978. ill. **HE23. 1110:ct**.

This is a series of eight books on children with handicaps, written for Head Start, day care, nursery school, and other preschool staff, and for parents of children with special needs. Each volume provides information on the handicapping condition and offers suggestions on how to deal with it in the classroom and at home.

383-1. **Children with Emotional Disturbances: A Guide to Teachers, Parents and Others Who Work with Emotionally Disturbed Preschoolers**. 147p. DHHS Publication No. (OHDS) 84-31115. S/N 017-092-00036-7. $6.50. **HE23.1110:Em6**.

383-2. **Children with Health Impairments: A Guide to Teachers, Parents and Others Who Work with Health Impaired Preschoolers.** 131p. DHEW Publication No. (OHDS) 78-31111. S/N 017-092-00031-6. $6.50. **HE23.1110:H34.**

383-3. **Children with Hearing Impairments: A Guide to Teachers, Parents and Other Who Work with Hearing Impaired Children.** 131p. DHHS Publication No. (OHDS) 81-31116. S/N 017-092-00032-4. $6.50. **HE23.1110:H35.**

383-4. **Children with Learning Disabilities: A Guide to Teachers, Parents and Others Who Work with Learning Impaired Preschoolers.** 133p. DHHS Publication No. (OHDS) 80-31117. S/N 017-092-00035-9. $6.50. **HE23.1110:L47.**

383-5. **Children with Mental Retardation: A Guide to Teachers, Parents and Others Who Work with Mentally Retarded Preschoolers.** 139p. DHHS Publication No. 81-31110. S/N 017-092-00029-4. $6.50. **HE23.1110:M42.**

383-6. **Children with Orthopedic Handicaps: A Guide for Teachers, Parents and Others Who Work with Orthopedically Handicapped Preschoolers.** 139p. DHHS Publication No. 81-31114. S/N 017-092-00034-1. $6.50. **HE23.1110:Or8.**

383-7. **Children with Speech and Language Impairments: A Guide for Teachers, Parents and Others Who Work with Speech and Language Impaired Preschoolers.** 167p. DHHS Publication No. (OHDS) 80-31113. S/N 017-092-00033-2. $6.50. **HE23.1110:Sp3.**

383-8. **Children with Visual Handicaps: A Guide for Teachers, Parents and Others Who Work with Visually Handicapped Preschoolers.** 127p. DHHS Publication No. (OHDS) 81-31112. S/N 017-092-00030-8. $6.00. **HE23.1110:V82.**

384. **No Easy Answers: The Learning-Disabled Child.** National Institute of Mental Health. 1978. 144p. DHEW Publication (ADM) 77-526. S/N 017-024-00687-4. $6.50. **HE20.8102:L47/2.**
Designed to help parents and teachers understand why certain children have difficulties in learning, why they behave as they do, and how the parents and teacher can help overcome those children's difficulties. Bibliography.

Citizenship, Immigration, and Naturalization

385. **Basic Guide to Naturalization**. Immigration and Naturalization Service. 1980. 115p. M-230. **J21.6/3:N21**.

Intended primarily as a teaching aid for counselors and instructors preparing persons for naturalization examinations. References.

386. **Directory of Voluntary Agencies**. Immigration and Naturalization Service. 1983. 199p. M-233. **J21.2:V88**.

Lists voluntary agencies, legal services corporations, and ethnic, religious, and community organizations which either counsel persons on immigration and resettlement matters or refer them to more experienced agencies.

387-389. **Federal Textbook on Citizenship [series]**. Immigration and Naturalization Service. **J21.9:ct**.

This series is intended for naturalization candidates in the United States to help them learn to read, speak, and write English and to familiarize them with United States history, customs, government, and civil rights and responsibilities. Those who must study at home for the naturalization examination may use these books with the help of a friend. Each student book contains reading text, discussion questions, and self-testing sections, as well as many diagrams and illustrations. The three groups available are listed below (entries 387-389).

387-1. **Becoming a Citizen Series. Book 1. Our American Way of Life**. Rev. July 1980. 111p. ill. M-161. S/N 027-002-00240-7. $5.50. **J21.9:C49/4/bk.1/980**.

Discusses the early history of the United States, our federal government, and how it works under the Constitution.

387-2. **Becoming a Citizen Series. Book 2. Our United States**. Rev. 1973 (repr. 1984). 141p. ill. M-162. S/N 027-002-00135-4. $6.50. **J21.9:C49/4/bk.2/973**.

Discusses the rights and responsibilities of citizenship and how to become an American citizen.

387-3. **Becoming a Citizen Series. Book 3. Our Government.** Rev. 1973 (repr. 1981). 149p. ill., maps. M-163. S/N 027-002-00136-2. $7.00. **J21.9:C49/4/bk.3/ 973.**

Designed to meet the needs of students able to absorb an advanced knowledge of matters relating to the government, the Constitution, and citizenship responsibility.

387-4. **Becoming a Citizen Series. Teachers Guide, Books 1-2-3.** 1971 (repr. 1976). 23p. M-164. S/N 027-002-00100-1. $2.50. **J21.9:C49/4/guide/971.**

Contains general suggestions for conducting classes, as well as a presentation of the text material in each of the three books above.

388-1. **Home Study Course. Section 1. English, Home and Community Life. For the Helper.** Rev. 1967 (repr. 1979). 56p. ill. M-40. S/N 027-002-00019-6. $4.50. **J21.9:En3/2/sec.1/979.**

388-2. **Home Study Course. Section 1. English, Home and Community Life. For the Student.** Rev. 1978. 112p. ill., maps. M-41. S/N 027-002-00209-1. $5.50. **J21.9:En3/sec.1/978.**

This series is intended for persons who speak English but have a limited ability in reading. Contains a vocabulary relating to home and community living and material for practice writing.

388-3. **Home Study Course. Section 2. English and Federal Government. For the Helper.** Rev. 1971 (repr. 1979). 99p. ill. M-42. S/N 027-002-00118-4. $5.00. **J21.9:En3/2/sec.2/971.**

388-4. **Home Study Course. Section 2. English and Federal Government. For the Student.** 1971 (repr. 1979). 179p. ill. M-43. S/N 027-002-00106-1. $6.50. **J21.9:En3/sec.2/971.**

Explains the work of the three branches of the federal government and how the Constitution works.

388-5. **Home Study Course. Section 3. English and State Government. For the Helper.** Rev. 1973 (repr. 1984). 76p. ill. M-44. S/N 027-002-00133-8. $4.75. **J21.9:En3/2/sec.3/973.**

388-6. **Home Study Course. Section 3. English and State Government. For the Student.** Rev. 1973 (repr. 1979). 126p. ill. M-45. S/N 027-002-00137-1. $5.50. **J21.9:En3/sec.3/973.**

Discusses state and local governments, their relation to the federal government, and responsibilities of the citizen in the community.

389-1. **Our Constitution and Government. Home Study Course. For the Helper.** Rev. 1978. 47p. M-40. S/N 027-002-00208-3. $4.25. **J21.9:C76/3/978.**

389-2. **Our Constitution and Government. Home Study Course. For the Student.** Rev. 1978. 161p. ill. M-39. S/N 027-002-00206-7. $6.00. **J21.9: C76/4/978.**

Intended for the candidate who cannot attend public school classes, but who can read and understand English. It is a study guide to the simplified edition below (entry 389-4).

389-3. **Our Constitution and Government. Lessons on the Constitution of the United States Government for Use in the Public Schools by Candidates for Citizenship. Regular Edition.** 1978 (repr. 1984). 408p. ill. M-7. S/N 027-002-00191-5. $9.50. **J21.9P:C76/978.**

389-4 **Our Constitution and Government: Lessons on the Constitution of the United States Government for Use in the Public Schools by Candidates for Citizenship. Simplified Edition.** Rev. 1973 (repr. 1982). 237p. ill. M-8. S/N 027-002-00132-0. $7.00. **J21.9:C76/2/973.**

390. **Gateway to Citizenship.** Immigration and Naturalization Service. Rev. 1979. 165p. M-74. S/N 027-002-00207-5. $3.25. **J21.6/3:C49/979.**

Provides material to be used in naturalization ceremonies and offers selected readings from government officials and naturalized Americans on the significance of American citizenship.

391. **Review of U.S. Refugee Resettlement Programs and Policies.** Congress. Senate. Committee on the Judiciary. July 1979. 350p. Committee Print, 96th Congress, 1st Session. S/N 052-070-05409-3. $7.50. **Y4.J89/2:R25/17/980.**

Discusses existing U.S. refugee admission procedures under immigration laws, and refugee assistance agencies and programs. Provides brief history of U.S. refugee programs since World War II. Footnote references.

392. **Selected Readings on U.S. Immigration Policy and Law: A Compendium.** Congress. Senate. Committee on the Judiciary. October 1980. 502p. charts, tables. Committee Print, 96th Congress, 2d Session. S/N 052-070-05456-5. $8.50. **Y4.J89/2: Im6/5.**

A collection of forty-seven articles organized under the following topics: illegal immigration, proposed solutions, enforcement and amnesty, temporary worker programs, and immigration goals. References.

393. **U.S. Immigration Law and Policy: 1952-1979.** Congress. Senate. Committee on the Judiciary. May 1979. 112p. tables. Committee Print, 96th Congress, 1st Session. S/N 052-070-04957-0. $4.75. **Y4.J89/2:Im6/4/952-79.**

Presents a comprehensive overview and analysis of the major policy issues related to immigration since 1952. Also traces the development of the Immigration and Naturalization Act of 1952 which with substantial amendments remains the basic law. Footnote references.

394. **United States Immigration Laws: General Information.** Immigration and Naturalization Service. Rev. April 1983. 27p. M-50. S/N 027-002-00287-3. $4.50. **J21.5/2:Im6/983.**

Provides information designed to help solve the kinds of problems most frequently encountered by aliens entering the United States.

395. **U.S. Immigration Policy and the National Interest.** Congress. House. Committee on the Judiciary. August 1981. 491p. charts, tables. Joint Committee Print No. 8. S/N 052-070-05628-2. $7.50. **Y4.J89/1:Im6/11.**

A reprint of the final report of the Select Commission on Immigration and Refugee Policy. Provides historical review and analysis of current immigration policy, and presents findings and recommendations of the Commission. References.

See also entry 464.

For additional publications on this topic see Subject Bibliography **SB-069, Immigration, Naturalization, and Citizenship.**

Cities and Urban Affairs

396. **Block Grants and You: A Citizen's Handbook**. Commission on Civil Rights. 1983. 71p. tables. **CR1.6/2:G76**.
Provides basic information on federal block grants to private citizens and groups. Footnote references.

397. **The Land Use and Urban Development Impacts of Beltways Final Report**. Department of Transportation. October 1980. 165p. tables. DOT-TPI-30-80-38. **TD1.20/6:30-80-38**.
Presents an assessment of beltways' land use and urban development impacts, and describes the urban and transportation policy implications. Bibliography.

398. **Neighborhood Planning Primer**. Department of Housing and Urban Development. September 1980. 110p. ill., charts, tables. HUD-NVACP-602. S/N 023-000-00644-8. $5.50. **HH1.2:N31/20**.
Intended for neighborhood preservation organizations involved in the design and implementation of neighborhood revitilization strategies. Describes the essential steps and processes involved in neighborhood planning. Bibliography. Index.

399. **People, Buildings, and Neighborhoods: Final Report to the President and the Congress of the United States**, National Commission on Neighborhoods. March 1979. 369p. S/N 052-003-00616-2. $9.00. **Y3.N31:1/979**.
The commission was established by the National Neighborhood Policy Act of 1977 to investigate the causes of neighborhood decline, and to recommend changes in public policy to become more supportive of neighborhood stability. Footnote references.

400. **The President's National Urban Policy, 1984**. Department of Housing and Urban Development. 1984. 75p. ill., charts, tables. HUD-909-PDR. S/N 023-000-00704-5. $3.25. **HH1.75:984**.
Discusses the three part strategy of the Reagan administration to maintain and improve the social and physical condition of America's cities and urban areas.

401.   **Remember the Neighborhoods: Conserving Neighborhoods through Historic Preservation**. Advisory Council on Historic Preservation. 1981. 20p. ill. S/N 052-003-00802-5. $2.00. **Y3.H62:2N31/2**.

Describes legal and governmental and financing techniques to preserve historic neighborhoods. Footnote references.

See also entries 189, 544, 693, 1519.

Climate and Weather

CLIMATE

402. **Climate Changes to the Year 2000: A Survey of Expert Opinion**. National Defense University. February 1978. 109p. ill., charts, tables. S/N 008-020-00738-2. $7.00. **D5.402:C61**.

Contains narrative and statistical descriptions of five climate scenarios, ranging from large global cooling to large global warming. Summarizes the opinions of twenty-four climatologists and compares their data across latitudinal zones, and across three time periods to the year 2000. References.

403. **Climates of the United States**. Environmental Data Service. 1973 (repr. 1982). 119p. charts, maps, tables. S/N 003-017-00211-0. $5.50. **C55.202:C61**.

Describes the weather conditions of the United States, their causes, and events of interest in the climatological history of the United States.

404. **Climatic Atlas of the United States**. National Oceanic and Atmospheric Administration. June 1968 (repr. 1984). 80p. maps. S/N 003-017-00512-7. $12.00. **C55.22:C61**.

Contains maps of the United States depicting average climatic elements such as temperature, precipitation, humidity, daylight, and more.

405. **Comparative Climatic Data for the United States through 1979**. National Climatic Center. 1980. 99p. tables. **C55.202:C61/2/979**.

Includes detailed tables showing average climatic conditions for each month at approximately 330 weather stations in the fifty states, Puerto Rico, and the Pacific Ocean. The sixteen tables provide data on conditions such as temperature, precipitation, wind, and humidity.

For additional publications on this topic see Subject Bibliography **SB-234, Climate and Weather**.

WEATHER AND WEATHER
INFORMATION

406.   **Aviation Weather for Pilots and Flight Operations Personnel**. Federal Aviation Administration. Rev. 1975 (repr. 1984). 232p. ill., maps. AC 00-6A. S/N 050-007-00283-1. $8.50. **TD4.408:W37/975**.
Part 1 explains weather facts every pilot should know. Part 2 contains topics of special interest such as high altitude, Arctic, tropical, and soaring weather. Glossary. Index.

407.   **Clouds**. National Oceanic and Atmospheric Administration. May 1983. folder, 8p. ill. NOAA/PA 71012. S/N 003-014-00016-9. $2.50. **C55.2:C62/974/rev**.
Gives a picture of each cloud type, the name, a brief description, and cloud code figure according to the International System of Cloud Classification.

408.   **Daily Weather Maps: Weekly Series**. National Environmental Satellite, Data and Information Service. Weekly. 8p. maps. S/N 703-021-00000-0. Symbol DWMW. $60.00 per yr. Single copy $1.50. **C55.213:date**.
This periodical features for each weekly period (Monday-Sunday) a surface weather map of the United States showing weather conditions at 7:00 a.m. Eastern Standard Time. Three other small maps on each page show patterns of wind and temperature, highest and lowest temperature at selected weather stations, and area over which precipitation was reported during the last twenty-four hours.

409.   **Explanation of the Daily Weather Map**. Environmental Data and Information Service. 1982. folder, 21x32". S/N 003-017-00505-4. $2.00. **C55.230:W37**.
Explains symbols and other detail on the daily weather map.

410.   **The Future of the Nation's Weather Services**. National Advisory Committee on Oceans and Atmosphere. July 1982. 82p. ill., charts, maps. tables. **Y3.Oc2:2W37**.
This study was undertaken to analyze budgetary cuts and shifting views about the role of public and private sectors in providing weather services.

411.   **NOAA Weather Radio: The Voice of the National Weather Service**. National Weather Service. Rev. April 1985. folder, 8p. ill., tables. NOAA/PA 76015. **C55.102:R11/4/985**.
Lists the location and frequency of the stations in the NOAA weather radio network.

412.   **A Pilot's Guide to Aviation Weather Services**. National Weather Service. 1979. folder, 18p. maps, tables. **C55.108:Av5/2**.
Provides brief information for private pilots on where to obtain weather information from the National Weather Service, and how to interpret that information.

413.   **Public's Guide to General Weather Information**. National Weather Service. Rev. August 1983. folder, 8p. ill. **C55.108:P96/983**.
Describes the types of weather information which the National Weather Service provides to the public, and how it is distributed.

See also entry 1619.

FLOODS

414.   **Floods, Flash Floods, and Warnings**. National Weather Service. Rev. 1981. folder, 6p. ill. NOAA/PA 81010. **C55.102:F65/3/981**.
   Discusses the dangers of floods and flash floods, and the warnings issued by the National Weather Service. Includes flood safety rules.

415.   **How to Read a Flood Insurance Rate Map**. Federal Emergency Management Administration. April 1981. 14p. maps. **FEM1.8:F65/3**.
   Intended for use by citizens, community officials, banks, and lending institutions to determine the degree of flood hazards in a specific area so that rates of flood insurance can be determined.

416.   **In the Event of a Flood: Tips to Minimize Loss of Life and Property**. Federal Insurance Administration. 1983. folder, 8p. FEM1.202:F65/3.
   Provides tips on how to minimize loss of life and property before, during, and after a flood.

417.   **Questions and Answers on the National Flood Insurance Program**. Federal Emergency Management Administration. Rev. 1983. 26p. FIA-2. **FEM1.2:F65/2/983**.
   Provides answers to some of the most frequently asked questions about the National Flood Insurance Program.

418.   **Tips on Handling Your Flood Insurance Claim after a Major Disaster**. Federal Emergency Management Administration. March 1983. 25p. L-134. **FEM1.11:134**.
   Provides tips on managing claims under the National Flood Insurance Program. Includes a nineteen-page inventory checklist section to aid in preparing an inventory of household furnishings and possessions for claims purposes.

   See also entry 567.

HURRICANES

419.   **Hurricane Warning: A Booklet for Boys and Girls**. National Weather Service. 1977. 16p. ill. NOAA/PA 77001. S/N 003-018-00075-0. $1.75. **C55.102:H94/7**.
   This cartoon book discusses in simple terms hurricane safety rules.

420.   **Perspectives on Hurricane Preparedness: Techniques in Use Today**. Federal Emergency Management Administration. October 1984. 51p. ill. **FEM1.2:H94**.
   Highlights successful efforts of government and industry in innovative hurricane awareness/education programs.

421.   **Preparing for Hurricanes and Coastal Flooding: A Handbook for Local Officials**. Federal Emergency Management Administration. October 1983. 143p. maps. FEMA-50. **FEM1.8:H94**.
   Designed to help communities choose a course of action to reduce damages from hurricanes and coastal flooding. It focuses on the Atlantic and Gulf coasts. References.

422. **Some Devastating North Atlantic Hurricanes of the 20th Century**. National Oceanic and Atmospheric Administration. Rev. May 1982. 19p. maps, tables. NOAA/PA 77019. **C55.2:H94/3/982.**

Includes maps of the North Atlantic and continental areas for seven historical periods showing the tracks of major hurricanes during the pre- and post-hurricane stages. Provides brief information on severity and damage.

See also entries 562, 567.

THUNDERSTORMS AND LIGHTNING

423. **Lightning Protection for the Farm**. Department of Agriculture. Rev. June 1978. 18p. ill. Farmers' Bulletin 2136. **A1.9:2136/4.**

Discusses the nature of lightning and the principles of lightning protection. Provides advice on installing protective devices on farm buildings.

424. **Owlie Skywarn's Lightning Book: A Booklet for Boys and Girls**. National Weather Service. 1978. 16p. ill. NOAA/PA 77023. S/N 003-018-00086-5. $1.75. **C55.102:L62/4.**

This cartoon book discusses in simple terms lightning and safety during thunderstorms.

425. **Thunderstorms and Lightning**. National Weather Service and Federal Emergency Management Administration. June 1984. folder, 6p. ill. NOAA/PA 83001. FEMA L-139. **C55.102:T42/2.**

Provides brief information on the occurrence of thunderstorms and lightning. Includes safety rules and first aid for lightning.

426. **Watch Out: Storms Ahead! Owlie Skywarn's Weather Book**. National Weather Service. Rev. February 1983. 28p. ill. NOAA/PA 82004. S/N 003-017-00513-5. $3.50. **C55.102:Sk9/4/983.**

This illustrated cartoon book describes in simple terms dangerous weather conditions such as hurricanes, tornadoes, lightning, flash floods, and winter storms.

TORNADOES

427. **Tornado Preparedness Planning**. National Weather Service. Rev. December 1978. 26p. charts. S/N 003-017-00434-1. $2.00. **C55.102:T63/2/978.**

Provides planning information to assist local communities and on-site assistance teams in developing community preparedness plans in tornado-prone areas.

428. **Tornado Warning: A Booklet for Boys and Girls**. National Weather Service. Rev. April 1981. 16p. ill. NOAA/PA 75012. **C55.102:T63/5/981.**

Discusses safety precautions which children in tornado country should learn. Includes crossword puzzle.

429.   **You Can Survive a Tornado: Safety Tips**. Federal Emergency Management Administration. 1982. 4p. ill. **FEM1.2:T63**.
Provides tips on how to protect yourself from injury during a tornado.

See also entries 562, 567.

WINTER STORMS

430.   **Safety Tips for Winter Storms**. Federal Emergency Management Administration. Rev. February 1984. folder, 8p. ill. L-96. **FEM1.11:96/2**.
Contains tips for surviving winter storms in the home and on the road.

431.   **Winter Storms**. National Weather Service. Rev. 1979. 8p. ill. NOAA/PA 79018. **C55.102:St7/979**.
Describes different types of winter storms, and how they are generated. Identifies the different types of watches and warnings for hazardous winter weather conditions which are issued by the National Weather Service.

See also entries 63, 69, 567.

Clothing Care and Repair

432. **Clothing Repairs**. Agricultural Research Service. 1965 (repr. 1976). 30p. ill. Home and Garden Bulletin 107. S/N 001-000-00778-5. $3.75. **A1.77:107**.
   Illustrates simple clothing repairs.

433. **Cutting a Fashionable Fit: Dressmaker's Drafting Systems in the United States**. Smithsonian Institution. 1979. 171p. ill., tables. Smithsonian Studies in History and Technology No. 42. S/N 047-000-00353-9. $6.50. **SI1.28:42**.
   Discusses drafting systems for cutting dresses which were popular with both amateur and professional dressmakers in the late nineteenth century. References. Bibliography.

434. **How to Prevent and Remove Mildew: Home Methods**. Department of Agriculture. Rev. November 1980. 15p. ill. Home and Garden Bulletin 68. S/N 001-000-04207-6. $2.50. **A1.77:68/8**.
   Discusses how to prevent mildew in the home and how to remove it from clothing, wood, books, leather, and other household articles.

435. **Sewing Menswear: Jackets**. Extension Service. February 1977.. 43p. ill. PA 1174. S/N 001-000-03658-1. $4.50. **A1.68:1174**.
   Provides advice on selecting styles, fabrics, and patterns and on sewing techniques for men's jackets.

436. **Sewing Menswear: Pants**. Extension Service. April 1975. 32p. ill. PA 1115. S/N 001-000-03412-0. $3.50. **A1.68:1115**.
   Provides advice on selecting styles, fabrics, and patterns and on sewing techniques for men's pants.

See also entry 481.

Coins, Medals, and Currency

437. **Domestic and Foreign Coins Manufactured by Mints in the United States**. Bureau of the Mint. Rev. 1981. 178p. tables. S/N 048-005-00025-0. $4.50. **T28.1/a: C666/2/793-980**.

Presents a complete historical record of the number of coins manufactured by U.S mints, including coins manufactured for foreign governments from 1793 to 1980. Does not include illustrations of the coins.

438. **Facts about United States Money**. Department of the Treasury. 1976. 28p. ill. S/N 048-000-00301-0. $1.50. **T1.40:976**.

Explains how money is coined and paper currency is printed, shows locations of important features on paper currency to detect counterfeiting, gives specifications for U.S. coins, and tells how to exchange mutilated paper currency.

439. **Know Your Money**. Secret Service. Rev. 1983. 20p. ill. S/N 048-006-00010-8. $3.25. **T34.2:M74/983**.

Describes and illustrates how to recognize counterfeit bills and forged U.S. government checks.

440. **Medals of the United States Mint Issued for Public Sale**. Bureau of the Mint. Rev. 1972. 315p. ill. S/N 048-004-00479-6. $12.00. **T28.2:M46/2/972**.

Describes 253 medals that have been authorized by Congress for Presidents, secretaries of the treasury, directors of the mint, and military heroes and victories. Includes brief biographies of the individuals or descriptions of the event.

441. **Official Coins and Medals Sold by the United States Mint**. Bureau of the Mint. 1983. 16p. ill. **T28.2:C66/10**.

Provides descriptions and prices of numismatic coins and medals sold by the U.S. Mint including annual proof coin sets, Olympic commemorative coins, gold medallions, and special souvenir sets.

For additional publications on this topic see Subject Bibliography **SB-198, Coins and Medals**.

Common Tools and Repairs

442. **Common Wood and Metal Repair**. Department of the Army. April 1979 (repr. 1982). 69p. ill. FM 43-4. S/N 008-020-00909-1. $5.00. **D101.20:43-4**.

Discusses preliminary inspection of wood and metal items, preparation for repair, repair procedures, inspection of finished work, and safety precautions. Intended as a guide to the repair of such items as furniture, food service equipment, tools, and implements.

443. **A Consumer's Guide to Safe Ladder Selection Care and Use**. Consumer Product Safety Commission. July 1980. 10p. ill. **Y3.C76/3:8L12**.

Provides advice on the proper selection, use, and care of stepladders, and single and extension ladders.

444. **Tools and Their Uses**. Bureau of Naval Personnel. 1971 (repr. 1985). 179p. ill. NAVPERS 10085. S/N 008-047-00145-2. $7.00. **D208.11:T61/2/971**.

Covers common hand tools and power tools, measuring tools and techniques, fastening components and procedures, grinding operations, metal cutting operations, and miscellaneous tasks. Index.

445. **Use and Care of Hand Tools and Measuring Tools**. Department of the Army. Rev. December 1982. 289p. ill. TM9-243. **D101.11:9-243/2**.

Provides information on the use and care of a large number of common hand tools and measuring tools. References. Index.

Computers and Data Processing

446. **An Assessment of Alternatives for a National Computerized Criminal History System**. Congress. Office of Technology Assessment. October 1982. 208p. charts, tables. OTA-CIT-161. S/N 052-003-00896-3. $7.00. **Y3.T22/2:2C86/2**.

Examines the current status of criminal history record systems, evaluates alternatives for a national computerized system, and discusses policy issues to be considered so that the beneficial aspects of a national system are maximized and adverse effects are minimized. Footnote references. Index.

447. **Computer Crime: Electronic Fund Transfer Systems and Crime**. Bureau of Justice Statistics. July 1982. 182p. NCJ 83736. S/N 027-000-01170-5. $7.00. **J29.2:El2**.

Examines the nature and extent of crime related to electronic funds transfer (EFT) systems. References.

448. **Computer Education: A Catalog of Projects Sponsored by the U.S. Department of Education**. National Institute of Education. 1984. 299p. S/N 065-000-00202-7. $9.00. **ED1.302:C73**.

Contains an overview of the general types of projects that were ongoing during 1983. Includes 275 project summaries with names and addresses of people to contact for more information.

449. **Computers on the Farm: Farm Uses for Computers, How to Select Software and Hardware, and Online Services in Agriculture**. Department of Agriculture. March 1984. 37p. ill. Farmers' Bulletin 2277. **A1.9:2277**.

Provides advice on selecting and buying computer hardware and software for use on the farm. Describes information services available online from the Department of Agriculture, states, and private sources.

450. **A Directory of Computer Software, 1984**. National Technical Information Service. 1984. 225p. **C51.11/2:984**.

Issued annually. Lists approximately five hundred machine-readable computer programs compiled in cooperation with over one hundred federal agencies and their contractors. Order information is provided. Five indexes: agency, accession number, subject, hardware, and language.

451. **A Directory of Computerized Data Files, 1984**. National Technical Information Service. 1984. 328p. **C51.11/2-2:984**.

Issued annually. An annotated catalog of over seven hundred numeric, statistical, and technical source files available in magnetic tape from NTIS for approximately fifty agencies. Arranged under twenty-seven topics. Agency, number, and subject indexes.

452. **Introduction to FORTRAN**. Naval Education and Training Command. 1980. 138p. NAVEDTRA 10078-1. S/N 008-047-00306-4. $6.50. **D207.208/2:F76**.

Serves as an introduction to FORTRAN (FORmula TRANslation), which is a general purpose, procedure-oriented, high-level computer programming language.

453. **Introduction to Programming in BASIC**. Naval Education and Training Command. Rev. 1983. 184p. NAVEDTRA 10079-1. S/N 008-047-000361-7. $4.50. **D207.208/2:P94/983**.

Provides a hands-on introduction to programming in BASIC. Each chapter includes exercises and suggested solutions. Designed for individual study.

454. **Instructional Use of Computers in Public Schools, Spring 1982**. National Center for Education Statistics. 1984. 27p. tables. FRSS (Fast Response Survey System) Report 14. NCES 84-201. S/N 065-000-00197-7. $1.00. **ED1.125:14**.

Provides summary data on the availability of computers in elementary and secondary schools and the extent of computer-based instruction.

455. **Micro-Computers for Use in Small Business: Small Business Management Training Instructor's Guide**. Small Business Administration. 1984. 82p. **SBA1.19:B96/3**.

Provides advice on selecting and using minicomputer hardware and software in a small business. References.

456. **Reference Manual for the Ada Programming Language**. Department of Defense. February 1983. 325p. ANSI/MIL-STD-1815A-1983. S/N 008-000-00394-7. $8.00. **D7.10:1815A-1983**.

Describes the Department of Defense sponsored Ada computer programming language, a common language for programming large scale and real-time systems.

457. **Selected Electronic Funds Transfer Issues: Privacy, Security, and Equity; Background Paper**. Congress. Office of Technology Assessment. March 1982. 85p. tables. OTA-BP-CIT-12. S/N 052-003-00868-8. $4.75. **Y3.T22/2:2El2**.

Analyzes possible implications of electronics fund transfer (EFT) for privacy, security, and equity. Footnote references.

See also entries 486, 487, 826, 1161.

For additional publications on this topic see Subject Bibliography **SB-051, Computers and Data Processing**.

Constitution and
Historic Documents

458. **Bill of Rights (Facsimile)**. National Archives and Records Service. 1958. poster, 31x33". S/N 022-002-00022-8. $2.75. **GS4.11/2:B49**.

A facsimile of the enrolled original Bill of Rights, reproduced in the yellowish tint and faded brown ink of the original.

459. **Constitution of the United States (Facsimile)**. National Archives and Records Service. 1958 (repr. 1976). poster, 31x38". S/N 022-002-00023-6. $2.75. **GS4.11/2:C76**.

Four sheets of the original document have been reproduced on one large page in the yellowish tint and faded brown ink of the original.

460. **The Declaration of Independence and the Constitution of the United States of America**. Congress. 1979 (repr. 1984). 56p. House Document 96-143. S/N 052-071-00596-0. $4.50. **X96-1:H.doc.143**.

Contains the text of the Declaration of Independence, the Constitution, amendments to the Constitution, and proposed amendments not ratified by the states. Index.

461. **Declaration of Independence (Facsimile)**. National Archives and Records Service. 1958. poster, 29x35". S/N 022-002-00024-4. $2.75. **GS4.11/2:D37**.

A facsimile reproduced in the yellowish tint and faded brown ink of the original 1776 document.

462. **Flag Manual**. Marine Corps. 1971 (repr. 1982). 92p. ill. MCO P10520.3A. S/N 008-055-00055-6. $6.00. **D214.9/2:F59**.

Gives a brief history of the American flag and lists the proper times and manner in which the flag is to be displayed and folded. Also includes information on Marine Corps flags, colors, standards, guidons, and plates and miscellaneous flags.

463.   **Washington's Farewell Address to the People of the United States**. Congress. 1979. 30p. Senate Document 96-5. S/N 052-071-00575-7. $3.75. **X96-1:S.doc.5**.

Includes the text of Washington's farewell address written in 1796 which was intended to take him out of contention for a third term, but has become a landmark document because of his wise advice.

464.   **A Welcome to U.S.A. Citizenship**. Immigration and Naturalization Service. 1980. 38p. M-76. **J21.9:C49/5**.

Includes the text of the Declaration of Independence, Constitution, Pledge of Allegiance to the Flag, Oath of Allegiance, and the Star Spangled Banner (song). Intended for new citizens at their naturalization ceremony.

See also entries 571, 1060, 1061-1.

Consumer Information and Protection

GENERAL

465. **A Business Guide to the Federal Trade Commission Mail Order Rule**. Federal Trade Commission. 1983. 19p. **FT1.8/2:B96**.

Provides guidance to mail order businesses on how to comply with FTC rules that require merchandise to be shipped on time, and in case of delays to notify customers and provide them with an option of accepting the delay or cancelling the order and receiving a prompt refund.

466. **Buying Lots from Developers**. Department of Housing and Urban Development. Rev. February 1982. 20p. ill. HUD-357-I(6). S/N 023-000-00694-4. $2.50. **HH1.2:L91/982**.

Provides advice to the consumer on buying lots from developers. Discusses protection against fraud and requirements for full disclosure which are available under the Interstate Land Sales Act of 1968.

467. **The Changing Telephone Industry: Access Charges, Universal Service, and Local Rates**. Congressional Budget Office. June 1984. 88p. charts, tables. S/N 052-070-05940-1. $3.25. **Y10.2:T23**.

Analyzes the consequences of the FCC decision which requires the telephone industry to alter the manner in which costs, particularly fixed costs, are allocated and recovered. Footnote references.

468. **Consumer Affairs Guide**. Department of the Treasury. Rev. 1982. 16p. S/N 048-000-00354-1. $2.00. **T1.10/2:C76/982**.

Contains information on a number of Treasury Department services including U.S. savings bonds, direct bank deposit, sale of uncut sheets of currency, commemorative silver half dollars, and IRS taxpayer assistance.

469. **The Difficult Consumer Problem: Where to Go When All Else Fails**. Office of Consumer Affairs. 1983. 11p. **HE1.502:D56**.

Includes lists of third-party dispute resolution programs, trade and professional associations offering formal complaint handling procedures, and other sources of help when traditional methods at the retailer and manufacturer level have failed.

470. **Directory of Better Business Bureaus**. Food and Drug Administration. May 1984. folder, 8p. **HE20.4002:B46**.

Contains list of addresses and telephone numbers of better business bureaus in major cities in the United States and Canada.

471. **Do You Speak "Credit"?** Federal Trade Commission. February 1981. 12p. ill. S/N 018 000 00290-6. $2.75. **FT1.2:C86/7**.

Designed to help the average consumer understand the content of a loan contract. Quotes legal clauses used in credit contracts and provides a plain English translation.

472. **Facts about Hearing and Hearing Aids**. National Bureau of Standards. Rev. 1979. 31p. ill. Consumer Information Series No. 4. S/N 003-003-02024-9. $3.50. **C13.53:4/3**.

Explains briefly how the ear functions, describes various types of hearing loss, explores different kinds of hearing aids available, and offers practical advice on selection, use, and maintenance of hearing aids.

473. **Give Yourself Credit: Guide to Consumer Credit Laws**. Congress. House. Committee on Banking, Finance and Urban Affairs. April 1983. 195p. tables. House Document 98-46. **Y1.1/7:98-46**.

Explains what credit is, how to apply for credit, how to use credit responsibly, and what your rights are under current consumer credit laws.

474. **A Guide to Funeral Planning**. Congress. House. Select Committee on Aging. 1984. 41p. Committee Publication No. 98-466. S/N 052-070-05982-6. $1.75. **Y4.Ag4/2:F96/8**.

Discusses the Federal Trade Commission's funeral rule, alternatives to traditional funerals, memorial societies, and death benefits.

475. **How to Advertise Consumer Protection: Complying with the Law**. Federal Trade Commission. June 1982. 20p. ill. S/N 018-000-00294-9. $48.00 per 50 copies. No single copies sold. **FT1.8/2:C86/3**.

Describes the disclosure statements which must be present in advertisements for open-end credit, closed-end credit, and consumer leases.

476. **How to Write a Wrong: Complain Effectively and Get Results**. Federal Trade Commission. 1983. 16p. ill. S/N 018-000-00298-1. $41.00 per 100 copies. No single copies sold. **FT1.2:W93**.

Written for senior citizens. Explains the rights of consumers and provides a step-by-step approach for writing a complaint letter. Emphasis is placed on door-to-door and mail order sales.

477. **Lost or Damaged Household Goods**. Interstate Commerce Commission. Rev. 1979. 16p. ill. Public Advisory No. 4. S/N 026-000-01147-7. $3.00. **IC1.31:4/979**.

Provides the householder with information on what to expect from the mover, and what to do when household goods are lost or damaged during an interstate move.

478. **Price of Death: A Survey Method and Consumer Guide for Funerals, Cemeteries, and Grave Markers**. Federal Trade Commission. 1975. 35p. Consumer Survey Handbook 3. S/N 018-000-00185-3. $4.50. **FT1.8/3:3**.

Contains information and instructions which will enable consumers to survey and compare funeral, cemetery, and grave marker prices in their communities in order to obtain the lowest price consistent with their needs and desires. Glossary.

479. **Shopper's Guide**. Department of Agriculture. 1974. 368p. ill., tables. Yearbook of Agriculture 1974. S/N 001-000-03300-0. $11.00, cloth. **A1.10:974**.

A compilation of articles by consumer specialists arranged under six topics: food, materials, equipment, gardening, services, and recreation. Information ranges from the number of servings you can expect from a package of food to how to deal with movers. References. Index.

480. **What You Should Know about Wine Labels**. Bureau of Alcohol, Tobacco and Firearms. Rev. September 1984. folder, 5p. ill. ATF P5100.11. **T70.2:G76/984**.

Describes what the wine label tells about the brand, vintage date, varietal designation of dominant grapes used, alcohol content, appellation of origin, viticultural area, and name or trade name.

481. **What's New about Care Labels**. Federal Trade Commission. April 1984. 9p. S/N 018-000-00304-0. $16.00 per 50 copies. No single copies sold. **FT1.2:L11/7**.

Brief explanation of the FTC's revised rule on the amount and type of information to be placed on care labels required in textile clothing.

See also entries 67, 176, 537, 912, 1414.

For additional publications on this topic see Subject Bibliography **SB-002, Consumer Protection**.

CONSUMER PRICE INDEX

482. **CPI Detailed Report**. Bureau of Labor Statistics. Monthly. approx. 80p. charts, tables. S/N 729-002-00000-3. Symbol CPI. $25.00 per yr. Single copy $4.00. **L2.38/3:yr/no**.

This periodical contains detailed data on Consumer Price Indexes for all urban consumers and for urban wage earners and clerical workers by separate groups and items of services and commodities, and for regions and major cities.

483. **A Description of Major Price Indexes and Their Energy Content**. Energy Information Administration. August 1982. 57p. DOE/EIA-0351. **E3.2:P93/2**.

Describes the content, structure, and treatment of energy within the most frequently used and best-known general price indexes, as well as the behavior of the energy and nonenergy components of these indexes over time. Bibliography.

484. **Relative Importance of Components in the Consumer Price Index, 1984.**
Bureau of Labor Statistics. Rev. May 1985. 44p. tables. Bulletin 2233. S/N
029-001-02844-0. $1.75. **L2.3:2233**.

Revised annually. Presents data on the relative importance of components in the
Consumer Price Index for Urban Consumers (CPI-U) and the Consumer Price Index
for Urban Wage Earners and Clerical Workers (CPI-W) as of the end of the year.
References.

Copyrights, Patents, and Trademarks

485. **Attorneys and Agents Registered to Practice before the U.S. Patent and Trademark Office, 1984**. Patent and Trademark Office. 1984. 342p. S/N 003-004-00609-9. $9.50. **C21.9/2:984**.

Provides name, address, telephone number, and registration number of registered attorneys and agents. Part 1 is an alphabetical list by surname. Part 2 is a geographic list by state and foreign country.

486. **Automating the Patent and Trademark Office**. Patent and Trademark Office. 1982. 27p. ill., charts, tables. **C21.2:Au8**.

Summarizes the master plan which is intended to fully automate the operations of the Patent and Trademark Office by 1990, and provide paperless operations with electronic text and computer-accessible image databases.

487. **Final Report of the National Commission on New Technological Uses of Copyrighted Works**. 1979. 171p. tables. S/N 030-002-00143-8. $6.50. **Y3.C79:1/978**.

Presents the commission's findings and recommendations relating to changes needed in copyright laws caused by new technologies of photocopying and computers in order to protect the rights of copyright owners while considering the concerns of the general public.

488. **General Information Concerning Patents: A Brief Introduction to Patent Matters**. Patent and Trademark Office. Rev. 1984. 44p. S/N 003-004-00607-2. $2.00. **C21.2:P27/984**.

Provides general information about patents and the operations of the Patent and Trademark Office. Intended especially for inventors, prospective applicants, and students.

489. **General Information Concerning Trademarks**. Patent and Trademark Office. Rev. 1984. 24p. S/N 003-004-00605-6. $1.75. **C21.26:984**.

Provides a brief introduction to the definition and functions of trademarks, and what applicants must do to register a trademark. Includes application forms.

490. **Patents and Inventions: An Information Aid for Inventors**. Patent and Trademark Office. Rev. August 1977 (repr. 1980). S/N 003-004-00545-9. $3.25. **C21.2:P27/10/977**.

A step-by-step guide to help the inventor decide whether to apply for a patent, obtain patent protection, and promote his invention.

491. **Patents and Trademark Style Manual: A Supplement to the United States Government Printing Office Style Manual**. Patent and Trademark Office. 1984. 136p. ill. S/N 003-004-00606-4. $5.50. **GP1.23/4:St9/984/supp**.

This supplement is intended to be used in conjunction with the *United States Government Printing Office Style Manual* (entry 172). It serves as a guide to writers, editors, and printers of patent and trademark materials. Index.

492. **Revolutionary Ideas: Patents and Progress in America**. Patent and Trademark Office. 1976. 28p. ill., tables. S/N 003-004-00537-8. $1.75. **C21.2:R32**.

Lists nearly two hundred famous and significant inventors and their patents, copies of which are available from the Patent and Trademark Office. The cover of this American Revolution Bicentennial commemorative publication is a facsimile of the first patent issued in 1790.

See also entry 1620.

For additional publications on this topic see Subject Bibliographies **SB-021, Patents and Trademarks** and **SB-126, Copyrights**.

Crime and Criminal Justice System

GENERAL

493. **Dictionary of Criminal Justice Data Terminology: Terms and Definitions Proposed for Interstate and National Data Collection and Exchange**. 2d ed. Bureau of Justice Statistics. 1981. 266p. NCJ-76939. **J29.9:NCJ-76939**.

Includes terms relating to crime and the criminal justice process and agency statistics where an adequate basis for national concensus on fact and language exists.

494. **Directory of Automated Criminal Justice Information Systems, 1983**. Bureau of Justice Statistics. Rev. 1983. 985p. tables. **J29.8:C86/983**.

Contains listings of the automated criminal justice information systems used by police, courts, corrections, and other criminal justice agencies. Indexes by state jurisdiction, systems name, systems functions, and CPU (computer processing unit) manufacturer.

495. **Report to the Nation on Crime and Justice: The Data**. Bureau of Justice Statistics. 1983. 112p. charts, tables. NCJ-87068. S/N 027-000-01175-6. $6.00. **J29.9:NCJ-87068**.

This first comprehensive picture of crime and the criminal justice system in the United States brings together a wide variety of data from a number of research and reference sources. References. Index.

496. **Sourcebook of Criminal Justice Statistics, 1983**. 11th ed. Bureau of Justice Statistics. 1984. 724p. tables. S/N 027-000-01200-1. $15.00. **J29.9:SD-SB-11**.

Issued annually. The data in this statistical compendium has been organized under the following topics: characteristics of the criminal justice system, public attitudes towards crime, nature and distribution of known offenses, persons arrested, disposition of civil and criminal cases in the courts, and corrections. References. Index.

497.   **Uniform Crime Reports: Crime in the United States, 1983**. Federal Bureau of Investigation. 1984. 397p. charts, tables. S/N 027-001-00035-1. $9.00. **J1.14/7:983**.

Issued annually. This is the official comprehensive statistical summary of the incidence of crime in the United States. The opening section provides general summary information about crime trends and a crime index. Subsequent sections deal with statistics of specific crimes and their rates in over fifteen thousand cities, counties, and suburban and rural areas.

See also entries 309, 362, 364, 371, 446, 697.

See also "Firearms, Explosives, and Gun Control" (entries 713-726).

For additional publications on this topic see Subject Bibliographies **SB-036, Crime and Criminal Justice** and **SB-074, Juvenile Delinquency**.

CRIME

498.   **The Cash Connection: Organized Crime, Financial Institutions, and Money Laundering**. President's Commission on Organized Crime. October 1984. 99p. S/N 041-001-00281-2. $3.75. **Pr40.8:C86/C26**.

Examines the problems of money laundering and law enforcement authorities' response to it. Provides ten case studies which show the diversity and magnitude of these schemes. Includes the recommendations of the commission.

499.   **The Future of Crime**. National Institute of Mental Health. 1980. 89p. Crime and Delinquency Issues Series. DHHS Publication No. (ADM) 80-912. S/N 017-024-01011-1. $4.75. **HE20.8114/3:C86**.

Analyzes sociological theories of crime causation with respect to six major aspects of the American social structure and considers the future of crime in America. Also considers unconventional crime such as white collar and political crime. Footnote references.

500.   **Intimate Victims: A Study of Violence among Friends and Relatives**. Law Enforcement Assistance Administration. January 1980. 57p. charts, tables. **J26.10:SD-NCS-N-14**.

Presents data and analyses of events occurring during the period 1973-1976 as derived from semiannual interviews of occupants of sixty thousand housing units nationwide. Discusses the setting, victim-offender interaction, and aftermath of violence among intimates.

501.   **President's Task Force on Victims of Crime: Final Report**. December 1982. 152p. S/N 040-000-00461-1. $7.00. **Pr40.8:V66/F49**.

Contains proposed constitutional amendment and recommendations for legislative and executive actions to protect and reimburse the victims of crime. Footnote references.

502.   **Robbery in the United States: An Analysis of Recent Trends and Patterns**. National Institute of Justice. September 1983. 32p. tables. **J28.2:R53**.

Analyzes recent trends and patterns of robbery with respect to weapon use, geographic distribution, robbery sites, characteristics of robbers and victims, and robbery careers. References.

503. **School Crime and Disruption: Prevention Models**. National Institute of Education. June 1978. 199p. S/N 017-080-01908-6. $7.00. **HE19.202:C86**.

A collection of seventeen papers which discuss probable causes of school crime and offer practical approaches to prevent or control it. Footnote references.

See also entries 447, 1707, 1709.

CRIME PREVENTION

504. **The Crime Prevention Coloring Book**. 2d ed. Department of the Army. 1979 (repr. 1984). 24p. ill. S/N 008-020-01006-5. $1.50. **D101.12:C86/4**.

A cartoon coloring book for children on crime prevention.

505. **Security and the Small Business Retailer**. National Institute of Law Enforcement and Criminal Justice. 1979. 128p. ill. S/N 027-000-00765-1. $6.00. **J28.9:Se2**.

Presents ways in which the small business owner can deal with robbery, burglary, shoplifting, and employee theft.

506. **Take a Bite out of Crime [series]**. Department of Justice.

This series of booklets has been prepared for the Crime Prevention Coalition, which consists of nearly one hundred national and state organizations. It is part of an overall public service campaign conducted in the public interest by the Advertising Council. Single copies of some of the titles listed below are available from the Crime Prevention Coalition, Box 6700, Rockville, MD 20850.

506-1. **Arson: How Not to Get Burned**. 1979. 12p. ill. S/N 027-000-00998-1. $2.25. **J26.2:C86/12/burned**.

Outlines briefly the impact and motives for arson and how to prevent it. Also tells what to do when arson fires are set.

506-2. **"Got a Minute? You Could Stop a Crime."** 1979. 20p. ill. S/N 027-000-00956-5. $1.50. **J26.2:C86/12/stop**.

Discusses the effectiveness of such community programs for crime prevention as neighborhood programs, and helping victims by appearing in court as a witness.

506-3. **How Not to Get Conned**. 1979. 20p. ill. S/N 027-000-00959-0. $2.50. **J26.2:C86/12/conned**.

Provides advice to protect against frauds such as repair and home improvement schemes, land and investment frauds, door-to-door sales frauds, bait and switch schemes, and other con games.

506-4. **How to Be Streetwise and Safe**. 1980. 8p. ill. S/N 027-000-00941-7. $1.00. **J26.2:C86/12/streetwise**.

Describes methods of reducing the likelihood of being mugged or raped, and includes suggestions for self-protection against attacks.

506-5. **How to Crimeproof Your Business**. 1979. 28p. ill. S/N 027-000-00984-1. $2.75. **J26.2:C86/12/business**.

Provides advice to help prevent burglary, robbery, shoplifting, embezzlement, pilferage, computer fraud, bribery, kickbacks, and insurance fraud.

506-6. **How to Crimeproof Your Home**. 1984. 20p. ill. S/N 027-000-00942-5. $2.50. **J26.8:C86/13**.

Practical hints for protecting your home against burglary. Discusses precautions for doors, locks, windows, and security alarms. Includes special tips for apartment dwellers.

506-7. **How to Prevent Rural Crime**. 1979. 12p. and poster. ill. S/N 027-000-01107-1. $4.00. **J26.2:C86/12/rural**.

Provides suggestions for farmers to protect their livestock, farm products, equipment and supplies, and their neighbor's property.

506-8. **How to Protect Children**. 1984. 20p. ill. S/N 027-000-01179-9. $1.50. **J1.2:P94/14**.

Provides advice to parents, teachers, and other adults on teaching children how to avoid trouble and crime. Describes community programs designed to protect children.

506-9. **How to Protect Your Neighborhood**. 1980. 20p. ill. S/N 027-000-00983-2. $2.50. **J26.2:C86/12/neighborhood**.

Describes measures that neighborhoods can take to prevent crime, such as neighborhood watch programs.

506-10. **How to Protect Yourself against Sexual Assault**. 1979. 16p. ill. S/N 027-000-01004-1. $2.25. **J26.2:C86/12/sexual**.

Provides advice to reduce the risk of rape, what to do if attacked, and what to do if victimized.

506-11. **How Your Organization Can Take Action against Crime**. 1979. 12p. ill. S/N 027-000-01105-5. $2.25. **J26.2:C86/12/organization**.

Suggests a number of projects which community groups can undertake to prevent crime.

506-12. **Senior Citizens against Crime**. 1980. 20p. ill. S/N 027-000-01003-2. $2.50. **J26.2:C86/12/senior**.

Provides advice to reduce the risk of crimes at home and on the street that particularly affect older persons. Describes special crime prevention programs for senior citizens, and how to start a local program.

507. **"Taking a Bite out of Crime": The Impact of a Mass Media Crime Prevention Campaign**. National Institute of Justice. February 1984. 83p. ill. **J28.2:C86/10**.

Addresses the impact of the national media campaign on citizen perceptions, attitudes, and behaviors regarding crime prevention, and how the findings may be applied to similar efforts in the future.

508.   **Youth and Crime Prevention: Youth Can Make a Difference**. Department of Justice. 1984. 24p. ill. S/N 027-000-01193-4. $40.00 per 100 copies. No single copies sold. **J1.2:Y8/2**.

Provides advice on how young people can protect themselves against crime on the street and at home. Describes ways youth can get together to reduce crime and protect their schools and communities.

See also entries 68, 187.

CRIMINAL INVESTIGATION

509.   **Crime Scene Search and Physical Evidence Handbook**. National Institute of Justice. 1973 (repr. 1984). 206p. ill. S/N 027-000-01195-1. $7.00. **J28.8:C86/3**.

Provides the investigating officer with guidance as to proper techniques for the collection of physical evidence at the scene of a crime.

510.   **Forensic Handbook**. Department of the Treasury. Rev. 1983. 108p. ill. S/N 048-012-00080-9. $4.50. **T1.10/2:F76/983**.

Intended as a quick-reference book on known procedures for the collection, preservation, and transmittal to a forensic laboratory for examination and analysis of many types of criminal physical evidence.

511.   **Forensics: When Science Bears Witness**. National Institute of Justice. October 1984. 30p. ill. S/N 027-000-01202-7. $1.50. **J1.2:F76/4**.

This illustrated booklet describes the role and contributions of forensic science to the criminal justice system. Bibliography.

512.   **Handbook of Forensic Science**. Federal Bureau of Investigation. Rev. March 1984. 134p. ill. S/N 027-001-00034-3. $5.00. **J1.14/16:F76/984**.

Discusses legally accepted and practical procedures for collecting, preserving, and handling criminal physical evidence. Describes the services and examinations available in the FBI crime laboratories.

513.   **The Science of Fingerprints: Classification and Uses**. Federal Bureau of Investigation. Rev. 1984. 211p. ill. S/N 027-001-00033-5. $5.50. **J1.14/2:F49/12/984**.

Discusses types of fingerprint patterns and their interpretation, classification and filing of fingerprint records, searching and referencing, techniques for taking good fingerprints, latent impressions, and preparation of fingerprint charts for court testimony.

514.   **Scientific Validity of Polygraph Testing: A Research Review and Evaluation**. Congress. Office of Technology Assessment. 1983. 131p. tables. Technical Memorandum OTA-TM-H-15. S/N 052-003-00934-0. $5.50. **Y3.T22/2:11Sci2**.

Focuses on the nature and application of polygraph (lie detector) tests, the scientific controversy over polygraph testing, data from the field and simulation studies, and factors that affect their validity.

POLICE AND LAW ENFORCEMENT

515. **Law Enforcement Officers Killed and Assaulted, 1983**. Federal Bureau of Investigation. 1984. 62p. charts, tables. Uniform Crime Reports. **J1.14/7-6:983**.

Issued annually. Contains data on law enforcement officers killed and assaulted during the year. Historic data are presented in many tables. Also includes descriptive summaries of felonious assaults during which officers were killed during the year.

516. **Police Use of Deadly Force: A Conciliation Handbook for Citizens and Police**. Community Relations Service. May 1982. 30p. **J1.8/2:P75/4**.

Proposes actions for police departments and community organizations to break down barriers to good relations and to deal constructively with the issue of deadly force in disputes. Footnote references. Bibliography.

517. **Police Strikes: Causes and Prevention**. National Institute of Justice. August 1980. 281p. **J28.2:P75**.

Describes events leading up to, during, and following police strikes in San Francisco, Tucson, Oklahoma City, Las Cruces, and Youngstown during 1975-1976. Includes recommendations. Bibliography.

518. **Who Is Guarding the Guardians? A Report on Police Practices**. Commission on Civil Rights. October 1981. 184p. tables. **CR1.2:G93/2**.

Presents the findings of a commission study which recommends standards in the following areas: recruitment, selection, and training of police officers; use of deadly force; receipt and processing of civilian complaints; discipline; and exercise of oversight by local authorities. Footnote references.

See also entry 709-3.

For additional publications on this topic see Subject Bibliography **SB-117, Law Enforcement**.

COURTS

519. **Glossary of Terms Used in the Federal Courts**. Administrative Office of the United States Courts. Rev. November 1980. 30p. **Ju10.2:T27/980**.

Includes a narrative description of civil actions in federal courts in which terms are used and defined, and an alphabetical glossary of terms.

520. **Judges of the United States**. 2d ed. Judicial Conference of the United States. 1983. 681p. S/N 028-004-00056-7. $20.00, cloth. **Ju10.2:J89/4/983**.

Contains brief biographies of federal judges appointed from 1780 through 1983. Indexes by personal name, year of appointment, and by appointing President.

521. **United States Court Directory**. Administrative Office of the United States Courts. October 1984. 304p. S/N 028-004-00059-1. $10.00. **Ju10.17:984-2**.

Issued semiannually. Contains the name, mailing address, and telephone number of judges of all federal courts nationwide.

522.   **The United States Courts: A Pictorial Summary for the Twelve Month Period Ended June 1984**. Administrative Office of the United States Courts. 1984. 21p. charts, tables. **Ju10.12:984**.

Issued annually. This chartbook presents summary statistics on the activities of the federal court system.

523.   **Victim Witness Handbook**. Department of Justice. 1984. 24p. **J1.8/2:V66**.

Designed to help a witness understand how the criminal justice system works in felony and misdemeanor cases, and to inform the witness of his/her rights and responsibilities.

Customs

524. **Know Before You Go.** Customs Service. Rev. 1983. 15p. ill. Customs Publication No. 512. **T17.2:C96/2/983.**
Explains briefly customs regulations which the traveler to a foreign country should know before leaving regarding customs declarations, exemptions, residency, restricted or prohibited articles, currency, medicine, and narcotics.

525. **United States Customs Guide for Private Flyers (General Aviation Pilots).** Customs Service. Rev. September 1983. 39p. Customs Publication No. 513. S/N 048-002-00091-9. $3.75. **T17.5/2:F67/984.**
Intended for the private and corporate pilot on business or pleasure flights to and from foreign countries. Presents basic customs requirements, and provides a list of airports at which customs clearance may be obtained.

526. **United States Customs Hints for Visitors (Nonresidents).** Customs Service. Rev. 1981. 13p. Customs Publication No. 511. **T17.2:C96/5/981.**
Provides advice on U.S. customs declarations, exemptions, gifts, other articles free of duty and subject to duty, and prohibited and restricted articles.

527. **U.S. Customs: Importing a Car.** Customs Service. Rev. 1984. 7p. Customs Publication No. 520. **T17.2:C17/984.**
Includes a brief description of customs regulations, as well as those of agencies other than Customs whose regulations the Customs Service enforces regarding imported cars, including the Environmental Protection Agency and Department of Transportation.

528. **U.S. Customs: Pets, Wildlife.** Customs Service. Rev. 1983. 7p. ill. Customs Publication No. 509. **T17.2:P44/2/983.**
Provides brief information about customs regulations, as well as regulations of the Department of Agriculture and Public Health Service regarding the importing of birds, cats, dogs, monkeys, turtles, and other wildlife.

529.   **U.S. Customs Pocket Hints: Capsule Information for Returning U.S. Residents about Their Customs Exemptions**. Customs Service. Rev. 1984. folder, 5p. Customs Publication No. 506. **T17.2:C96/13/984**.

Provides brief information on duty-free exemptions, restricted and prohibited articles, and the customs declaration.

See also entry 283.

For additional publications on this topic see Subject Bibliography **SB-027, Customs, Immunization, and Passport Publications**.

Debate Topics

Public Law 88-246 requires the Library of Congress to compile annually information guides pertaining to the National Debate Topic for High Schools and the Intercollegiate Debate Topic. These guides are usually in the form of excerpts reprinted from a variety of sources both inside and outside the federal government, and include an extensive bibliography of additional sources. The high school debate topic guide is published each year as a Senate Document, and the intercollegiate debate topic guide as a House Document. Each is an excellent guide to a topic of current interest. Subject Bibliographies **SB-043** and **SB-176** are revised each year to list in-print government publications relating to the high school and intercollegiate debate topics, respectively for that year. The guides for the years 1979-1980 to 1984-1985 are listed below.

INTERCOLLEGIATE DEBATE TOPIC

530. 1979-1980. **Should the Federal Government Significantly Strengthen the Regulation of Mass Media Communication in the United States?** 1979. 434p. House Document 96-167. **X96-1:H.doc. 167.**

531. 1980-1981. **Should the United States Significantly Increase Its Foreign Military Commitments?** 1980. 489p. ill., map. House Document 96-366. **X96-2: H.doc.366.**

532. 1981-1982. **Should the Federal Government Significantly Contain the Power of Labor Unions in the United States?** 1981. 696p. ill. House Document 97-89. **Y1.1/7:97-89.**

533. 1982-1983. **Should the United States Be Prohibited from Intervention in the Western Hemisphere?** 1982. 373p. House Document 97-226. **Y1.1/7:97-226.**

534.   1983-1984.   **Should Producers of Hazardous Waste Be Legally Responsible for Injuries Caused by the Waste?** 1983. 594p. House Document 98-93. **Y1.1/7:98-93**.

535.   1984-1985.   **Should the U.S. Federal Government Significantly Increase the Exploration and/or Development of Space beyond the Earth's Mesosphere?** 1984. 1616p. ill. House Document 98-257. **Y1.1/7:98-257**.

NATIONAL DEBATE TOPIC
FOR HIGH SCHOOLS

536.   1979-1980.   **What Should Be the Future Direction of the Foreign Policy of the United States?** 1979. 718p. charts, tables. Senate Document 96-17. **X96-1:S.doc.17**.

537.   1980-1981.   **How Can the Interests of the United States Consumers Best Be Protected?** 1980. 643p. Senate Document 96-43. **X96-2:S.doc.43**.

538.   1981-1982.   **How Can the United States Elementary and Secondary Education Systems Best Be Improved?** 1981. 730p. charts, tables. Senate Document 97-3. S/N 052-071-00631-1. $10.00. **Y1.1/3:97-3**.

539.   1982-1983.   **What Should Be the Level of United States Commitments for National Defense?** 1982. 883p. maps. Senate Document 97-24. S/N 052-071-00648-6. $8.50. **Y1.1/3:97-24**.

540.   1983-1984.   **What Changes Are Most Needed in the Procedures Used in the U.S. Justice System?** 1983. 945p. ill. Senate Document 98-5. **Y1.1/3:98-5**.

541.   1984-1985.   **How Can the Federal Government Best Decrease Poverty in the United States.** 1984. 856p. charts, tables. Senate Document 98-25. **Y1.1/3:98-25**.

Demography and Statistics

542. **America's Fact Finder: The Census Bureau**. Bureau of the Census. 1984. folder, 8p. ill. **C3.2:C33/37**.

Provides brief information on the activities of the Census Bureau in collecting facts on American life, and where and how the public can use that information when published.

543. **Census '80: Continuing the Fact Finder Tradition**. Bureau of the Census. January 1980. 508p. ill., charts, tables. S/N 003-024-02262-1. $9.00. **C3.2:C33/34**.

Developed as a textbook for the Experimental Student Intern Program for the 1980 Census of Population and Housing. Provides detailed background on the collection, processing, publication, and use of census data. References.

544. **County and City Data Book, 1983: A Statistical Abstract Supplement**. 10th ed. Bureau of the Census. 1983. 1060p. maps, tables. S/N 003-024-05833-2. $24.00, cloth. **C3.134/2:C83/2/983**.

Presents a broad variety of 216 statistical data items for each state and county in the United States, 170 data items for 952 incorporated cities having a population of over twenty-five thousand, and 15 data items for 9,969 places of twenty-five hundred or more. References. Index.

545. **Estimates of the Population of States: 1970 to 1983**. Bureau of the Census. October 1984. 17p. maps, tables. Current Population Reports, Series P-25, No. 957. S/N 003-001-91454-9. $1.50. **C3.186:P-25/957**.

Presents estimates of the population of states on 1 July 1981, 1982, and 1983 and changes from 1980 to 1983 due to births, deaths, and migration. Also presents annual estimates for each year from 1970 to 1980.

546. **Estimates of the Population of the United States by Age, Sex, and Race: 1980 to 1984**. Bureau of the Census. March 1985. 38p. charts, tables. Current Population Reports, Series P-25, No. 965. **C3.186:P-25/965**.

Provides estimates of the population by age (1-84 and 85 +), sex, and race (white, black, other races) as of 1 July 1980, 1981, 1982, 1983, and 1984.

547.   **Factfinder for the Nation [series].** Bureau of the Census. ill., charts, maps, tables. Available at prices indicated from Customer Services, Bureau of the Census, Washington, DC 20233. **C3.252:no.**
This series provides general information on statistics collected, organized, and made available by the Bureau of the Census. Each publication tells how long and how often statistics on a particular topic have been collected and made available, how they are organized and published, what a typical statistical table looks like, whether the statistics are updated between periods, and who is likely to find the statistics useful.

547-1.   No. 1.   **Statistics on Race and Ethnicity.** 1981. 4p. $0.25.

547-2.   No. 2.   **Availability of Census Records about Individuals.** 1983. 4p. $0.25.

547-3.   No. 3.   **Agricultural Statistics.** 1983. 4p. $0.25.

547-4.   No. 4.   **History and Organization.** 1979. 12p. $0.30.

547-5.   No. 5.   **Reference Sources.** 1984. 10p. $0.25.

547-6.   No. 6.   **Housing Statistics.** 1981. 4p. $0.25.

547-7.   No. 7.   **Population Statistics.** 1981. 4p. $0.25.

547-8.   No. 8.   **Census Geography-Concepts and Products.** 1982. 8p. $0.30.

547-9.   No. 9.   **Construction Statistics.** 1983. 4p. $0.25.

547-10.   No. 10.   **Retail Trade Statistics.** 1983. 4p. $0.25.

547-11.   No. 11.   **Wholesale Trade Statistics.** 1983. 4p. $0.25.

547-12.   No. 12.   **Statistics on Service Industries.** 1983. 4p. $0.25.

547-13.   No. 13.   **Transportation Statistics.** 1983. 4p. $0.25.

547-14.   No. 14.   **Foreign Trade Statistics.** 1978. 4p. $0.25.

547-15.   No. 15.   **Statistics on Manufacturers.** 1983. 4p. $0.25.

547-16.   No. 16.   **Statistics on Mineral Industries.** 1983. 4p. $0.25.

547-17.   No. 17.   **Statistics on Governments.** 1983. 4p. $0.25.

547-18.   No. 18.   **Census Bureau Programs and Products.** 1982. 16p. $0.40.

547-19.   No. 19.   **Enterprise Statistics.** 1983. 4p. $0.25.

547-20.   No. 20.   **Energy and Conservation Statistics.** 1980. 4p. $0.25.

547-21.   No. 21.   **International Programs.** 1981. 4p. $0.25.

547-22.   No. 22.   **Data for Small Communities.** 1981. 12p. $0.30.

548. **A Framework for Planning U.S. Federal Statistics for the 1980s.** Office of Federal Statistical Policy and Standards. July 1978. 447p. S/N 003-005-00183-2. $11.00. **C1.2:F84/2.**

Provides an overview of the U.S. federal statistical system through a discussion of subject areas, statistical agencies, and important related cross-cutting issues. Intended to contribute toward improved coordination among federal agencies by providing a future agenda. Bibliography.

549. **Geographical Mobility: March 1982 to March 1983.** Bureau of the Census. October 1984. 148p. tables. Current Population Reports, Series P-20, No. 393. S/N 003-001-90792-5. $5.00. **C3.186:P-20/393.**

Issued annually. Data are derived by comparing the location of each respondent's residence at the starting date with current residence at the closing date. Includes data from earlier surveys for comparison purposes. References.

550. **Historical Statistics of the United States, Colonial Times to 1970.** 2 vols. Bureau of the Census. 1975. 1248p. tables. S/N 003-024-00120-9. $35.00(set), cloth. **C3.134/2:H62/789-970/pt.1,2.**

A massive collection of statistics on almost every conceivable aspect of American life. Contains statistical information on the population, national income and wealth, transportation and more.

551. **Population Profile of the United States, 1982.** Bureau of the Census. 1983. 86p. tables. Current Population Reports, Series P-23, No. 130. S/N 003-001-91546-4. $4.00. **C3.186:P-23/130.**

Issued annually. Presents a statistical profile of the population of the United States by selected demographic, social, and economic characteristics. References.

552. **Projections of the Population of the United States by Age, Sex, and Race: 1983 to 2080.** Bureau of the Census. May 1984. 175p. charts, tables. Current Population Reports, Series P-25, No. 952. S/N 003-001-91449-2. $5.50. **C3.186:P-25/952.**

Presents estimates of the population of the United States by age, sex, and race for each year from 1983 to 2000, and then every five years from 2000 to 2080.

553. **Provisional Projections of the Population by States, by Age and Sex: 1980 to 2000.** Bureau of the Census. August 1983. 50p. charts, tables. Current Population Reports, Series P-25, No. 937. S/N 003-001-91434-4. $4.00. **C3.186:P-25/937.**

Presents projections of the resident population of each state by five-year age groups and sex for 1 July 1990 and 2000. Also presents similar actual count data from the 1980 Census of Population.

554. **Reflections of America: Commemorating the Statistical Abstract Centennial.** Bureau of the Census. December 1980. 212p. ill., charts, tables. S/N 003-024-02921-9. $10.00. **C3.2:Am3/5.**

A collection of twenty-six essays by notable American authors on American social and cultural history during the past one hundred years illustrated with statistical evidence from the *Statistical Abstract* and photographs. The first edition of the *Statistical Abstract* was published in 1879. Footnote references.

555.   **Revolution in United States Government Statistics, 1926-1976.** Office of Federal Statistical Policy and Standards. October 1978. 266p. S/N 003-005-00181-6. $7.50. **C1.2:St2/10/926-76.**

Reviews revolutionary developments in federal statistics collection, processing, and dissemination during the past fifty years. Reviews federal government statistics prior to 1933, and the attempts to develop a coordinated statistics system from 1933 to 1976. Footnote references. Bibliography. Index.

556.   **Social Indicators III: Selected Data on Social Conditions and Trends in the United States.** Bureau of the Census. 1980. 645p. charts, tables. S/N 003-024-02683-0. $19.00. **C3.2:So1/2/979.**

Presents a wide variety of current and historical data on social conditions and trends in the United States. Glossary. Index.

557.   **State and Metropolitan Area Data Book, 1982: A Statistical Abstract Supplement.** Bureau of the Census. August 1982. 701p. tables. S/N 003-024-04932-5. $15.00. **C3.134/5:982.**

This compendium presents a wide variety of current and historical data—social, demographic, and economic—for standard metropolitan statistical areas (SMSAs), central cities of SMSAs, census regions and divisions, and states. References. Index.

558.   **Statistical Abstract of the United States: National Data Book and Guide to Sources, 1984.** 105th ed. Bureau of the Census. 1985. 1019p. and folder, *Statistics in Brief, 1985.* charts, tables. S/N 003-024-06135-0. $19.00, paper. S/N 003-024-06136-8. $23.00, cloth. **C3.134:985.**

Issued annually. This volume is the standard summary of social, political, and economic statistics for the United States. It serves as a convenient volume for statistical reference data and as a guide to more comprehensive statistical publications and sources. Index.

559.   **Statistics in Brief for 1985: A Supplement to the Statistical Abstract of the United States.** Bureau of the Census. 1985. folder, 9p. tables. S/N 003-024-06192-9. $1.00. Included free with publication described in entry 558. **C3.134/2:St2/985.**

Issued annually. Presents statistical highlights in significant areas from the *Statistical Abstract* (entry 558). Formerly titled *USA Statistics in Brief.*

560.   **Twenty Censuses: Population and Housing Questions, 1790-1980.** Bureau of the Census. October 1979. 91p. ill. S/N 003-024-01874-8. $5.00. **C3.2:C33/33.**

Contains reproductions of census schedules for the twenty decennial census, 1790-1980 showing the questions which were asked regarding population and housing. Bibliography.

561.   **We, the Americans.** Bureau of the Census. Rev. January 1984. 16p. ill., charts, tables. S/N 003-024-05692-5. $1.00. **C3.2:Am3/6/no.1/984.**

Presents statistical highlights from the 1980 Census of Population and Housing and recent surveys on the characteristics of the American people.

See also entries 700, 702, 911, 1320, 1681.

For additional publications on this topic see Subject Bibliography, **SB-273, Statistical Publications.**

Disaster Preparedness and Emergency Management

562. **Aboveground Home Fallout Shelter**. Federal Emergency Management Administration. November 1983. 8p. ill. H-12-2. **FEM1.2:F19**.

Provides instructions and plans for constructing an aboveground shelter for six persons to protect against nuclear blasts, as well as hurricanes, tornadoes, and earthquakes.

563. **Coping with Children's Reactions to Earthquakes and Other Disasters**. Federal Emergency Management Administration. September 1983. 12p. ill. FEMA-48. **FEM1.2:C44**.

Provides advice for parents, teachers, and other adults concerned with how to deal with a child's fears and anxieties following a disaster.

564. **The Demands of Humanity: Army Medical Disaster Relief**. Army Center of Military History. 1983. 188p. ill. Special Studies Series. S/N 008-029-00124-1. $5.00. **D114.17:H88**.

This history describes the humanitarian contributions made by army medical personnel during disaster situations in the United States and abroad. It examines the problems encountered by medical units in relief operations, and traces the development of the army's role with other organizations such as the Red Cross. Footnote references. Index.

565. **Directory of Governors and State Officials Responsible for Disaster Operations and Emergency Planning**. Federal Emergency Management Administration. Rev. April 1984. 22p. map. FEMA-9. **FEM1.2:D62/984**.

Includes the name, address, and telephone number of the governor, state emergency director, and responsible senior official in each state. Also includes similar information for the Federal Emergency Management Administration regional directors.

566. **Home Blast Shelter**. Federal Emergency Management Administration. November 1983. 8p. ill. H-12-3. **FEM1.2:B61**.

Provides instructions and plans for building a six-person home blast shelter which will provide protection against the thermal effects, fallout radiation, and blast effects from a nuclear explosion.

567. **In Time of Emergency: A Citizen's Handbook**. Federal Emergency Management Administration. Rev. February 1984. 41p. ill. H-14. **FEM1.8:Em3/3**.

Provides general guidance to insure survival in the event of a natural or man-made disaster with separate chapters on the following: floods, hurricanes, tornadoes, winter storms, earthquakes, tidal waves (tsunamies), nuclear power plant accidents, fire, and nuclear attack.

568. **Natural Disaster Assistance Available from the U.S. Department of Agriculture**. Department of Agriculture. August 1984. 7p. PA 1328. **A1.68:1328**.

Describes the types of assistance available, the USDA agencies which administer the programs, and where to apply for assistance.

569. **What You Should Know about Nuclear Preparedness**. Federal Emergency Management Administration. November 1983. 14p. L-138. **FEM1.11:138**.

Provides answers to commonly asked questions about how to prepare for a nuclear attack.

See also "Earthquakes" (entries 876-882), "Floods" (entries 414-418), "Hurricanes" (entries 419-422), "Tornadoes" (entries 427-429), "Winter Storms" (entries 430-431), and "Volcanoes" (entries 883-886).

Discrimination, Civil Rights, and Equal Opportunity

CIVIL RIGHTS

570. **American Indian Civil Rights Handbook**. Commission on Civil Rights. Rev. September 1980. 78p. Clearinghouse Publication 35. S/N 035-000-00245-1. $4.75. **CR1.10:35/2**.

Informs native Americans about the basic rights which they have, both on and off the reservation.

571. **Citizen's Guide to Individual Rights under the Constitution of the United States of America**. 6th ed. Congress. Senate. Committee on the Judiciary. July 1980. 52p. Committee Print, 96th Congress, 2d Session. S/N 052-070-05355-1. $4.25. **Y4.J89/2:R44/980**.

Discusses individual rights in the Constitution as originally adopted, in the Bill of Rights or the first ten amendments, and in subsequent amendments. Includes the text of the Constitution, plus amendments. Glossary.

572. **Federal Civil Rights Laws: A Sourcebook**. Congress. Senate. Committee on the Judiciary. November 1984. 154p. Committee Print, 98th Congress, 2d Session. S/N 052-070-05975-3. $4.25. **Y4.J89/2:S.prt.98-245**.

Includes the full text or excerpts and legislative history of constitutional amendments and statutes dealing with civil rights, the text of executive orders, and summaries of Supreme Court cases on civil rights. Bibliography.

573. **Personal Justice Denied: Report of the Commission on Wartime Relocation and Internment of Civilians**. 1983. 467p. S/N 052-003-00897-1. $8.50. **Y3.W19/10:2J98**.

This is the final report of a commission which was established to review the facts and circumstances of the relocation and internment of American citizens during World War II, mainly those of Japanese ancestry and Alaska Aleut civilians. Footnote references. Index.

574.   **President Reagan's 50 States Project: "Status of the States." 1982 Year-End Report**. White House. Office of Public Liaison. 1983. 140p. **Pr40.2:St2**.
Provides information for each state on current and past legislation pertaining to discrimination on the basis of sex.

575.   **Religion in the Constitution: A Delicate Balance**. Commission on Civil Rights. September 1983. 84p. Clearinghouse Publication 80. **CR1.10:80**.
Reviews the history of separation of church and state, and the interpretation of the First Amendment with regard to education, conscientious objectors, and native Americans. Examines religious discrimination in employment and religious freedom in prisons. Footnote references.

See also "Minorities and Ethnics Studies" (entries 1312-1334) and "Women" (entries 1678-1709).

For additional publications on this topic see Subject Bibliography **SB-207, Civil Rights and Equal Opportunity**.

EQUAL EDUCATIONAL OPPORTUNITY

576.   **Being a Man: A Unit of Instructional Activities on Male Role Stereotyping**. Office of Education. 1977. 70p. S/N 017-080-01777-6. $5.00. **HE19.102:M31**.
Contains classroom activities and a curriculum for junior high school teachers who wish to teach a course on how the male role is stereotyped in our society. Footnote references. Bibliography.

577.   **Citizen's Guide to School Desegregation Law**. National Institute of Education. July 1978. 60p. S/N 017-080-01896-9. $4.75. **HE19.208:Sch6/2**.
Explains how our judicial systems works, provides a brief overview of school desegregation law since 1954, and discusses recent Supreme Court decisions that set standards for desegregation cases.

578.   **Freedom of Reach for Young Children: Nonsexist Early Childhood Education**. Office of Education. 1977. 64p. S/N 017-080-01778-4. $4.75. **HE19.108:N73**.
Focuses on concepts, strategies, and activities for assisting early education teachers to implement nonsexist education for preschool children through the early elementary school years.

579.   **Higher Education Opportunities for Minorities and Women: Annotated Selections**. Department of Education. Rev. 1984. 71p. S/N 065-000-00226-4. $3.00. **ED1.42:984**.
Provides information on loans, scholarships, and fellowships in various academic disciplines which are available to minorities and women.

580.   **More Hurdles to Clear: Women and Girls Competitive Athletics**. Commission on Civil Rights. July 1980. 94p. ill., charts, tables. Clearinghouse Publication 63. **CR1.10:63**.
Provides historical background on women and girls in athletics. Discusses the status in the last 1970s of the implementation of Title IX of the Educational

Amendments of 1972, and the extent of participation by females in school and college competitive athletics. Footnote references.

581. **Title 9: The Half Full, Half Empty Glass.** National Advisory Council on Women's Educational Programs. 1981. 62p. ill. S/N 065-000-00117-9. $5.00. **Y3.Ed8/6:2T53.**

Provides an explanation of Title IX which prohibits sex discrimination in schools receiving federal financial assistance. Describes changes in the educational system resulting from the law.

582. **With All Deliberate Speed: 1954-19??.** Commission on Civil Rights. November 1981. 51p. Clearinghouse Publication 69. **CR1.10:69.**

Reviews the historical background of segregation in schools, and the landmark 1954 Supreme Court decision in *Brown* v. *Board of Education*. Discusses the southern response, desegregation in the North, transportation of students, and the effect of desegregation on public education. Footnote references.

EQUAL EMPLOYMENT OPPORTUNITY

583. **Affirmative Action in the 1980s: Dismantling the Process of Discrimination.** Commission on Civil Rights. November 1981. 62p. Clearinghouse Publication 70. **CR1.10:70.**

Discusses civil rights law and affirmative action, and argues that affirmative action plans provide a remedy for discrimination. Footnote references. Bibliography.

584. **Equal Employment Opportunity for Women: U.S. Policies.** Women's Bureau. 1982. 43p. tables. **L36.102:Em7/5.**

Provides data on women workers, and discusses U.S. policies to promote equality of employment opportunities for women. Prepared for an international conference. References.

585. **Minority Teachers in an Era of Retrenchment: Early Lessons in an Ongoing Dilemma.** Commission on Civil Rights. December 1982. 67p. tables. **CR1.2:T22/3.**

Describes the effects of budget cuts and declining enrollment in Massachusetts on the employment of minority teachers, many of whom lack seniority to retain their jobs during retrenchments. Examines implications of civil rights on nonwhites. Footnote references.

586. **Sexual Harassment on the Job: A Guide to Employers.** Commission on Civil Rights. October 1983. 21p. **CR1.6/2:H21/3.**

Discusses sexual harassment and the law. Provides advice to employers on how to comply with the law and how to recognize situations of potential trouble. Bibliography.

See also entries 103, 893, 1699.

Education

GENERAL

587. **All about ERIC: Educational Resources Information Center**. Department of Education. 1983. 31p. S/N 065-000-00147-1. $4.25. **ED1.302:Ed8/2**.

Describes the information products and services of the Educational Resources Information Center (ERIC) and tells how to obtain them. References.

588. **American Education**. Department of Education. Monthly, except January/ February and August/September (combined). approx. 40p. ill. S/N 765-001-00000-5. Symbol AMED. $23.00 per yr. Single copy $2.50. **ED1.10:vol/no**.

This periodical is dedicated to informing the public of trends in education, the basis and purpose of federal policies affecting education, and the continuing exploration of the meaning of excellence in education and how to achieve it. Articles are grouped under the following topics: policy, practice, and research forum. Departments include Recent Publications and Statistic of the Month.

589. **The Condition of Education, 1984**. National Center for Education Statistics. 1984. 240p. tables. NCES 84-401. S/N 065-000-00200-1. $7.00. **ED1.109:984**.

Issued annually. Discusses the condition of American elementary and secondary education, higher education, vocational and adult education, and teacher preparation. Current and historical data are presented on enrollment, number of institutions, staffing, and finances. References. Index.

590. **Digest of Education Statistics, 1983-84**. National Center for Education Statistics. 1983. 226p. tables. S/N 065-000-00191-8. $6.50. **ED1.113:983-84**.

Issued annually. Contains current and historical data on a wide variety of subjects on American education from kindergarten to graduate school.

591. **Educational Attainment in the United States: March 1981 and 1980**. Bureau of the Census. August 1984. 94p. charts, tables. Current Population Reports, Series P-20, No. 390. S/N 003-001-90789-5. $3.25. **C3.186:P-20/390**.

Issued annually. Presents national statistics on educational attainment by age, sex, race, and Spanish origin.

592. **Educational Governance in the States: A Status Report on State Boards of Education, Chief State School Officers, and State Education Agencies**. Department of Education. February 1983. 278p. charts, tables. S/N 065-000-00172-1. $8.50. **ED1.2:Ed8/6**.

Provides a state-by-state description of state boards of education, chief state school officers, state education agencies, and statewide coordinating agencies for higher education. Also provides a comparative analysis and summary of policies in educational governance across the country. References. Bibliography.

593. **Educational Testing Facts and Issues: A Layperson's Guide to Testing in Schools**. National Institute of Education. September 1981. 53p. charts, tables. **ED1.308:T28**.

Discusses the role, purposes, and uses of testing in public education, and current issues regarding testing. Bibliography.

594. **How to Help Your Children Achieve in School**. National Institute of Education. 1983. 28p. S/N 065-000-00176-4. $3.75. **ED1.302:C43/3**.

Explains how to help your children improve their study skills, both at home and in school. Provides tips on maintaining interest and attention, and techniques for effective notetaking. Bibliography.

595. **Informational Technology and Its Impact on American Education**. Congress. Office of Technology Assessment. 1982. 269p. ill., tables. OTA-CIT-187. S/N 052-003-00888-2. $8.00. **Y3.T22/2:2In3/2**.

Provides an overview of the issues relating to application of new information technologies in American education. Examines a variety of new information products and services, and surveys the effect that the application of new technologies may have on current education providers. Footnote references. Index.

596. **A Nation at Risk: The Imperative for Educational Reform. A Report to the Nation and the Secretary of Education**. National Commission on Excellence in Education. April 1983. 70p. S/N 065-000-00177-2. $4.50. **ED1.2:N21**.

This slim document had a major impact on the discussion of educational policy in the United States. It includes the findings and recommendations of the commission created in August 1981 by the secretary of education. Appendices include list of commissioned papers and hearings.

597. **Nation Responds: Recent Efforts to Improve Education**. Department of Education. May 1984. 229p. S/N 065-000-00198-5. $7.50. **ED1.2:N21/2**.

Describes responses to recent studies in education, including the report of the National Commission on Excellence in Education (entry 596). Includes an overview of national developments, and a state-by-state profile of recent activities. Also provides an informal sampling of efforts by local schools and districts, colleges, associations, and the private sector.

598. Opportunities Abroad for Educators, 1983-1984: Teaching, Seminars. Department of Education. 1982. 35p. S/N 065-000-00141-1. $4.25. **ED1.19:983-84**.

Issued annually. Describes international exchange programs and seminars administered by the Department of Education for educators under the Fullbright Grants Program.

599. Overseas American-sponsored Elementary and Secondary Schools Assisted by the U.S. Department of State. Department of State. January 1984. 31p. **S1.2:Sch6/2**.

Lists the names and addresses of overseas schools which received direct or indirect assistance from the Department of State for providing educational services to dependents of U.S. government personnel overseas.

600. Overseas Employment Opportunities for Educators, Department of Defense Dependents Schools, School Year 1985-1986. Department of Defense. 1984. 50p. ill. **D1.68:985-86**.

Issued annually. Describes position categories, eligibility, and special requirements for elementary and secondary school educators who seek employment in Defense Department dependents' schools overseas. Includes information on entitlements and living conditions, and application blanks with filing instructions.

601. Progress of Education in the United States of American, 1980-81 through 1982-83. Department of Education. 1984. 141p. charts, tables. **ED1.41:980-83**.

This report was prepared for the thirty-ninth International Conference of Education sponsored by the United Nations Educational, Cultural, and Scientific Organization (UNESCO). Provides a brief summary of current educational priorities in the United States and describes various systems of education. Summarizes recent major legislation, present issues for reform, and national programs. References.

602. Projections of Education Statistics to 1990-91. 16th ed. 2 vols. National Center for Education Statistics. 1982. Vol. 1. **Analytical Report**. 122p. charts, tables. NCES 82-402-A. S/N 065-000-00144-6. $6.00. Vol. 2. **Methodological Report**. 44p. tables. NCES 82-402-B. S/N 065-000-00151-9. $4.75. **ED1.120:990-91/v1,2**.

Issued biennially. Volume 1 contains a variety of tables, charts, and narrative presenting enrollment, teacher, graduate, and expenditure data for the past eleven years and projections for the next ten years for elementary and secondary education, and higher education. Volume 2 gives detailed technical explanations of the methods used to develop the projections. References.

603. The Rights and Responsibilities of Students: A Handbook for the School Community. Administration for Children, Youth and Families. 1978. 52p. ill. DHEW Publication No. (OHDS) 79-32001. S/N 017-090-00041-1. $4.50. **HE23.1308:St9**.

Discusses the rights and responsibilities of students under the Constitution and federal laws. Provides a model code for the school community and guidelines for preparing a code. Footnote references.

604. Strength through Wisdom: A Critique of United States Capability; A Report to the President. President's Commission on Foreign Language and International Studies. 1979. 156p. S/N 017-080-02065-3. $7.00. **HE19.102:F76**.

Explains why competence in foreign languages and international understanding is important to all Americans in relation to national security and economic viability.

604-A. **President's Commission on Foreign Language and International Studies: Background Papers and Studies.** November 1979. 312p. S/N 017-080-02070-0. $9.00. **HE19.102:F76/papers.**

Contains twenty-three papers dealing with instruction in foreign languages and international studies in American schools, and how to improve the use of foreign languages and increase students' knowledge and appreciation of foreign cultures. References.

See also entries 448, 503, 650, 960, 1321, 1459.

See also "Equality Educational Opportunity" (entries 576-582).

For additional publications on this topic see Subject Bibliography **SB-083, Educational Statistics.**

ELEMENTARY AND SECONDARY EDUCATION

605. **High School and Beyond: A National Longitudinal Study for the 1980's.** National Center for Education Statistics.

High School and Beyond is a program to study longitudinally the educational, vocational, and personal development of high school students and the familial, social, institutional, and cultural factors that affect that development. The program has a base year of 1980 and includes over thirty thousand sophomores, and over twenty-eight thousand seniors in over a thousand public and private schools. Follow-ups are scheduled every two years. The following entries are examples of recent reports.

605-1. **High School Seniors: A Comparative Study of the Classes of 1972 and 1980.** 1984. 51p. tables. NCES 84-202. S/N 065-000-00204-3. $2.25. **ED1.102:H53/3.**

Describes differences between the classes of 1972 and 1980 with regard to school experiences, behavior, attitudes, problems, values, and plans. Data are also analyzed to detect instances where changes varied for subgroups defined by sex, race, socioeconomic status, academic achievement level, high school program, or region.

605-2. **Two Years after High School: A Capsule Description of 1980 Seniors.** 1984. 47p. NCES 84-209. S/N 065-000-00209-4. $2.25. **ED1.102:H53/4.**

Provides a general overview of the activities and experiences of 1980 high school seniors using information from the base year and first follow-up survey. Topics covered include postsecondary education, labor force participation, military service, family formation, and attitudes and values.

605-3. **Two Years in High School: The Status of 1980 Sophomores in 1982.** 1984. 47p. tables. NCES 84-207. S/N 065-000-00212-4. $2.25. **ED1.102:H53/5.**

Presents summary information from the first follow-up survey in 1982 about sophomores in the 1980 base study. Among topics discussed are courses taken, grades earned, discipline problems, dropouts, and college plans.

606.   **Public Elementary and Secondary Education in the United States, 1981-1982: A Statistical Compendium.** National Center for Education Statistics. 1984. 114p. charts, tables. NCES 84-104. S/N 065-000-00210-8. $4.00. **ED1.112/2:981-82.**

This compendium is the fourth in a series of statistical compilations of institutional pupil, staff, and financial data about local education agencies presented in summary and profile form for each state. Profiles show how each state ranks with respect to other states on each of the selected variables.

607.   **Statistics of Public Elementary School Systems: Schools, Pupils, and Staff, Fall 1980.** National Center for Education Statistics. 1982. 40p. tables. NCES 82-119. S/N 065-000-00156-0. $4.50. **ED1.112:980.**

Provides basic statistics on public elementary and secondary education in each state, the District of Columbia, and outlying territories for fall 1980. Statistical data are presented on the number of school systems, pupils and staff, and high school graduates for school years 1978-1979 and 1979-1980.

See also entries 454, 1411, 1420.

For additional publications on this topic see Subject Bibliographies **SB-096, Elementary Education** and **SB-068, Secondary Education**.

HIGHER EDUCATION

608.   **Accredited Postsecondary Institutions and Programs, including Institutions Holding Preaccredited Status as of September 1, 1980.** 5th ed. Department of Education. 1981. 222p. S/N 065-000-00081-4. $7.50. **ED1.38:980.**

Lists institutions accredited by regional associations, and by national specialized, professional, and technical accrediting agencies. Lists nationally recognized accrediting agencies and associations, and agencies recognized by the Education Department for preaccreditation.

609.   **College Costs: Basic Student Charges, 2-Year and 4-Year Institutions, 1983-84.** National Center for Education Statistics. 1984. 25p. tables. NCES 84-307. S/N 065-000-00199-3. $1.75. **ED1.121/3:983-84.**

Lists annual basic student charges for public and private two- and four-year colleges and universities in the United States for full-time undergraduate and graduate studies. Charges include tuition and fees (in-state and out-of-state), room, and board.

610.   **Education Directory: Colleges and Universities, 1983-84.** National Center for Education Statistics. 1984. 396p. NCES 84-300. S/N 065-000-00201-9. $10.00. **ED1.111:983-84.**

Issued annually. Arranged alphabetically by state. Entries include name, address, and telephone number; date established; control; undergraduate tuition fees (in-state); semester; highest degree; and accreditation.

611.   **Fall Enrollment in Colleges and Universities, 1982.** National Center for Education Statistics. 1984. 165p. tables. NCES 84-305. S/N 065-000-00205-1. $5.50. **ED1.124:982.**

Presents national and state data on enrollment by sex, attendance status, type of institution and control. Also presents data on the one hundred largest public institutions and the fifty largest private institutions of higher education.

612. **Historically Black Colleges and Universities: Fact Book**. 3 vols. Department of Education. January 1983. 1178p. **HE1.2:B56/v.1-3**.

Each volume contains uniform descriptive data prepared by the institutions. Volume 1 contains fact sheets from fifteen junior and community colleges; volume 2 from twenty-nine private colleges and graduate schools; and volume 3 from twenty-five public colleges and graduate schools.

613. **Institutions of Higher Education: Index by State and Congressional District, 1983-84**. National Center for Education Statistics. 1984. 118p. tables. NCES 84-304. S/N 065-000-00203-5. $4.75. **ED1.116/2:983-84**.

Lists by state and congressional district those institutions that offer at least a one-year program of college-level study leading towards a degree. Information is also provided on enrollment, tuition and fees, room and board, and days open per week.

614. **Look Out for Yourself! Helpful Hints for Selecting a School or College**. Education Division. 1977. 16p. S/N 017-080-01776-8. $2.75. **HE19.2:H59**.

Tells how to decide what's important to you and how to find the information you need in choosing a college.

615. **Traditionally Black Institutions of Higher Education: Their Identification and Selected Characteristics**. National Center for Education Statistics. 1978. 15p. tables. NCES 79-305. S/N 017-080-01949-3. $2.75. **HE19.302:B56**.

Identifies 106 traditionally black schools, explains the procedures for classifying them, and provides descriptive information about each.

See also entries 670, 816, 888, 899, 1160, 1204, 1224, 1455.

For additional publications on this topic see Subject Bibliographies **SB-085, Financial Aid to Students** and **SB-217, Higher Education**.

VOCATIONAL AND ADULT EDUCATION

616. **The Adult Illiterate Speaks Out: Personal Perspectives on Learning to Read and Write**. National Institute of Education. September 1980. 57p. **ED1.302:Ad9/2**.

Includes comments of former illiterate adults on the following topics: what it's like to be illiterate, making the decision to become literate, and the process of becoming literate.

617. **DANTES Guide to External Degree Programs, 1983-1984**. Defense Activity for Non-Traditional Education Support (DANTES). 1983. 60p. tables. DOD 1322.8-C. **D1.6/2:D36/983-84**.

Describes twenty-three undergraduate and four graduate external degree programs designed to fit the needs of the military student. An external degree program is one that has no, or minimal requirements for on-campus attendance.

618.   **Free Universities and Learning Referral Centers, 1981.** National Center for Education Statistics. 1983. 38p. tables. NCES 83-110. S/N 065-000-00185-3. $3.75. **ED1.102:Un3.**

Presents aggregate statistical data on registrations and referrals, expenditures, revenues, fees, and staff for 1980 and 1981. Also includes a directory of free universities and learning referral centers by state.

619.   **Participation in Adult Education, 1981.** National Center for Education Statistics. July 1982. 41p. charts, tables. NCES 82-335. S/N 065-000-00149-7. $4.75. **ED1.123:981.**

Reports the results of the 1981 survey of participation in adult education, which is the fifth and last of the triennial series begun in 1969. Includes national data on the demographic and socioeconomic characteristics of the students, course subjects, type of school, and reasons for taking course.

620.   **Terms, Definitions, Organizations, and Councils Associated with Adult Learning.** National Advisory Council on Adult Education. July 1980. 52p. S/N 052-003-00761-4. $3.75. **Y3.Ed8/4:2Ad9/3.**

Includes dictionaries of adult learning, legislative, and school finance and tax terms; text of federal laws and regulations relating to adult education; and a list of adult education associations and organizations. References.

See also entry 709-1.

For additional publications on this topic see Subject Bibliographies **SB-110, Vocational and Career Education** and **SB-214, Adult Education.**

EDUCATION IN FOREIGN COUNTRIES

621.   **Education in the USSR: Current Status of Higher Education.** Office of Education. 1980. 70p. tables. OE 79-19140. S/N 017-080-02060-2. $4.50. **HE19.102:Un3/5.**

Discusses the following topics: administration of higher education, admission to higher education, programs, teacher education and certification, and growth of higher education in the 1970s. Footnote references. Bibliography.

622.   **Education in the USSR: Research and Innovation.** Office of Education. 1978. 37p. OE 77-19130. S/N 017-080-01815-2. $4.25. **HE19.102:Un3/4.**

Discusses recent developments and emerging trends in research and innovation in education in the Soviet Union. Footnote references. Bibliography.

623.   **Educational System of. . . [series].** Department of Education. charts, maps, tables. **ED1.36:ct.**

This series provides basic information on the educational system of a foreign country. Each discusses briefly history, organization, structure, administration, financing, academic calendar, grading system, and levels of education. Each includes a selected reading list and glossary of selected educational terms.

623-1.   . . . **Austria.** 1980. 39p. E-80-14011. S/N 065-000-00061-0. $4.50. **ED1.36:Au7.**

623-2.　. . . **Costa Rica**. 1980. 33p. E-80-14005. **ED1.36:C82**.

623-3.　. . . **Greece**. 1981. 21p. E-80-14012. S/N 065-000-00055-5. $3.25. **ED1.36:G81**.

623-4.　. . . **New Zealand**. 1981. 23p. E-80-14016. **ED1.36:N42z**.

623-5.　. . . **Yugoslavia**. 1982. 116p. **ED1.36:Y9**.

For additional publications on this topic see Subject Bibliography **SB-235, Foreign Education**.

Elections

624. **Absentee Voting: How to Do It**. American Forces Information Service. 1984. folder, 6p. FS-13. **D2.14:FS-13**.

Provides information on absentee voting with emphasis on military personnel and their dependents.

625. **Campaign Finance Law 84: A Summary of Campaign Finance Laws with Quick Reference Charts**. Federal Election Commission. Rev. 1984. 347p. S/N 052-006-00030-9. $9.50. **Y3.El2/3:2L44/2/984**.

Provides summaries of the campaign finance law in each state and the District of Columbia in effect through 31 December 1983. Two quick reference charts provide summary information on filing requirements and contribution limits. Footnote references.

626. **Campaign Guide for Congressional Candidates and Committees**. Federal Election Commission. Rev. September 1982. 49p. ill. **Y3.El2/3:8C15/2/982**.

Focuses on federal requirements for congressional candidates and their committees to disclose their campaign receipts and disbursements and to abide by certain contribution limits and prohibitions.

627. **Campaign Guide for Political Party Committees**. Federal Election Committee. Rev. March 1984. 64p. ill. **Y3.El2/3:13P75/984**.

Describes federal requirements for record keeping of contributions and expenditures, and reports to the Federal Election Commission. Includes samples of completed FEC forms.

628. **Election Directory, 1984**. Federal Election Commission. Rev. 1984. 37p. S/N 052-006-00031-7. $2.25. **Y3.El2/3:14/984**.

Lists state election agencies and officials and describes their functions and duties.

629. **The Law of Political Broadcasting and Cablecasting: A Political Primer**. Federal Communications Commission. Rev. 1984. 87p. ill. **CC1.2:B78/30/984**.

Discusses the laws, rules, and policies which govern political broadcasting and cablecasting, including equal time, censorship, reasonable access, and the Fairness Doctrine.

630. **Nomination and Election of the President and Vice-President of the United States including the Manner of Selecting Delegates to National Political Conventions**. Congress. Senate. Committee on Rules and Administration. Rev. February 1984. 383p. tables. **Y4.R86/2:S.prt.98-150**.

A compilation of constitutional provisions, federal and state laws, and rules of the two major political parties. Lists states holding presidential preference primaries, and the dates of such primaries.

631. **Public Funding of Presidential Elections**. Federal Election Commission. July 1983. 13p. **Y3.El2/3:2P96**.

Gives a brief history of presidential election funding and an overview of how the process works.

632. **Senate Election Law Guidebook, 1984**. Congress. Senate. Committee on Rules and Administration. 1984. 305p. tables. Senate Document 98-23. **Y1.1/3:98-23**.

Includes constitutional and federal statutory provisions regarding the nomination and election of Senators, standing rules of the Senate regarding election of Senators, and an analysis of state election laws relative to candidates for the U.S. Senate.

633. **Voting Assistance Guide, 84/85**. American Forces Information Service. Rev. 1984. 208p. DOD GEN-6K. S/N 008-001-00142-8. $5.50. **D2.14:GEN-6K**.

Prepared especially for members of the armed forces, members of the U.S. merchant marine, their spouses and dependents, and U.S. citizens living in other countries who are not able to vote in person. Separate sections for each state list requirements for absentee registration and voting.

For additional publications on this topic see Subject Bibliography **SB-245, Voting and Elections**.

Electricity and Electronics

634. **Basic Electricity**. Bureau of Naval Personnel. 1969 (repr. 1983). 497p. ill. NAVPERS 10086-B. S/N 008-047-00069-3. $11.00. **D208.11:El2/3/969**.

A comprehensive illustrated guide to fundamentals of electricity. Covers basic concepts of electricity, batteries, DC circuits, electrical conductors, generators, transformers, motors, amplifiers, and servomechanisms. Index.

635. **Basic Electronics**.

635-1. **Basic Electronics. Vol. 1**. Bureau of Naval Personnel. 1971 (repr. 1982). 571p. NAVPERS 10087-C. S/N 008-047-00134-7. $12.00. **D208.11: El2/10/971/v.1**.

Provides general information concerning naval electronic equipment, testing devices, safety precautions, basic transistor and electronic tube circuits, and electronic communications. Index.

635-2. **Basic Electronics. Vol. 2**. Naval Education and Training Command. 1979. 327p. NAVEDTRA 10087-C1. S/N 008-047-00296-3. $8.50. **D207.208/2: El2/8/979/v.2**.

Covers direct trace oscilloscopes, the operation and application of pulse forming, and pulse staying circuits and microwave devices. Also presents detailed coverage of microwave receiving, transmitting, and indicating systems.

636. **Commonsense Electrical Safety**. Bureau of Mines. January 1984. 164p. ill. **I28.2:El2**.

Discusses the fundamentals of electricity, effects of electricity, and safety equipment and procedures. Describes safety procedures both on the surface and in underground mines. Glossary. Index.

See also entries 1, 1091.

For additional publications on this topic see Subject Bibliography **SB-053**, **Electricity and Electronics**.

Energy

GENERAL

637. **Annual Energy Outlook, 1984 with Projections to 1995.** Energy Information Administration. 1985. 384p. tables. DOE/EIA-0383(84). S/N 061-003-00419-9. $10.00. **E3.1/4:984**.

Issued annually. Provides yearly projections from 1984 through 1995 of the consumption and supply of energy by fuel, and by end sector use. References.

638. **Annual Energy Review, 1984.** Energy Information Administration. 1985. 283p. tables. DOE/EIA-0384(84). S/N 061-003-00430-0. $10.00. **E3.1/2:984**.

Issued annually. Presents current data for the year on energy production, consumption, exploration and development for petroleum, natural gas, electricity, nuclear power, and geothermal and solar energy. Historical data back to 1952 are provided for many series. References.

639. **DOE This Month.** Department of Energy. Monthly. approx. 8p. ill. S/N 761-004-00000-0. Symbol EINS. $19.00 per yr. Single copy $1.75. **E1.54:vol/no**.

This periodical uses a newspaper tabloid format. It includes news items concerning activities and operations of the Department of Energy related to energy research and development and policy.

640. **Energy Information Directory.** Energy Information Administration. Quarterly. 81p. charts. DOE/EIA-0205. **E3.33:yr/no**.

Lists under twenty topics many of the federal government offices that are involved in energy matters. Also includes state energy offices, DOE research and development and field facilities. Subject and personal name indexes.

641. **International Energy Annual, 1983.** Energy Information Administration. 1984. 117p. tables. DOE/EIA-0219(83). S/N 061-003-00413-0. $4.75. **E3.11/20:983**.

Issued annually. Presents current data and trends for production, consumption, stocks, imports, and exports for primary energy commodities in more than 190 countries. Also includes prices on petroleum products in selected countries. References.

642. **International Energy Prices, 1979-1983**. Energy Information Administration. 1984. 164p. DOE/EIA-0424(83). S/N 061-003-00397-4. $5.50. **E3.11/20-2:979-83**.

Presents quarterly energy price and tax information from 1979 through 1983 for the United States and nine major energy-consuming countries. Data are presented for petroleum, coal, natural gas, and electricity.

643. **Monthly Energy Review**. Energy Information Administration. Monthly. 118p. charts, tables. DOE/EIA-0035. S/N 761-007-00000-9. Symbol MER. $42.00 per yr. Single copy $3.75. **E3.9:yr/mo**.

This periodical provides current and historical energy data under the following topics: energy summary, consumption, petroleum, natural gas, oil and gas resource development, coal, electrical utilities, nuclear energy, prices, and international. Glossary.

644. **The National Energy Policy Plan**. Department of Energy. 1983. 25p. DOE/S-0014/1. **E1.60:0014/1**.

Issued biennially. This report is required by the Department of Energy Organization Act of 1977. It discusses current programs, goals and strategy, energy markets, and energy projections to 2010.

645. **State Energy Data Report, 1960 through 1982**. Energy Information Administration. 1984. 720p. tables. DOE/EIA-0214(82). S/N 061-003-00378-8. $15.00. **E3.42:960-82**.

645-A. . . . **Supplement**. 1984. 106p. charts, tables. S/N 061-003-00379-6. $3.00. **E3.42:960-82/supp**.

This statistical compilation presents estimates of annual energy consumption at state and national levels by major economic sector and by principal energy types for 1960 through 1982.

646. **State Energy Overview, 1982**. Energy Information Administration. 1984. 456p. DOE/EIA-0354(82/2). S/N 061-003-00399-1. $13.00. **E3.42/2:982-2**.

Presents an overview of selected energy-related data for the United States, each state and the District of Columbia. Also provides for each state selected demographic and energy-related information that has been ranked and expressed as a percent of the national total. References.

647. **State Energy Price and Expenditure Report, 1970-1981**. Energy Information Administration. 1984. 241p. tables. DOE/EIA-0376(81). S/N 061-003-00385-1. $8.00. **E3.2:P93/4/970-81**.

Presents estimated average energy prices and annual energy expenditures in the United States and each of the fifty states and the District of Columbia for 1970 through 1981. Provides estimates by type of energy and economic sector.

See also entries 483, 547-20.

ENERGY CONSERVATION AND USE

648. **Cutting Energy Costs.** Department of Agriculture. 1980. 407p. ill., charts, tables. Yearbook of Agriculture 1980. S/N 001-000-04173-8. $12.00, cloth. **A1.10:980**.

Its forty-eight articles on energy conservation are grouped under the following topics: agriculture and forestry, family living, communities, and alternate energy sources. Glossary. References. Index.

649. **Energy Activities with Energy Ant.** Department of Energy. 1979. 28p. ill. S/N 061-000-00307-0. $3.50. **E1.2:An8**.

A coloring book for children on energy conservation. Includes games to play.

650. **Energy Education Guidebook.** Community Services Administration. 1980. 218p. CSA Pamphlet 6143-17. S/N 059-000-00063-2. $7.50. **CSA1.9:6143-17**.

Provides an overview of the type of energy education activities now under way. Contains an overview of energy audit procedures for school facilities, as well as eighteen classroom activities and projects. References. Bibliography.

651. **How to Save Money by Using Less Electricity, Natural Gas, and Water: A Do-It-Yourself Guide.** Department of Energy. 1979. 24p. **E1.8:M74**.

Suggests what to look for and changes to consider regarding heating and air conditioning systems, kitchen appliances, lighting, and water use.

652. **Residential Energy Consumption Survey: Consumption Expenditures, April 1982 through March 1983.** 2 pts. Energy Information Administration. 1984. 539p. ill., charts, maps. DOE/EIA-0321/1,2(82). Pt. 1. S/N 061-003-00411-3. $7.00. Pt. 2. S/N 061-003-00357-5. $8.00. **E3.43:C76/982-83/pt.1,2**.

Issued annually. Provides data on consumption and residential use of natural gas, electricity, fuel oil and kerosene, and liquified petroleum gas. Data are classified by selected socioeconomic characteristics of households and families, housing characteristics, and annual heating and cooling days. Part 1 provides national data, and part 2 provides similar data for four census regions and nine census divisions.

653. **Residential Energy Consumption Survey: Household Characteristics, 1982.** Energy Information Administration. 1984. 245p. charts, maps. DOE/EIA-0314(82). S/N 061-003-00393-1. $7.00. **E3.43:H81/982**.

Issued annually. Presents data on household fuel use, appliance use, characteristics of the housing unit, heating equipment, conservation activities, and consumption of wood fuel.

654. **Save Energy: Save Money!** Community Services Administration. Rev. August 1977. 48p. ill. CSA Pamphlet 6143-5. S/N 059-000-00002-1. $4.75. **CSA1.9:6143-5/2**.

Designed especially for people without the skills, ability, or resources to undertake major winter-proofing alterations. Provides a series of simple low-cost repairs and modifications around the house to save energy and money.

655. **Tips for Energy Savers.** Department of Energy. November 1983. 29p. ill., map. DOE/CE-0049. **E1.89:0049**.

Contains tips on saving energy and money in the home and on the road.

COAL

656. **Annual Outlook for U.S. Coal, 1984 with Projections to 1995**. Energy Information Administration. 1984. 37p. ill., charts, tables. DOE/EIA-0333(84). S/N 061-003-00400-8. $2.25. **E3.11/7-8:984**.

Discusses future (1985 to 1995) as well as historical trends of coal production and consumption. Footnote references. Bibliography.

657. **Coal Data: A Reference, 1984**. Energy Information Administration. Rev. 1985. 85p. ill., maps. DOE/EIA-0064(84). S/N 061-003-00421-1. $3.00. **E3.11/7-7:984**.

Contains summary information about coal as an important energy source. Includes overview of coal, section on coal terminology, and related information and statistical data.

658. **Coal Data Book**. President's Commission on Coal. February 1980. 235p. charts, tables. S/N 052-003-00738-0. $8.00. **Pr39.8:C63/C63/2/980**.

Contains data on coal production and consumption, including information on demand, reserves, prices, labor force, transportation and technology.

659. **Coal Production, 1983**. Energy Information Administration. 1984. 132p. ill. DOE/EIA-0118(83). S/N 061-003-00403-2. $4.75. **E3.11/7-3:983**.

Issued annually. Provides comprehensive data about coal production, number of mines, prices, productivity, employment, productive capacity, reserves, and stocks of coal in the United States. References.

See also entry 1305.

ELECTRIC AND NATURAL
GAS UTILITIES

660. **Electric Power Annual, 1983**. Energy Information Administration. 1984. 147p. tables. DOE/EIA-0348(83). S/N 061-003-00396-6. $5.50. **E3.11/17-10:983**.

Issued annually. Presents summary of electric utility statistics at national, regional, and state levels. Topics include generating capacity, amount generated, peak load capability, fuel consumption and cost, electric power retail prices, revenues, and incomes. Ten-year projections for peak load are presented as well as annual historical aggregates for the previous five years. References.

661. **Financial Statistics of Selected Electric Utilities, 1983**. Energy Information Administration. 1985. 986p. tables. DOE/EIA-0437(83). S/N 061-003-00424-5. $20.00. **E3.18/4:983**.

Issued annually. This volume combines two annual reports which were previously published separately for many years: "Statistics of Privately Owned Electrical Utilities," and "Statistics of Publicly Owned Utilities."

662. **Natural Gas Annual, 1983**. 2 vols. Energy Information Administration. 1985. 458p. charts, tables. DOE/EIA-0131(83/1,2). Vol. 1. S/N 061-003-00426-1. $7.00. Vol. 2. S/N 061-003-00427-0. $7.50. **E3.11/2-2:983/v.1,2**.

Issued annually. Presents summary data on the quantity and average price of natural gas production at the state and national levels, as well as total gas supply/disposition balances. References.

663. **Statistics of Interstate Natural Gas Pipeline Companies, 1983**. Energy Information Administration. 1984. 412p. tables. DOE/EIA-0145(83). S/N 061-003-00404-1. $11.00. **E3.25:983**.

Issued annually. Presents financial and operating statistics on the nearly one hundred classes A and B interstate natural gas pipeline companies operating in the United States.

664. **Typical Electrical Bills, January 1, 1984**. Energy Information Administration. 1984. 368p. tables. DOE/EIA-0040(84). S/N 061-003-00417-2. $10.00. **E3.22:984**.

Issued annually. Presents typical monthly electrical bills for residential service for communities over twenty-five hundred population for five levels of service; for commercial service for communities over fifty thousand population at six levels of service; and for industrial service for communities over fifty thousand population.

See also entries 306, 694.

OIL AND PETROLEUM

665. **Oil Shale: A Potential Source of Energy**. Geological Survey. Rev. 1980. 15p. ill. **I19.2:Oi5/4/980**.

Discusses the history and formation of oil shale deposits, where they are located in the United States, potential resources, and products and use of oil shale.

666. **U.S. Vulnerability to an Oil Import Curtailment: The Oil Replacement Capability**. Congress. Office of Technology Assessment. September 1984. 166p. ill., charts, tables. OTA-E-243. S/N 052-003-00963-3. $5.50. **Y3.T22/2:2Oi5/6**.

Analyzes the technical potential for replacing large quantities of oil in the United States over a five-year period by fuel substitution and conservation in the event of an extended oil supply shortfall. Footnote references.

SOLAR ENERGY

667. **Going Solar: A Buyer's Guide to Solar Energy**. Department of Energy. January 1981. folder, 12p. ill. WSUN-24R. **E1.88:24R**.

Contains tips for the homeowner on buying a solar heating system. References.

668. **Homeowner's Solar Sizing Workbook: A Simplified Method for Sizing Active Solar Space Heating Systems**. Department of Energy. 1980. 45p. ill., tables. SERI/SP-722-342. S/N 065-000-00468-8. $4.50. **E1.28:SERI/SP-722-342**.

Presents a simplified method of determining the size of the solar heating system needed to heat the home. Also includes advice on general conservation measures for the home. Bibliography.

669. **Hot Water from the Sun: A Consumer Guide to Solar Water Heating**. Department of Housing and Urban Development. 1980. 123p. ill. HUD-PDR-548. S/N 023-000-00620-1. $6.50. **HH1.6/3:Su7/2**.

Describes and illustrates the cost and efficiency factors involved in deciding whether to install a solar hot water system, in choosing the right system and dealer, and in protecting your investment.

670. **National Solar Energy Education Directory**. 3d ed. Department of Energy. 1981. 285p. SERI/SP-751-1049. S/N 061-000-00537-4. $8.00. **E1.28:SERI/SP-751-1049**.

Provides information on educational institutions and organizations involved in solar educational activities beyond the secondary school level. Index.

671. **Solar Energy: A Brief Assessment**. Western Area Power Administration. September 1983. 52p. ill., maps. **E6.2:So4**.

Provides information on solar resources technologies including active and passive heating and cooling systems, process heat, solar ponds, and photovoltaic power systems.

672. **Solar Hot Water and Your Home**. Department of Housing and Urban Development. August 1979. 13p. ill. HUD-PDR-466. **HH1.2:So4/16**.

Discusses the design and choice of different types of solar hot water systems, and indicates some possible pitfalls to avoid. References.

673. **U.S.A.: Living with the Sun**. Department of Energy. 1981. 31p. ill. DOE/CE-0017. S/N 061-000-00551-0. $3.25. **E1.89:0017**.

Describes how people in the United States have acted on their own initiative to resolve their energy problems through innovative use of simple renewable energy techniques (wind, water, solar power). Buildings and homes are described.

See also entry 1094.

For additional publications on this topic see Subject Bibliography **SB-009, Solar Energy**.

WIND ENERGY

674. **Capturing Energy from the Wind**. National Aeronautics and Space Administration. 1982. 87p. ill., maps. NASA SP-455. S/N 033-000-00850-3. $6.00. **NAS1.21:455**.

Provides brief background on the use of wind-driven machines to generate energy. Describes current developments of small wind-driven machines and big turbines to generate energy. Index.

675. **Wind Energy Developments in the 20th Century**. National Aeronautics and Space Administration. Rev. 1981. 32p. ill., charts, tables. S/N 033-000-00819-8. $4.50. **NAS1.2:W72/981**.

Describes developments in the twentieth century and the status of projects to develop wind turbines for the creation of energy. Bibliography.

676.   **Wind Machines**. National Science Foundation. 1975 (repr. 1980). 77p. ill., charts. NSF-RA-N-75-051. S/N 038-000-00272-4. $5.50. **NS1.2:W72/2**.

Discusses the history, taxonomy, current usefulness, and future potential of various types and sizes of wind machines that might be used to help meet future U.S. energy demands. Bibliography.

677.   **Wind Power and Windmills**. Department of Agriculture. March 1980. 11p. charts, tables. PA 1256. S/N 001-000-04136-3. $2.25. **A1.68:1256**.

Describes and illustrates the uses of windmills for pumping water and generating electricity. Includes estimates for the costs of necessary equipment.

Environmental Protection and Ecology

GENERAL

678. **Common Environmental Terms**. Environmental Protection Agency. Rev. November 1977. 16p. S/N 055-000-00163-4. $4.50. **EP1.2:T27/977**.
A comprehensive dictionary of common environmental words and phrases.

679. **Description of the Ecoregions of the United States**. Forest Service. 1980. 81p. ill., map. Miscellaneous Publication 1391. S/N 001-000-04241-6. $6.00. **A1.38:1391**.
Briefly describes and illustrates the nation's four ecoregions (polar domain, humid temperature domain, dry domain, and humid tropical domain). The description of each region includes a discussion of land-surface forms, climate, vegetation, soil, and fauna. References.

680. **Environmental Contaminants in Food**. Congress. Office of Technology Assessment. December 1979. 237p. charts, tables. OTA-F-103. S/N 052-003-00724-0. $7.00. **Y3.T22/2:2C76/2**.
Examines the regulatory approaches and monitoring strategies for coping with food contaminated by chemicals or radioactive substances, which inadvertently find their way into food through agriculture, mining, industrial operations, or energy production. Footnote references.

681. **Environmental Quality, 1983**. Council on Environmental Quality. 1983. 352p. ill. S/N 041-011-00077-7. $8.00. **PrEx14.1:983**.
Issued annually. Presents highlights of activities, conditions, and trends during the year in the protection of the environment dealing with air quality, water quality, waste management, toxic substances, and natural resources. Statistical appendix includes current and historical data on environmental topics. References. Index.

682.   **Environmental Trends**. Council on Environmental Quality. July 1981. 351p. charts. S/N 041-011-00058-1. $11.00. **PrEx14.2:En8/10**.

A chart book with illustrations and text to highlight trends in people and the land, transportation, materials use and solid waste, toxic substances, cropland, forests and range land, wildlife, energy, water resources and quality, air quality, and biosphere. References. Index.

683.   **EPA Journal**. Environmental Protection Agency. Monthly, except January/February and July/August (combined). approx. 36p. ill. S/N 755-001-00000-7. Symbol EPAJ. $20.00 per yr. Single copy $2.00. **EP1.67:vol/no**.

This periodical contains short articles of general interest on protection of the environment and related topics. Departments include Update (review of recent major EPA activities and developments in pollution control); Appointments at EPA (includes brief biographies of new major appointments); and book reviews.

684.   **Fun with the Environment**. Environmental Protection Agency. Rev. 1977. 16p. ill. S/N 055-000-00161-8. $2.75. **EP1.2:F96/977**.

A cartoon book designed to teach children about protecting the environment.

685.   **Global Future: Time to Act; Report to the President on Global Resources, Environment and Population**. Council on Environmental Quality. January 1981. 262p. S/N 041-011-00056-4. $7.50. **PrEx14.2:G51/3**.

Presents assessments and ideas for U.S. action in response to the probable changes in world population, resources, and environment through the end of the century as reported in the *Global 2000 Report* (entry 686). Index.

686.   **Global 2000 Report to the President: Entering the Twenty-First Century**. 3 vols. Council on Environment Quality. **PrEx14.2:G51/2/2000/v.1-3**.

686-1.   Vol. 1.   **Summary Report**. 1980. 47p. S/N 041-011-00037-8. $5.00.

An interagency study directed by President Carter to investigate probable changes in the world's population, resources, and environment through the end of the twentieth century. This interpretative report summarizes the findings in nontechnical terms.

686-2.   Vol. 2.   **Technical Report**. 1980. 803p. charts, maps, tables. S/N 041-011-00038-6. $14.00.

Presents projections and analyses in great detail with respect to population, gross national product, climate, technology, food, fisheries, forestry, energy, water, fuel and nonfuel minerals, and environment. References.

686-3.   Vol. 3.   **Documentation on the Government's Global Sectoral Models: The Government's "Global Model."** 1981. 410p. charts, tables. S/N 041-011-00051-3. $9.50.

Presents information on the long-term sectoral models used by the U.S. government to project global trends in population, resources, and the environment. Footnote references.

687. **Learning about the Environment**. Bureau of Land Management. Rev. May 1979. 19p. ill. **I53.2:En8/2/979**.

Explains what is meant by ecology, environment, conservation, and pollution and the relationships between plants, animals, and people. Describes the different environments that the bureau manages, and its environmental protection programs.

688. **Understanding the Game of Environment: An Illustrated Guide to Understanding Ecological Principles**. Forest Service. 1979. 174p. ill. Agriculture Information Bulletin 426. S/N 001-001-00498-7. $9.00. **A1.75:426**.

This colorfully illustrated publication translates major ecological principles into a game in which living organisms interact with each other and their environment. Includes the playing fields, rules of the game, changing players and playing fields, fouls and penalties, and improving the game. Glossary.

689. **Using Our Natural Resources**. Department of Agriculture. 1983. 611p. ill., charts, tables. Yearbook of Agriculture 1983. S/N 001-000-04387-1. $7.00, cloth. **A1.10:983**.

Tells the fabulous story of our nation's resources, mainly in terms of land, water, forests and woodlands, plants, farmlands, people, and urban and suburban greenbelts. Various views are expressed in a number of essays prepared by Department of Agriculture specialists. Index.

690. **Your World, Your Environment**. Environmental Protection Agency. 1979. 12p. ill. S/N 055-000-00175-8. $2.50. **EP1.2:W89/6**.

Intended for children, this publication explains pollution of the environment in simple terms.

See also entries 107, 202, 203, 310, 709-2, 836, 1083, 1153, 1664, 1668, 1672.

For additional publications on this topic see Subject Bibliography **SB-088, Environmental Education and Protection**.

AIR POLLUTION

691. **Acid Rain: A Survey of Data and Current Analysis**. Congress. House. Committee on Energy and Commerce. May 1984. 966p. ill., charts, tables. Committee Print, 98th Congress, 2d Session. S/N 052-070-05930-5. $14.00. **Y4.En2/3:98-X**.

Part 1 provides a review of the literature on acid rain. Part 2 is a compilation of articles under the following topics: background, sources of emissions, atmospheric processes, impact of acid precipitation, strategies to mitigate acid deposition, and costs and benefits of control. References.

692. **Acid Rain: Research Summary**. Environmental Protection Agency. October 1979. 23p. ill., maps. EPA-600/8-79-028. S/N 055-000-00185-5. $3.25. **EP1.2:Ac4**.

Reviews the causes, chemistry, and effects of acid rain and summarizes related research.

693. **A Citizen's Guide to Clean Air and Transportation: Implications for Urban Revitalization**. Environmental Protection Agency. October 1980. 61p. ill., charts. **EP1.8:C49.**

Discusses the problem of air pollution due to motor vehicle use. Provides a guide for community air quality and transportation planning to reduce pollution and revitalize urban areas. Footnote references.

694. **The Clean Air Act, the Electric Utilities, and the Coal Market**. Congressional Budget Office. April 1982. 109p. maps, tables. S/N 052-070-05724-6. $5.50. **Y10.2:C58.**

Discusses the interrelated issues of achieving and maintaining clean air and the assurance of a reliable and low-cost supply of electricity derived from coal. Analyzes alternate emission standards to promote the use of coal. Footnote references.

695. **To Breathe Clean Air: Report of the National Commission on Air Quality**. March 1981. 371p. charts, tables. S/N 052-003-00806-8. $9.00. **Y3.Ai7/5:2Ai7.**

The commission was established under the Clean Air Act Amendments of 1977 to make an independent analysis of air pollution control and alternative strategies for achieving the goals of the act. Includes the findings and recommendations of the commission. References.

696. **Trends in the Quality of the Nation's Air**. Environmental Protection Agency. Rev. January 1985. 19p. ill., charts. **EP1.2:Q2/13/985.**

Reports national trends from 1975 to 1982 in reducing amounts of the following pollutants in the air: lead, carbon monoxide, particulate matter, ozone, nitrogen dioxide, and sulphur dioxide.

See also entry 182.

For additional publications on this topic see Subject Bibliography **SB-046, Air Pollution**.

Families

697. **Attorney General's Task Force on Family Violence; Final Report**. Department of Justice. September 1984. 164p. S/N 027-000-01197-7. $4.50. **J1.2:F21/2**.

Presents the findings, conclusions, and recommendations of a federal task force on family violence with respect to the role of the judicial system, federal and state lawmakers, the media, and victim assistance. Footnote references.

698. **Family Economics Review**. Agricultural Research Service. Quarterly. approx. 36p. charts, tables. S/N 701-019-00000-8. Symbol FAMER. $12.00 per yr. Single copy $3.25. **A77.708:yr/no**.

This periodical contains articles on a wide variety of home economics subjects, usually of a statistical nature. The following departments provide current data: Consumer Prices, Cost of Food at Home for Food Plans at 4 Cost Levels for a Family of 2, and of 4, and Updated Estimated Costs of Raising a Child.

699. **Family Violence: Intervention Strategies**. Children's Bureau. May 1980. 98p. DHHS Publication No. (OHDS) 80-30258. S/N 017-092-00065-1. $5.50. **HE23.1210/4:V81**.

Provides information on the nature, causes, and effects of family violence; identification of violent families; intervention strategies; and program development techniques. Bibliography.

700. **Household and Family Characteristics: March 1984**. Bureau of the Census. 1985. 244p. tables. Current Population Reports, Series P-20, No. 398. S/N 003-001-90797-6. $8.50. **C3.186:P-20/398**.

Issued annually. Presents detailed national data on household and family characteristics of the population by selected demographic, social, and economic characteristics. Introductory text highlights recent changes and trends. References.

701. **Listening to America's Families: Action for the 80's. The Report to the President, Congress, and Families of the Nation**. White House Conference on Families. October 1980. 249p. ill. S/N 040-000-00429-7. $7.50. **Y3.W58/22:1/980.**

This is the final report of a conference called by President Carter to examine the strengths of American families, the difficulties they face, and ways in which family life is affected by public policies. References.

702. **Marital Status and Living Arrangements: March 1983**. Bureau of the Census. 1984. 68p. tables. Current Population Reports, Series P-20, No. 389. S/N 003-001-90788-7. $2.75. **C3.186:P-20/389.**

Issued annually. Presents detailed national data on marital status and living arrangements of the noninstitutionalized population of the United States by age, sex, race, and Spanish origin. Introductory text highlights recent changes and trends. References.

703. **Single-Parent Families**. Administration for Children, Youth and Families. March 1981. 41p. ill. DHHS Publication No. (OHDS) 79-30247. S/N 017-091-00229-1. $4.50. **HE23.1002:Si6.**

Provides suggestions for single parents on all aspects of raising children and on coping with divorce or death in the family. References.

704. **Yours, Mine and Ours: Tips for Stepparents**. National Institute of Mental Health. 1978. 27p. DHEW Publication No. (ADM) 78-676. S/N 017-024-00833-8. $3.50. **HE20.8102:Y8/2.**

Suggests steps to take before remarriage to ease the transition into the family. Discusses problems many step-families have encountered and indicates ways to deal with them. References.

See also entries 81, 127, 257, 365, 366, 500, 1068, 1312.

Films and
Audiovisual Materials

705. **Catalog of Captioned Films for the Deaf, 1982-1983**. Office of Special Education and Rehabilitation Services. 1983. 83p. ill. **ED1.209/2:982-83**.

Lists and describes captioned films which are available for loan under a federal program for showing to groups of deaf persons. Films are listed in three sections: feature films and short subjects, adult education, and video cassettes.

706. **Catalog of United States Coast Guard Films, 1983**. Coast Guard. Rev. 1983. 11p. **TD5.2:F48/983**.

This annotated catalog lists general interest boating safety 16mm films which are available on loan from Coast Guard film libraries. The films are also sold by the National Audiovisual Center.

707. **Documentary Film Classics Produced by the United States Government**. National Audiovisual Center. 1980. 48p. ill. **GS4.2:F48/2**.

Describes notable documentary films, particularly from the Great Depression of the 1930s and World War II which were produced by the U.S. government and are available for sale. Order information is provided. Bibliography.

708. **A Guide to Audiovisual and Print Materials on Safety Belts and Child Safety Seats**. National Highway Traffic Safety Administration. July 1983. 41p. ill. DOT HS 806 418. **TD8.8:Au2**.

Describes selected 16mm films and other audiovisual materials on the use of automobile safety belts and child car safety seats which are suitable for the general public and elementary and secondary school students. References.

709. **A List of Audiovisual Materials Produced by the United States Government for. . . .** National Audiovisual Center. **GS4.17/5-2:ct**.

The following catalogs list and describe audiovisual materials which were produced by federal agencies and are available to the public for sale or rent from the National

Audiovisual Center. Most listed items are films, but other materials such as slide sets, audiotapes, filmstrips, multimedia kits, videocassettes, and other formats may be included.

709-1. . . . **Career Education**. Rev. March 1983. 9p. **GS4.17/5-2:C18/983**.

709-2. . . . **Environment and Energy Conservation**. Rev. August 1982. 18p. **GS4.17/5-2:En8/982**.

709-3. . . . **Fire/Law Enforcement [and] Emergency Medical Services**. Rev. June 1982. 18p. **GS4.17/5-2:F51/982**.

709-4. . . . **Flight and Meteorology**. Rev. August 1983. 12p. **GS4.17/5-2: F64/983**.

709-5. . . . **Foreign Language Instruction**. Rev. 1983. 6p. **GS4.17/5-2: F76/983**.

709-6. . . . **History**. Rev. October 1982. 26p. **GS4.17/5-2:H62/982**.

709-7. . . . **Industrial Safety**. Rev. August 1982. 17p. **GS4.17/5-2:In2/982**.

709-8. . . . **Library and Information Sciences**. Rev. October 1983. 8p. **GS4.17/5-2:L61/983**.

709-9. . . . **Nursing**. Rev. June 1982. 18p. **GS4.17/5-2:N93/982**.

710. **NASA Films**. National Aeronautics and Space Administration. Rev. January 1982. 31p. PAM 172. **NAS1.2:F48/982**.
This annotated catalog lists 16mm films, filmstrips, and audiotapes produced by NASA which describe its programs and achievements, and which are available to the public. Title index.

711. **NASA Photography Index, 1983**. National Aeronautics and Space Administration. Rev. 1983. 198p. ill. S/N 033-000-00885-6. $5.00. **NAS1.43/4:983**.
Lists representative space photographs from NASA launches and activities which are available free to the information media. The general public may obtain these materials at a laboratory service charge through a photographic contractor.

712. **National Science Foundation Films**. National Science Foundation. Rev. 1984. 20p. **NS1.2:F43/984**.
An annotated list of films produced by the National Science Foundation to report the progress of scientific research and its applications to the public. Includes information on availability. Title index.

For additional publications on this topic see Subject Bibliography **SB-073, Motion Pictures, Films, and Audiovisual Information**.

Firearms, Explosives, and Gun Control

EXPLOSIVES

713. **Bomb Threats and Search Techniques**. Bureau of Alcohol, Tobacco and Firearms. April 1975. 18p. ill. ATF P7550.2. S/N 048-004-00810-6. $2.75. **T70.2:B63**.

Provides advice on how to prepare for and handle telephone and written bomb threats, and on searching rooms and buildings for bombs or explosives. Includes checklist and report form.

714. **Explosives Incidents, 1982**. Bureau of Alcohol, Tobacco and Firearms. May 1983. 48p. ill., charts, tables. ATF P5400.10. **T70.11:982**.

Issued annually. Presents statistics and descriptive highlights of bombings, stolen explosives and recoveries, and other explosives incidents which were reported to the bureau during the year.

715. **Explosives Tagging: Scientific "Finger Printing" for Law Enforcement**. Bureau of Alcohol, Tobacco and Firearms. December 1979. 13p. **T70.2:Ex7**.

Explains how the addition of taggants (small microscopic plastic chips) to explosives during manufacture can assist in the detection and identification of explosives used illegally.

716. **Taggants in Explosives**. Congress. Office of Technology Assessment. April 1980. 270. ill., charts, tables. OTA-ISC-116. S/N 052-003-00747-9. $8.00. **Y3.T22/2:2Ex7**.

Taggants are materials added to explosives during manufacture to aid law enforcement agencies in identification and detection of unlawful use. This report assesses whether they work, and, if so, the possible safety hazards and cost effectiveness. Footnote references.

717. **Uniform Crime Reports: Bomb Summary, 1983**. Federal Bureau of Investigation. 1984. 24p. charts, tables. **J1.14/7-4:B63/983**.

Issued annually. Presents statistics on actual and attempted bombing incidents reported to the FBI during the year.

FIREARMS AND GUN CONTROL

718. **Federal Regulation of Firearms**. Congress. Senate. Committee on the Judiciary. May 1982. 267p. tables. Committee Print, 97th Congress, 2d Session. S/N 052-070-05732-7. $6.50. **Y4.J98/2:F51/4**.

Discusses federal policies and proposals on firearm regulations. Includes five studies on gun control and crime, and a survey of selected state firearms control laws. Footnote references. Bibliography.

719. **Firearms Identification: A Visual Guide**. Federal Bureau of Investigation. 1984. 54p. ill. S/N 027-001-00036-0. $1.75. **J1.14/2:F51**.

Contains photographs of common types of hand guns, typical rifles, common shotguns, and submachine guns and carbines.

720. **Identification of Firearms within the Purview of the National Firearms Act**. Bureau of Alcohol, Tobacco and Firearms. Rev. 1984. 36p. ill. ATF P5300.1. S/N 048-012-00083-3. $2.00. **T70.2:F51/984**.

Presents illustrations of firearms and destructive devices which must be registered with the bureau regardless of condition. This includes selected machine guns and machine pistols, shotguns, rifles, revolvers and pistols, and destructive devices such as mortars and explosives.

721. **Issued Revolver Preventive Maintenance Guide**. Secret Service. 1982. 44p. ill. S/N 048-002-00076-1. $3.50. **T34.8:R32**.

Provides preventive maintenance instructions for the Smith & Wesson .38 caliber Special and .357 caliber Magnum revolvers used by the Secret Service.

722. **Project Indentification: A Study of Handguns Used in Crime**. Bureau of Alcohol, Tobacco and Firearms. May 1976. 65p. ill., tables. ATF P3310.1. S/N 048-012-00016-7. $5.00. **T70.2:Id2**.

Reflects a total of 10,617 crime guns submitted by police of sixteen cities for tracing. Handguns are categorized by price, size of barrel, and region of sale with special focus on "Saturday Night Specials."

723. **Revolver Preventive Maintenance Guide**. Federal Bureau of Investigation. 1984. 37p. ill. **J1.14/16:R32**.

Provides preventive maintenance instructions for the Smith & Wesson .38 Special revolvers, model no. 13, model no. 10-6 or 10-8, and model no. 10.

724. **The Right to Keep and Bear Arms**. Congress. Senate. Committee on the Judiciary. February 1982. 184p. Committee Print, 97th Congress, 2d Session. S/N 052-070-05686-0. $5.00. **Y4.J89/2:Ar5/5**.

Provides historical background and case law regarding the Second Amendment right to "keep and bear arms." Discusses firearms law enforcement regarding the

Second Amendment. Includes selected articles and statements presenting arguments for and against gun control. Footnote references.

725.   State Laws and Published Ordinances: Firearms. Bureau of Alcohol, Tobacco and Firearms. Rev. December 1983. 147p. ATF P5300.5. S/N 048-012-00081-7. $4.25. **T70.5:F51/2/983**.
    Provides a compilation of the texts of state laws together with selected municipal ordinances dealing with possession and use of firearms.

726.   Your Guide to Federal Firearms Regulations, 1984-85. Bureau of Alcohol, Tobacco and Firearms. April 1984. 85p. S/N 048-012-00082-5. $3.00. **T70.8:F51/3**.
    Includes the text of federal laws and regulations, and Treasury Department rulings, procedures and industry circulars relating to firearms. Also includes questions and answers and miscellaneous items of information regarding firearms. References.

Fires, Fire Prevention, and Safety

727. **After the Fire: Returning to Normal**. Federal Emergency Management Administration. October 1984. 13p. FA-46. **FEM1.2:F51/8**.

Provides advice for the homeowner on steps to take following a fire, including insurance reports, replacement of valuable documents and records, and salvaging household goods.

728. **Arson Resource Directory**. 2d ed. Federal Emergency Management Administration. 1982. 308p. FA-58. **FEM1.102:Ar7**.

Lists organizations and programs concerned with the management of arson prevention and control activities, investigation and prosecution of arson, economic and behavioral factors in arson, and miscellaneous anti-arson organizations. Indexes of organizations and persons.

729. **Fire in the United States: Deaths, Injuries, Dollar Loss, and Incidents at the National, State, and Local Levels in 1978**. 2d ed. Federal Emergency Management Administration. July 1982. 181p. charts, maps, tables. **FEM1.2:F51/2**.

Presents national estimates of deaths, injuries, and property damage due to fires in 1978. Also discusses firefighter death and injury situations, the arson problem, and the effects of social and economic characteristics on the fire problem. References.

730. **Indirect Costs of Residential Fires**. Fire Administration. July 1979. 36p. ill., tables. S/N 064-000-00004-7. $2.50. **FEM1.102:C82/2**.

Discusses the nature of indirect losses due to fires, such as costs of temporary shelter, medical care, lost wages, etc. Presents national estimates for indirect fire costs, and provides techniques for making local estimates of these costs.

731. **What You Should Know about Home Fire Safety**. Consumer Product Safety Commission. Rev. October 1983. 9p. ill. **Y3.C76/3:2H75/3/983**.

Calls attention to fire hazards in the home including flammable liquids and fabrics; and ignition sources such as space heaters, matches, and lighters. Provides advice on surviving a fire, including use of smoke detectors.

732. **What You Should Know about Smoke Detectors**. Consumer Product Safety Commission. Rev. 1985. 4p. ill. **Y3.C76/3:2Sm7/985**.

Discusses why to have a smoke detector; how ionization and photoelectric detectors work; and how to select, install, and maintain a detector.

733. **Winter Fires: Winter Fire Safety Tips for the Home**. Federal Emergency Management Administration. May 1984. folder, 6p. ill. L-97. **FEM1.11:97**.

Offers safety tips on using regular and alternate sources for home heating such as space heaters and fireplaces.

See also entries 506-1, 567, 709-3, 824.

First Aid and Emergency Treatment

734. **Camper's First Aid**. Army Corps of Engineers. 1980. 14p. ill. S/N 008-022-00143-3. $2.50. **D103.6/5:C15**.

A handy booklet of basic first aid information for the camper to use until medical assistance is obtained. Topics include bleeding, broken bones, burns, choking, snake bites, and shock.

735. **First Aid Book**. Mine Safety and Health Administration. 1980. 232p. ill. S/N 029-017-00003-4. $7.00. **L38.8:F51**.

Provides basic first aid knowledge with many illustrations for use by mine workers. Covers treatment for shock, wounds, burns, fractures, and other medical emergencies. Bibliography. Index.

736. **Medical Guide and Glossary**. English edition. Office of Refugee Settlement. February 1980. 86p. ill. S/N 017-000-00233-3. $5.50. **HE1.6/3:M46/2/English**.

This guide was developed in response to concerns about the health needs of Indochinese refugees and is also prepared in Cambodian, Laotian, and Vietnamese editions. Provides useful information on common diseases, symptoms, medication, reproductive concerns, preventive health care, and first aid. Bibliography.

737. **The Ship's Medicine Chest and Medical Aid at Sea**. Public Health Service. Rev. 1984. looseleaf, 517p. ill. DHHS Publication No. (PHS) 84-2024. S/N 917-010-00000-5. Symbol SMCMA. $44.00 (includes basic manual plus supplements for an indeterminate period). **HE20.8:M46**.

This manual is intended primarily for the information and guidance of the ship's master and other crew members responsible for medical care on U.S. merchant ships at sea which do not have a doctor aboard.

738. **Standard First Aid Training Course: Instructor's Syllabus**. Naval Education and Training Command. Rev. 1982. 168p. ill. NAVEDTRA 10081-D. S/N 008-047-00340-4. $5.00. **D207.208/2:F51/3/982**.

This manual is designed to provide instructional and reference materials on first aid procedures for nonmedical naval personnel. Index.

See also entries 11, 13.

Food and Nutrition

GENERAL

739. **Food News for Consumers**. Food Safety and Inspection Service. Quarterly. approx. 16p. ill. S/N 701-025-00000-8. Symbol FONC. $9.50 per yr. No single copies sold. **A110.10:vol/no**.

This periodical includes short news items organized under the following topics: consumer education, food safety, health and nutrition, looking ahead, consumer almanac, food programs, and buying and eating trends.

740. **Fun with Good Foods**. Food and Nutrition Service. October 1978. 48p. ill. PA 1204. S/N 001-000-03868-1. $4.75. **A1.68:1204**.

A coloring book intended to teach young children about food and nutrition.

741. **The Good Foods Coloring Book**. Food and Nutrition Service. Rev. June 1973 (repr. 1978). 32p. ill. PA 912. S/N 001-000-02940-1. $4.50. **A1.68:912/2**.

Includes illustrations of nutritious foods for children to color along with a description telling why each item is good for them.

742. **Packet for the Bride**. 10 books. Department of Agriculture. 1983. 249p. S/N 001-000-04385-4. $7.00. **A1.2:B76/983**.

Includes the following pamphlets: *How to Buy Fresh Fruits* (entry 756), *Calories and Weight* (entry 745), *The Sodium Content of Your Food* (entry 752), *Conserving the Nutritive Values in Foods* (entry 747), *Vegetables in Family Meals* (entry 799), *Lamb in Family Meals* (entry 780), *Poultry in Family Meals* (entry 782), *Pork in Family Meals* (entry 781), *Guide to Budgeting for the Family* (entry 245), and *Keeping Food Safe to Eat* (entry 769).

743. **What's to Eat? and Other Questions Kids Ask about Foods**. Department of Agriculture. 1979. 142p. ill. Yearbook of Agriculture 1979. S/N 001-000-04041-3. $8.50. **A1.10:979**.

From cover to cover it's a full-color feast of stories, games, jokes, cartoons, craft projects, recipes, and fun facts for children of all ages. Dedicated to children for the 1979 International Year of the Child.

See also entries 74, 85, 97, 110, 689, 1440.

NUTRITION

744. **Building a Better Diet**. Food and Nutrition Service. September 1979. 16p. ill. PA 1241. **A1.68:1241**.
Intended primarily for food stamp recipients, this booklet tells how to buy and eat healthy foods.

745. **Calories and Weight: The USDA Pocket Guide**. Department of Agriculture. Rev. May 1981. 80p. ill., tables. Agriculture Information Bulletin 364. S/N 001-000-04164-9. $2.25. **A1.75:364/3**.
Contains tables of common food items with the calorie count for specific servings. Also includes advice on losing weight.

746. **Composition of Food: Raw, Processed, Prepared**. Department of Agriculture. Rev. 1976- . looseleaf. tables. Agriculture Handbook 8. **A1.76:8-no**.
This revision of the 1963 edition is being issued in numbered sections to expedite release of data to the public. Each section contains a table of nutrient data for a major food group. Each page in the table contains the nutrient profile of a single food item, given on the 100-gram basis in two common measures and in the edible portion of one pound (453.6 grams) as purchased. Values are provided for proximate composition, minerals, vitamins, lipids, and amino acides.

746-1. . . . **Baby Foods**. December 1978. 237p. S/N 001-000-03900-8. $8.00. **A1.76:8-3**.

746-2. . . . **Breakfast Cereals**. July 1982. 171p. S/N 001-000-04283-1. $7.00. **A1.76:8-8**.

746-3. . . . **Dairy and Egg Products**. November 1976. 157p. S/N 001-000-03635-1. $7.00. **A1.76:8-1**.

746-4. . . . **Fats and Oils**. June 1979. 148p. S/N 001-000-03984-9. $7.00. **A1.76:8-4**.

746-5. . . . **Fruits and Fruit Juices**. August 1982. 283p. S/N 001-000-04287-4. $9.00. **A1.76:8-9**.

746-6. . . . **Nuts and Seed Products**. September 1984. 142p. S/N 001-000-04429-0. $5.50. **A1.76:8-12**.

746-7. . . . **Pork Products**. 1983. 212p. S/N 001-000-04368-4. $7.50. **A1.76:8-10**.

746-8. . . . **Poultry Products**. August 1979. 336p. S/N 001-000-04008-1. $9.50. **A1.76:8-5**.

746-9. . . . **Sausages and Luncheon Meats**. September 1980. 98p. S/N 001-000-04183-5. $6.00. **A1.76:8-7**.

746-10. . . . **Soups, Sauces and Gravies**. February 1980. 227p. S/N 001-000-04114-2. $8.00. **A1.76:8-6**.

746-11. . . . **Spices and Herbs**. 1977. 43p. S/N 001-000-03646-7. $6.50. **A1.76:8-2**.

746-12. . . . **Vegetables and Vegetable Products**. August 1984. 508p. S/N 001-000-04427-3. $16.00. **A1.76:8-11**.

747. **Conserving the Nutritive Values in Foods**. Human Nutrition Information Service. Rev. April 1983. 11p. Home and Garden Bulletin 90. S/N 001 000 04304 8. $2.25. **A1.77:90/6**.
Calls attention to some of the important nutrients in food that are affected by different handling and preparation practices, and suggests ways in which these nutrients can be preserved.

748. **Dietary Goals for the United States**. 2d ed. Congress. Senate. Select Committee on Nutrition. December 1977. 124p. charts, tables. Committee Print, 95th Congress, 1st Session. S/N 052-070-04376-8. $5.00. **Y4.N95:D56/977-2**.
Examines and documents harmful trends in our national diet and sets forth seven basic goals for the development of healthier eating habits. Each goal is carefully explained. Footnote references. Bibliography.

749. **Ideas for Better Eating: Menus and Recipes to Make Use of the Dietary Guidelines**. Department of Agriculture. January 1981. 30p. S/N 001-000-04217-3. $1.75. **A106.8:Ea8**.
Offers ideas and recipes to help use the revised Department of Agriculture dietary guidelines published in 1980.

750. **Nutrition and Your Health: Dietary Guidelines for Americans**. Department of Agriculture. 20p. Home and Garden Bulletin 232. S/N 001-000-04248-3. $2.25. **A1.77:232**.
Provides a brief explanation of the USDA seven dietary guidelines for Americans to maintain good health. Discusses what foods should be eaten, what foods should be avoided, how to lose weight, and the importance of *moderate* consumption of alcohol. Minor changes to the guidelines are to be published in 1985.

751. **Nutritive Value of Foods**. Department of Agriculture. Rev. April 1981. 34p. tables. Home and Garden Bulletin 72. S/N 001-000-04232-7. $4.50. **A1.77:72/7**.
Consists primarily of detailed tables showing the nutritive value of common foods including amounts of protein, fat, fatty acids, carbohydrates, and various minerals in each.

752. **The Sodium Content of Your Food**. Human Nutrition Information Service. Rev. February 1983. 43p. tables. Home and Garden Bulletin 233. **A1.77:233/2**.

Lists in tabular format the sodium content (in milligrams) of standard portions of 791 food items. It also lists the sodium content of twenty-three selected nonprescription drugs including aspirin, antacids, and laxatives.

See also entries 349, 950, 951, 953.

BUYING GUIDES

753.   **Do You Use Food Labels to Make Smart Choices?** Department of Agriculture. July 1984. folder, 6p. ill. PA 1345. **A1.68:1345.**
Provides brief advice on unit pricing and other labels and information on food products in supermarkets.

754.   **How Do You Find the Best Meat Buys?** Department of Agriculture. July 1984. 6p. ill. PA 1347. **A1.68:1347.**
Provides brief advice on picking the best meat buys for your family's meals.

755.   **How to Buy Dairy Products**. Agricultural Marketing Service. Rev. February 1983. 16p. ill. Home and Garden Bulletin 201. **A1.77:201/5.**
Provides advice on how to buy milk, cream, butter, cheese, yogurt, and frozen desserts.

756.   **How to Buy Fresh Fruits**. Agricultural Marketing Service. Rev. 1984. 23p. ill. Home and Garden Bulletin 141. S/N 001-000-04406-1. $1.50. **A1.77:141/3.**
Provides brief advice on how to buy fresh fruits.

757.   **How to Buy Fresh Fruits and Vegetables**. 5 books. Department of Agriculture. 1982. 118p. ill. S/N 001-000-04309-9. $7.00.
A packet of the following five Home and Garden Bulletins: *How to Buy Fresh Fruits* (no. 141), *How to Buy Fresh Vegetables* (no. 143), *How to Buy Canned and Frozen Vegetables* (no. 167), *How to Buy Canned and Frozen Fruits* (no. 191), and *How to Buy Economically* (no. 235).

758.   **How to Buy Lamb**. Department of Agriculture. Rev. April 1979. 16p. ill. Home and Garden Bulletin 195. **A1.77:195/2.**
Provides practical advice on buying different grades and cuts of lamb.

759.   **How to Buy Meat for Your Freezer**. Food Safety and Quality Service. Rev. November 1980. 28p. ill. Home and Garden Bulletin 166. **A1.77:166/5.**
Provides advice on buying wholesale and retail cuts of beef, lamb, and pork for the home freezer.

760.   **How to Buy Meat, Poultry, and Dairy Products**. 7 books. Department of Agriculture. 1981. 114p. ill. S/N 001-000-04308-1. $9.00.
A packet of the following Home and Garden Bulletins: *How to Buy Eggs* (no. 144), *How to Buy Beef Steaks* (no. 145), *How to Buy Poultry* (no. 146), *How to Buy Meat for Your Freezer* (no. 166), *How to Buy Cheese* (no. 193), *How to Buy Lamb* (no. 195), and *How to Buy Dairy Products* (no. 201).

761. **Meat and Poultry Labels Wrap It Up**. Food Safety and Inspection Service. March 1984. folder, 8p. ill. Home and Garden Bulletin 238. **A1.77:238**.

Provides six easy steps to reading labels for product name, ingredients and weight, inspection marks, nutrition information, special handling instructions and dating, and company name and lot.

762. **Which Brand Is the Best Buy?** Department of Agriculture. July 1984. folder, 6p. ill. PA 1344. **A1.68:1344**.

Provides brief advice on comparing brands of food in the supermarket.

763. **Your Money's Worth in Foods**. Human Nutrition Information Service. Rev. September 1984. 39p. tables. Home and Garden Bulletin 183. S/N 001-000-04431-1. $2.25. **A1.77:183/8**.

Brings together information on meal planning and good shopping to make food dollars count more for nutrition. Cost comparison tables have been updated to reflect 1984 prices.

PRESERVATION AND STORAGE

764. **Freezing Combination Main Dishes**. Agricultural Research Service. Rev. June 1976. 22p. ill. Home and Garden Bulletin 40. S/N 001-000-03559-2. $2.25. **A1.77:40/5**.

Describes the types of food, equipment, and packaging materials required to freeze your meals. Also include recipes.

765. **Home Canning of Fruits and Vegetables**. Extension Service. Rev. May 1983. 31p. ill., tables. Home and Garden Bulletin 8. S/N 001-000-04331-1. $1.50. **A1.77:8/12**.

Describes the various types of canning equipment that can be used and provides illustrated instructions for canning more than thirty different fruits and vegetables.

766. **Home Canning of Meat and Poultry**. Agricultural Research Service. Rev. June 1977. 24p. ill. Home and Garden Bulletin 106. S/N 001-000-04111-8. $2.25. **A1.77:106/7**.

Describes general canning methods and techniques and provides specific directions for canning meat and poultry. Index.

767. **Home Freezing of Fruits and Vegetables**. Extension Service. Rev. April 1982. 48p. ill., tables. Home and Garden Bulletin 10. S/N 001-000-02448-5. $2.00. **A1.77:10/8**.

Includes illustrated directions for freezing many fruits and vegetables so they retain their freshness and nutritive value. Also tells what fruits and vegetables can be frozen and how to prepare them for freezing.

768. **How to Make Jellies, Jams, and Preserves at Home**. Extension Service. Rev. 1977 (repr. 1982). 34p. ill. Home and Garden Bulletin 56. S/N 001-000-04268-8. $2.50. **A1.77:56/9**.

Tells how to make various kinds of jellies, jams, and conserves with and without added pectin. Also includes recipes for marmalades and preserves made with no added pectin.

769.   **Keeping Food Safe to Eat: A Guide for Homemakers**. Department of Agriculture. Rev. October 1978. 12p. ill. Home and Garden Bulletin 162. S/N 001-000-03832-0. $2.25. **A1.77:162/4**.

Describes and illustrates the dangers of food poisoning and offers suggestions regarding proper methods for storing, preparing, freezing, and canning foods.

770.   **Making Pickles and Relishes at Home**. Department of Agriculture. Rev. 1978. 33p. ill. Home and Garden Bulletin 92. S/N 001-000-03766-8. $2.00. **A1.77:92/5**.

Includes recipes for such old favorites as pickled peaches and sauerkraut and for the newer dills, such as sweet gherkins, crosscut pickle slices, and green beans.

771.   **Practices Used for Home Canning of Fruits and Vegetables**. Department of Agriculture. April 1979. 69p. charts, tables. Home Economics Research Report 43. S/N 001-000-03949-1. $4.25. **A1.87:43**.

Reports the results of a nationwide survey on fruit and vegetable canning procedures and equipment used by households, their sources of instruction, and the food spoilage observed.

772.   **The Safe Food Book: Your Kitchen Guide**. Food Safety and Inspection Service. July 1984. 32p. ill., tables. Home and Garden Bulletin 241. **A1.77:241**.

Discusses how food spoils and describes bacteria that causes food poisoning. Provides advice on storing and cooking foods, and what to do when the freezer fails. Index.

773.   **Storing Vegetables and Fruits in Basements, Cellars, Outbuildings, and Pits**. Agricultural Research Service. Rev. January 1978. 20p. ill. Home and Garden Bulletin 119. S/N 001-000-02942-8. $2.25. **A1.77:119/4**.

Provides general information on different types of storage facilities and procedures. Includes advice on the storage of specific types of vegetables and fruits.

For additional publications on this topic see Subject Bibliography **SB-005, Canning, Freezing, and Storage of Food**.

BREADS, DESSERTS, AND SNACKS

774.   **Apples in Appealing Ways**. Agricultural Research Service. Rev. November 1977. 20p. ill. Home and Garden Bulletin 161. S/N 001-000-03665-3. $2.75. **A1.77:161/2**.

Provides useful information on the characteristics of apple varieties, recipes for many favorite apple dishes, and some new or unusual ways of preparing and serving apples.

775.   **Breads, Cakes, and Pies in Family Meals: A Guide for Consumers**. Department of Agriculture. Rev. January 1979. 38p. ill. Home and Garden Bulletin 186. S/N 001-000-03915-6. $4.25. **A1.77:186/4**.

The recipe section offers popular quick breads, cakes, pastries, and cookies. Also offers advice on selecting and measuring ingredients, and on mixing, baking, and storing ingredients and baked products.

776. **Cereals and Pasta in Family Meals: A Guide for Consumers**. Department of Agriculture. Rev. June 1979. 37p. ill. Home and Garden Bulletin 150. S/N 001-000-03750-1. $4.25. **A1.77:150/2**.

A guide to buying, storing, and cooking cereals and pasta including recipes for a variety of foods from appetizers to desserts. Index.

777. **Snack Facts**. National Institute of Dental Health. August 1982. folder, 9p. ill. NIH Publication No. 82-1680. **HE20.3402:Sn1/2**.

Suggests snacks that are nutritious and contain little sugar, sugar being a major cause of tooth decay.

778. **A Snack Is a Mini-Meal**. Department of Agriculture. July 1984. folder, 6p. ill. PA 1346. **A1.68:1346**.

Provides brief advice on selecting nutritional snacks.

MEAT AND POULTRY

779. **Beef and Veal in Family Meals: A Guide for Consumers**. Agricultural Research Service. Rev. January 1978. 38p. ill. Home and Garden Bulletin 118. **A1.77:118/5**.

Provides advice on buying, storing, and cooking beef and veal. Includes recipes. Index.

780. **Lamb in Family Meals: A Guide for Consumers**. Agricultural Research Service. Rev. 1982. 21p. ill. Home and Garden Bulletin 124. S/N 001-000-04098-7. $3.00. **A1.77:124/6**.

Provides advice on buying, storing, and cooking lamb. Includes recipes. Index.

781. **Pork in Family Meals: A Guide for Consumers**. Department of Agriculture. Rev. 1982. 34p. ill., tables. Home and Garden Bulletin 160. S/N 001-000-03640-8. $4.25. **A1.77:160/4**.

Shows how to identify fresh and cured pork cuts in the meat market and provides tips on how to select good quality pork, how to estimate the right quantity to buy, and how to cook it properly. Also includes recipes.

782. **Poultry in Family Meals: A Guide for Consumers**. Department of Agriculture. Rev. 1982. 36p. ill. Home and Garden Bulletin 110. S/N 001-000-03895-8. $1.75. **A1.77:110/6**.

Provides advice on buying, storing, and preparing chickens, turkeys, ducks, and geese. Includes recipes for main dishes, salads, sandwiches, soups, stuffings, sauces, and gravies. Index.

783. **Talking about Turkey: How to Buy, Store, Thaw, Stuff, and Prepare Your Holiday Bird**. Department of Agriculture. June 1984. 20p. ill. Home and Garden Bulletin 243. **A1.77:243**.

Provides advice on buying, storing, thawing, roasting, and carving a turkey. Includes recipes for stuffings, gravies, and leftovers.

SEAFOOD

784.   **A Little Fish Goes a Long Way**. National Marine Fisheries Service. 1973 (repr. 1979). 32p. ill. S/N 003-020-00074-6. $1.50. **C55.302:F52/2**.
This pocket-sized booklet contains twenty-five tasty recipes using fish fillets, breaded fish sticks, or portions of canned fish and shellfish.

785.   **Nautical Notions for Nibbling**. National Marine Fisheries Service. 1976. 24p. ill. S/N 003-020-00109-2. $1.50. **C55.302:N51**.
This colorful booklet is loaded with recipes for flavorful and exciting finger foods from the sea.

786.   **Sea Fare from NOAA**. National Oceanic and Atmospheric Administration. 1980. 15p. ill. S/N 003-017-00484-8. $1.00. **C55.2:Se1/7**.
Includes seafood recipes which were originally published in *NOAA*, the official magazine of the National Oceanic and Atmospheric Administration.

787.   **A Seafood Heritage: From Plymouth to the Prairies**. National Marine Fisheries Service. 1976. 29p. ill. S/N 003-020-00122-0. $2.50. **C55.302:Se1/4**.
Includes thirty-one recipes which feature fish and cooking techniques typical from New England to the prairies. Provides historical background on each dish.

788.   **A Seafood Heritage: From the Plains to the Pacific**. National Marine Fisheries Service. 1976. 29p. ill. S/N 003-020-00124-6. $1.75. **C55.302:Se1/5**.
Includes thirty-four recipes which feature fish and cooking techniques typical from the Great Plains to the Pacific Coast, including Alaska and Hawaii. Provides historical background on each dish.

789.   **A Seafood Heritage: From the Rappahannock to the Rio Grande**. National Marine Fisheries Service. 1976. 29p. ill. S/N 003-020-00118-1. $1.75. **C55.302:Se1/3**.
Includes forty-four recipes which feature fish and cooking techniques typical from Virginia to Texas. Includes historical background on each dish.

790.   **Seafoods for Health**. National Marine Fisheries Service. 1978. 16p. ill. S/N 003-020-00144-1. $2.00. **C55.302:Se1/6**.
Explains how seafood can help regulate fat intake and furnish nutrients needed by the body.

RECIPES

791.   **Cooking for Two**. Food and Nutrition Service. Rev. June 1977. 91p. ill. PA 1043. S/N 001-000-03698-0. $5.50. **A1.68:1043/3**.
Provides recipes, helpful hints on planning and serving meals, and information on nutrition through the four basic food groups. Recipes are basic and cover all types of menu items.

792.   **Eating for Better Health**. Food and Nutrition Service. August 1981. 28p. ill. PA 1290. S/N 001-000-04243-2. $3.50. **A1.68:1290**.
Examines breakfast, lunch, dinner, snack, and low-calorie menus and recipes that are low cost and easy to prepare.

793. **Family Fare: A Guide to Good Nutrition**. Department of Agriculture. Rev. June 1978. 94p. Home and Garden Bulletin 1. S/N 001-000-03777-3. $5.50. **A1.77:1/11**.

Provides advice on planning nutritious meals that include family favorites, foods in season, and foods that fit the family budget. Index.

794. **Favorite American Recipes: A Collection of Classics from around the Country**. Food and Nutrition Service. July 1974 (repr. 1979). 79p. FNS 109. S/N 001-024-00197-0. $4.50. **A98.9:109**.

Contains over one hundred recipes divided into six menu classifications: soups, main dishes, vegetables, salads and salad dressings, bread, and desserts.

795. **Food: A Publication on Food and Nutrition**. Department of Agriculture. 1979. 64p. ill. Home and Garden Bulletin 228. S/N 001-000-03881-8. $6.00. **A1.77:228**.

Contains three sections: the hassle-free guide to a better diet; "good morning!" breakfasts; and tips on snacking. Includes sixty recipes. Index.

796. **Food 2: Getting Down to Basics; A Dieter's Guide, plus 42 Great Recipes**. Department of Agriculture. 1982. 42p. ill. **A1.11/3:F73**.

Reviews up-to-date facts about weight loss and supplies commonsense tips for effective weight control. Includes forty-two low-calorie recipes for main dishes, vegetables, salads, breads, soups, and desserts.

797. **Food 3: Eating the Moderate Fat and Cholestoral Way plus New Ideas for Traditional Recipes**. Department of Agriculture. 1982. 16p. ill. **A1.11/3:F73/2**.

Provides practical advice to reduce fat and cholestoral in the diet. Includes recipes for main dishes, vegetables, breads, soups and sauces, and desserts.

798. **For the Family: A Cost Saving Plan**. Department of Agriculture. Rev. December 1978. 22p. tables. Home and Garden Bulletin 209. **A1.77:209/2**.

Provides advice on planning low-cost meals. Includes sample menus and food lists, and recipes for main dishes, breads, desserts, soups and salads, and sandwiches and snacks. Index.

799. **Vegetables in Family Meals: A Guide for Consumers**. Department of Agriculture. Rev. 1980. 29p. ill. Home and Garden Bulletin 105. S/N 001-000-04150-9. $3.75. **A1.77:105/8**.

Contains practical tips on buying, cooking, and storing vegetables. Includes recipes for main dishes, soups and chowders, and salads. Index.

See also entry 985.

For additional publications on this topic see Subject Bibliography **SB-065, Cookbooks and Recipes**.

Foreign Area Studies

GENERAL

800.   **Atlas of the Caribbean Basin**. 2d ed. Department of State. Rev. July 1984. 16p. charts, maps. Department of State Publication 9398. S/N 044-000-02022-0. $1.50. **S1.3/a:C19/984**.

Illustrates economic and political features of the Caribbean Basin which includes the islands of the Caribbean Sea as well as countries on its shores except the larger countries of the region.

801.   **Handbook of Economic Statistics, 1984**. Central Intelligence Agency. September 1984. 241p. charts, tables. CPAS-84-10002. S/N 041-015-00158-2. $7.50. **PrEx3.17:984**.

Issued annually. Presents economic data for selected non-communist and all communist countries of the world. Data are presented for each fifth year 1960-1975, and for each year 1979-1983. Index.

802.   **Status of the World's Nations**. Department of State. Rev. June 1983. 19p. map, tables. Geographic Bulletin. Department of State Publication 8735. S/N 044-000-01982-5. $3.00. **S1.119/2:W89/983**.

Presents brief information on the 167 nations of the world. Appendices provide alphabetical and chronological lists of 94 nations which gained independence since 1943.

803.   **World Factbook, 1984**. Central Intelligence Agency. 1984. 284p. S/N 041-015-00157-4. $11.00. **PrEx3.15:984**.

Issued annually. This reference book provides brief information on the following topics for nearly two hundred countries of the world: land, people, government, economy, communications, and defense forces.

804. **World Population and Fertility Planning Technologies: The Next 20 Years**. Congress. Office of Technology Assessment. February 1982. 256p. ill., charts, tables. OTA-HR-157. S/N 052-003-00867-0. $7.50. **Y3.T22/2:2P81**.

Discusses how government policies and programs view birth control technologies, and how international population assistance has changed world population growth in the last twenty years. Assesses future birth control technologies and their impact. Footnote references.

805. **World Population, 1984: Recent Demographic Estimates for Countries and Regions of the World**. Bureau of the Census. 1984. 600p. tables. ISP-WP-84. **C3.215/3:WP-84**.

Issued annually. Presents summary demographic information for over two hundred countries and territories of the world, and aggregated data for the world, regions, and subregions.

FOREIGN AREA STUDIES

806. **Background Notes**. Department of State. Revised irregularly. maps, tables. S/N 844-002-00000-9. Symbol BBN. $32.00 per yr. (subscription includes all updated or new *Background Notes* published during the next twelve month period). Single copy price varies. S/N 044-000-00000-9. $32.00(set) (includes all currently available *Background Notes*). **S1.123:ct**.

These short factual pamphlets about various countries and territories of the world provide concise information on the country's land, people, history, government, political conditions, economy, and foreign relations. References.

806-1. **Index**. December 1984. 2p. S/N 044-000-93602-0. $1.00. **S1.123/2: 984-3**.

806-2. **Afghanistan**. April 1983. 8p. Department of State Publication 7795. S/N 044-000-92744-6. $2.00. **S1.123:Af3/983**.

806-3. **Albania**. August 1984. 6p. Department of State Publication 8217. S/N 044-000-93576-7. $1.00. **S1.123:Al1/984**.

806-4. **Algeria**. August 1983. 8p. Department of State Publication 7821. S/N 044-000-93519-8. $2.00. **S1.123:Al3/983**.

806-5. **Andorra**. August 1984, 4p. Department of State Publication 8992. S/N 044-000-93577-5. $1.00. **S1.123:An2/984**.

806-6. **Angola**. September 1979 (repr. 1985). 7p. Department of State Publication 7962. S/N 044-000-91288-1. $2.00. **S1.123:An4/979**.

806-7. **Argentina**. May 1984. 8p. Department of State Publication 7836. S/N 044-000-93564-3. $1.00. **S1.123:Ar3/984**.

806-8. **ASEAN [Association of South East Asia Nations]**. November 1983. 8p. Department of State Publication 9375. S/N 044-000-93539-2. $2.00. **S1.123:As7**.

806-9. **Australia**. May 1984. 6p. Department of State Publication 8149. S/N 044-000-93568-6. $1.00. **S1.123:Au7/2/984**.

806-10.   **Austria**. August 1983. 8p. Department of State Publication 7935. S/N 044-000-93520-1. $2.00. **S1.123:Au7/983**.

806-11.   **Bahamas**. December 1984. 4p. Department of State Publication 8242. S/N 844-002-10001-1. $1.00. **S1.123:B14/2/984**.

806-12.   **Bahrain**. August 1982. 4p. Department of State Publication 8013. S/N 044-000-92710-1. $2.00. **S1.123:B14/982**.

806-13.   **Bangladesh**. July 1984. 7p. Department of State Publication 8698. S/N 044-000-93572-4. $1.00. **S1.123:B22/984**.

806-14.   **Barbados**. August 1984. 4p. Department of State Publication 8242. S/N 044-000-93581-3. $1.00. **S1.123:B23/984**.

806-15.   **Belgium**. June 1983. 8p. Department of State Publication 8087. S/N 044-000-93507-4. $2.00. **S1.123:B41/983**.

806-16.   **Belize**. September 1984. 4p. Department of State Publication 8332. S/N 044-000-93596-1. $1.00. **S1.123:B41/2/984**.

806-17.   **Benin**. November 1984. 6p. Department of State Publication 8993. S/N 044-000-93603-8. $1.00. **S1.123:B43/984**.

806-18.   **Bermuda**. August 1983. 4p. Department of State Publication 7901. S/N 044-000-93521-0. $2.00. **S1.123:B45/983**.

806-19.   **Bhutan**. May 1983. 4p. Department of State Publication 8334. S/N 044-000-93501-5. $2.00. **S1.123:B46/983**.

806-20.   **Bolivia**. October 1983. 7p. Department of State Publication 8032. S/N 044-000-93533-3. $2.00. **S1.123:B63/983**.

806-21.   **Botswana**. May 1983. 4p. Department of State Publication 8046. S/N 044-000-93502-3. $2.00. **S1.123:B65/983**.

806-22.   **Brazil**. December 1982. 8p. Department of State Publication 7756. S/N 044-000-92732-2. $2.00. **S1.123:B73/982**.

806-23.   **Bulgaria**. April 1983. 7p. Department of State Publication 7882. S/N 044-000-92745-4. $2.00. **S1.123:B87/983**.

806-24.   **Burma**. August 1984. 7p. Department of State Publication 7931. S/N 044-000-93585-6. $1.00. **S1.123:B92/984**.

806-25.   **Burundi**. September 1983. 4p. Department of State Publication 8084. S/N 044-000-93525-2. $2.00. **S1.123:B95/983**.

806-26.   **Cameroon**. February 1983. 7p. Department of State Publication 8010. S/N 044-000-92736-5. $2.00. **S1.123:C14/983**.

806-27.   **Canada**. March 1983. 7p. Department of State Publication 7769. S/N 044-000-92740-3. $2.00. **S1.123:C16/983**.

806-28.   **Cape Verde**. June 1984. 4p. Department of State Publication 8874. S/N 044-000-93573-2. $1.00. **S1.123:C17/984**.

806-29.   **Central African Republic**. October 1983. 4p. Department of State Publication 7970. S/N 044-000-93540-6. $2.00. **S1.123:C33af/983**.

806-30.   **Chad**. December 1977. 4p. Department of State Publication 7669. S/N 044-000-91191-4. $2.00. **S1.123:C34/979**.

806-31.   **Chile**. November 1983. 8p. Department of State Publication 7998. S/N 044-000-93541-4. $2.00. **S1.123:C43/983**.

806-32.   **China**. December 1983. 16p. Department of State Publication 8318. S/N 044-000-93544-9. $2.00. **S1.123:C44/983**.

806-33.   **Colombia**. November 1982. 8p. Department of State Publication 7767. S/N 044-000-92723-3. $2.00. **S1.123:C71/982**.

806-34.   **Comoros**. December 1982. 4p. Department of State Publication 8963. S/N 044-000-92728-4. $2.00. **S1.123:C73/982**.

806-35.   **Congo**. May 1983. 4p. Department of State Publication 7896. S/N 044-000-93503-1. $2.00. **S1.123:C76/2/983**.

806-36.   **Costa Rica**. November 1982. 4p. Department of State Publication 7768. S/N 044-000-92724-1. $2.00. **S1.123:C82/982**.

806-37.   **Cuba**. April 1983. 8p. Department of State Publication 8347. S/N 044-000-92746-2. $2.00. **S1.123:C89/983**.

806-38.   **Cyprus**. October 1984. 12p. Department of State Publication 7392. S/N 044-000-93604-6. $1.00. **S1.123:C99/2/984**.

806-39.   **Czechoslovakia**. October 1983. 7p. Department of State Publication 7758. S/N 044-000-93534-1. $2.00. **S1.123:C99/983**.

806-40.   **Denmark**. March 1983. 7p. Department of State Publication 8298. S/N 044-000-93560-1. $1.00. **S1.123:D41/984**.

806-41.   **Djibouti**. June 1982. 4p. Department of State Publication 8429. S/N 044-000-92705-5. $2.00. **S1.123:D64/982**.

806-42.   **Dominica**. November 1981. 4p. Department of State Publication 9235. S/N 044-000-92663-6. $2.00. **S1.123:D71/2**.

806-43.   **Dominican Republic**. October 1981. 7p. Department of State Publication 7759. S/N 044-000-92660-1. $2.00. **S1.123:D71/981**.

806-44.   **Ecuador**. July 1984. 8p. Department of State Publication 7771. S/N 044-000-93605-4. $1.00. **S1.123:Ec9/984**.

806-45.   **Egypt**. February 1985. 12p. Department of State Publication 8152. S/N 844-002-10009-7. $1.00. **S1.123:Eg9/985**.

806-46.   **El Salvador**. February 1985. 8p. Department of State Publication 7794. S/N 844-002-10008-9. $1.00. **S1.123:El7/985**.

806-47.   **Equatorial Guinea**. June 1984. 8p. Department of State Publication 8025. S/N 044-000-93569-4. $1.00. **S1.123:Eq2/984**.

806-48.   **Ethiopia**. August 1981. 7p. Department of State Publication 7785. S/N 044-000-92645-8. $2.00. **S1.123:Et3/981**.

806-49.   **European Community**. November 1984. 8p. Department of State Publication 9155. S/N 844-002-10002-0. $1.00. **S1.123:Eu7/984**.

806-50. **Fiji**. September 1983. 4p. Department of State Publication 8486. S/N 044-000-93526-1. $2.00. **S1.123:F47/983**.

806-51. **Finland**. May 1982. 7p. Department of State Publication 8262. S/N 044-000-92698-9. $2.00. **S1.123:F49/982**.

806-52. **France**. March 1984. 8p. Department of State Publication 8209. S/N 044-000-93549-0. $2.00. **S1.123:F84/984**.

806-53. **French Antilles and Guiana**. December 1983. 7p. Department of State Publication 8856. S/N 044-000-93534-7. $2.00. **S1.123:F88an/983**.

806-54. **Gabon**. July 1983. 4p. Department of State Publication 7968. S/N 044-000-93514-7. $2.00. **S1.123:G11/983**.

806-55. **Gambia**. November 1982. 4p. Department of State Publication 8014. S/N 044-000-92725-0. $2.00. **S1.123:G14/982**.

806-56. **German Democratic Republic [East Germany]**. November 1984. 8p. Department of State Publication 7957. S/N 844-002-10003-8. $1.00. **S1.123:G31/2/984**.

806-57. **Germany, Federal Republic of [West Germany]**. 1985. 8p. Department of State Publication 7834. S/N 844-002-10014-3. $1.00. **S1.123:G31/985**.

806-58. **Ghana**. June 1983. 8p. Department of State Publication 8089. S/N 044-000-93508-2. $2.00. **S1.123:G34/983**.

806-59. **Greece**. February 1982. 8p. Department of State Publication 8198. S/N 044-000-92677-6. $2.00. **S1.123:G81/982**.

806-60. **Grenada**. February 1984. 4p. Department of State Publication 8822. S/N 044-000-93550-3. $2.00. **S1.123:G86/984**.

806-61. **Guatemala**. September 1984. 6p. Department of State Publication 7798. S/N 044-000-93606-2. $1.00. **S1.123:G93/984**.

806-62. **Guinea**. July 1983. 4p. Department of State Publication 8057. S/N 044-000-93515-5. $2.00. **S1.123:G94/983**.

806-63. **Guinea-Bissau**. July 1982. 4p. Department of State Publication 7966. S/N 044-000-92706-3. $2.00. **S1.123:G94/2/982**.

806-64. **Guyana**. January 1985. 8p. Department of State Publication 8095. S/N 844-002-10010-1. $1.00. **S1.123:G99/985**.

806-65. **Haiti**. June 1984. 4p. Department of State Publication 8287. S/N 044-000-93570-8. $1.00. **S1.123:H12/984**.

806-66. **Honduras**. September 1984. 6p. Department of State Publication 8184. S/N 044-000-93590-2. $1.00. **S1.123:H75/2/984**.

806-67. **Hong Kong**. October 1983. 4p. Department of State Publication 8126. S/N 044-000-93535-0. $2.00. **S1.123:H75/983**.

806-68. **Hungary**. April 1983. 8p. Department of State Publication 7915. S/N 044-000-92747-1. $2.00. **S1.123:H89/983**.

806-69.   **Iceland**. July 1984. 4p. Department of State Publication 8227. S/N 044-000-93582-1. $1.00. **S1.123:Ic2/984**.

806-70.   **India**. June 1982. 7p. Department of State Publication 7847. S/N 044-000-92699-7. $2.00. **S1.123:In2/2/982**.

806-71.   **Indonesia**. September 1983. 7p. Department of State Publication 7786. S/N 044-000-93527-9. $2.00. **S1.123:In2/983**.

806-72.   **Iran**. May 1982. 7p. Department of State Publication 7760. S/N 044-000-92700-4. $2.00. **S1.123:Ir1/982**.

806-73.   **Iraq**. December 1984. 8p. Department of State Publication 7975. S/N 844-002-10004-6. $1.00. **S1.123:Ir1/2/984**.

806-74.   **Ireland**. May 1984. 6p. Department of State Publication 7974. S/N 044-000-93561-9. $1.00. **S1.123:Ir2/984**.

806-75.   **Israel**. October 1984. 8p. Department of State Publication 7752. S/N 044-000-93597-0. $1.00. **S1.123:Is7/984**.

806-76.   **Italy**. September 1984. 8p. Department of State Publication 8874. S/N 044-000-93586-4. $1.00. **S1.123:It1/984**.

806-77.   **Ivory Coast**. February 1983. 6p. Department of State Publication 8119. S/N 044-000-92737-3. $2.00. **S1.123:Iv7/983**.

806-78.   **Jamaica**. October 1984. 6p. Department of State Publication 8080. S/N 044-000-93607-1. $1.00. **S1.123:J22/984**.

806-79.   **Japan**. May 1983. 8p. Department of State Publication 7770. S/N 044-000-93505-8. $2.00. **S1.123:J27/983**.

806-80.   **Jordan**. June 1981. 8p. Department of State Publication 7956. S/N 044-000-92637-7. $2.00. **S1.123:J76/981**.

806-81.   **Kampuchea [Cambodia]**. May 1984. 10p. Department of State Publication 7747. S/N 044-000-93565-1. $1.00. **S1.123:K12**.

806-82.   **Kenya**. September 1982. 7p. Department of State Publication 8024. S/N 044-000-92715-2. $2.00. **S1.123:K42/982**.

806-83.   **Kuwait**. June 1983. 7p. Department of State Publication 7855. S/N 044-000-93509-1. $2.00. **S1.123:K96/983**.

806-84.   **Laos**. February 1984. 7p. Department of State Publication 8301. S/N 044 000 93556 2. $2.00. **S1.123:L29/984**.

806-85.   **Lebanon**. September 1984. 7p. Department of State Publication 7816. S/N 044-000-93598-8. $1.00. **S1.123:L49/984**.

806-86.   **Lesotho**. August 1984. 4p. Department of State Publication 8091. S/N 044-000-93578-3. $1.00. **S1.123:L56/984**.

806-87.   **Liberia**. June 1984. 4p. Department of State Publication 7991. S/N 044-000-93571-6. $1.00. **S1.123:L61/2/984**.

806-88.   **Libya**. April 1983. 6p. Department of State Publication 7815. S/N 044-000-92748-9. $2.00. **S1.123:L61/983**.

806-89.   **Liechtenstein**. April 1983. 4p. Department of State Publication 8610. S/N 044-000-92749-7. $2.00. **S1.123:L62/983**.

806-90.   **Luxembourg**. October 1984. 4p. Department of State Publication 8325. S/N 044-000-93591-1. $1.00. **S1.123:L97/984**.

806-91.   **Macau**. 1985. 4p. Department of State Publication 8352. S/N 844-002-10015-1. $1.00. **S1.123:M11/985**.

806-92.   **Madagascar**. October 1984. 4p. Department of State Publication 8015. S/N 044-000-93599-6. $1.00. **S1.123:M26/984**.

806-93.   **Malawi**. August 1983. 4p. Department of State Publication 7790. S/N 044-000-93523-6. $2.00. **S1.123:M29/2/983**.

806-94.   **Malaysia**. October 1983. 7p. Department of State Publication 7753. S/N 044-000-93536-8. $2.00. **S1.123:M29/983**.

806-95.   **Maldives**. June 1984. 4p. Department of State Publication 8026. S/N 044-000-93566-0. $1.00. **S1.123:M29/4/984**.

806-96.   **Mali**. February 1984. 8p. Department of State Publication 8056. S/N 044-000-93551-1. $2.00. **S1.123:M29/5/984**.

806-97.   **Malta**. March 1981. 4p. Department of State Publication 8220. S/N 044-000-92624-5. $2.00. **S1.123:M29/6/981**.

806-98.   **Mauritania**. February 1985. 6p. Department of State Publication 8169. S/N 844-002-10016-0. $1.00. **S1.123:M44/2/985**.

806-99.   **Mauritius**. December 1982. 4p. Department of State Publication 8023. S/N 044-000-92730-6. $2.00. **S1.123:M44/982**.

806-100.   **Mexico**. June 1983. 8p. Department of State Publication 7865. S/N 044-000-93510-4. $2.00. **S1.123:M57/983**.

806-101.   **Monaco**. March 1983. 4p. Department of State Publication 8670. S/N 044-000-92742-0. $2.00. **S1.123:M74/2/983**.

806-102.   **Mongolia**. December 1983. 6p. Department of State Publication 8318. S/N 044-000-93546-5. $2.00. **S1.123:M74/983**.

806-103.   **Morocco**. April 1982. 8p. Department of State Publication 7954. S/N 044-000-92688-1. $2.00. **S1.123:M82/982**.

806-104.   **Mozambique**. January 1983. 6p. Department of State Publication 7965. S/N 044-000-92733-1. $2.00. **S1.123:M87/983**.

806-105.   **Namibia [Southwest Africa]**. January 1983. 7p. Department of State Publication 8168. S/N 044-000-92734-9. $2.00. **S1.123:N15/983**.

806-106.   **Nauru**. December 1981. 4p. Department of State Publication 8595. S/N 044-000-92671-7. $2.00. **S1.123:N22/981**.

806-107.   **Nepal**. August 1984. 7p. Department of State Publication 7904. S/N 044-000-93592-9. $1.00. **S1.123:N35/984**.

806-108.   **Netherlands**. November 1984. 7p. Department of State Publication 7967. S/N 844-002-10005-4. $1.00. **S1.123:N38/984**.

806-109.   **Netherlands Antilles.** October 1983. 4p. Department of State Publication 8223. S/N 044-000-93537-6. $2.00. **S1.123:N38/2/983.**

806-110.   **New Zealand.** October 1984. 7p. Department of State Publication 8251. S/N 044-000-93587-2. $1.00. **S1.123:N42z/984.**

806-111.   **Nicaragua.** January 1983. 4p. Department of State Publication 7772. S/N 044-000-92735-7. $2.00. **S1.123:N51/983.**

806-112.   **Niger.** December 1984. 7p. Department of State Publication 8293. S/N 844-002-10006-2. $1.00. **S1.123:N56/984.**

806-113.   **Nigeria.** September 1984. 7p. Department of State Publication 7953. S/N 044-000-93593-7. $1.00. **S1.123:N56/2/984.**

806-114.   **[North] Korea.** April 1984. 7p. Department of State Publication 8369. S/N 044-000-93555-4. $2.00. **S1.123:N81k/984.**

806-115.   **Norway.** March 1984. 4p. Department of State Publication 8228. S/N 044-000-93557-1. $2.00. **S1.123:N83/984.**

806-116.   **Oman.** December 1983. 7p. Department of State Publication 8070. S/N 044-000-93543-1. $2.00. **S1.123:Om1/983.**

806-117.   **Pakistan.** April 1984. 8p. Department of State Publication 7748. S/N 044-000-93558-9. $2.00. **S1.123:P17/984.**

806-118.   **Panama.** February 1982. 7p. Department of State Publication 8022. S/N 044-000-92678-4. $2.00. **S1.123:P19/982.**

806-119.   **Papua New Guinea.** June 1984. 7p. Department of State Publication 8824. S/N 044-000-93574-1. $1.00. **S1.123:P19/2/984.**

806-120.   **Paraguay.** September 1984. 4p. Department of State Publication 8098. S/N 044-000-93600-3. $1.00. **S1.123:P21/984.**

806-121.   **Peru.** February 1985. 4p. Department of State Publication 7799. S/N 844-002-10017-8. $1.00. **S1.123:P43/985.**

806-122.   **Philippines.** September 1983. 8p. Department of State Publication 7750. S/N 044-000-93528-7. $2.00. **S1.123:P53/983.**

806-123.   **Poland.** June 1983. 7p. Department of State Publication 8020. S/N 044-000-93511-2. $2.00. **S1.123:P75/983.**

806-124.   **Portugal.** March 1985. 8p. Department of State Publication 8074. S/N 844-002-10018-6. $1.00. **S1.123:P83/2/985.**

806-125.   **Qatar.** January 1985. 4p. Department of State Publication 7606. S/N 844-002-10011-9. $1.00. **S1.123:Q1/985.**

806-126.   **Romania.** July 1983. 7p. Department of State Publication 7890. S/N 044-000-93516-3. $2.00. **S1.123:R44/983.**

806-127.   **Rwanda.** August 1983. 4p. Department of State Publication 7916. S/N 044-000-93524-4. $2.00. **S1.123:R94/983.**

806-128.   **St. Lucia.** August 1984. 6p. Department of State Publication 9234. S/N 044-000-93575-9. $1.00. **S1.123:Sa2/984.**

806-129.   **San Marino.** February 1985. 4p. Department of State Publication 9223. S/N 844-002-10019-4. $1.00. **S1.123:Sa5/985.**

806-130.   **Sao Tome and Principe.** September 1983. 4p. Department of State Publication 8871. S/N 044-000-93530-9. $2.00. **S1.123:Sa6t/983.**

806-131.   **Saudi Arabia.** February 1983. 8p. Department of State Publication 7835. S/N 044-000-92738-1. $2.00. **S1.123:Sa8/983.**

806-132.   **Senegal.** June 1984. 6p. Department of State Publication 7820. S/N 044-000-93583-0. $1.00. **S1.123:Se5/984.**

806-133.   **Seychelles.** June 1983. 4p. Department of State Publication 8246. S/N 044-000-93512-1. $2.00. **S1.123:Se9/983.**

806-134.   **Sierra Leone.** February 1984. 7p. Department of State Publication 8069. S/N 044-000-93552-0. $2.00. **S1.123:Si1/984.**

806-135.   **Singapore.** August 1984. 7p. Department of State Publication 8240. S/N 044-000-93588-1. $1.00. **S1.123:Si6/984.**

806-136.   **Solomon Islands.** October 1981. 6p. Department of State Publication 8941. S/N 044-000-92662-8. $2.00. **S1.123:So4/981.**

806-137.   **Somalia.** March 1984. 7p. Department of State Publication 7881. S/N 044-000-93559-7. $2.00. **S1.123:So5/984.**

806-138.   **South Africa.** July 1982. 8p. Department of State Publication 8021. S/N 044-000-92709-8. $2.00. **S1.123:So8af/982.**

806-139.   **[South] Korea.** October 1983. 8p. Department of State Publication 7782. S/N 044-000-93542-2. $2.00. **S1.123:K84/983.**

806-140.   **Spain.** March 1985. 8p. Department of State Publication 7800. S/N 844-002-10020-8. $1.00. **S1.123:Sp1/985.**

806-141.   **Sri Lanka.** June 1983. 8p. Department of State Publication 7757. S/N 044-000-93517-1. $2.00. **S1.123:Sr3/983.**

806-142.   **Sudan.** November 1982. 7p. Department of State Publication 8022. S/N 044-000-92726-8. $2.00. **S1.123:Su2/982.**

806-143.   **Surinam.** October 1984. 8p. Department of State Publication 8268. S/N 044-000-93601-1. $1.00. **S1.123:Su7/984.**

806-144.   **Swaziland.** March 1983. 6p. Department of State Publication 8174. S/N 044-000-92741-1. $2.00. **S1.123:Sw2/983.**

806-145.   **Sweden.** October 1982. 8p. Department of State Publication 8033. S/N 044-000-92721-7. $2.00. **S1.123:Sw3/982.**

806-146.   **Switzerland.** February 1985. 8p. Department of State Publication 8132. S/N 844-002-10007-1. $1.00. **S1.123:Sw6/985.**

806-147.   **Syria.** January 1984. 7p. Department of State Publication 7761. S/N 044-000-93547-3. $2.00. **S1.123:Sy8/984.**

806-148.   **Tanzania.** February 1984. 8p. Department of State Publication 8097. S/N 044-000-93553-8. $2.00. **S1.123:T15/984.**

806-149.   **Taiwan.** September 1983. 8p. Department of State Publication 7791. S/N 044-000-93531-7. $2.00. **S1.123:T13/983.**

806-150.   **Thailand.** February 1983. 8p. Department of State Publication 7961. S/N 044-000-92739-0. $2.00. **S1.123:T32/983.**

806-151.   **Togo.** July 1984. 4p. Department of State Publication 8325. S/N 044-000-93594-5. $1.00. **S1.123:T57/984.**

806-152.   **Tonga.** December 1979 (repr. 1985). 4p. Department of State Publication 8594. S/N 044-000-91299-6. $2.00. **S1.123:T61/979.**

806-153.   **Trinidad and Tobago.** September 1984. 4p. Department of State Publication 8306. S/N 044-000-93595-3. $1.00. **S1.123:T73/984.**

806-154.   **Tunisia.** September 1984. 7p. Department of State Publication 8142. S/N 044-000-93584-8. $1.00. **S1.123:T83/984.**

806-155.   **Turkey.** December 1984. 7p. Department of State Publication 7850. S/N 844-002-10012-7. $1.00. **S1.123:T84/984.**

806-156.   **Uganda.** February 1982. 7p. Department of State Publication 7958. S/N 044-000-92679-2. $2.00. **S1.123:Ug1/982.**

806-157.   **United Arab Emirates.** August 1982. 7p. Department of State Publication 7901. S/N 044-000-92717-9. $2.00. **S1.123:Un34a/2/982.**

806-158.   **United Kingdom.** January 1984. 8p. Department of State Publication 8099. S/N 044-000-93548-1. $2.00. **S1.123:Un34k/984.**

806-159.   **United Nations.** August 1984. 20p. Department of State Publication 8933. S/N 044-000-93579-1. $1.00. **S1.123:Un34n/984.**

806-160.   **Upper Volta [Faso Burkina].** April 1984. 7p. Department of State Publication 7857. S/N 044-000-93562-7. $1.00. **S1.123:Up6v/984.**

806-161.   **Uruguay.** December 1982. 4p. Department of State Publication 7857. S/N 044-000-92731-4. $2.00. **S1.123:Ur8/982.**

806-162.   **U.S.S.R.** September 1981. 15p. Department of State Publication 7842. S/N 044-000-92655-5. $2.00. **S1.123:Un33/981.**

806-163.   **Vatican City.** November 1984. 3p. Department of State Publication 8258. S/N 044-000-93608-9. $1.00. **S1.123:V45/984.**

806-164.   **Venezuela.** May 1984. 6p. Department of State Publication 7749. S/N 044-000-93563-5. $1.00. **S1.123:V55/984.**

806-165.   **Vietnam.** May 1984. 8p. Department of State Publication 8955. S/N 044-000-93567-8. $1.00. **S1.123:V67/2/984.**

806-166.   **Western Somoa.** September 1983. 4p. Department of State Publication 8977. S/N 044-000-93532-5. $2.00. **S1.123:W52s/983.**

806-167.   **Yemen [North].** January 1985. 6p. Department of State Publication 8170. S/N 844-002-10013-5. $1.00. **S1.123:Y3/985.**

806-168.   **Yemen [South].** December 1980. 4p. Department of State Publication 8368. S/N 044-000-92615-6. $2.00. **S1.123:Y3/2/980.**

806-169.   **Yugoslavia**. June 1983. 8p. Department of State Publication 7773. S/N 044-000-93518-0. $2.00. **S1.123:Y9/983**.

806-170.   **Zaire**. October 1983. 8p. Department of State Publication 7793. S/N 044-000-93538-4. $2.00. **S1.123:Z1/2/983**.

806-171.   **Zambia**. August 1984. 4p. Department of State Publication 7841. S/N 044-000-93589-9. $1.00. **S1.123:Z1/984**.

806-172.   **Zimbabwe**. October 1982. 7p. Department of State Publication 8104. S/N 044-000-92722-5. $2.00. **S1.123:Z6/982**.

807.   **Country Demographic Profiles [series]**. Bureau of the Census. charts, tables. ISP-DP-series. **C3.205/3:DP-no.**

This series brings together a variety of demographic, economic, and social data for selected countries of the world. Data are based on the most current national census and current available data and estimates. The reports also include bibliographies of major sources.

807-1.   **Bangladesh**. December 1982. 65p. **C3.205/3:DP-26**.

807-2.   **Botswana**. June 1981. 41p. **C3.205/3:DP-27**.

807-3.   **Brazil**. January 1981. 43p. **C3.205/3:DP-19**.

807-4.   **Chile**. February 1978. 20p. **C3.205/3:DP-13**.

807-5.   **China, Republic of**. February 1978. **C3.205/3:DP-12**.

807-6.   **Colombia**. October 1979. 44p. **C3.205/3:DP-20**.

807-7.   **Costa Rica**. August 1977. 20p. **C3.205/3:DP-4**.

807-8.   **Ghana**. September 1977. 21p. **C3.205/3:DP-5**.

807-9.   **Guatemala**. October 1977. 23p. **C3.205/3:DP-6**.

807-10.   **Honduras**. December 1977. 21p. **C3.205/3:DP-10**.

807-11.   **India**. November 1978. 29p. **C3.205/3:DP-16**.

807-12.   **Indonesia**. May 1979. 45p. **C3.205/3:DP-18**.

807-13.   **Jamaica**. November 1977. 21p. **C3.205/3:DP-9**.

807-14.   **Kenya**. January 1978. 17p. **C3.205/3:DP-11**.

807-15.   **Korea, Republic of**. June 1978. 26p. **C3.205/3:DP-17**.

807-16.   **Liberia**. March 1982. 50p. **C3.205/3:DP-28**.

807-17.   **Malaysia**. November 1979. 37p. **C3.205/3:DP-22**.

807-18.   **Mexico**. September 1979. 34p. **C3.205/3:DP-14**.

807-19.   **Morocco**. July 1980. 57p. **C3.205/3:DP-23**.

807-20.   **Nepal**. November 1979. 34p. **C3.205/3:DP-21**.

807-21.   **Pakistan**. March 1980. 45p. **C3.205/3:DP-24**.

807-22.   **Panama**. November 1977. 22p. **C3.205/3:DP-7**.

807-23.   **Sri Lanka**. November 1977. 20p. **C3.205/3:DP-8**.

807-24.   **Thailand**. April 1978. 36p. **C3.205/3:DP-15**.

807-25.   **Turkey**. August 1980. 47p. S/N 003-024-02126-9. $4.25. **C3.205/3:DP-25**.

808.   **Country Study [series]**. Department of the Army. ill., maps, tables. DA Pamphlet 550-no. **D101.22:550-no**.

This series provides detailed analyses of the social, political, and economic institutions of most of the countries of the world. Each volume contains an extensive bibliography. It was formerly called the Area Handbook series until the late 1970s when the present series title was adopted. In the listing below no differentiation is made between those which were published as an *Area Handbook* or a *Country Study*. Whenever an *Area Handbook* is reprinted, the new series title is adopted.

808-1.   **Afghanistan**. 4th ed. 1973 (repr. 1978). 607p. S/N 008-020-00461-8. $13.00. **D101.22:550-65/2**.

808-2.   **Albania**. 1971 (repr. 1976). 237p. S/N 008-020-00362-0. $10.00. **D101.22:550-98**.

808-3.   **Algeria**. 3d ed. 1979. 390p. S/N 008-020-00791-9. $11.00. **D101.22: 550-44/3**.

808-4.   **Angola**. 2d ed. 1979. 309p. S/N 008-020-00816-8. $11.00. **D101.22: 550-59/2**.

808-5.   **Argentina**. 2d ed. 1974. 418p. S/N 008-020-00536-3. $12.00. **D101.22:550-73/2**.

808-6.   **Australia**. 1974 (repr. 1980). 476p. S/N 008-020-00540-1. $13.00, cloth. **D101.22:550-169**.

808-7.   **Austria**. 1976. 292p. S/N 008-020-00598-3. $11.00. **D101.22:550-176**.

808-8.   **Bangladesh**. 1976. 364p. S/N 008-020-00591-6. $11.00. **D101.22: 550-175**.

808-9.   **Belgium**. 1974. 280p. S/N 008-020-00544-4. $10.00. **D101.22:550-170**.

808-10.   **Bolivia**. 2d ed. 1974 (repr. 1979). 431p. S/N 008-020-00506-1. $12.00. **D101.22:550-66**.

808-11.   **Brazil**. 4th ed. 1983. 439p. S/N 008-020-00975-0. $11.00, cloth. **D101.22:550-20/4**.

808-12.   **Bulgaria**. 1974. 344p. S/N 008-020-00528-2. $11.00. **D101.22: 550-168**.

808-13.   **Burma**. 3d ed. 1984. 355p. S/N 008-020-00981-4. $14.00, cloth. **D101.22:550-61/3**.

808-14.   **Burundi**. 1969. 217p. S/N 008-020-00219-4. $9.50. **D101.22:550-83**.

808-15.   **Cameroon, United Republic of.** 1974. 349p. S/N 008-020-00488-0. $11.00. **D101.22:550-166**.

808-16.   **Chad.** 1972. 275p. S/N 008-020-00423-5. $10.00. **D101.22:550-159**.

808-17.   **Chile.** 2d ed. 1982. 315p. S/N 008-020-00930-0. $13.00. **D101.22: 550-77/2**.

808-18.   **China.** 1981. 621p. S/N 008-020-00888-5. $12.00. **D101.22:550-60/3**.

808-19.   **China, Republic of [Taiwan].** March 1969. 449p. S/N 008-020-00437-5. $12.00, cloth. **D101.22:550-63**.

808-20.   **Colombia.** 3d ed. 1977 (repr. 1984). 522p. S/N 008-020-00647-5. $13.00. **D101.22:550-26/3**.

808-21.   **Congo, People's Republic of [Congo Brazzaville].** 1971. 268p. S/N 008-020-00346-8. $10.00. **D101.22:550-91**.

808-22.   **Costa Rica.** 2d ed. 1984. 367p. S/N 008-020-01009-0. $14.00, cloth. **D101.22:550-90/2**.

808-23.   **Cuba.** 1976. 550p. S/N 008-020-00626-2. $13.00. **D101.22:550-152/2**.

808-24.   **Cyprus.** 3d ed. 1980. 336p. S/N 008-020-00831-1. $11.00. **D101.22: 550-22/3**.

808-25.   **Czechoslovakia.** 2d ed. 1982. 381p. S/N 008-020-00911-3. $12.00. **D101.22:550-158/2**.

808-26.   **Dominican Republic.** 2d ed. 1973 (repr. 1982). 275p. S/N 008-020-00484-7. $11.00, cloth. **D101.22:550-54/2**.

808-27.   **East Germany.** 2d ed. 1982. 379p. S/N 008-020-00918-1. $12.00. **D101.22:550-155/2**.

808-28.   **Ecuador.** 1973. 416p. S/N 008-020-00449-9. $12.00. **D101.22: 550-52/2**.

808-29.   **Egypt.** 4th ed. 1983. 399p. S/N 008-020-00956-3. $8.00. **D101.22: 550-43/4**.

808-30.   **El Salvador.** 1971. 271p. S/N 008-020-00367-1. $10.00, cloth. **D101.22:550-150**.

808-31.   **Ethopia.** 3d ed. 1981. 395p. S/N 008-020-00870-2. $12.00. **D101.22: 550-28/3**.

808-32.   **Federal Republic of Germany.** 2d ed. 1983. 486p. S/N 008-020-00943-1. $11.00, cloth. **D101.22:550-173/2**.

808-33.   **Finland.** 1974. 273p. S/N 008-020-00514-2. $10.00, cloth. **D101.22: 550-167**.

808-34.   **Ghana.** 1971. 463p. S/N 008-020-00382-4. $12.00. **D101.22:550-153**.

808-35.   **Greece.** 2d ed. 1977. 298p. S/N 008-020-00718-8. $11.00. **D101.22: 550-87/2**.

808-36. **Guatemala.** 2d ed. 1984. 286p. S/N 008-020-00987-3. $7.50. **D101.22:550-78/2.**

808-37. **Guinea.** 2d ed. 1975. 400p. S/N 008-020-00587-8. $12.00. **D101.22: 550-174.**

808-38. **Guyana.** 1969 (repr. 1980). 392p. S/N 008-020-00218-6. $11.00. **D101.22:550-82.**

808-39. **Haiti.** 1973 (repr. 1979). 203p. S/N 008-020-00486-3. $9.50. **D101.22:550-164.**

808-40. **Honduras.** 2d ed. 1984. 327p. S/N 008-020-00997-1. $13.00, cloth. **D101.22:550-151/2.**

808-41. **Hungary.** 1973 (repr. 1978). 353p. S/N 008-020-00485-5. $11.00. **D101.22:550-165.**

808-42. **India.** 3d ed. 1975 (repr. 1980). 664p. S/N 008-020-00572-0. $15.00. **D101.22:550-21/3.**

808-43. **Indian Ocean, Five Island Countries [Madagascar, Mauritius, Comoros, Seychelles, Maldives].** 2d ed. 1983. 374p. S/N 008-020-00957-1. $9.50, cloth. **D101.22:550-154/2.**

808-44. **Indonesia.** 4th ed. 1983. 373p. S/N 008-020-00965-2. $8.00, cloth. **D101.22:550-39/4.**

808-45. **Iran.** 3d ed. 1978. 520p. S/N 008-020-00761-7. $13.00, cloth. **D101.22:550-68/2.**

808-46. **Iraq.** 3d ed. 1979. 341p. S/N 008-020-00818-4. $11.00. **D101.22: 550-31/3.**

808-47. **Israel.** 2d ed. 1979. 442p. S/N 008-020-00790-1. $12.00, cloth. **D101.22:550-25/2.**

808-48. **Italy.** 1977. 310p. S/N 008-020-00648-3. $11.00. **D101.22:550-182.**

808-49. **Ivory Coast.** 2d ed. 1973. 515p. S/N 008-020-00481-2. $13.00, cloth. **D101.22:550-69.**

808-50. **Jamaica.** 1976. 346p. S/N 008-020-00604-1. $11.00, cloth. **D101.22: 550-177.**

808-51. **Japan.** 4th ed. 1983. 421p. S/N 008-020-00937-7. $14.00, cloth. **D101.22:550-30/4.**

808-52. **Jordan.** 3d ed. 1980. 334p. S/N 008-020-00839-7. $11.00, cloth. **D101.22:550-34/3.**

808-53. **Kenya.** 3d ed. 1984. 352p. S/N 008-020-00992-0. $13.00. **D101.22: 550-56/3.**

808-54. **Khmer Republic [Cambodia].** 1973. 403p. S/N 008-020-00445-6. $12.00. **D101.22:550-50/3.**

808-55. **Laos.** 2d ed. 1972 (repr. 1979). 351p. S/N 008-020-00467-1. $11.00, cloth. **D101.22:550-58/2.**

808-56. **Lebanon.** 2d ed. 1974 (repr. 1979). 400p. S/N 008-020-00553-3. $12.00, cloth. **D101.22:550-24/2.**

808-57. **Liberia.** 2d ed. 1972. 435p. S/N 008-020-00414-6. $12.00, cloth. **D101.22:550-38/2.**

808-58. **Libya.** 3d ed. 1979. 378p. S/N 008-020-00817-6. $11.00, cloth. **D101.22:550-85/3.**

808-59. **Malawi.** 1975 (repr. 1980). 367p. S/N 008-020-00567-3. $12.00, cloth. **D101.22:550-172.**

808-60. **Malaysia.** 4th ed. 1985. 399p. S/N 008-020-01017-1. $14.00, cloth. **D101.22:550-45/4.**

808-61. **Mauritania.** 1972. 197p. S/N 008-020-00438-3. $9.50, cloth. **D101.22:550-161.**

808-62. **Mexico.** 2d ed. 1975 (repr. 1983). 468p. S/N 008-020-00585-1. $13.00, cloth. **D101.22:550-79/2.**

808-63. **Mongolia.** 1970. 514p. S/N 008-020-00509-6. $13.00, cloth. **D101.22:550-76/2.**

808-64. **Morocco.** 4th ed. 1978. 426p. S/N 008-020-00762-5. $12.00, cloth. **D101.22:550-49/3.**

808-65. **Mozambique.** 2d ed. 1977. 258p. S/N 008-020-00716-1. $10.00, cloth. **D101.22:550-64/2.**

808-66. **Nepal, Bhutan, and Sikkim.** 1973 (repr. 1980). 501p. S/N 008-020-00480-4. $13.00, cloth. **D101.22:550-35/2.**

808-67. **Nicaragua.** 2d ed. 1982. 308p. S/N 008-020-00932-6. $12.00. **D101.22:550-88/2.**

808-68. **Nigeria.** 4th ed. 1982. 386p. S/N 008-020-00913-0. $12.00, cloth. **D101.22:550-157/3.**

808-69. **North Korea,** 3d ed. 1981. 333p. S/N 008-020-00908-3. $11.00, cloth. **D101.22:550-81/3.**

808-70. **North Vietnam.** 1967 (repr. 1981). 504p. S/N 008-020-00202-0. $13.00, cloth. **D101.22:550-57.**

808-71. **Oceania: A Regional Study.** Rev. 1985. 586p. S/N 008-020-01026-0. $16.00, cloth. **D101.22:550-94/2.**

808-72. **Pakistan.** 5th ed. 1984. 401p. S/N 008-020-01003-1. $14.00, cloth. **D101.22:550-48/4.**

808-73. **Panama.** 3d ed. 1981. 300p. S/N 008-020-00868-1. $11.00, cloth. **D101.22:550-46/2.**

808-74. **Paraguay.** 1972. 330p. S/N 008-020-00402-2. $11.00, cloth. **D101.22:550-156.**

808-75. **Persian Gulf States [Bahrain, Kuwait, Oman, Qatar, United Arab Emirates].** 1977. 462p. S/N 008-020-00682-3. $12.00, cloth. **D101.22:550-185.**

808-76.   **Peru.** 3d ed. 1981. 329p. S/N 008-020-00869-9. $11.00, cloth. **D101.22:550-42/3.**

808-77.   **Philippines.** 3d ed. 1984. 401p. S/N 008-020-01004-9. $15.00, cloth. **D101.22:550-72/3.**

808-78.   **Poland.** 2d ed. 1984. 514p. S/N 008-020-00986-5. $13.00, cloth. **D101.22:550-162/2.**

808-79.   **Portugal.** 1977. 470p. S/N 008-070-00630-1. $12.00, cloth. **D101.22:550-181.**

808-80.   **Romania.** 1972 (repr. 1979). 333p. S/N 008-020-00433-2. $11.00, cloth. **D101.22:550-160.**

808-81.   **Rwanda.** 1969. 226p. S/N 008-020-00220-8. $9.50, cloth. **D101.22: 550-84.**

808-82.   **Saudi Arabia.** 4th ed. 1984. 444p. S/N 008-020-01020-1. $15.00, cloth. **D101.22:550-51/4.**

808 83.   **Senegal.** 2d ed. 1974 (repr. 1977). 424p. S/N 008-020-00521-5. $11.00, cloth. **D101.22:550-70/2.**

808-84.   **Sierra Leone.** 1976. 414p. S/N 008-020-00625-4. $12.00, cloth. **D101.22:550-180.**

808-85.   **Singapore.** 1977. 230p. S/N 008-020-00651-3. $10.00, cloth. **D101.22:550-184.**

808-86.   **Spain.** 1976 (repr. 1985). 442p. S/N 008-020-00611-4. $13.00, cloth. **D101.22:550-179.**

808-87.   **Somalia.** 3d ed. 1982. 373p. S/N 008-020-00926-1. $13.00, cloth. **D101.22:550-86/3.**

808-88.   **South Africa.** 2d ed. 1981. 493p. S/N 008-020-00892-3. $12.00, cloth. **D101.22:550-93/2.**

808-89.   **South Korea.** 3d ed. 1982. 331p. S/N 008-020-00921-1. $12.00, cloth. **D101.22:550-41/4.**

808-90.   **South Vietnam.** 1967 (repr. 1978). 524p. S/N 008-020-00333-6. $13.00, cloth. **D101.22:550-55.**

808-91.   **Soviet Union.** 1971 (repr. 1979). 845p. S/N 008-020-00335-2. $17.00, cloth. **D101.22:550-95.**

808-92.   **Sudan.** 3d ed. 1983. 392p. S/N 008-020-00955-5. $10.00, cloth. **D101.22:550-27/3.**

808-93.   **Syria.** 3d ed. 1979. 287p. S/N 008-020-00813-3. $11.00, cloth. **D101.22:550-47/3.**

808-94.   **Tanzania.** 2d ed. 1978. 363p. S/N 008-020-00767-6. $11.00, cloth. **D101.22:550-62/2.**

808-95.   **Thailand.** 5th ed. 1981. 381p. S/N 008-020-00859-1. $11.00, cloth. **D101.22:550-53/4.**

808-96.   **Trinidad and Tobago**. 1976. 318p. S/N 008-020-00610-6. $11.00, cloth. **D101.22:550-178**.

808-97.   **Tunisia**. 2d ed. 1979. 344p. S/N 008-020-00792-7. $11.00, cloth. **D101.22:550-89/2**.

808-98.   **Turkey**. 3d ed. 1980. 398p. S/N 008-020-00832-0. $12.00, cloth. **D101.22:550-80/3**.

808-99.   **Uganda**. 1969 (repr. 1976). 472p. S/N 008-020-00212-7. $12.00, cloth. **D101.22:550-74**.

808-100.   **Uruguay**. 1971 (repr. 1976). 453p. S/N 008-020-00361-1. $12.00, cloth. **D101.22:550-97**.

808-101.   **Venezuela**. 3d ed. 1977. 367p. S/N 008-020-00676-9. $11.00, cloth. **D101.22:550-71/2**.

808-102.   **Yemens [North and South]**. 1977. 278p. S/N 008-020-00650-5. $10.00, cloth. **D101.22:550-183**.

808-103.   **Yugoslavia**. 2d ed. 1982. 363p. S/N 008-020-00920-2. $12.00, cloth. **D101.22:550-99/2**.

808-104.   **Zaire**. 3d ed. 1979. 353p. S/N 008-020-00776-5. $11.00, cloth. **D101.22:550-67/2**.

808-105.   **Zambia**. 3d ed. 1979. 333p. S/N 008-020-00814-1. $11.00, cloth. **D101.22:550-75/3**.

808-106.   **Zimbabwe**. 2d ed. 1983. 393p. S/N 008-020-00964-4. $8.00, cloth. **D101.22:550-171/2**.

See also "Marketing in. . . series" (entry 285), "Pocket Guide series" (entry 1541), "Port Guide series" (entry 1542), and "Post Report series" (entry 1543).

For additional publications on this topic see Subject Bibliography **SB-166, Foreign Area Studies**.

FOREIGN LANGUAGES

809-812.   **Foreign Service Institute Foreign Language Manuals and Readers**.
The School of Area Studies of the Foreign Service Institute produces a series of language manuals and readers for use in teaching Foreign Service personnel and other federal employees the language of the country or area in which they will be serving. Listed below are samples of texts for several common languages. Manuals are also available for Amharic, Arabic, Bulgarian, Cambodian, German, Greek, Hindi, Hungarian, Italian, Korean, Lao, Polish, Russian, Saudi Arabian, Serbo-Croatian, Swahili, Turkish, and Vietnamese. In-print titles are listed in Subject Bibliography **SB-082, Foreign Languages**.

809-1.   **French Basic Course, Units 1-12 Revised**. 1976 (repr. 1981). 475p. S/N 044-000-01643-5. $11.00. **S1.114/2:F88/units 1-12/976**.

809-2. **French Basic Course, Units 13-24 Revised**. 1976 (repr. 1982). 575p. S/N 044-000-01653-2. $12.00. **S1.114/2:F88/units 13-24/976**.

810-1. **French Phonology Programmed Instruction: Instructor's Manual**. 1978. 129p. S/N 044-000-01681-8. $5.50. **S1.114/2:F88/2/instructor**.

810-2. **French Phonology Programmed Instruction: Student's Manual**. 1977. 1408p. S/N 044-000-01654-1. $9.50. **S1.114/2:F88/2/student**.

811-1. **Portuguese Programmatic Course [Units 1-25]**. 1980. 807p. **S1.114/2: P83/3/980/v.1**.

811-2. **Portuguese Programmatic Course [Units 26-48]**. 1980. 627p. S/N 044-000-01775-0. $13.00. **S1.114/2:P83/3/v.2**.

812-1. **Spanish Basic Course, Units 1-15**. 1961 (repr. 1983). 699p. S/N 044-000-00287-7. $12.00. **S1.114/2:Sp2/units 1-15**.

812-2. **Spanish Basic Course, Units 16-30**. 1961 (repr. 1984). 716p. S/N 044-000-00279-5. $13.00. **S1.114/2:Sp2/units 16-30**.

812-3. **Spanish Basic Course, Units 31-45**. 1959 (repr. 1981). 614p. S/N 044-000-00277-9. $12.00. **S1.114/2:Sp2/units 31-45**.

812-4. **Spanish Basic Course, Units 46-55**. 1962 (repr. 1981). 462p. S/N 044-000-00280-9. $10.50. **S1.114/2:Sp2/units 46-55**.

813. **Translation Card [series]**. Naval Military Personnel Command. card. **D208.6/5:D22**.
These pocket-sized cards have translations of commonly used phrases in foreign languages of countries in which naval personnel may be on leave.

813-1. **Danish**. 1978. NAVPERS 15354. **D208.6/5:D22**.

813-2. **Dutch**. 1978. NAVPERS 15350. **D208.6/5:D95**.

813-3. **Egyptian-Arabic**. 1984. NAVPERS 15358. **D208.6/5:Eg9**.

813-4. **España [Spanish]**. 1978. NAVPERS 15286. **D208.6/5:Es6**.

813-5. **French**. 1978. NAVPERS 15269. **D208.6/5:F88**.

813-6. **German**. 1985. NAVPERS 15353. **D208.6/5:G31/985**.

813-7. **Greek**. 1978. NAVPERS 15355. **D208.6/5:G81**.

813-8. **Napoli [Italian]**. 1978. NAVPERS 15268. **D208.6/5:N16/2**.

813-9. **Norwegian**. 1978. NAVPERS 15356. **D208.6/5:N83**.

813-10. **Portuguese**. 1978. NAVPERS 15351. **D208.6/5:P83**.

813-11. **Turkish**. 1978. NAVPERS 15352. **D208.6/5:T84**.

See also entry 709-5.

For additional publications on this topic see Subject Bibliography **SB-082, Foreign Languages**.

Forests and Forestry

814.   **An Assessment of the Forest and Range Land Situation in the United States.**
Forest Service. October 1981. 380p. ill., charts, tables. Forest Resource Report No. 22.
S/N 001-001-00562-2. $9.00. **A13.50:22.**
This second comprehensive study of the renewable resources of forest and range
land and associated waters shows that the nation's demands for outdoor recreation,
wildlife and fish, range grazing, timber, and water have grown rapidly. Footnote
references. Index.

815.   **Checklist of United States Trees (Native and Naturalized).** Forest Service.
September 1979. 379p. Agriculture Handbook 541. S/N 001-000-03846-0. $13.00, cloth.
A1.76:541.
Compiles the accepted scientific names and current synonyms, approved common
names and others in use, and the geographic ranges of the native and naturalized trees
of the United States, including Alaska, but not Hawaii.

816.   **Forestry Schools in the United States.** Forest Service. Rev. October 1983. 34p.
map. **A13.2:Sch6/983.**
Describes undergraduate and graduate degree programs in forestry and related
fields at American colleges and universities. Arranged alphabetically by state, then by
name of institution.

817.   **Important Forest Trees of the United States.** Forest Service. June 1978. 72p. ill.,
maps. Agriculture Handbook 519. S/N 001-000-03722-6. $5.00. **A1.76:519.**
A popular, illustrated, compact reference for identifying important and common
trees in the forests. Approximately one-fourth of the native tree species of the
continental United States are included, arranged geographically. References. Index.

818.   **Land Areas of the National Forest System as of September 1983.** Forest Service.
Rev. 1983. 80p. tables. FS-383. **A13.10:983.**

Provides data on the gross and net area of national forest and other land administered by the Forest Service broken down by state, congressional district, and county.

819. **Mountaineers and Rangers: A History of Federal Forest Management in the Southern Appalachians, 1900-81.** Forest Service. April 1983. 219p. ill. FS-380. S/N 001-001-00602-5. $7.00. **A13.2:M86/3.**

Assesses the impact of federal land acquisition and land management on the peoples of the Southern Appalachian region. Three periods of federal involvement are emphasized: 1911-1920, the 1930s, and the 1960s when Appalachia was rediscovered. Footnote references. Bibliography.

820. **Silvicultural Systems for the Major Forest Types of the United States.** Forest Service. Rev. December 1983. 195p. Agriculture Handbook 445. S/N 001-000-04322-6. $11.00. **A1.76:445/3.**

Summarizes the silvicultural systems that appear biologically feasible for each of the forty-eight major forest types in the United States. Footnote references.

821. **Trees of Our National Forests: Their Beauty and Use.** Forest Service. Rev. 1980. 32p. ill., maps. PA 1124. S/N 001-000-04187-8. $3.75. **A1.68:1124/2.**

Describes the great trees of the American forests including the Douglas fir, ponderosa, and southern pine, yellow-poplar, sugar maple, and white oak.

822. **U.S. Timber Production, Trade, Consumption, and Price Statistics, 1950-80.** Forest Service. August 1981. 85p. charts, tables. Miscellaneous Publication 1408. **A1.38:1408.**

Presents national statistical data on the production, trade, consumption, and price of timber produced in the United States from 1950 to 1980. Some data are also shown for states, regions, and Canada. Bibliography.

823. **What Good Is a Forest?** North Central Forest Experiment Station. 1979. 16p. ill. S/N 001-001-00490-1. $3.00. **A13.82/2:F76/4.**

Describes and illustrates the value that forests have for recreation, wood production, wildlife, and water purification.

824. **You and Forest Fires.** Forest Service. Rev. May 1980. 16p. ill. PA 64. **A1.68:64/6.**

Discusses how forest fires start, how you can help prevent them, and what the Forest Service is doing to prevent and control forest fires.

See also entry 689.

For additional publications on this topic see Subject Bibliography **SB-086, Trees, Forest Products, and Forest Management.**

Freedom of Information,
Privacy, and Information Policy

825. **A Compilation of State Sunset Statutes with Background Information on State Sunset Laws**. Congress. House. Committee on Rules. October 1983. 716p. Committee Print, 98th Congress, 1st Session. **Y4.R86/1:Su7/2**.

This compilation contains the text of "sunset" statutes in thirty-seven states which have adopted such legislation since 1976. Sunset laws usually provide for a termination date for existing programs or agencies in their authorizing legislation.

826. **Computer-based National Information Systems: Technology and Public Policy Issues**. Congress. Office of Technology Assessment. September 1981. 176p. ill., charts. OTA-CIT-146. S/N 052-003-00852-1. $6.50. **Y3.T22/2:2C73/6**.

Provides a broad introductory examination of computer-based national information systems and related technology and public policy issues that Congress is likely to face in the future including privacy, security, and constitutional rights. Footnote references.

827. **Federal Information Centers**. General Services Administration. October 1983. folder, 8p. **GS2.2:In3**.

Lists the names and addresses of federal information centers.

828. **Federal Register: Privacy Act Issuances, 1982/83 Compilation**. 5 vols. Office of the Federal Register. 1984. 5000p. **GS4.107/a:P939/2/982-83/v.1-5**.

This compilation contains descriptions of systems of records maintained on individuals by federal agencies which were published in the *Federal Register* as required by the Privacy Act of 1974, and the rules of each agency which set out the procedures that agencies will follow to assist individuals who request information about their records.

829. **FOIA Update**. Department of Justice. Quarterly. approx. 8p. ill. S/N 727-002-00000-6. Symbol FOIA. $10.00 per yr. Single copy $2.75. **J1.58:vol/no**.

This periodical is intended for federal officials responsible for administering the Freedom of Information Act (FOIA). It includes news items and guidelines. Departments include significant new court decisions, FOIA training activities, and the profile of an FOIA official.

830. **Freedom of Information Case List**. Department of Justice. September 1984. 372p. S/N 027-000-01201-9. $9.00. **J1.56:984**.

Issued annually. This list is an alphabetical compilation of judicial decisions of precedential significance, both published and unpublished addressing issues under the Freedom of Information Act (FOIA) and the Privacy Act of 1974. Separate lists of access cases under the government in the Sunshine Act and the Federal Advisory Committee Act are included as well as a list of reverse FOIA cases. Topical index.

831. **Issues in Information Policy**. National Telecommunications and Information Administration. February 1981. 108p. NTIA-SP-80-9. S/N 003-000-00575-5. $5.00. **C60.9:80-9**.

A collection of papers on dissemination of information, access to government data, privacy, property rights, and information markets. Footnote references.

832. **Public Sector/Private Sector Interaction in Providing Information Services**. National Commission on Libraries and Information Science. February 1982. 104p. S/N 052-003-00866-1. $5.50. **Y3.L61:2P96/2**.

Presents the results of a two-year study by a task force of members from both the private and public sectors on the interactions between government and private sector information activities.

833. **Your Right to Federal Records: Questions and Answers on the Freedom of Information Act and the Privacy Act**. General Services Administration. 1984. 17p. **GS1.2:F13/2**.

Provides answers to questions which citizens most frequently ask at the federal information centers about the Freedom of Information Act and the Privacy Act.

See also entries 457, 1164, 1169.

Gardens and Gardening

GENERAL

834. **Gardening for Food and Fun**. Department of Agriculture. 1977. 432p. ill., tables. Yearbook of Agriculture 1977. S/N 001-000-03679-3. $12.00, cloth. **A1.10:977**.

A practical book for gardeners of all types and ages. Articles are grouped under four sections: introduction to gardening, home garden vegetables, fruits and nuts, and home food preservation. References. Index.

835. **Home Gardening Kit**. 8 books. Department of Agriculture. 1963-1981. 180p. ill. S/N 001-000-04280-7. $5.50.

Includes the following Home and Garden Bulletins: *Growing Flowering Perennials* (no. 114), *Selecting and Growing House Plants* (no. 82), *Indoor Gardening* (no. 220), *Summer Flowering Bulbs* (no. 151), *Growing Boxwoods* (no. 120), *Growing Chrysanthemums* (no. 65), *Growing Camelias* (no. 86), and *Growing Peonies* (no. 126).

836. **Landscape for Living**. Department of Agriculture. 1972. 416p. ill., maps, tables. Yearbook of Agriculture 1972. S/N 001-000-02441-8. $12.00, cloth. **A1.10:972**.

Contains more than forty articles, discussing ways to use plants to improve the environment. Includes sections on gardening, landscaping, attracting birds, brightening neighborhoods, rent-a-gardens, and more. References. Index.

See also "Pests and Pest Control" (entries 1375-1398).

For additional publications on this topic see Subject Bibliographies **SB-041, The Home** and **SB-301, Gardening**.

GROWING FLOWERS

837. **Growing Azaleas and Rhododendrons**. Department of Agriculture. Rev. August 1980. 8p. ill. Home and Garden Bulletin 71. S/N 001-000-04171-1. $1.75. **A1.77:71/7**.
Provides brief advice on selecting, planting, and caring for azaleas and rhododendrons in the home garden.

838. **Growing Camellias**. Department of Agriculture. Rev. April 1981. 12p. ill. Home and Garden Bulletin 86. S/N 001-000-04229-7. $2.00. **A1.77:86/7**.
Provides advice on buying, planting, and maintaining garden and potted camellias, and on preventing against and treating them for disease and insect infestations.

839. **Growing Chrysanthemums in the Home Garden**. Department of Agriculture. Rev. 1981. 8p. ill. Home and Garden Bulletin 65. S/N 001-000-04212-2. $2.00. **A1.77:65/7**.
Provides advice on selecting, planting, propagating, growing, and caring for chrysanthemums in the home garden.

840. **Growing Dahlias**. Department of Agriculture. Rev. November 1978. 8p. ill. Home and Garden Bulletin 131. **A1.77:131/5**.
Provides brief advice on selecting, planting, caring for, and propagating dahlias in the home garden.

841. **Growing Flowering Crabapples**. Department of Agriculture. Rev. May 1978. 11p. ill. Home and Garden Bulletin 135. S/N 001-000-03784-6. $1.75. **A1.77:135/2**.
Describes and illustrates varieties of flowering crabapples and provides suggestions for their care.

842. **Growing Flowering Perennials**. Department of Agriculture. Rev. 1970 (repr. 1979). 32p. ill. Home and Garden Bulletin 114. S/N 001-000-00783-1. $2.50. **A1.77:114/3**.
Provides instructions for planting the garden, mulching, fertilizing, and cultivating. Also gives directions for starting perennials indoors and transplanting them later.

843. **Growing Peonies**. Department of Agriculture. Rev. April 1981. 12p. ill. Home and Garden Bulletin 126. S/N 001-000-04234-3. $2.25. **A1.77:126/6**.
Describes garden and tree peonies and how they grow. Provides advice on selecting, planting, and caring for them.

844. **Roses for the Home**. Department of Agriculture. Rev. November 1978. 25p. ill. Home and Garden Bulletin 25. S/N 001-000-03848-6. $2.25. **A1.77:25/12**.
Describes and illustrates plant selection, planting sites, soil preparation, and planting and pruning of bush roses and climbing roses.

845. **Summer Flowering Bulbs**. Department of Agriculture. Rev. September 1978 (repr. 1983). 16p. ill. Home and Garden Bulletin 151. S/N 001-000-03833-8. $2.50. **A1.77:151/4**.

Describes nineteen types of summer flowering bulbs. Provides advice on selecting and planting bulbs, and caring for the plants.

GROWING FRUITS

846. **Controlling Diseases of Raspberries and Blackberries**. Department of Agriculture. Rev. September 1980. 17p. ill. Farmers' Bulletin 2208. **A1.9:2208/5**.
Describes thirteen raspberry diseases and seven blackberry diseases, and provides advice on how to control them.

847. **Growing American Bunch Grapes**. Agricultural Research Service. Rev. December 1977. 26p. ill., maps. Farmers' Bulletin 2123. S/N 001-000-03733-1. $2.25. **A1.9:2123/6**.
Describes different varieties of American bunch grapes. Provides advice on site selection, planting, training and pruning, soil management, and control of insects and diseases.

848. **Growing Raspberries**. Department of Agriculture. Rev. June 1979. 15p. ill. Farmers' Bulletin 2165. **A1.9:2165/8**.
Describes types of raspberries and where they are grown. Provides advice on site selection, planting, training and pruning, thinning, care, harvesting, and controlling insects and diseases.

849. **Strawberry Diseases**. Agricultural Research Service. Rev. January 1978. 27p. ill. Farmers' Bulletin 2140. S/N 001-000-03752-8. $2.25. **A1.9:2140/7**.
Describes the diseases, identifies their symptoms, provides advice on the care of infected plants, and discusses the most effective preventive measures.

850. **Strawberry Varieties in the United States**. Department of Agriculture. Rev. June 1979. 26p. ill., maps, tables. Farmers' Bulletin 1043. S/N 001-000-03976-8. $2.50. **A1.9:1043/5**.
Describes thirty-eight varieties of strawberries based on regional differences and whether they are primarily commercial or garden types. Describes new varieties now being tested. Index.

GROWING VEGETABLES

851. **Growing Cauliflower and Broccoli**. Extension Service. Rev. 1984. 14p. ill. Farmers' Bulletin 2239. S/N 001-000-04426-5. $1.00. **A1.9:2239/6**.
Describes different varieties of cauliflower and broccoli. Provides advice on planting, caring for, controlling insects and diseases, and harvesting and packing.

852. **Growing Table Beets**. Department of Agriculture. Rev. January 1980. 6p. ill. Leaflet 360. **A1.35:360/12**.
Provides advice on selecting, planting, and growing beets and protecting them from insects and diseases.

853. **Growing Tomatoes in the Home Garden**. Department of Agriculture. Rev. April 1981. 13p. ill. Home and Garden Bulletin 180. S/N 001-000-04225-4. $2.00. **A1.77:180/4**.

Provides advice on soil preparation, seeding, care and cultivation, and harvesting of tomatoes and controlling insects and diseases.

854. **Growing Vegetables in the Home Garden**. Department of Agriculture. Rev. September 1980. 49p. ill., map, tables. Home and Garden Bulletin 202. **A1.77:202/3**.

A step-by-step guide for the home gardener in selecting a site, preparing the soil, choosing garden tools, planting, and caring for the backyard garden. Includes advice on growing specific types of vegetables. Index.

855. **Insects and Diseases of Vegetables in the Home Garden**. Department of Agriculture. Rev. November 1980. 56p. ill. Agriculture Information Bulletin 380. S/N 001-000-04019-7. $4.25. **A1.75:380/2**.

Describes insects under the vegetables (arranged alphabetically) which they damage. Includes types of damage, regional distribution, control measures, and pesticide precautions.

856. **Minigardens for Vegetables**. Department of Agriculture. Rev. January 1981. 13p. ill., tables. Home and Garden Bulletin 163. **A1.77:163/5**.

Provides advice on containers, soil, light, planting dates, fertilizers, watering, and cultivating vegetables in minigardens. Also discusses ornamental vegetables.

857. **Radish Production**. Department of Agriculture. September 1979. 5p. ill. Leaflet 566. S/N 001-000-03942-3. $1.75. **A1.35:566**.

Describes and illustrates types and varieties of radishes and offers suggestions for their cultivation from commercial and home gardening perspectives.

INDOOR GARDENING

858. **Building Hobby Greenhouses**. Agricultural Research Service. Rev. July 1977. 20p. ill. Agriculture Information Bulletin 357. S/N 001-000-03692-1. $2.75. **A1.75:357/3**.

Discusses the different types of greenhouses, designing a greenhouse and selecting a site for it, construction materials, types of frames, heating and cooling systems, and more.

859. **Indoor Gardening: Artificial Lighting, Terrariums, Hanging Baskets, and Plant Selection**. Agricultural Research Service. Rev. February 1978. 47p. ill., tables. Home and Garden Bulletin 220. S/N 001-000-03758-7. $4.25. **A1.77:220/2**.

Includes plans for constructing eleven types of indoor gardens. Provides advice on starting and caring for the garden. Discusses special gardening including terrariums and hanging baskets.

860. **Selecting and Growing House Plants**. Agricultural Research Service. Rev. 1963 (repr. 1983). 32p. ill. Home and Garden Bulletin 82. S/N 001-000-00863-3. $2.50. **A1.77:82/2**.

Provides advice on selecting and growing plants indoors.

LAWN AND YARD CARE

861. **Better Lawns: Establishment, Maintenance, Renovation, Lawn Problems, Grasses**. Department of Agriculture. Rev. August 1979. 36p. ill., tables. Home and Garden Bulletin 51. **A1.77:51/12**.

Provides advice on the establishment, maintenance, and renovation of lawns and on dealing with lawn problems. Describes common lawn grasses and ground cover plants, where they grow best by climatic region, and how to establish them.

862. **Lawn Diseases: How to Control Them**. Department of Agriculture. Rev. July 1978. 22p. ill., tables. Home and Garden Bulletin 61. S/N 001-000-03806-1. $2.50. **A1.77:61/7**.

Discusses how to control lawn diseases which are caused primarily by fungi. Describes other causes of poor turf and suggests remedies.

863. **Weed Control in Lawns and Other Turf**. Agricultural Research Service and Extension Service. May 1984. 41p. ill., tables. Home and Garden Bulletin 239. S/N 001-000-04420-6. $2.00. **A1.77:239**.

Describes and illustrates twenty-three common lawn weeds. Provides advice on controlling weeds through fertilizing, liming, watering, mowing, and herbicide treatments.

TREES, SHRUBS, AND VINES

864. **Dwarf Fruit Trees: Selection and Care**. Agricultural Research Service. Rev. December 1976. 8p. ill. Leaflet 407. S/N 001-000-03563-1. $2.00. **A1.35:407/8**.

Provides brief advice on selecting, planting, caring for, and training dwarf fruit trees.

865. **Growing Boxwoods**. Department of Agriculture. Rev. June 1979. 15p. ill., map. Home and Garden Bulletin 120. S/N 001-000-03986-5. $2.00. **A1.77:120/5**.

Describes and illustrates varieties of boxwood and offers advice for their care and protection against insects and related pests.

866. **Growing Ornamental Bamboo**. Department of Agriculture. Rev. August 1978. 11p. ill. Home and Garden Bulletin 76. S/N 001-000-03815-0. $2.25. **A1.77:76/2**.

Tells how to select a proper bamboo variety of either clump or running bamboo and how to propagate it successfully.

867. **Homeowner's Guide for Beautiful, Safe, and Healthy Trees**. Northeastern Forest Experiment Station. 1984. folder, 8p. S/N 001-001-00605-0. $13.00 per 100 copies. No single copies sold. **A13.42/25:NE-INF-58-84**.

Provides brief advice on growing and maintaining healthy trees.

868. **Pruning Shade Trees and Repairing Their Injuries**. Agricultural Research Service and Extension Service. Rev. November 1983. 13p. ill. Home and Garden Bulletin 83. S/N 001-000-04399-4. $1.00. **A1.77:83/3**.

Discusses seasons for pruning, pruning techniques, repairing injuries, and special pruning problems and equipment.

869.   **Salt Injury to Ornamental Shrubs and Ground Covers**. Department of Agriculture. July 1980. 10p. ill. Home and Garden Bulletin 231. S/N 001-000-04144-4. $2.50. **A1.77:231**.

Discusses how salt accumulations in the soil may damage ornamental shrubs and ground covers. Provides advice on selecting plants and reducing soil salinity.

870.   **Shade Tree Pruning**. National Park Service. Rev. 1955 (repr. 1979). 30p. ill., tables. Tree Preservation Bulletin No. 4. S/N 024-005-00147-6. $2.00. **I29.26:4/2**.

Describes proper methods for pruning deciduous trees and conifers.

871.   **Shade Trees for the Home**. Agricultural Research Service. December 1972. 48p. ill., tables. Agriculture Handbook 425. S/N 001-000-02496-5. $4.50. **A1.76:425**.

Provides brief description of various shade trees suitable for planting around houses in the continental United States. Tells how to select, plant, and care for them, and reveals the climate and type of soil best suited for propagation. Does not include small ornamental trees.

872.   **Shrubs, Vines and Trees for Summer Color**. Department of Agriculture. Rev. June 1980. 21p. Ill., map. Home and Garden Bulletin 181. **A1.77:181/3**.

Describes forty-two types of shrubs, nine types of vines, and six types of trees which will add summer color to the home garden. Includes common and scientific names and climate zones suitable for growing them.

873.   **Trees for Shade and Beauty: Their Selection and Care**. Department of Agriculture. Rev. June 1979. 8p. ill. Home and Garden Bulletin 117. S/N 001-000-04112-6. $2.00. **A1.77:117/6**.

Discusses the important factors in tree selection and care, including form, size, and undesirable characteristics.

Geology

GENERAL

874. **Geologic Story of the Great Plains**. Geological Survey. 1980. 55p. ill., maps. Bulletin 1493. S/N 024-001-03381-0. $5.00. **I19.3:1493**.
Provides a nontechnical description of the origin and evolution of the landscape of the Great Plains. References. Index.

875. **Our Changing Continent**. Geological Survey. Rev. 1985. 23p. ill., maps. S/N 024-001-02033-5. $1.50. **I19.2:C76/985**.
Discusses and presents maps reflecting changes during the Great Ice Age, the Age of Dinosaurs, and the Coal Age.

See also entry 665.

EARTHQUAKES

876. **Earthquake History of the United States**. Environmental Data and Information Service. Rev. 1982. 270p. ill., maps, tables. **C55.228:41-1/2**.
Presents a history of prominent earthquakes in the United States from historical times through 1970 arranged in nine seismic regions. Also includes 1971-1980 supplement and an addenda and corrigenda section. References. Bibliography.

877. **Earthquake Safety Checklist**. Federal Emergency Management Administration. September 1983. 18p. FEMA-46. **FEM1.2:Ea7/2**.
This checklist is designed to help one plan for and survive a major earthquake.

878. **Learning to Live in Earthquake Country: Preparedness in Apartments and Mobile Homes.** Federal Emergency Management Administration. October 1984. 15p. L-143. **FEM1.11:143.**

Contains tips on how to protect life and property before, during, and after an earthquake with emphasis on apartment and mobile home dwellers.

879. **Safety and Survival in an Earthquake.** Geological Survey. Rev. 1980. folder, 12p. ill. S/N 024-001-00001-6. $1.75. **I19.2:Ea7/3/980.**

Describes and illustrates the damage caused by earthquakes and contains suggestions for taking measures that can reduce the dangers before, during, and after earthquakes.

880. **Safety Tips for Earthquakes.** Federal Emergency Management Administration. Rev. July 1983. folder, 8p. ill. L-111. **FEM1.11:111/2.**

Contains tips on protecting life and property before, during, and after an earthquake.

881. **The Severity of an Earthquake.** Geological Survey. Rev. 1979. 15p. ill., map. **I19.2:Ea7/16/979.**

Describes how the severity of an earthquake is expressed in magnitude on the Richter Scale and in intensity on the Modified Mercalli Scale.

882. **United States Earthquakes, 1981.** Geological Survey. 1984. 144p. ill., maps, tables. S/N 024-001-03512-0. $5.00. **I19.65/2:981.**

Issued annually. Describes all earthquakes that were reported felt in the United States and nearby territories during the year. Arrangement is alphabetical by state, then chronological. References.

See also entries 562, 567.

VOLCANOES

883. **Eruption of Mount St. Helens: Past, Present, and Future.** Geological Survey. 1984. 50p. ill., maps. S/N 024-001-03527-8. $2.75. **I19.2:M86/2.**

This colorfully illustrated booklet discusses briefly the geological history of the Mount St. Helens area, and provides highlights of the major eruptions of May 1980. It speculates about the possible future behavior of this volcanic peak. References.

884. **The 1980 Eruptions of Mount St. Helens, Washington.** Geological Survey. 1981. 871p. ill., charts, maps, tables. Professional Paper 1250. S/N 024-001-03452-2. $35.00, cloth. **I19.16:1250.**

Presents detailed early results of volcanic events in 1980 at Mount St. Helens; geophysical monitoring of activity; and studies of volcanic deposits, effects, and potential behavior. References. Index.

885. **Volcanic Eruptions of 1980 at Mount St. Helens: The First 100 Days.** Geological Survey. 1982. 133p. ill., maps. Professional Paper 1249. S/N 024-001-03488-3. $8.50. **I19.16:1249.**

This nontechnical, colorfully illustrated report of the Mount St. Helens's volcanic eruptions was prepared for the general public. It presents a chronology of events from 20 March to 27 June 1980. Bibliography.

886. **Volcanoes**. Geological Survey. 1982. 45p. ill., maps. S/N 024-001-03472-7. $3.25. **I19.2:V88/8**.

Presents a generalized summary of the nature, workings, and hazards of the common types of volcanoes around the world with a brief introduction to the techniques of volcano monitoring. References.

Handicapped

GENERAL

887. **American Rehabilitation**. Rehabilitation Services Administration. Quarterly. 32p. ill. S/N 765-002-00000-1. Symbol ARHB. $11.00 per yr. Single copy $3.00. **ED1.211:vol/no**.

This periodical includes short articles of general interest on handicapping conditions and rehabilitation of the handicapped. Departments provide short news items, book reports, and announcements of new contract research reports. A regular feature is Language Use or Used Language which discusses current word use, or misuse and gobbledygook.

888. **The College Student with a Disability: A Faculty Handbook**. President's Committee on Employment of the Handicapped. 1981. 35p. S/N 040-000-00428-9. $4.50. **PrEx1.10/8:St9**.

Suggests various adjustments that can be made in the environment or in teaching style for blind, partially sighted, deaf or hearing-impaired, or speech-impaired students. Glossary. References.

889. **Digest of Data on Persons with Disabilities**. Office of Special Education and Rehabilitative Services. June 1984. 192p. tables. S/N 065-000-00211-6. $5.50. **ED1.2:D26/3**.

A compilation of both published and previously unpublished statistical data on persons with disabilities. Includes such topics as impairments, work disabilities, limitation of activity, and employment. Highlights and explanatory notes accompany each table.

890. **Directory of Living Aids for the Disabled Person**. Veterans Administration. 1982. 308p. S/N 051-000-00158-3. $7.50. **VA1.2:D63/3**.

Lists alphabetically products which are living aids and their manufacturers, and lists by state the living aids available. Includes dressing aids, telephone aids, exercisers, special eating utensils, ramps, and wheel chairs.

891. **Directory of National Information Sources on Handicapping Conditions and Related Services.** 3d ed. Office of Special Education and Rehabilitative Services. August 1982. 263p. S/N 065-000-00142-0. $8.00. **ED1.202:H19/2.**

Lists public and private organizations at the national level that are providers of information and direct services on handicapping conditions.

892. **Disabled USA.** President's Committee on Employment of the Handicapped. Quarterly. approx. 32p. ill. S/N 741-001-00000-4. Symbol DIUSA. $11.00 per yr. Single copy $3.00. **PrEx1.10/3-2:vol/no.**

This periodical presents articles and short news items with timely information on opportunities for handicapped workers, developments in rehabilitation, and new ideas on coping with a disability.

893. **The Law and Disabled People: Selected Federal and State Laws Affecting Employment and Certain Rights of People with Disabilities.** President's Committee on Employment of the Handicapped. 1980. 179p. tables. S/N 040-000-00432-7. $6.50. **PrEx1.10:L41.**

Analyzes federal and state laws dealing with architectural accessibility and barrier removal; equal employment opportunity and employment programs; and education, transportation, and housing. Footnote references.

894. **People Just like You: About Handicaps and Handicapped (An Activity Guide).** President's Committee on Employment of the Handicapped. 1979. 36p. ill. S/N 040-000-00405-0. $4.50. **PrEx1.10/8:P39.**

Acquaints students at all levels with handicapped persons in order to provide them with first-hand awareness of the problems and human experiences of handicapped people.

895. **Pocket Guide to Federal Help for the Disabled Person.** Department of Education. Rev. February 1985. S/N 065-000-00227-2. $1.00. **ED1.8:D63/985.**

Describes federal programs which benefit blind, deaf, and developmentally disabled persons. Includes names and addresses of agencies to which to apply for benefits or request more information.

896. **Recreation and Leisure for Handicapped Individuals: Information, Resources, Funding Guide, Publications Available from Federal Sources.** Office for Handicapped Individuals. December 1980. 102p. S/N 065-000-00076-8. $5.50. **ED1.8:R26/2.**

Describes information resources which are primarily national in scope, and covers all handicapping conditions. References.

897. **Rehabilitation for Independent Living: A Selected Bibliography.** President's Committee on Employment of the Handicapped. Rev. 1982. 60p. S/N 040-000-00457-2. $4.50. **PrEx1.10/9:R26/982.**

This annotated bibliography of books, journal articles, and audiovisual materials covers materials on independent living as a means of rehabilitation for the physically handicapped and mentally retarded.

See also entries 705, 1342, 1687.

See also "Handicapped Children" (entries 381-384).

For additional publications on this topic see Subject Bibliographies **SB-037, The Handicapped**, and **SB-081, Rehabilitation.**

ARCHITECTURAL AND TRANSPORTATION BARRIERS

898. **Access Travel, Airports: A Guide to Accessibility of Terminals.** Federal Aviation Administration. Rev. September 1979. 23p. tables. **TD4.8:T67/3/979.**
   Lists in tabular format the design features, facilities, and services that are important to the handicapped at 282 airports in forty countries.

899. **Adapting Historic Campus Structures for Accessibility.** Department of Education. 1980. 100p. ill. **ED1.2:C15.**
   Gives ideas for possible solutions to architectural barriers to handicapped persons in older campus buildings.

900. **Designing for Everyone.** Architectural and Transportation Barriers Compliance Board. April 1980. 8p. ill. **Y3.B27:2D46.**
   Provides barrier-free, accessible, universal design sketches for curb ramps, toilets, and rest rooms.

901. **The Feasibility of Accommodating Physically Handicapped Individuals on Pedestrian Over and Undercrossing Structures; Final Report.** Federal Highway Administration. September 1980. 102p. ill. FHWA-RD-79-146. S/N 050-001-00206-0. $5.00. **TD2.30:79-146.**
   Describes the evaluation of a sampling of over and under-crossing pedestrian structures, which found that 86 percent had at least one major access barrier. Analyzes alternate solutions for cost-effectiveness.

LIBRARY SERVICES FOR THE BLIND AND PHYSICALLY HANDICAPPED

902. **Address List: Regional and Subregional Libraries for the Blind and Physically Handicapped.** National Library Service for the Blind and Physically Handicapped. Rev. 1983. 26p. **LC19.17:983.**
   Lists alphabetically by state those regional and subregional libraries through which the Library of Congress provides a free library service to persons who are unable to read or use standard printed materials because of a visual or physical handicap.

903. **Braille Books, 1982.** National Library Service for the Blind and Physically Handicapped. 1982. 187p. **LC19.9/2:982.**
   Issued annually. Lists press braille and handcopied braille books produced by the Library of Congress during the year. Index.

904. **Braille Scores Catalog.** Pt. 1. **Classical, Music and Musicians.** Pt. 2. **Popular, Music and Musicians.** National Library Service for the Blind and Physically Handicapped. 1983. 337p. **LC19.2:M97/13/pt.1,2.**
   Lists braille vocal music in the collections of the Library of Congress.

905.   **Cassettee Books, 1983**. National Library Service for the Blind and Physically Handicapped. 1983. 375p. **LC19.10/3:983**.

Issued annually. This annotated catalog lists cassette books produced by the Library of Congress during the year which are suitable for adult and young readers. Author and title indexes.

906.   **For Younger Readers: Braille and Talking Books, 1982-1983**. National Library Service for the Blind and Physically Handicapped. 1983. 133p. **LC19.11:Y8/982-83**.

Issued biennially. This annotated catalog lists books produced for young readers on disc and cassette, and in press braille and handcopied braille. Arranged by topic in two broad categories: nonfiction and fiction. Author and title indexes.

907.   **Historical Fiction**. National Library Service for the Blind and Physically Handicapped. 1983. 79p. **LC19.11:H62**.

This annotated bibliography is a guide to selected historical works covering the period prior to 1900 which are available on disc or cassette, or in braille through the interlibrary network of the National Library Service for the Blind and Physically Handicapped.

908.   **Talking Books: Adult, 1982-83**. National Library Service for the Blind and Physically Handicapped. 1983. 159p. **LC19.10/2:982-83**.

Issued biennially. This annotated catalog lists disc books produced by the Library of Congress during 1982 and 1983.

Health and Medical Care

GENERAL

909. **Books That Help Children Deal with a Hospital Experience**. Bureau of Community Health Services. Rev. 1978. 23p. DHEW Publication No. (HSA) 78-5224. **HE20.5102:B64/978**.

An annotated list of books for children that discuss hospital experiences and illnesses — most are written for preschool or elementary school children. Title index.

910. **Directory of United States Poison Control Centers and Services, 1983**. Food and Drug Administration. Rev. 1983. 52p. **HE20.4003/2-2:983**.

Lists the name, address, and telephone number of state coordinators and poison control centers in the United States. Entries are arranged alphabetically by state, then by city. References.

911. **Facts of Life and Death**. National Center for Health Statistics. Rev. November 1978. 50p. tables. DHEW Publication No. (PHS) 79-1222. S/N 017-022-00645-6. $2.75. **HE20.6202:L62/978**.

Presents statistics on population; birth; life expectancy; fetal, infant, and maternal mortality; marriage and divorce; health characteristics; physical measurement; health resources; and mortality.

912. **FDA Consumer**. Food and Drug Administration. Monthly, except July/August and December/January (combined). 48p. ill. S/N 717-009-00000-2. Symbol FDAP. $17.00 per yr. Single copy $2.00. **HE20.4010:vol/no**.

This periodical includes articles of general interest to consumers regarding safe production and use of foods and drugs. Departments include short news items regarding FDA regulatory activities and related matters, samples of reports from field investigators on contaminated products, and summaries of court decisions.

913. **Health Information Resources in the Federal Government.** Public Health Service. 1984. 130p. DHHS Publication No. (PHS) 84-50146. **HE20.2:In3/2.**

Lists 113 agencies and offices in the federal government that provide health information to professionals and to the public. Entries include description of services, publications, and databases.

914. **Health United States, 1984.** National Center for Health Statistics. 1985. 195p. charts, maps, tables. DHHS Publication No. (PHS) 85-1232. S/N 017-022-00861-1. $6.50. **HE20.6223:984.**

Issued annually. Presents statistics comparing and contrasting recent trends in the health care sector. The report is divided into two parts. Part 1 is a chart book of twenty-five maps illustrating geographic variations in health statistics. Part 2 contains ninety-four statistical tables around four major subjects.

915. **Healthy People. The Surgeon General's Report on Health Promotion and Disease Prevention.** Public Health Service. 1979. 177p. charts, tables. DHEW Publication No. (PHS) 79-55071. S/N 017-001-00416-2. $6.00. **HE20.2:H34/5.**

Reviews the state of health of the American people, and the status of current health promotion and disease prevention programs. Shows how a national commitment to efforts for preventing disease and promoting health can further improve the health of the American people. References.

915-A. . . . **Background Papers.** 1979. 491p. DHHS Publication No. (PHS) 79-55071-A. S/N 017-001-00417-1. $8.00. **HE20.2:H34/5/papers.**

Provides a summary of the Surgeon General's Report. Includes nineteen background papers on a wide variety of topics dealing with disease prevention and health promotion. Footnote references.

916. **Inside the Cell: The New Frontier of Medical Science.** National Institute of General Medical Sciences. 1978. 96p. ill. NIH Publication No. 79-1051. S/N 017-040-00439-7. $4.75. **HE20.3459:C33.**

A fully illustrated, layperson's language guide to the basic characteristics and functions of a cell. Glossary.

917. **Medicines and You.** National Institute of General Medical Sciences. April 1981. 62p. ill. NIH Publication No. 81-2140. S/N 017-040-00480-0. $4.50. **HE20.3459:M46.**

Contains chapters on biological individuality, the birth of pharmacology, biotransformation, genes, and using medicines rationally and safely. Glossary.

918. **National Listing of Providers Furnishing Kidney Dialysis and Transplant Services; Sequence: State, City.** Health Care Financing Administration. January 1985. 240p. HCFA Publication No. 03199. S/N 017-060-00179-3. $8.50. **HE22.25:985.**

Issued annually. Lists medical institutions and other facilities which are providers of kidney dialysis and transplant services in alphabetical sequence by state, and city within each state. Entries includes name and address, intermediary number, services provided, and other information.

919. **Postmarketing Surveillance of Prescription Drugs.** Congress. Office of Technology Assessment. November 1982. 70p. OTA-H-189. S/N 052-003-00893-9. $5.00. **Y3.T22/2:2D84/3.**

Describes the drug-approval process, the history and objectives of postmarketing surveillance, the methods used to accomplish it, and current activities in postmarketing surveillance. Index.

920. **Staying Healthy: A Bibliography of Health Promotion Materials**. Public Health Service. Rev. November 1984. 48p. S/N 017-001-00449-9. $2.00. **HE20.11/2: H34/4/984**.

This annotated bibliography of publications and audiovisual materials on health promotion is arranged by topic. Most of the titles are government publications many of which are available free. Order information is provided. Title index.

921. **Uniformed Services Medical/Dental Facilities in the U.S.A.** American Forces Information Service. Rev. 1984. 23p. PA-17. **D2.14:PA-17/3**.

Lists hospitals, medical clinics, and dental facilities for service members and their dependents. Arranged in alphabetical order by state.

922. **When Your Child Goes to the Hospital**. Children's Bureau. 1976. 36p. ill. DHEW Publication No. (OHDS) 79-30092. S/N 017-091-00217-7. $4.25. **HE1.452:C43/3**.

Intended especially for parents and other family members as a guide to help them prepare their child or children for an expected visit to the hospital. References.

See also entries 77, 79, 312, 1475, 1476, 1477, 1479, 1480.

For additional publications on this topic see Subject Bibliographies **SB-008, Diseases in Humans**, and **SB-154, Medicine and Medical Science**.

ALLERGIES

923. **Allergies: Medicine for the Layman**. National Institutes of Health. September 1981. 25p. ill. NIH Publication No. 81-1948. **HE20.3031:Al5**.

Describes the causes, incidence, and treatment of allergies and asthma, and the status of current research.

924. **Allergies: Questions and Answers**. National Institute of Allergy and Infectious Diseases. August 1984. folder, 8p. NIH Publication No. 84-189. S/N 017-044-00049-4. $16.00 per 100 copies. No single copies sold. **HE20.3252:Al5/2**.

Provides answers to the most frequently asked questions about the causes, prevention, and treatment of allergies.

925. **Asthma**. National Institute of Allergy and Infectious Diseases. July 1983. 11p. NIH Publication No. 83-525. S/N 017-044-00033-8. $2.25. **HE20.3252:As8/2**.

Discusses the causes, symptoms, and treatment of asthma.

926. **Drug Allergy**. National Institute of Allergy and Infectious Diseases. Rev. January 1982. 22p. NIH Publication No. 82-703. **HE20.3252:D84/982**.

Discusses the causes, symptoms, diagnosis, and treatment of drug allergy. Discusses which drug reactions are nonallergic, the major culprits, and the status of current research.

927. **Dust Allergy**. National Institute of Allergy and Infectious Diseases. Rev. November 1982. 12p. NIH Publication No. 83-490. S/N 017-044-00040-1. $21.00 per 100 copies. No single copies sold. **HE20.3252:D94/982**.

Discusses types of house dusts, and the causes and treatment of dust allergy including preventive measures.

928. **Insect Allergy**. National Institute of Allergy and Infectious Diseases. Rev. October 1981. 23p. NIH Publication No. 82-1046. **HE20.3252:In7/981**.

Discusses the causes, symptoms, diagnosis, and treatment of reactions to stinging insects.

929. **Mold Allergy**. National Institute of Allergy and Infectious Diseases. Rev. July 1983. 16p. NIH Publication No. 84-797. S/N 017-044-00042-7. $26.00 per 100 copies. No single copies sold. **HE20.3252:M73/983**.

Discusses the causes, symptoms, diagnosis, and treatment of allergic reactions to fungi and molds.

930. **Poison Ivy Allergy**. National Institute of Allergy and Infectious Diseases. Rev. March 1982. 16p. NIH Publication No. 82-697. S/N 017-044-00039-7. $2.00. **HE20.3252:P75/982**.

Discusses the causes, symptoms, treatment, and prevention of dermatitis due to allergy to poison ivy, poison oak, or poison sumac.

ALZHEIMER'S DISEASE

931. **Alzheimer's Disease**. Congress. House. Select Committee on Aging. January 1984. 65p. Committee Publication No. 98-402. **Y4.Ag4/2:Al9/2**.

Discusses the cause, diagnosis, and treatment of Alzheimer's disease. Discusses financing the treatment, and provides a guide to the families of victims.

932. **Progress Report on Alzheimer's Disease; Volume II**. National Institute on Aging. July 1984. 27p. ill. NIH Publication No. 84-2500. S/N 017-062-00133-2. $1.50. **HE20.3852:Al9/2/v.2**.

Provides an overview of the state of medical, psychosocial, and clinical research on Alzheimer's disease which is regarded as the major form of old age senility.

ARTHRITIS

933. **Arthritis: Medicine for the Layman**. National Institutes of Health. December 1982. 27p. ill. NIH Publication No. 83-1945. **HE20.3031:Ar7**.

Describes inflammation of the joints, and joint replacement surgery. Discusses treatment of gout, osteoarthritis, and rheumatoid arthritis. References.

934. **How to Cope with Arthritis**. National Institute of Arthritis, Diabetes, and Digestive and Kidney Diseases. Rev. October 1981. 19p. NIH Publication No. 82-1092. S/N 017-045-00100-4. $2.50. **HE20.3302:Ar7/2/981**.

Describes the different types of arthritis and how to cope with them.

BREAST CANCER

935. **After Breast Cancer: A Guide to Followup Care**. National Cancer Institute. March 1984. 11p. ill. NIH Publication No. 84-2400. **HE20.3158:B74/6**.
Provides helpful suggestions for taking care of oneself after breast cancer treatment; how to cope with emotional needs; what to expect during the follow-up examinations; and how to spot signs of reoccurrence.

936. **Breast Biopsy: What You Should Know**. National Cancer Institute. March 1984. 11p. ill. NIH Publication No. 84-657. **HE20.3152:B74/15**.
Discusses different types of breast biopsy as well as treatment for breast cancer. Glossary.

937. **The Breast Cancer Digest: A Guide to Medical Care, Emotional Support, Educational Programs, and Resources**. 2d ed. National Cancer Institute. April 1984. 212p. NIH Publication No. 84-1691. **HE20.3158:B74/2/984**.
This sourcebook provides a broad range of information on the causes, detection, diagnosis, and treatment of breast cancer; rehabilitation after surgery; breast reconstruction; coping by patients and family; educational programs; and resources and services. References. Index.

938. **Breast Cancer: Understanding Treatment Options**. National Cancer Institute. October 1984. 19p. ill. NIH Publication No. 84-2675. **HE20.3152:B74/14/corr**.
Discusses treatment options for breast cancer including various degrees of breast surgery and radiation therapy. Glossary. References.

939. **Breast Exams: What You Should Know**. National Cancer Institute. Rev. April 1985. 14p. ill. NIH Publication No. 85-2000. **HE20.3152:B74/7/985**.
Provides answers to questions about breast cancer screening methods, including medical history, X-ray, mammography, breast self-examination, and future technologies.

940. **Breast Reconstruction: A Matter of Choice**. National Cancer Institute. Rev. March 1984. 19p. ill. NIH Publication No. 84-2151. **HE20.3152:B74/9/984**.
Describes three common reconstructive surgery procedures, and provides practical information on making a decision on whether to have breast reconstruction after mastectomy. Glossary.

941. **Mastectomy: A Treatment for Breast Cancer**. National Cancer Institute. March 1984. 24p. ill. NIH Publication No. 84-658. **HE20.3152:M39**.
Designed to ease some of the mastectomy patient's fears by letting her know what to expect from the time of entering the hospital to recovery at home, and after. References.

942. **Questions and Answers about Breast Lumps**. National Cancer Institute. Rev. September 1983. 14p. ill. NIH Publication No. 83-2401. **HE20.3152:B74/12/983**.
Provides answers to some common questions about breast lumps as an indication of cancer. Includes instructions on breast self-examination.

943. **Radiation Therapy: A Treatment for Early State Breast Cancer**. National Cancer Institute. March 1984. 20p. ill. NIH Publication No. 84-659. **HE20.3152:R11/2**.
Describes the procedures used in radiation therapy and tells the patient what to expect from the beginning of treatment to recovery at home.

944. **What You Need to Know about Cancer of the Breast**. National Cancer Institute. Rev. 1984. 16p. ill. NIH Publication No. 84-1566. **HE20.3152:B74/6/984**.
Provides a brief explanation of the causes, diagnosis, and treatment of cancer of the breast.

CANCER

Single copies of many of the publications which are listed below and in the section above on breast cancer are available free from the National Institute of Cancer, Office of Cancer Communications, Bethesda, MD 20205.

945. **Advanced Cancer: Living Each Day**. National Cancer Institute. April 1985. 30p. ill. NIH Publication No. 85-856. **HE20.3152:Ad9/985**.
Intended to help make living with advanced cancer easier by providing practical information and addressing questions that are often asked by patients. References.

946. **Cancer Treatment: Medicine for the Layman**. National Institutes of Health. September 1979. 32p. ill. NIH Publication No. 80-1807. **HE20.3031:C16**.
Describes surgical, radiation, and chemical treatment of cancer. Discusses testing of new drugs, and how cancer drugs work.

947. **Cancer: What Is It? Medicine for the Layman**. National Institutes of Health. February 1980. 28p. ill. NIH Publication No. 80-1806. **HE20.3031:C16/2**.
Provides an overview of the nature of cancer, the terminology used in discussing it, its effects, its biology, and its causes.

948. **Cancer: What to Know; What to Do about It**. National Cancer Institute. Rev. April 1981. 25p. ill. NIH Publication No. 81-211. **HE20.3152:C16/2/981**.
Provides information about the causes, detection, and treatment of cancer. Glossary.

949. **Decade of Discovery: Advances in Cancer Research, 1971-1981**. National Cancer Institute. 1981. 74p. ill. NIH Publication No. 81-2323. S/N 017-042-00158-7. $5.50. **HE20.3152:D63/971-81**.
Presents highlights of advances in cancer research during the decade 1971-1981.

950. **Diet and Nutrition: A Resource for Parents of Children with Cancer**. National Cancer Institute. December 1979. 57p. ill. NIH Publication No. 80-2038. S/N 017-042-00148-0. $4.50. **HE20.3152:D56/3**.
Discusses the importance of nutrition, side effects of cancer and cancer treatment, and encouraging your child to eat. Includes menus for seven special diets. Glossary.

951. **Diet, Nutrition, and Cancer Prevention: A Guide to Food Choices**. National Cancer Institute. Rev. November 1984. 51p. ill. NIH Publication No. 85-2711. **HE20.3158:N95/984.**

It has been estimated that 35 percent of all cancers may be related to the way we eat. This guide describes what is known about diet, nutrition, and cancer prevention. Includes recommended menus.

952. **Early Detection of Oral Cancer May Save Your Live**. National Cancer Institute. 1978. folder, 5p. ill. NIH Publication No. 78-1814. **HE20.3152:D48.**

An illustrated guide to self-examination of the face, neck, lip, cheek, and mouth for early detection of oral cancer.

953. **Eating Hints: Recipes and Tips for Better Nutrition during Cancer Treatment**. National Cancer Institute. January 1980. 89p. ill. NIH Publication No. 80-2079. S/N 017-042-00154-4. $7.50. **HE20.3152:Ea8.**

Written to help cancer patients and their families and friends find ways to eat well and to enjoy eating, particularly at those times when cancer treatment or the disease itself causes problems. Includes recipes.

954. **Everything Doesn't Cause Cancer**. National Cancer Institute. Rev. February 1984. 16p. ill. **HE20.3152:C16/19/984.**

Discusses agents which cause cancer, how research identifies such agents and their effects, and ways to prevent cancer.

955. **Help Yourself: Tips for Teenagers with Cancer**. National Cancer Institute. September 1983. 36p. ill. **HE20.3152:T22.**

Provides advice for teenagers on how to cope with the effects of cancer based on the experiences of persons who had cancer as teenagers. References.

956. **Radiation Risks and Radiation Therapy: Medicine for the Layman**. National Institutes of Health. December 1982. 27p. ill. NIH Publication No. 83-2367. **HE20.3031:R11.**

Describes the types and medical applications of radiation. Discusses the measurement of radiation dose and the assessment of radiation risk.

957. **Radiation Therapy and You: A Guide to Self-Help during Treatment**. National Cancer Institute. August 1980. 32p. ill. NIH Publication No. 80-2227. **HE20.3158:R11.**

Intended to help the patient understand what radiation therapy is about, and to provide useful information on the possible side effects and what can be done about them. Glossary.

958. **Science and Cancer**. National Cancer Institute. Rev. 1980. 117p. ill., charts, tables. NIH Publication No. 80-568. **HE20.3152:Sci2/980.**

Describes the nature of cancer, its effects on the organism in which it resides, and efforts of scientists and physicians to learn more about it. Addressed primarily to informed readers outside the scientific community.

959. **State Legislated Actions Affecting Cancer Prevention: A Fifty State Profile**. National Cancer Institute. September 1984. 102p. NIH Publication No. 84-2686. **HE20.3152:St2.**

Indicates for each state the following legislation or programs if applicable: health education, dedicated tax on cigarettes, limitations on smoking, cancer registries, cancer research or control center, cancer screening procedures, control of carcinogens, and cancer insurance.

960. **Students with Cancer: A Resource for the Educator**. National Cancer Institute. Rev. May 1984. 23p. ill. NIH Publication No. 84-2086. **HE20.3152:C16/20/984**.
Provides a general explanation of cancer, its treatment, and effects; suggests approaches for dealing with the student, classmates, and parents; and includes guidelines for school reentry. References.

961. **Taking Time: Support for People with Cancer and the People Who Care about Them**. National Cancer Institute. September 1980. 70p. NIH Publication No. 80-2059. S/N 017-042-00152-8. $4.50. **HE20.3152:T48**.
Provides suggestions on handling relationships with the family and friends of cancer patients.

962. **What Black Americans Should Know about Cancer**. National Cancer Institute. Rev. April 1982. 28p. ill. NIH Publication No. 82-1635. **HE20.3152:B56/982**.
Provides general information on the causes, detection, and treatment of cancer and specific information related to the incidence of cancer among blacks.

963. **What You Need to Know about Adult Leukemia**. National Cancer Institute. Rev. April 1984. 20p. ill. NIH Publication No. 84-1572. **HE20.3152:L57/4/984**.
Provides information on the causes, detection, and treatment of adult leukemia.

964. **What You Need to Know about Childhood Leukemia**. National Cancer Institute. Rev. April 1984. 20p. ill. NIH Publication No. 84-1573. **HE20.3152: L57/5/984**.
Provides information on the causes, detection, and treatment of childhood leukemia.

965. **What You Need to Know about Cancer**. National Cancer Institute. 1979. 19p. ill. NIH Publication No. 79-1566. **HE20.3152:C16/4**.
Provides information about causes, detection, and treatment of cancer.

966. **What You Need to Know about Cancer(s) of the . . . .** National Cancer Institute.
The following booklets provide information about the causes, detection, and treatment of cancer in specific locations of the body.

966-1. **. . . Bladder**. Rev. March 1981. 18p. ill. NIH Publication No. 81-1559. **HE20.3152:B56/2/981**.

966-2. **. . . Bone**. 1979. 20p. ill. NIH Publication No. 79-1571. **HE20.3152: B64**.

966-3. **. . . Brain and Spinal Cord**. 1979. 18p. ill. NIH Publication No. 79-1558. **HE20.3152:B73**.

966-4. . . . **Colon and Rectum**. Rev. May 1984. 26p. ill. NIH Publication No. 84-1552. **HE20.3152:C71/2/984.**

966-5. . . . **Esophagus**. Rev. January 1980. 13p. ill. NIH Publication No. 80-1557. **HE20.3152:Es5/980.**

966-6. . . . **Kidney**. Rev. January 1981. 20p. ill. NIH Publication No. 81-1569. **HE20.3152:K54/981.**

966-7. . . . **Larynx**. Rev. October 1984. 16p. ill. NIH Publication No. 84-1568. **HE20.3152:L32/2/984.**

966-8. . . . **Lung**. Rev. April 1984. 19p. ill. NIH Publication No. 84-1553. **HE20.3152:L97/984.**

966-9. . . . **Mouth**. Rev. January 1980. 16p. ill. NIH Publication No. 80-1574. **HE20.3152:M86/2/980.**

966-10. . . . **Ovary**. 1979. 16p. NIH Publication No. 79-1561. **HE20.3152: Ov1.**

966-11. . . . **Pancreas**. 1979. 18p. ill. NIH Publication No. 79-1560. **HE20.3152:P19.**

966-12. . . . **Prostate and Other Male Genito-Urinary Organs**. January 1980. 17p. ill. NIH Publication No. 80-1576. **HE20.3152:P94/2.**

966-13. . . . **Skin**. Rev. June 1980. 14p. ill. NIH Publication No. 80-1564. **HE20.3152:Sk3/3/980.**

966-14. . . . **Stomach**. March 1985. 15p. ill. NIH Publication No. 85-1554. **HE20.3152:St6.**

966-15. . . . **Testis**. 1979. 16p. ill. NIH Publication No. 79-1565. **HE20.3152: T28.**

966-16. . . . **Uterus**. Rev. March 1980. 19p. ill. NIH Publication No. 80-1562. **HE20.3152:Ut2/2/980.**

967. **What You Need to Know about Dysplasia, Very Early Cancer and Invasive Cancer of the Cervix**. National Cancer Institute. Rev. July 1984. 15p. ill. NIH Publication No. 84-2047. **HE20.3152:D99/984.**

968. **What You Need to Know about Hodgkin's Disease**. National Cancer Institute. March 1985. 15p. ill. NIH Publication No. 85-1555. **HE20.3152:H66/2.**

969. **What You Need to Know about Melanoma**. National Cancer Institute. 1979. 14p. ill. NIH Publication No. 79-1653. **HE20.3152:M48.**

970. **What You Need to Know about Multiple Myeloma**. National Cancer Institute. Rev. May 1985. 15p. ill. NIH Publication No. 85-1575. **HE20.3152:M99/985.**

971. **What You Need to Know about Non-Hodgkin's Lymphoma**. National Cancer Institute. 1979. 16p. ill. NIH Publication No. 79-1567. **HE20.3152:L98.**

972. **What You Need to Know about Wilms' Tumor**. National Cancer Institute. Rev. May 1985. 20p. ill. NIH Publication No. 85-1570. **HE20.3152:W68/985**.
Wilms' Tumor is a form of kidney cancer in children.

973. **When Cancer Returns: Meeting the Challenge Again**. National Cancer Institute. October 1984. 34p. ill. NIH Publication No. 85-2709. **HE20.3152:M47**.
Discusses types of recurrent cancers and their treatment. Provides advice to patients on handling the situation. References.

974. **Young People with Cancer: A Handbook for Parents**. National Cancer Institute. April 1982. 100p. ill. NIH Publication No. 82-2378. **HE20.3158:Y8/2**.
Provides parents with information on the most common types of cancer, on treatment and its side effects, and on the common issues that arise when a child is diagnosed with cancer. References. Bibliography.

CARDIOVASCULAR DISEASES

975. **Exercise and Your Heart**. National Heart, Lung and Blood Institute. 1983. 43p. ill. NIH Publication No. 83-1677. **HE20.3202:Ex3**.
Topics include amount of exercise needed, benefits of exercise, the heart and exercise, risk factors, myths about exercise, keys to success, ways to avoid injuries, walking and jogging, and more.

976. **A Handbook of Heart Terms**. National Heart, Lung and Blood Institute. Rev. 1978. 58p. ill. NIH Publication No. 78-131. S/N 017-040-00428-1. $4.50. **HE20.3208: H35/978**.
This illustrated booklet is a layperson's dictionary and language guide to frequently used terms and phrases in the heart field.

977. **Heart Attacks: Medicine for the Layman**. National Institutes of Health. July 1979. 32p. ill. NIH Publication No. 79-1803. **HE20.3031:H35**.
Discusses the causes, symptoms, and effects of a heart attack; what to do and where to go for the help; life after a heart attack; treatment; and preventive measures.

978. **The Heart: Diagnosis and Treatment: Medicine for the Layman**. National Institutes of Health. November 1980. 27p. ill. NIH Publication No. 81-1809. **HE20.3031:H35/2**.
Describes the action of the heart and the causes of coronary artery diseases. Discusses diagnosis and treatment of heart disease.

979. **High Blood Pressure: Medicine for the Layman**. National Institutes of Health. 1979. 21p. ill. NIH Publication No. 79-1808. **HE20.3031:B62**.
Discusses blood pressure changes and measurement; blood pressure and life expectancy; causes and effects of hypertension; and drug therapy.

980. **How Doctors Diagnose Heart Disease**. National Heart, Lung and Blood Institute. 1978. 17p. ill. NIH Publication No. 78-753. S/N 017-043-00089-7. $3.00. **HE20.3202:H35/11**.

Intended to inform the public about the variety of procedures which physicians may follow in diagnosing possible heart disease. Describes warning signals of a heart attack.

981. **Protect Your Lifeline! Fight High Blood Pressure**. Veterans Administration. 1981. 24p. tables. S/N 051-000-00149-4. $2.00. **VA1.2:P94/3**.
Defines blood pressure and tells how it is measured. Describes the causes, effects, and symptoms of high blood pressure. Provides diet suggestions.

For additional publications on this topic see Subject Bibliography **SB-104, Heart and Circulatory System**.

DENTAL HEALTH

982. **Fluoride to Protect Your Children's Teeth**. National Institute of Dental Health. Rev. February 1981. folder, 6p. NIH Publication No. 81-1141. **HE20.3402:F67/3/981**.
Discusses the sources of fluoridation to protect teeth through water fluorination; fluoride tables, drugs, and dentifrices; and professional applications.

983. **Prepaid Dental Care: A Glossary**. Bureau of Health Professions. Rev. August 1980. 30p. DHHS Publication No. (HRA) 80-50. S/N 017-022-00705-3. $3.75. **HE20.6002:D43/3/980**.
This dictionary is divided into two parts: the first contains definitions of insurance terms, and the second dental terms.

984. **Tooth Decay**. National Institute of Dental Health. Rev. 1980. folder, 6p. NIH Publication No. 80-1146. **HE20.3402:T61/2/980**.
Discusses the cause and prevention of tooth decay.

See also entry 777.

DIABETES

985. **Cookbooks for People with Diabetes: Selected Annotations**. National Institute of Arthritis, Diabetes, and Digestive and Kidney Diseases. Rev. May 1981. 19p. NIH Publication No. 81-2177. **HE20.3316:C77/981**.
An annotated list of forty-four cookbooks that emphasize recipes for people with diabetes. Author and title indexes.

986. **Diabetes and Your Eyes**. National Eye Institute. Rev. June 1983. 16p. ill. NIH Publication No. 83-2171. **HE20.3002:D54/4/983**.
Describes how diabetes may cause eye disease and loss of vision. Discusses treatment and preventive measures. Glossary.

987. **Educational Materials for and about Young People with Diabetes**. National Diabetes Information Clearinghouse. Rev. September 1983. 90p. NIH Publication No. 83-1871. **HE20.3316:Ed8/983**.

This annotated bibliography of print and audiovisual materials for and about infants, children, and adolescents with diabetes is divided into two sections: one contains materials for the general public, the other for professionals. Author, title, and subject indexes.

988. **Facts about Insulin-dependent Diabetes**. National Institute of Arthritis, Metabolism, and Digestive Diseases. April 1980. 11p. NIH Publication No. 80-2098. S/N 017-045-00095-4. $2.50. **HE20.3302:In7**.
Discusses the causes, effects, and treatment of insulin-dependent diabetes, which is the most serious form of this disease.

989. **Feet First: A Booklet about Foot Care for Older People and People Who Have Diabetes**. Bureau of Health Professions. 1970 (repr. 1980). 45p. ill. DHEW Publication No. (HRA) 75-81. S/N 017-041-00011-8. $4.50. **HE20.3102:F32**.
Discusses why the feet of older people and those with diabetes need special care, and what should be done about it.

990. **How to Cope with Diabetes**. National Institute of Arthritis, Metabolism, and Digestive Diseases. 1977. 16p. NIH Publication No. 77-987. S/N 017-045-00082-2. $2.75. **HE20.3302:D54**.
Discusses the causes, symptoms, and treatment of diabetes.

991. **Understanding Diabetes Mellitus**. Veterans Administration. March 1981. 92p. ill. Information Bulletin 11-73. S/N 051-000-00152-4. $5.50. **VA1.22:11-73**.
Printed in large type, includes discussions of nutrition for diabetics, guidelines for administering insulin, daily care procedures, and chronic complications of diabetes. Glossary. References.

INFECTIOUS DISEASES

992. **Genital Herpes**. Centers for Disease Control. September 1983. 9p. NIH Publication No. 84-2005. S/N 017-044-00043-5. $21.00 per 100 copies. No single copies sold. **HE20.7302:G28**.
Provides answers to commonly asked questions about the causes, diagnosis, transmission, effects, and treatment of genital herpes.

993. **Immunology: Its Role in Disease and Health**. National Institute of Allergy and Infectious Diseases. Rev. April 1980. 168p. ill., charts, tables. NIH Publication No. 80-940. S/N 017-044-00035-4. $5.50. **HE20.3252:Im6/2/980**.
Evaluates present knowledge on immunology and its role in the cause, prevention, and treatment of disease. Intended for the general reader. Glossary.

994. **Rubella [German Measles]**. Bureau of Community Health Services. Rev. 1980. 14p. DHHS Publication No. (HSA) 80-5225. S/N 017-026-00093-3. $2.75. **HE20.5102: R82/980**.
Provides a brief explanation of the causes, symptoms, diagnosis, care, and prevention of rubella, commonly known as German measles.

995.   **Sexually Transmitted Diseases**. National Institute of Allergy and Infectious Diseases. June 1979. 24p. NIH Publication No. 79-909. S/N 017-044-00032-0. $3.50. **HE20.3252:Se9**.

   Discusses the causes, symptoms, and treatment of gonorrhea, syphilis, genital herpes, and other venereal diseases.

996.   **Tales of Shots and Drops for Parents of Young Children**. Administration for Children, Youth and Families. October 1979. 22p. ill., tables. DHHS Publication No. (OHDS) 79-31128. S/N 017-092-00058-8. $3.25. **HE23.1002:Sh8**.

   Describes immunization procedures which should be taken against the "big seven" childhood diseases: diptheria, whooping cough, lockjaw, polio, red or hard measles, mumps, and German measles.

997.   **Tuberculosis in the United States, 1980**. Centers for Disease Control. November 1983. 57p. charts, tables. DHHS Publication No. (CDC) 83-8322. **HE20.7310:980**.

   Issued annually. Contains statistical data and analysis of tuberculosis morbidity and mortality in the United States during the year. Includes historical and trend data back to 1970.

998.   **Understanding the Immune System**. National Institute of Allergy and Infectious Diseases. October 1983. 22p. ill. NIH Publication No. 84-529. S/N 017-044-00044-3. $1.50. **HE20.3252:Im6/5**.

   Describes the immune system in the human body and how it works. Glossary.

999.   **What You Should Know about Influenza and Flu Shots**. Centers for Disease Control. Rev. October 1984. 8p. ill. **HE20.7002:In3/3/984**.

   Discusses who should get flu shots, other methods of preventing flu, and treatment of the flu.

   See also entry 1526.

MENTAL HEALTH
AND MENTAL DISORDERS

1000.   **Depression and Manic-Depressive Illness**. National Institutes of Health. February 1982. 29p. ill. NIH Publication No. 82-1940. **HE20.3031:D44**.

   Discusses the incidence, causes, symptoms, and treatment of manic-depressive illnesses.

1001.   **Depressive Disorders: Causes and Treatment**. National Institute of Mental Health. 1981. 13p. DHHS Publication No. (ADM) 81-1081. S/N 017-024-01093-6. $2.00. **HE20.8102:D44/4**.

   Describes the types of depressive disorders, and their causes and treatment.

1002.   **Mental Health Directory, 1985**. National Institute of Mental Health. Rev. 1985. 364p. DHHS Publication No. (ADM) 85-1375. S/N 017-024-01230-1. $9.00. **HE20.8123:985**.

   Lists government, public, and private agencies and institutions whose primary objective is to provide mental health services and which are classified as psychiatric hospitals, outpatient clinics, residential treatment centers, partial care organizations, and halfway houses.

1003. **Mental Health, United States 1983**. National Institute of Mental Health. 1983. 158p. DHHS Publication No. (ADM) 83-1275. S/N 017-024-01168-1. $5.50. **HE20.8137:983**.

Provides statistical data on the number of patients, facilities, and staff in the nation's mental health services delivery system. References.

1004. **Schizophrenia: Is There an Answer?** National Institute of Mental Health. Rev. 1981. 20p. DHHS Publication No. (ADM) 81-74. **HE20.8102:Sch3/981**.

Describes the causes, symptoms, and treatment of schizophrenia and the status of current research.

1005. **You Are Not Alone: Facts about Mental Health and Mental Illness**. National Institute of Mental Health. 1981. 11p. DHHS Publication No. (ADM) 81-1178. S/N 017-024-01121-5. $2.25. **HE20.8102:Al7**.

Provides basic facts about mental health and mental illness.

For additional publications on this topic see Subject Bibliography **SB-167, Mental Health**.

NEUROLOGICAL AND COMMUNICATIVE DISORDERS AND STROKE

1006. **Amyotrophic Lateral Sclerosis (ALS), Lou Gehrig's Disease: Hope through Research**. National Institute of Neurological and Communicative Disorders and Stroke. Rev. 1984. 26p. NIH Publication No. 84-196. S/N 017-049-00131-0. $1.50. **HE20.3502: Am9/984**.

Describes the causes, symptoms, and treatment of ALS and the status of current research.

1007. **Aphasia: Hope through Research**. National Institute of Neurological and Communicative Disorders and Stroke. November 1979. 16p. ill. NIH Publication No. 80-391. S/N 017-049-00108-5. $2.75. **HE20.3502:Ap1**.

Describes the causes, symptoms, and treatment of aphasia, and outlines current research into prevention and treatment methods. Aphasia is the loss of ability to make sense of language.

1008. **Brain in Aging and Dementia: Medicine for the Layman**. National Institutes of Health. December 1983. 33p. ill., charts. NIH Publication No. 83-2625. **HE20.3031: B73/2**.

Describes brain anatomy and physiology, and the aging process of the brain. Discusses the causes, characteristics, and types of dementia and the population affected.

1009. **The Brain: Medicine for the Layman**. National Institutes of Health. July 1979. 20p. ill. NIH Publication No. 79-1813. **HE20.3031:B73**.

Discusses what the brain does, how it works, what may go wrong, and how doctors diagnose the problem.

1010. Brain Tumors: Hope through Research. National Institute of Neurological and Communicative Disorders and Stroke. December 1981. 24p. ill. NIH Publication No. 82-504. S/N 017-049-00125-5. $3.00. **HE20.3502:B73/4**.

Describes the causes, symptoms, and treatment of brain tumors, and outlines current research into prevention and treatment methods.

1011. Cerebral Palsy: Hope through Research. National Institute of Neurological and Communicative Disorders and Stroke. Rev. 1980. 24p. ill. NIH Publication No. 80-159. S/N 017-049-00117-4. $2.50. **HE20.3502:C33/2/980**.

Describes the causes, symptoms, and treatment of cerebral palsy and outlines current research into prevention and new treatment methods.

1012. Chronic Pain: Hope through Research. National Institute of Neurological and Communicative Disorders and Stroke. April 1982. 29p. ill. NIH Publication No. 82-2406. S/N 017-049-00127-1. $3.75. **HE20.3502:P16**.

Describes the causes, symptoms, and treatment of chronic pain, and outlines current research into prevention and new treatment methods.

1013. Dementias: Hope through Research. National Institute of Neurological and Communicative Disorders and Stroke. March 1981. 32p. ill. NIH Publication No. 81-2252. S/N 017-049-00119-1. $2.75. **HE20.3502:D39**.

Describes the causes, symptoms, and treatment of dementias, and outlines current research into prevention and new treatment methods.

1014. Epilepsy: Hope through Research. National Institute of Neurological and Communicative Disorders and Stroke. Rev. 1981. 28p. ill. NIH Publication No. 81-156. S/N 017-049-00121-2. $2.75. **HE20.3052:Ep4/981**.

Describes the causes, symptoms, and treatment of epilepsy, and outlines current research into improved prevention and treatment methods.

1015. Epilepsy: Medicine for the Layman. National Institutes of Health. June 1982. 24p. ill. NIH Publication No. 82-2369. **HE20.3031:Ep4**.

Discusses the function of the nerve cell and the causes of epilepsy. Describes partial and generalized seizures, and therapy for epilepsy.

1016. Handbook of Hearing Aid Measurement. Veterans Administration. March 1983. 361p. charts, tables. Information Bulletin IB 11-75. **VA1.22:11-75**.

Issued annually. Presents the results of the VA's programs for measuring and evaluating the performance characteristics of commercially available hearing aids for possible acquisition. Regular hearing aids and special hearing aids are evaluated in alternate years.

1017. Head Injury: Hope through Research. National Institute of Neurological and Communicative Disorders and Stroke. August 1984. 37p. ill. NIH Publication No. 84-2478. S/N 017-049-00130-1. $2.00. **HE20.3502:H34/3**.

Describes penetrating injuries and closed head injuries and their treatment. Discusses rehabilitation, coping with personality changes, regaining quality of life, and the impact on the family. Outlines current research to reduce damage and aid rehabilitation.

1018. **Headache: Hope through Research**. National Institute of Neurological and Communicative Disorders and Stroke. 1984. 36p. ill. NIH Publication No. 84-158. S/N 017-049-00132-8. **HE20.3502:H34/4.**

Describes diagnosis of headaches and improved methods of treatment.

1019. **Hearing Loss: Hope through Research**. National Institute of Neurological and Communicative Disorders and Stroke. Rev. January 1982. 36p. ill. NIH Publication No. 82-157. S/N 017-049-00126-3. $4.25. **HE20.3502:H35/2/982.**

Discusses how we hear, causes of hearing loss, treatment and programs to help, and the state of current research.

1020. **Huntington's Disease: Hope through Research**. National Institute of Neurological and Communicative Disorders and Stroke. Rev. October 1979. 28p. ill. NIH Publication No. 80-49. **HE20.3502:H92/979.**

Discusses the causes, symptoms, and treatment of Huntington's disease, and outlines current research into improved prevention and treatment methods.

1021. **Learning Disabilities due to Minimal Brain Dysfunction: Hope through Research**. National Institute of Neurological and Communicative Disorders and Stroke. 1977. 22p. ill. NIH Publication No. 77-154. S/N 017-002-00129-1. $2.50. **HE20.3502:L47.**

Describes the causes, symptoms, and treatment of minimal brain dysfunction in children and the status of current research.

1022. **Learning to Talk: Speech, Hearing, and Language Problems in the Pre-School Child**. National Institute of Neurological and Communicative Disorders and Stroke. Rev. 1977. 48p. ill. NIH Publication No. 77-43. S/N 017-049-00082-8. $4.50. **HE20.3502:T14/977.**

Discusses the physiology of speech and hearing; reviews learning patterns; and describes common speech, hearing, and language problems as they are manifested in preschool children.

1023. **Multiple Sclerosis: Hope through Research**. National Institute of Neurological and Communicative Disorders and Stroke. 1979. 17p. ill., map. NIH Publication No. 79-75. S/N 017-049-00101-8. $2.50. **HE20.3502:M91/2.**

Discusses the causes, symptoms, and treatment of multiple sclerosis (MS) as well as the status of current research.

1024. **National Survey of Stroke**. National Institute of Neurological and Communicative Disorders and Stroke. January 1980. 14p. ill., charts, tables. NIH Publication No. 80-2069. **HE20.3502:St8/3.**

Presents summary results of a survey of patients who were hospitalized for stroke during the years 1971, 1973, 1975, and 1976.

1025. **Parkinson's Disease: Hope through Research**. National Institute of Neurological and Communicative Disorders and Stroke. Rev. June 1983. 27p. ill. NIH Publication No. 83-139. **HE20.3502:P22/2/983.**

Describes the causes, symptoms, and treatment of Parkinson's disease, and outlines current research into prevention and new treatment methods.

1026. **Shingles: Hope through Research**. National Institute of Neurological and Communicative Disorders and Stroke. Rev. November 1981. 16p. ill. NIH Publication No. 82-307. S/N 017-049-00124-7. $3.00. **HE20.3502:Sh6/981**.

Discusses the disease chickenpox and the second attack later in life by the same virus causing the same disease. Describes the causes, symptoms, and treatment of shingles, and the status of current research.

1027. **Spinal Cord Injury: Hope through Research**. National Institute of Neurological and Communicative Disorders and Stroke. February 1981. 32p. ill. NIH Publication No. 81-160. **HE20.3502:Sp4/4**.

Discusses the causes, symptoms, and treatment of spinal cord injury, and the status of current research.

1028. **Stroke: Hope through Research**. National Institute of Neurological and Communicative Disorders and Stroke. August 1983. 32p. ill. NIH Publication No. 83-2222. S/N 017-049-00129-8. $1.75. **HE20.3502:St8/4**.

Describes the causes, symptoms, and treatment of stroke and outlines current research into prevention and new treatment methods.

1029. **Stuttering: Hope through Research**. National Institute of Neurological and Communicative Disorders and Stroke. May 1981. 17p. ill. NIH Publication No. 81-2250. S/N 017-049-00120-4. $2.25. **HE20.2:St9**.

Discusses theories as to why stuttering occurs since no scientific explanation has been found. Describes improved methods of therapy and the status of current research.

1030. **What You Should Know about Stroke and Stroke Prevention**. National Institute of Neurological and Communicative Disorders and Stroke. June 1979 (repr. 1981). 10p. NIH Publication No. 81-1909. S/N 017-049-00107-7. $2.00. **HE20.3502:St8/2**.

Discusses the causes, symptoms, prevention, and treatment of stroke.

See also entry 78.

MISCELLANEOUS HEALTH AND MEDICAL PROBLEMS

1031. **About Sleep, As You Grow Older**. Alcohol, Drug Abuse and Mental Health Administration. 1981. 5p. DHHS Publication No. (ADM) 81-1110. **HE20.8002:Sl2**.

Provides answers to questions frequently asked about sleep.

1032. **Are Routine Chest X-Rays Really Necessary?** Center for Devices and Radiological Health. 1984. folder, 6p. DHHS Publication No. (FDA) 84-8205. **HE20.4602:C42**.

Provides a brief summary of the findings of a panel of experts who conclude that chest x-rays should be given only to persons who have symptoms of possible chest disease or are at high risk of developing chest disease. Includes x-ray record card to record x-ray examinations.

1033. **Blood Transfusions, Benefits and Risks: Medicine for the Layman**. National Institutes of Health. January 1981. 32p. ill. NIH Publication No. 81-1949. **HE20.3031: B62/2**.

Describes human blood and its components and groups. Discusses risks and benefits of blood transfusions.

1034. **Chronic Obstructive Pulmonary Disease**. National Heart, Lung and Blood Institute. August 1981. 13p. NIH Publication No. 81-2020. S/N 017-043-00106-1. $2.50. **HE20.3202:P96/5**.

Discusses the causes, symptoms, diagnosis, treatment, and prevention of chronic obstructive pulmonary disease.

1035. **Crib Death: Sudden Infant Death Syndrome**. Bureau of Community Health Services. 1981. 20p. ill. DHHS Publication No. (HSA) 81-5262. S/N 017-026-00097-6. $3.00. **HE20.5102:C86**.

Offers suggestions to parents on how to handle emotions and misunderstandings regarding sudden infant death syndrome in their child.

1036. **Facts about Anorexia Nervosa**. National Institute of Child Health and Human Development. 1983. folder, 8p. **HE20.3352:An3**.

Discusses the causes, symptoms, and treatment of anorexia nervosa, a disorder of self-starvation.

1037. **Facts about Down Syndrome**. National Institute of Child Health and Human Development. 1984. 16p. **HE20.3352:D75/3**.

Discusses the causes and effects of down syndrome, a genetic birth defect associated with mental retardation.

1038. **Facts about Peptic Ulcer**. National Institute of Arthritis, Metabolism and Digestive Diseases. Rev. 1978. 16p. ill. NIH Publication No. 79-38. **HE20.3302: Ul1/978**.

Discusses the causes, symptoms, treatment, and complications of peptic ulcer.

1039. **Facts about Sudden Infant Death Syndrome**. Bureau of Community Health Services. 1978. 11p. S/N 017-026-00067-4. $2.25. **HE20.5102:In3/10**.

Provides answers to frequently asked questions about sudden infant death syndrome.

1040. **Learning Together: A Guide for Families with Genetic Disorders**. Bureau of Community Health Services. 1980. 21p. DHHS Publication No. (HSA) 80-5131. S/N 017-026-00088-7. $3.50. **HE20.5102:L47**.

Provides information on organizing a group of parents with children that have genetic disorders. Suggests activities for the group and lists national organizations that may help.

1041. **The Lungs: Medicine for the Layman**. National Institutes of Health. July 1979. 23p. ill. NIH Publication No. 79-1802. **HE20.3031:L97**.

Discusses how the lungs function, how they protect us, and how the doctor evaluates your lungs. Describes industrial and nonindustrial causes of lung disease.

1042. **Myths and Facts about Sleep**. Alcohol, Drug Abuse, and Mental Health Administration. 1981. 10p. DHHS Publication No. (ADM) 81-1108. **HE20.8002:Sl2/2**. Provides facts about sleep to dispel common myths.

1043. **Obesity and Energy Metabolism: Medicine for the Layman**. National Institutes of Health. September 1979. 23p. ill. NIH Publication No. 79-1805. **HE20.3031:Ob2**. Discusses the causes and health consequences of obesity and its relation to energy metabolism.

1044. **Prevention and Treatment of Kidney Stones**. National Institute of Arthritis, Diabetes, and Digestive and Kidney Diseases. August 1983. 15p. NIH Publication No. 83-2495. S/N 017-053-00078-7. $24.00 per 100 copies. No single copies sold. **HE20.3302:K54/2**. Discusses the causes, symptoms, diagnosis, and treatment of kidney stones.

1045. **Understanding Paget's Disease**. National Institute of Arthritis, Diabetes, and Digestive and Kidney Diseases. April 1985. 11p. NIH Publication No. 85-2241. **HE20.3302:P14/985**. Discusses the causes, symptoms, and treatment of Paget's disease which is a chronic disease of the skeleton that occurs most frequently in persons over fifty years of age.

See also entries 363, 472, 1383.

See also "Birth Control" (entries 216-230), "First Aid and Emergency Treatment" (entries 734-738), "Handicapped" (entries 887-908), and "Handicapped Children" (entries 381-384).

MEDICARE AND MEDICAL INSURANCE

1046. **CHAMPUS Handbook**. American Forces Information Service. January 1983. 89p. CHAMPUS 6010.46-H. **D2.8:C35**. Provides basic information on CHAMPUS (Civilian Health and Medical Program of the Uniformed Services) which is a medical insurance program for families of active duty, retired, and deceased members, and for retirees.

1047. **Guide to Health Insurance for People with Medicare**. Health Care Financing Administration. Rev. January 1985. 19p. tables. HCFA Publication No. 02110. S/N 017-060-00171-2. $29.00 per 100 copies. No single copies sold. **HE22.8:H34/985**. Discusses what Medicare pays for and doesn't pay for, and provides hints on shopping for supplementary private insurance.

1048. **The Medicare and Medicaid Data Book, 1983**. Health Care Financing Administration. December 1983. 161p. charts, tables. HCFA Publication No. 03156. S/N 017-070-00399-1. $4.75. **HE22.19/4-2:D26/983**. Provides a brief overview of the Medicare and Medicaid programs, discusses trends in the evolution of the programs, describes program characteristics, and provides detailed data on the programs.

1049. **Medicare and the Health Costs of Older Americans: The Extent and Effects of Cost Sharing**. Congress. Senate. Special Committee on Aging. April 1984. 47p. charts, tables. Committee Print, 98th Congress, 2d Session. S/N 052-070-05916-8. $2.00. **Y4.Ag4:S.prt.98-166**.

Provides data on Medicare coverage and the extent and effect of cost sharing of medical expenses by the aged. Footnote references.

1050. **Medicare: Benefits and Financing; Report of the 1982 Advisory Council on Social Security**. March 1984. 310p. charts, tables. S/N 017-060-00153-4. $9.50. **Y3.Ad9/3:2R29/982**.

Section 706 of the Social Security Act requires the appointment of an Advisory Council on Social Security every four years. This council appointed in September 1982 was directed to review the complex financial structure of the Medicare program.

1051. **Your Medicare Handbook**. Health Care Financing Administration. Rev. April 1985. 72p. HCFA Publication No. 10050. S/N 017-060-00172-1. $1.75. **HE22.8:M46/4/985**.

Provides information on the hospital and medical insurance benefits available under the Medicare program.

History and Biography

GENERAL

1052. Adams National Historic Site: A Family's Legacy to America. National Park Service. 1983. 75p. ill., maps. S/N 024-005-00821-7. $6.00. **I29.2:Ad1**.

This guidebook provides background on the Adams family's homestead in Quincy, Massachusetts, whose first occupant was John Adams, the nation's second President. It also describes the distinctive porcelain in the house, and its eighteenth-century garden.

1053. Boundary Markers of the Nation's Capital: A Proposal for Their Preservation and Protection. National Capital Planning Commission. 1976. 45p. ill., maps, tables. S/N 034-000-00008-5. $4.75. **NC2.2:B66/corr**.

Contains detailed street maps showing the location of the forty stone markers, each of them one mile apart to mark the original boundary of the District of Columbia in Maryland and Virginia. Describes their present condition, and presents a proposal for their preservation.

1054. Frederick Douglass: The Clarion Voice. National Park Service. 1976. 76p. ill. S/N 024-005-00656-7. $4.75. **I29.2:D74**.

Provides a biography of Frederick Douglass (1818-1895), the noted black leader — once a slave — abolitionist, editor, reformer, and politician.

1055. Historic America: Buildings, Structures, Sites. Library of Congress. 1983. 734p. ill., tables. S/N 030-000-00149-4. $29.00, cloth. **LC1.2:H62/5**.

Commemorates the fiftieth anniversary of the Historic American Buildings Survey. Part 1 contains sixteen essays on the origins and work of the survey. Part 2 is a comprehensive list of the buildings and sites recorded in the *Historic American Buildings Survey* and the *Historic American Engineering Record*. Index.

1056. **National Park Service Guide to the Historic Places of the American Revolution**. 1974. 135p. ill., maps. S/N 024-005-00517-0. $6.50. **I29.9/2:Am3/975**.

Describes national, state, and local historic sites related to the American Revolution located in eighteen eastern states. Includes chronology of political and military events of the American Revolution.

1057. **National Register of Historic Places**. 2 vols. National Park Service. vol. 1. 1976. 961p. ill. S/N 024-005-00645-1. $22.00, cloth. vol. 2. 1979. 638p. ill. S/N 024-005-00747-4. $19.00, cloth. **I29.76:976/v.1,2**.

Volume 1 contains descriptions of all properties listed in the *National Register of Historic Places*. through 1974. Volume 2 contains descriptions of additions during 1975 and 1976.

1058. **The Old Executive Office Building: A Victorian Masterpiece**. Executive Office of the President. 1984. 59p. ill., map. S/N 040-000-00479-3. $3.50. **PrEx1.2:Ol1**.

Provides historical background and a description of the Old Executive Office Building, located adjacent to the White House which was completed in 1888. It was originally known as the State, War, and Navy Building since it served as offices for those cabinet departments until the 1940s. References. Bibliography.

1059. **Revolutionary America, 1763-1789: A Bibliography**. 2 vols. Library of Congress. 1984. 1752p. S/N 030-000-00125-7. $38.00(set), cloth. **LC1.12/2:R32/4/763-89/ v.1,2**.

This bibliography is a guide to the more important printed primary and secondary works on the American Revolution in the collections of the Library of Congress. The nearly fifteen thousand entries are arranged in twelve topical-chronological chapters. Index.

1060. **Signers of the Constitution: Historic Places Commemorating the Signing of the Constitution**. National Park Service. 1976. 355p. ill., maps. National Survey of Historic Sites and Buildings, vol. 19. S/N 024-005-00649-4. $13.00, cloth. **I29.2:H62/9/v.19**.

Tells the story of the Constitution, recounts the lives of the men who conceived it, and describes the sites and buildings commemorating them. References.

See also entries 433, 550, 554, 707, 709-6, 1148, 1520.

NATIONAL PARK SERVICE HISTORICAL HANDBOOKS

The National Park Service publishes visitors' guides to the national parks and other historical or recreational sites which it administers. These folders provide brief background information on the historical events or persons associated with the site, a description of the site, and suggestions for visiting or using the site. These folders are available at the site, usually at the visitors' center, and are free. They are not listed in this book. In addition to these visitors' guides, the National Park Service has published handbooks on selected sites of historic events or on persons which provide more detailed information on the events and persons associated with the site. The first series of these detailed guides were called Historical Handbooks. They were replaced in the late 1970s by the Handbook series, printed on glossy paper and illustrated with color photographs, maps, sketches, and reproductions unlike the earlier Historical Handbooks, which were black and white.

1061.**National Park Service Handbook Series**. National Park Service. ill., maps. References. Index. **I29.9/5:no**.

1061-1. No. 103. **Framing of the Federal Constitution**. 1979 (repr. 1984). 111p. S/N 024-005-00740-7. $6.00.
Describes the events at the Federal Constitutional Convention held in Philadelphia in the summer of 1789 at which the Constitution of the United States was developed. References.

1061-2. No. 104. **Wind Cave National Park, South Dakota**. 1979. 143p. o.p.
Discusses the history of the early explorations of this cave in the Black Hills of South Dakota. Describes the animal and plant life in the park. Provides a travel guide for park visitors.

1061-3. No. 105. **Overland Migrations: Settlers to Oregon, California, and Utah**. 1980. 111p. S/N 024 005 00772 5. $110.50 per 50 copies. No single copies sold.
Discusses the overland migration of the pioneers in the mid-nineteenth century along the Mormon, Oregon, and California trails. Provides a travel guide to historic sites and parks along the trails.

1061-4. No. 106. **Assateague Island, National Seashore, Maryland and Virginia**. 1980. 175p. S/N 024-005-00776-8. $6.00.
Discusses the natural history of the barrier island and the Chincoteague National Wildlife Refuge Center and the behavior of the wild ponies found there. Provides a travel guide to attractions in the park and local areas.

1061-5. No. 107. **Agate Fossil Beds National Monument, Nebraska**. 1981. 95p. S/N 024-005-00785-7. $6.00.
Discusses prehistoric animal and plant life in this area of western Nebraska. Describes the geological and ecological evidence of the park's past and present. Provides a travel guide to the site, and to other National Park Service areas with fossil exhibits.

1061-6. No. 108. **Petrified Forests of Yellowstone: Yellowstone National Park, Wyoming, Montana, and Idaho**. 1980. 31p. S/N 024-005-00786-5. $3.75.
Describes the geological formation of the petrified forests in Yellowstone National Park.

1061-7. No. 109. **Appomattox Court House, National Historical Park, Virginia**. 1980. 111p. S/N 024-005-00778-4. $6.00.
Describes the retreat of General Robert E. Lee and the Army of Northern Virginia from the Petersburg area on 2 April, resulting in the Confederate surrender at Appomattox Court House on 9 April 1865. Provides travel guide to the site.

1061-8. No. 110. **Clara Barton National Historic Site, Maryland**. 1981. 80p. S/N 024-005-00806-3. $5.50.

Provides a chronology of Clara Barton and her times, and a biographical essay on this humanitarian and women's rights advocate who founded the American Red Cross. Provides a travel guide to the site in Glen Echo, Maryland.

1061-9. No. 111. **Devils Tower National Monument, Wyoming**. 1981. 80p. S/N 024-005-00899-3. $3.50.

Discusses the geological and natural history of Devil's Tower. Describes the animal life of the area, especially that of the protected prairie dog communities. Provides advice on climbing the tower.

1061-10. No. 112. **Great Smoky Mountains National Park, North Carolina and Tennessee**. 1981. 128p. S/N 024-005-00815-2. $6.50.

Describes the plants, animals, and peoples of the Great Smoky Mountains. Provides a travel guide for park visitors.

1061-11. No. 113. **Fort Vancouver National Historic Site, Washington**. 1982. 144p. S/N 024-005-00806-1. $7.00.

Part 1 introduces the fort, a fur trading post in southwest Washington during the nineteenth century. Part 2 tell the area's history with a focus on the major personalities of the time. Part 3 is a travel guide to the site, and nearby attractions.

1061-12. No. 114. **Benjamin Franklin's "Good House": The Story of Franklin Court, Independence National Historical Park, Philadelphia, Pennsylvania**. 1981. 64p. S/N 024-005-00907-8. $3.25.

Tells the story of the only house that Benjamin Franklin ever owned, and of his family who lived there during his prolonged absences abroad. Describes its destruction, and the memorial raised on the original site.

1061-13. No. 115. **Independence: A Guide to Independence National Park, Philadelphia, Pennsylvania**. 1982. 64p. S/N 024-005-00913-2. $3.00.

Discusses historical events and life in colonial Philadelphia. Describes the historic structures and sites within Independence National Park, Philadelphia.

1061-14. No. 116. **Exploring the American West, 1803-1879**. 1982. 128p. S/N 024-005-00834-9. $6.50.

Discusses the contribution of early explorers, mountain men, and scientists to the exploration and settlement of the lands west of the Mississippi River, 1803-1879.

1061-15. No. 117. **Carl Sandburg Home National Historic Site, North Carolina**. 1982. 128p. S/N 024-005-00835-7. $6.50.

Provides a biographical essay on Carl Sandburg and his work. Provides tourist information and a guide for visitors to the site.

1061-16. No. 118. **Fort Laramie National Historic Site, Wyoming**. 1983. 160p. S/N 024-005-00900-1. $4.75.

Describes the role which successive forts at this site played in the changing frontier on centers of trade, diplomacy, and warfare in the northern plains.

1061-17. No. 119. **Big Bend National Park, Texas.** 1983. 128p. S/N 024-005-00908-6. $5.50.

Provides a natural history of Big Bend country in west Texas which features the Rio Grande River and its canyons, the Chisos Mountains, and the Chihuahuan Desert. Provides a travel guide to attractions in the area.

1061-18. No. 120. **Morristown: A History and Guide, Morristown National Historical Park, New Jersey.** 1983. 112p. S/N 024-005-00905-1. $4.50.

Describes the winter encampments of the Continental Army at Morristown in 1777, and 1779-1780. Provides a guide to historic sites in the park.

1061-19. No. 121. **Nez Perce Country: A Handbook for Nez Perce National Historical Park, Utah.** 1983. 224p. S/N 024-005-00906-0. $6.50.

Tells the history of the Nez Perce Indians and their interactions with traders, trappers, missionaries, settlers, and soldiers. Provides general advice to tourists and a guide to historic sites in the park.

1061-20. No. 122. **Grand Teton: A Guide to Grand Teton National Park, Wyoming.** 1984. 96p. S/N 024-005-00903-5. $2.75.

Outlines the natural history, geology, and history of the mountains, valleys, and rivers which are part of Grand Teton National Park. Provides a concise travel guide to the park.

1061-21. No. 123. **Glacier Bay: A Guide to Glacier Bay National Park and Preserve, Alaska.** 1983. 128p. S/N 024-005-00901-9. $4.50.

Discusses the dynamics of tidewater glaciers and the natural history of both bay and landscape at Glacier Bay. Provides a travel guide to the park and preserve.

1061-22. No. 124. **Hopewell Furnace: A Guide to Hopewell Village National Historic Site, Pennsylvania.** 1983. 96p. S/N 024-005-00904-3. $2.75.

Presents an overview of the ironmaking industry during colonial times. Recounts the history of Hopewell's operations from 1771 to 1883 when the last furnace was shut down. Provides a guide to the main points of interest in the historic village.

1061-23. No. 125. **At Home in the Smokies: A Historical Handbook for Great Smoky Mountains National Park, North Carolina and Tennessee.** 1984. 159p. S/N 024-005-00902-7. $6.00.

Provides a brief introduction to the park and its historic sites. Presents a history of the region and its peoples from the early Cherokee Indian days to the establishment of the park in 1934.

1061-24. No. 127. **Fort Sumter, Anvil of War: Fort Sumter National Monument, South Carolina.** 1984. 63p. S/N 024-005-00909-1. $3.00.

Describes the military operations at Fort Sumter in April 1861 and during the struggle for Charleston, 1863-1865. Describes the fort today, and provides a tourist guide to it and to nearby historic sites.

1062.　**National Park Service Historical Handbook Series.** ill., maps. References.
I29.58:no.

    1062-1.　No. 1.　**Custer Battlefield National Monument, Montana.** Rev. 1969
(repr. 1978). 94p. S/N 024-005-00160-3. $165.00 per 100 copies. No single copies
sold. **I21.58:1/3.**
    Provides an interpretation of Custer's expedition against American Indians
in 1876, the battle of the Little Big Horn including American Indian accounts,
and a photographic essay.

    1062-2.　No. 3.　**Ford's Theatre and the House Where Lincoln Died.** Rev. 1969
(repr. 1977). 43p. S/N 024-005-00895-1. $2.50. **I29.58:3/4.**
    Relates the story of the assassination and death of President Abraham
Lincoln in April 1865, as well as the story of his life. Includes material on the
restored theater and museum, and the house across the street where Lincoln
died.

    1062-3.　No. 5.　**Fort McHenry National Monument and Historic Shrine,
Maryland.** 1954 (repr. 1975). 38p. S/N 024-005-00191-3. $4.25. **I29.58:5.**
    Relates the history of Fort McHenry, Baltimore, Maryland, including the
bombardment of the fort in September 1814 which inspired Francis Scott Key to
write the "Star Spangled Banner."

    1062-4.　No. 6.　**Custis-Lee Mansion, Robert E. Lee Memorial, Virginia.** Rev.
1962 (repr. 1973). 48p. S/N 024-005-00192-1. $4.25. **I29.58:6/3.**
    Relates the story of the Custis-Lee Mansion, a national memorial to one of
America's greatest men, Robert E. Lee, and the lives of the families of George
Washington Park Custis and General Lee who lived there.

    1062-5.　No. 8.　**Hopewell Village Historic Site, Pennsylvania.** Rev. 1954. 44p.
S/N 024-005-00195-6. $4.50. **I29.58:8/3.**
    Hopewell Village, which was abandoned in the late nineteenth century after
a century of activity provides an authentic display of social, cultural, and
economic environment of life in an ironmaking community of colonial and early
America.

    1062-6.　No. 9.　**Gettysburg National Military Park, Pennsylvania.** Rev. 1962
(repr. 1977). 64p. S/N 024-005-00196-4. $4.50. **I29.58:9/2.**
    Relates the story of the campaign and battle of Gettysburg, 1-3 July 1863,
one of the great decisive battles in American history. Also includes the story of
the establishment and dedication of the national cemetery on 19 November 1863.

    1062-7.　No. 10.　**Shiloh National Military Park, Tennessee.** 1955 (repr. 1981).
47p. S/N 024-005-00161-1. $4.50. **I29.58:10.**
    Describes the preliminary campaign, the first and second day of the battle,
6-7 April 1862 and the results of the battle of Shiloh.

    1062-8.　No. 12.　**Fort Sumter National Monument, South Carolina.** Rev. 1962
(repr. 1979). 47p. S/N 024-005-00163-8. $4.50. **I29.58:12/2.**
    Describes in detail the construction of Fort Sumter, and the events leading
to the firing of the "first shot" of the Civil War in 1861.

1062-9.　No. 15.　**Manassas (Bull Run) National Battlefield Park, Virginia.**
Rev. 1957 (repr. 1977). 48p. S/N 024-005-00227-8. $4.50. **I29.58:15/2**.
Relates the history of two of the more famous battles of the Civil War: the
opening engagement, 21 July 1861 and the second battle fought approximately
one year later paving the way for General Lee's first invasion of the North.

1062-10.　No. 18.　**Fort Pulaski National Monument, Georgia.** 1954 (repr.
1984). 55p. S/N 024-005-00890-0. $2.25. **I29.58:18**.
Relates the history of the Civil War battles around Fort Pulaski, near
Savannah, Georgia.

1062-11.　No. 20.　**Fort Laramie National Monument, Wyoming.** 1954 (repr.
1976). 43p. S/N 024-005-00171-9. $4.25. **I29.58:20**.
Relates the history of Fort Laramie, site of a fur trading post and the
principal military post guarding the covered wagon trails to Oregon, Utah, and
California from 1834-1890. Provides a brief description of historic points
nearby.

1062-12.　No. 21.　**Vicksburg National Military Park, Tennessee.** 1954 (repr.
1982). 60p. S/N 024-005-00228-6. $4.50. **I29.58:21**.
Relates the history of the campaign and seige of Vicksburg, the last
Confederate stronghold on the Mississippi River in June 1863. Describes the
principal points of interest in the park.

1062-13.　No. 23.　**Bandelier National Monument, New Mexico.** 1955 (repr.
1975). 44p. S/N 024-005-00173-5. $4.25. **I29.58:23**.
Discusses the life of the early American Indians who lived in this area from
approximately 1200-1500 A.D. Describes the principal ruins and sites in the park
area.

1062-14.　No. 24.　**Ocmulgee National Monument, Georgia.** 1956 (repr. 1976).
58p. S/N 024-005-00174-3. $4.50. **I29.58:24**.
Tells the story of the life and culture of the early American Indians as told
from the excavation of the mounds on the site which is preserved as the
Ocumulgee National Monument.

1062-15.　No. 25.　**Chickamauga and Chattanooga Battlefields, Chickamauga
and Chattanooga National Military Park, Georgia-Tennessee.** 1956 (repr. 1979).
60p. S/N 024-005-00229-4. $4.50. **I29.58:25**.
Describes the Civil War battle of Chickamauga in September 1863, and the
seige of Chattanooga in November 1863.

1062-16.　No. 26.　**George Washington Birthplace National Monument,
Virginia.** 1956 (repr. 1975). 44p. S/N 024-005-00175-1. $4.25. **I29.58:26**.
Tells the story of the Washington family, the Memorial Mansion, and the
Washington family burial ground located in Westmoreland County, Virginia.

1062-17.　No. 27.　**Montezuma National Monument, Arizona.** 1958 (repr.
1980). 40p. S/N 024-005-00176-0. $4.25. **I29.58:27**.

Describes and illustrates the ruins of pueblos in and around Montezuma Castle, Arizona. Describes the culture, history, and trade relations of the native American tribes who settled here.

1062-18. No. 28. **Scotts Bluff National Monument, Nebraska.** 1958. 64p. S/N 024-005-00891-8. $2.25. **I29.58:28.**

Discusses the activities of nineteenth century traders, missionaries, gold rush miners, cowboys, the pony express, and early railroads in the settlement of the Great Plains, and the American West. Describes the natural history of Scotts Bluff which was a landmark along the Oregon Trail.

1062-19. No. 29. **Chalmette National Historical Park, Louisiana.** 1958 (repr. 1975). 55p. S/N 024-005-00178-6. $4.50. **I29.58:29.**

Describes the people and events in Louisiana that played important roles in the period during the War of 1812 and the decisive battle of New Orleans in 1815 against the British.

1062-20. No. 30. **Guilford Courthouse National Military Park, North Carolina.** 1959 (repr. 1975). 40p. S/N 024-005-00179-4. $4.25. **I29.58:30.**

Describes the battle of Guilford Courthouse fought 15 March 1781, which marked the beginning of the end of the Revolutionary War. Also describes the campaign leading up to the battle, and the campaign after the battle.

1062-21. No. 31. **Antietam National Battlefield Site, Maryland.** Rev. 1961 (repr. 1984). 60p. S/N 024-005-00892-6. $2.25. **I29.58:31/2.**

Describes Lee's invasion of Maryland in 1862 which ended in the bloody battle at Antietam Creek, Sharpsburg, Maryland, in September 1862.

1062-22. No. 32. **Vanderbilt Mansion National Historic Site, New York.** 1960 (repr. 1977). 52p. S/N 024-005-00181-6. $4.50. **I29.58:32.**

Presents the history of the mansion and the Vanderbilt family, with a detailed, illustrated description of the mansion and its grounds.

1062-23. No. 33. **Richmond National Battlefield Park, Virginia.** 1961 (repr. 1979). 52p. S/N 024-005-00182-4. $4.25. **I29.58:33.**

Describes the major events and battles in the Richmond area during McClellan's Peninsular Campaign in the summer of 1862, and during the final year of the Civil War, 1864-1865, after Grant assumed command of the Union Armies.

1062-24. No. 34. **Wright Brothers National Monument, North Carolina.** 1961 (repr. 1976). 64p. S/N 024-005-00183-2. $82.00 per 100 copies. No single copies sold. **I29.58:34.**

Describes the Wright brothers' experiments at Dayton, Ohio, and Kitty Hawk, North Carolina, which resulted in the first manned flight of an airplane in 1903.

1062-25. No. 35. **Fort Union National Monument, New Mexico.** 1962 (repr. 1984). 72p. S/N 024-005-00893-4. $2.25. **I29.58:35.**

Describes and illustrates the history of Fort Union between 1851 and 1891. Includes a list of commanding officers during that period.

1062-26. No. 36. **Aztec Ruins National Monument, New Mexico.** 1962 (repr. 1973). 66p. S/N 024-005-00185-9. $4.50. **I29.58:36**.

Describes the life of early humans in the San Juan Valley in the Four Corners Country. Discusses explorations and excavations in the area, and describes the Aztec ruins as they exist today in the park.

1062-27. No. 37. **Whitman Mansion National Historic Site, Washington: Here They Labored among the Cayuse Indians.** 1964 (repr. 1977). 92p. S/N 024-005-00894-2. $3.00. **I29.58:37**.

This is the site of a mission founded in 1836 by Marcus and Narcissa Whitman to minister among the Cayuse Indians and assist emigrants on the Oregon Trail. The Whitmans were killed and the mission destroyed in 1847.

1062-28. No. 38. **Fort Davis National Historic Site, Texas.** 1965 (repr. 1977). 62p. S/N 024-005-00187-5. $4.50. **I29.58:38**.

Portrays the role that the Fort Davis garrison played in the settlement of west Texas, 1854-1891. It displays the history, culture, and lifestyles of Fort Davis as shown in illustrations of various aspects of the pioneer era.

1062-29. No. 39. **Where a Hundred Thousand Fell: The Battles of Fredericksburg, Chancellorsville, the Wilderness, and Spotsylvania Court House.** 1971 (repr. 1977). 56p. S/N 024-005-00188-3. $5.50. **I29.58:39**.

Contains information and descriptive material on some of the scenes of four great battles of the Civil War, where within a radius of seventeen miles over one hundred thousand casualties occurred at the battles of Fredericksburg in 1862, Chancellorsville in 1983 and the Wilderness and Spotsylvania Court House in 1864.

1062-30. No. 40. **Golden Spike [National Historic Site, Utah].** 1969 (repr. 1982). 61p. S/N 024-005-00190-5. $4.75. **I29.58:40**.

Discusses the origin and building of the Central Pacific Railroad and Union Pacific Railroad. Describes the Great Railroad Race, the dash to Promontory Point, Utah, and the driving of the last (golden) spike at the juncture ceremony on 10 May 1869.

For additional publications on this topic see Subject Bibliography **SB-016, Historical Handbook Series.**

HISTORIC SITES PRESERVATION

1063. **Gaslighting in America: A Guide to Historic Preservation.** Heritage Conservation and Recreation Service. 1978. 279p. ill. S/N 024-016-00094-3. $8.50. **I70.8:G21**.

Provides chronological, illustrated descriptions of the types and styles of gas fixtures which appeared in the rooms and streets of nineteenth- and early twentieth-century America. Footnotes references. Bibliography. Index.

1064. **Rehabilitation of Historic Buildings: An Annotated Bibliography.** Heritage Conservation and Recreation Service. 1980. 21p. S/N 024-016-00130-3. $3.50. **I70.15:H62/2**.

Consists of citations which deal with tax benefits, building codes, design and construction, and case studies of rehabilitating historic buildings.

1065. **Technical Preservation Services Publications and Price List**. National Park Service. Rev. 1983. 12p. **I29.82:T22/983**.

An annotated list of publications of the National Park Service Technical Preservation Services dealing with preservation of historic sites and buildings. Order information is provided.

1066. **Where to Look: A Guide to Preservation Information**. Advisory Council on Historic Preservation. 1982. 87p. ill. S/N 052-003-00879-3. $5.50. **Y3.H62:8P92**.

Describes the basic introductory works and general bibliographies in the field, as well as institutional sources of information and handbooks. Includes chapters on identifying and recording cultural resources, protective strategies, preserving and restoring structural fabric, publicity, and education and training.

See also entry 401.

Housing

GENERAL

1067. **Construction Review**. International Trade Administration. Bimonthly. approx. 80p. tables. S/N 703-016-00000-6. Symbol CORE. $17.00 per yr. Single copy $3.00. **C62.10:vol/no**.

This periodical is a primary source of current statistics on construction. It includes forty series under the following topics: construction put in place, housing, building permits, contract awards, costs, prices, and interest rates; construction materials; and contract construction employment. Also includes short articles.

1068. **Families and Housing Markets: Obstacles to Locating Suitable Housing**. Department of Housing and Urban Development. December 1980. 64p. tables. HUD-PDR-654. **HH1.2:F21/4**.

Examines the national housing situation which finds that some families are denied access to some housing markets, and others are disproportionately located in inadequate housing. Footnote references.

1069. **Handbook for the Home**. Department of Agriculture. 1973. 400p. ill. Yearbook of Agriculture 1973. S/N 001-000-02960-6. $12.00, cloth. **A1.10:973**.

Intended as a guide to help families use their income to best advantages. Its seventy-eight articles cover a wide variety of topics from keeping home financial records to selecting luggage for a vacation trip. References. Index.

1070. **Housing: A Reader**. Congress. House. Committee on Banking, Finance and Urban Affairs. July 1983. 195p. tables. Committee Print 98-5. S/N 052-070-05863-3. $4.75. **Y4.B22/1:H81/72**.

A collection of papers dealing with housing issues including inflation and housing finance, tax subsidies, assistance programs for the poor, discrimination, community development, and policymaking.

1071.   **How Restrictive Rental Practices Affect Families with Children**. Department of Housing and Urban Development. August 1980. 35p. tables. HUD-PDR-592. **HH1.2:R29/9**.

Presents national statistics and examples of families that had difficulty in finding adequate housing because they had children, or had too many children or those of the wrong sex.

1072.   **The Report of the President's Commission on Housing**. 1982. 313p. charts, tables. **Pr40.8:H81/H81**.

Section 1 discusses housing for low-income Americans and presents a new system for government aid. Section 2 considers the role of private institutions. Section 3 analyzes the housing finance system. Section 4 discusses government regulation of housing. Footnote references.

1073.   **A Survey of Homeowner Experience with New Residential Housing**. Department of Housing and Urban Development. August 1980. 148p. tables. HUD-PDR-622. **HH1.2:H75/18**.

Reports the results of a national survey of new home buyers regarding the incidence of builder-resolved and nonbuilder-resolved problems costing over one hundred dollars to repair.

1074.   **The Tax Treatment of Homeownership: Issues and Options**. Congressional Budget Office. September 1981. 96p. tables. S/N 052-070-05641-0. $5.50. **Y10.2:T19/2**.

Examines current federal tax provisions benefitting home ownership, and their effect on nonresidential investment, the housing market, and the tax system. Evaluates alternatives to current tax provisions. Footnote references.

DESIGNS, PLANS, AND DRAWINGS

1075.   **Design for Affordable Housing: Cost Effective/Energy Conserving Homes**. Department of Housing and Urban Development. 1983. 48p. ill. HUD-PDR-722. **HH1.2:Af2/3**.

This catalog presents floor plans and descriptions of affordable energy-efficient single-family attached or detached houses that were developed through federally funded research. These include six small houses, twelve medium-sized houses, and four large houses. Information is provided on ordering the complete house plans.

1076.   **Designing Affordable Houses**. Department of Housing and Urban Development. 1983. 21p. ill. HUD-PDR-749. S/N 023-000-00702-9. $1.75. **HH1.2:D46/3**.

Demonstrates a wide variety of options available to the designer of compact single houses. Sample floor plans are shown for different sizes and arrangements of building components.

1077.   **Designs for Low-Cost Wood Homes**. Forest Service. November 1978. 28p. ill. S/N 001-001-00019-1. $3.75. **A13.2:H75/3/978**.

Provides floor plans and brief descriptions of eleven low-cost wood homes. Working plans for construction of these homes are available from the GPO.

CONSTRUCTION AND BUILDING TECHNIQUES

1078. **Carpenter**. Department of the Army. 1971 (repr. 1979). 196p. ill., tables. TM 5-551B. S/N 008-020-00487-1. $7.00. **D101.11:5-551B**.

Provides information supplemented by hundreds of illustrations on construction techniques, building layout, forming for concrete, frame carpentry, roofing, and many related subjects. Glossary. Index.

1079. **House Construction: How to Reduce Costs**. Agricultural Research Service. Rev. April 1977. 16p. ill. Home and Garden Bulletin 168. S/N 001-000-03729-3. $2.50. **A1.77:168/5**.

Provides advice on location, style and design, interior arrangement, selection of building materials, construction techniques, and utilities.

1080. **Low-Cost Wood Homes for Rural America: Construction Manual**. Forest Service. Rev. September 1979. 116p. ill. Agriculture Handbook 364. S/N 001-000-04021-9. $5.50. **A1.76:364/3**.

An illustrated easy-to-understand text explaining construction techniques for wood houses. Glossary. References.

1081. **Minimum Property Standards, One and Two Family Buildings**. Department of Housing and Urban Development. Rev. 1982. 294p. ill. S/N 023-000-00698-7. $8.50. **HH1.6/9:On2/982**.

Provides minimum property standards for the construction of one- and two-family houses under the numerous programs of the Department of Housing and Urban Development. It provides standards for general acceptability criteria, site design, building design, materials, and construction.

1082. **Wood-Frame House Construction**. Forest Service. Rev. April 1975. 228p. ill. Agriculture Handbook 73. S/N 001-000-03528-2. $7.50. **A1.76:73/975**.

Presents sound principles for wood-frame house construction and suggestions for selecting suitable materials that will assist in the construction. Intended as a guide for those without construction experience. Glossary. References. Index.

HOME IMPROVEMENT, MAINTENANCE, AND REPAIR

1083. **Asbestos in the Home**. Consumer Product Safety Commission. August 1982. 12p. ill. S/N 052-011-00239-9. $2.75. **Y3.C76/3:2As1**.

Describes asbestos, where it may be found in the home, and the possible dangers of exposure to asbestos. References.

1084. **Condensation Problems in Your House: Prevention and Solution**. Forest Service. September 1974 (repr. 1980). 39p. ill. Agriculture Information Bulletin 373. S/N 001-000-03318-2. $4.50. **A1.75:373**.

A guide to understanding and preventing problems with house moisture. Contains recommendations for correct methods of installing vapor barriers, thermal insulation, and inlet and outlet ventilators.

1085.   **New Life for Old Dwellings: Appraisal and Rehabilitation**. Forest Service. Rev. September 1979. 100p. ill. Agriculture Handbook 481. S/N 001-000-02988-6. $5.50. **A1.76:481/2.**

The appraisal section deals with evaluating the suitability of various parts of a house for rehabilitation. The rehabilitation section provides detailed instructions on how to accomplish such changes.

1086.   **Painting Inside and Out**. Department of Agriculture. Rev. March 1980. 29p. ill., tables. Home and Garden Bulletin 222. **A1.77:222/2.**

Describes and illustrates surface preparation, paint selection, and application of paint, whitewash, and stains for both exterior and interior surfaces.

1087.   **Renovate an Old House?** Forest Service. Rev. November 1984. 23p. ill. Home and Garden Bulletin 212. **A1.77:212/2.**

Provides advice on how to inspect an older wood-frame house for possible rehabilitation, and how to evaluate other factors involving cost, location, and sentimental value to determine if rehabilitation is worth the time, money, and effort. References.

1088.   **Roofing Farm Buildings**. Department of Agriculture. Rev. 1983. 28p. ill. Farmers' Bulletin 2170. S/N 001-000-04384-6. $1.50. **A1.9:2170/6.**

Describes different types of roofing suitable for farm buildings. Offers advice on selecting the proper type of roofing, on repairing roofs, and on installing new roofing over old.

1089.   **Simple Home Repairs: Inside**. Department of Agriculture. Rev. November 1979. 23p. ill. PA 1034. **A1.68:1034/2.**

Prepared in easy step-by-step sections to help the most inexperienced person do simple home repair jobs inside the house, such as repairing a leaky faucet or replacing a broken window.

1090.   **Simple Home Repairs: Outside**. Extension Service. January 1978. 40p. ill. PA 1193. S/N 001-000-03749-8. $2.00. **A1.68:1193.**

Provides step-by-step instructions for doing simple home repairs outside.

1091.   **Was Your Home Built after 1964? Do You Have an Electrical System with Aluminum Wiring?** Consumer Product Safety Commission. Rev. 1980. 12p. ill. **Y3.C76/3:2H75/4/980.**

Outlines hazards inherent in electrical systems with aluminum wiring and describes what can be done to reduce or eliminate the fire hazards in these systems.

1092.   **Wood Decay in Houses: How to Prevent and Control It**. Forest Service. Rev. August 1977. 17p. ill. Home and Garden Bulletin 73. S/N 001-000-04096-1. $2.75. **A1.77:73/5.**

Describes how to safeguard from decay woodwork close to the ground and parts of the house exposed to rain. Also provides general safeguards and preventive measures against wood decay.

1093. **Wood Siding: Installing, Finishing, Maintaining**. Forest Service. Rev. December 1983. 23p. ill. Home and Garden Bulletin 203. S/N 001-000-04358-7. $1.50. **A1.77:203/4**.

Provides advice on selecting and installing wood siding, and selecting and applying wood finishes. Also includes advice on refinishing.

See also entries 423, 506-6, 654, 1397, 1398.

HOME HEATING, COOLING, AND ENERGY CONSERVATION

1094. **Drying Wood with the Sun: How to Build a Solar-Heated Firewood Dryer**. Department of Energy. 1983. 24p. ill. DOE/CE-15089-3. S/N 061-000-00613-3. $3.50. **E1.89:15096-3**.

Provides instructions on the construction of the "Virginian," a solar-heated firewood dryer. Gives helpful hints for stacking wood for drying, determining when it is ready for burning, and burning wood safely and efficiently.

1095. **Energy Conserving Features Inherent in Older Homes**. Department of Housing and Urban Development. 1982. 39p. ill. S/N 023-000-00838-1. $4.75. **HH1.2:En2/25**.

Designed to enable the homeowner to understand and utilize existing architectural features in older homes to achieve energy conservation.

1096. **Energy Management Checklist for the Home**. Extension Service. Rev. January 1983. 11p. tables. PA 1168. **A1.68:1118/2**.

Contains checklist items related to the following: home insulation, lighting, water heating, laundry, house cleaning and maintenance, household appliances, and transportation.

1097. **Find and Fix the Leaks: A Guide to Air Infiltration Reduction and Indoor Air Quality Control**. Department of Energy. 1981. 28p. ill. DOE/CE-0006. S/N 061-000-00538-2. $2.50. **E1.89:0006**.

Provides answers to questions on air leakage and describes step-by-step procedures to reduce costly air leaks while maintaining or improving indoor air quality.

1098. **Firewood for Your Fireplace: Selection, Purchase, Use**. Forest Service. Rev. June 1978. folder, 8p. tables. Leaflet 559. S/N 001-000-03805-2. $11.00 per 100 copies. No single copies sold. **A1.35:559/4**.

Provides brief advice on the selection, purchase, and use of wood for the home fireplace.

1099. **Heat Pumps**. Department of Energy. May 1979. 6p. ill. DOE/CE-0088. **E1.89:0088**.

Describes different types of heat pumps and their operating characteristics, and provides advice on determining whether a heat pump is more economical than conventional heating and cooling methods.

1100. **Heating with Wood**. Department of Energy. May 1980. 20p. ill. DOE/CS-0158. S/N 061-000-00416-5. $3.00. **E1.26:0158**.

Provides valuable hints about buying wood, outlines the theory of stove operation, offers guidance on purchasing a wood stove, and more.

1101. **Home Heating: Systems, Fuels, Controls**. Agricultural Research Service. Rev. November 1977. 24p. ill. Farmers' Bulletin 2235. S/N 001-000-03823-1. $1.75. **A1.9:2235/3**.

Discusses systems for warm air heating, hot water and steam heating, and electric heating. Discusses comparative costs for four commonly used fuels (wood, coal, oil, and gas) and describes automatic control systems.

1102. **In the Bank or Up the Chimney? A Dollars and Cents Guide to Energy-Saving Home Improvements**. 2d ed. Department of Housing and Urban Development. August 1977. 76p. ill., tables. HUD-PDR-89(4). S/N 023-000-00411-9. $5.00. **HH1.6/3: En2/2/977**.

Shows how to determine where you can conserve energy in the home, how to make an accurate dollar estimate of the costs and savings, and how to make the improvements.

1103. **Moisture and Home Energy Conservation: How to Detect, Solve, and Avoid Related Problems**. Department of Energy. 1983. 36p. ill. DOE/CE-15095-4. S/N 061-000-00615-0. $4.25. **E1.89:15095-4**.

Provides information on why and where most moisture problems occur; symptoms, causes, and possible solutions to excess moisture; remedies for moisture problems; and general methodology to test for moisture.

1104. **On the Side of Safety . . . Caution: Choosing and Using Your Gas Space Heater**. Consumer Product Safety Commission. 1982. 4p. ill. **Y3.C76/3:8C31**.

Provides safety precautions regarding the selection and use of gas space heaters.

1105. **Questions and Answers on Home Insulation**. Consumer Product Safety Commission. 1978. 18p. ill. **Y3.C76/3:2H75/2**.

Describes different types of home insulation, and provides advice on proper installation. Bibliography.

1106. **Warm Up to Wood Safety**. Federal Emergency Management Administration. Rev. June 1984. folder, 8p. ill. L-110. **FEM1.11:110/2**.

Contains advice on installing a wood stove, stovepipe, and chimney; on starting wood fires; and on cleaning chimneys and preventing chimney fires.

1107. **What about Fireplaces?** Department of Energy. 1980. 20p. ill. DOE/TIC-11297. S/N 061-000-00487-4. $2.75. **E1.28:DOE/TIC-11297**.

Provides answers to questions about wood heating in fireplaces, describes how fireplaces work, and suggests ways to make them more efficient. Also shows how to calculate the cost of using a fireplace.

1108. **Window Insulation: How to Sort Through the Options**. Department of Energy. 1984. 34p. ill. DOE/CE-15096-12. S/N 061-000-00632-0. $2.50. **E1.89:15096-12**.

Describes window insulation and how it differs from noninsulating window coverings. Discusses various options and how to decide on the best method of insulation.

See also entry 733.

BUYING A HOME

1109. **Energy-Wise Homebuyer: A Guide to Selecting an Energy-Efficient Home**. Department of Housing and Urban Development. March 1979. 63p. ill. HUD-PDR-412(2). S/N 023-000-00518-2. $5.50. **HH1.6/3:En2/7**.
Describes and illustrates the features that should be looked for when purchasing a new or existing home. Discusses measures that can be employed to make homes more energy-efficient.

1110. **The Home Buyer's Estimator of Monthly Housing Cost**. Department of Housing and Urban Development. Rev. September 1978. 12p. **HH1.6/3:H75/2/978**.
Includes a slide rule "Estimator," which helps to compare total monthly housing costs of different homes based on input of mortgage payment, property tax and insurance, utility costs, special fees, and other costs.

1111. **Home Buyer's Information Package: A Guidebook for Buying and Owning a Home**. Department of Housing and Urban Development. 1979. 129p. ill. **HH1.6/3: H75/4**.
The eight sections in this guidebook follow the steps in buying and owning a home: to buy or not to buy, search for a house, purchase contracts, financing the house, money management, maintaining your home, and definitions. Includes checklists, worksheets, and sample legal documents.

1112. **The Mortgage Money Guide**. Federal Trade Commission. 1982. 16p. tables. S/N 018-000-00292-2. $50.00 per 100 copies. No single copies sold. **FT1.8/2:M84**.
Intended to help the consumer learn some of the basic concepts needed in shopping for a home loan. Describes different types of mortgages.

1113. **Rent or Buy? Evaluating Alternatives in the Shelter Market**. Bureau of Labor Statistics. 1979. 26p. tables. Bulletin 2016. S/N 029-001-02309-0. $3.50. **L2.3:2016**.
Discusses the differences between owning and renting a home; analyzes shelter costs; and shows how to compare investment returns from owning and from renting.

1114. **Selecting and Financing a Home**. Department of Agriculture. Rev. June 1980. 24p. tables. Home and Garden Bulletin 182. S/N 001-000-04149-5. $3.00. **A1.77:182/6**.
Provides advice on selecting a house, and whether to buy or rent.

1115. **Settlement Costs: A HUD Guide**. Department of Housing and Urban Development. Rev. June 1983. 44p. tables. S/N 023-000-00699-5. $3.50. **HH1.6/3:Se7/983**.
Presents an item-by-item explanation of settlement services and costs with sample forms and worksheets to help the consumer make cost comparisons.

1116.   **Wise Home Buying**. Department of Housing and Urban Development. Rev. October 1978. 28p. ill. HUD-267-H(8). **HH1.2:H98/978**.

Provides advice on shopping for a house, inspecting your selection, financing and purchasing, and maintaining the property. Glossary.

International Social
and Political Problems

GENERAL

1117. **Atlas of U.S. Foreign Relations: International Organizations.** Department of State. June 1982. 21p. maps. S/N 044-000-01905-1. **S1.3/a:At6/international.**

Illustrates the membership and history of major international organizations: League of Nations and the United Nations, Organization of American States (OAS), Organization for Economic Cooperation and Development (OECD), European Communities, North Atlantic Treaty Organization (NATO) and Warsaw Pact, League of Arab States, and Organization of Petroleum Exporting Countries (OPEC).

1118. **Country Reports on Human Rights Practices for 1984.** Congress. Senate. Committee on Foreign Relations. 1985. 1462p. Committee Print, 99th Congress, 1st Session. S/N 052-070-05999-1. $19.00. **Y4.F76/2:S.prt.99-6.**

Issued annually. Contains the reports on human rights practices in individual countries which have been prepared by the Department of State in accordance with the Foreign Assistance Act. Issued in odd years by the House Committee on Foreign Affairs, and in even years by the Senate Committee on Foreign Relations.

1119. **Human Rights Documents: Compilation of Documents Pertaining to Human Rights.** Congress. House. Committee on Foreign Affairs. September 1983. 782p. Committee Print, 98th Congress, 1st Session. S/N 052-070-05876-5. $7.50. **Y4.F76/1: H88/25.**

This compilation assembles the provisions in current U.S. laws relating to human rights and the texts of key international human rights instruments adopted by the United Nations, regional organizations, and the International Red Cross.

1120. **International Relations Dictionary.** Department of State. 1980. 84p. Department and Foreign Service Series 221-2. S/N 044-000-01853-5. $5.00. **S1.69:221-2.**

Identifies and provides information about terms, phrases, acronyms, catch words, and abbreviations used in the conduct of foreign affairs. References.

1121. **Problems of Communism**. United States Information Agency. Bimonthly. 140p. ill. S/N 725-002-00000-9. Symbol PROC. $16.00 per yr. Single copy $2.75. **IA1.8:vol/no**.

This periodical includes scholarly articles which provide analyses and significant information about contemporary affairs of the Soviet Union, China, and other countries and political movements that are part of world communism. Also contains book reviews.

1122. **Overcoming World Hunger: The Challenge Ahead. Report of the Presidential Commission on World Hunger**. March 1980. 264p. **Pr39.8:W89/3/H89/3**.

Examines the causes, dimensions, and future implications of world hunger. Presents the findings and recommendations of the commission that the United States must do more to address the inequities that allow poverty and hunger to persist in the world.

1123. **President's Commission on the Holocaust: Report to the President**. September 1979. 47p. **Pr39.8:H74/H74**.

This is the final report of a commission to recommend a fitting memorial in the United States to the Jewish victims of the Nazi Holocaust.

1124. **The Quest for Peace: Principal United States Public Statements and Documents Relating to the Arab-Israeli Peace Process, 1967-1983**. Department of State. 1983. 141p. Department of State Publication 9373. S/N 044-000-01997-3. $4.00. **S1.2:P31/25**.

This compilation presents the texts of principal U.S. public statements and related documents concerning U.S. efforts since the June 1967 war to help resolve the Arab-Israeli dispute. Background information is presented on pertinent topics.

ARMS CONTROL AND DISARMAMENT

1125. **Arms Control and Disarmament Agreements: Texts and Histories of Negotiations**. 5th ed. Arms Control and Disarmament Agency. August 1982. 297p. tables. ACDA Publication 105. S/N 002-000-00082-2. $6.50. **AC1.2:Ar5/3/982**.

This compilation contains the text and brief background discussion of the Geneva Protocol of 1925 and in chronological order all major arms control agreements in which the United States has been a participant since World War II, as well as a list of signatories and parties to those agreements.

1126. **Security and Arms Control: The Search for a More Stable Peace**. Department of State. Rev. September 1984. 76p. ill., charts. S/N 044-000-02027-1. $2.50. **S1.2:Se2/4/984**.

Presents the Reagan administration's policy on national security and arms control.

1127. **A Short Guide to U.S. Arms Control Policy**. Department of State. October 1984. 34p. ill., charts, maps. **S1.71/5:Ar5**.

Discusses U.S. arms control policy with respect to strategic arms, intermediate range nuclear forces, conventional and chemical weapons, nuclear weapons, and space arms. Glossary.

1128. **World Military Expenditures and Arms Transfers, 1972-1982**. Arms Control and Disarmament Agency. 1984. 126p. tables. ACDA Publication 115. S/N 002-000-00086-5. $4.25. **AC1.16:972-82**.

Issued annually. Provides statistical data over a ten-year period for over 140 countries on their military expenditures and arms transfers. Data are also presented on population, size of armed forces, gross national product, and total imports and exports. Financial data are expressed in current and constant dollars.

For additional publications on this topic see Subject Bibliography **SB-127, Disarmament and Arms Control**.

TERRORISM

1129. **Countering Terrorism: Security Suggestions for U.S. Business Representatives Abroad**. Department of State. August 1982. 16p. Department and Foreign Service Series 157. Department of State Publication 8884. **S1.69:157**.

Discusses precautionary measures against terrorism, and security measures for home and family and for the office.

1130. **Hostage Negotiation: A Matter of Life and Death**. Department of State. October 1983. 27p. **S1.2:H79**.

Describes the U.S. government's policy regarding terrorism and provides general advice on principles of negotiation to secure the release of hostages. References.

1131. **Hostage Taking: Preparation, Avoidance, and Survival**. Department of State. October 1984. 38p. ill. Department and Foreign Service Series 390. Department of State Publication 9400. **S1.69:390**.

Provides advice on personal protection and precautions against hostage taking, and how to act during capture, transport, holding, interrogation, release, and after. Bibliography.

1132. **Report of the DoD Commission on Beirut International Airport Terrorist Act, October 23, 1983**. Department of Defense. December 1983. 147p. ill., maps. S/N 008-000-00400-5. $4.75. **D1.2:B39**.

This is the report of an independent inquiry headed by Admiral Robert J. L. Long, USN (retired) into the October 1983 terrorist attack on the Marine Corps headquarters in Beirut. It examines the circumstances resulting in the death of 241 military personnel, and the immediate aftermath. Popular name is the "Admiral Long Commission Report."

Labor and Employment

1133. Automation and the Workplace: Selected Labor, Education, and Training Issues: A Technical Memorandum. Congress. Office of Technology Assessment. March 1983. 105p. charts, tables. OTA-TM-CIT-25. S/N 052-003-00900-5. $5.50. **Y3.T22/2: 11Au8**.

Discusses procedures for evaluating potential employment changes and education and training problems associated with the expansion of programmable automation technologies. Footnote references.

1134. Brief History of the American Labor Movement. Bureau of Labor Statistics. Rev. 1976 (repr. 1984). 110p. ill. Bulletin 1000. S/N 029-001-01955-6. $5.50. **L2.3:1000/5**.

Discusses attempts to organize labor during the Revolutionary War era, the development of the modern labor movement, changes in the labor movement between the two world wars and between 1947 and 1975, and trends in collective bargaining. References.

1135. Comparison of State Unemployment Insurance Laws. Unemployment Insurance Service. Rev. January 1985. looseleaf, 241p. tables. S/N 929-002-00000-8. Symbol CSUIL. $41.00 (includes basic manual and semiannual revisions). **L37.212:985**.

Reports by state the types of workers and employers that are covered under state law, methods of financing the program, benefits payable, conditions to be met for payment, and administrative organizations.

1136. Employment and Training Report of the President, 1982. Department of Labor. 1983. 340p. charts, tables. S/N 029-000-00413-7. $10.00. **L1.42/2:982**.

Issued annually. Reviews significant employment and unemployment developments and describes federal employment and training programs during the year. A lengthy statistical appendix contains current and historical data on employment and training and related economic topics.

1137. **Employment and Wages: Annual Averages, 1982**. Bureau of Labor Statistics. June 1984. 525p. tables. Bulletin 2215. **L2.3:2215**.

Presents complete count of employment and wages covered by unemployment insurance programs during 1982 for 11 broad industry divisions, 84 major industry groups, and almost all the 1,005 four-digit-coded industries.

1138. **Employment Projections for 1995**. Bureau of Labor Statistics. March 1984. 189p. tables. Bulletin 2197. S/N 029-001-02805-9. $5.50. **L2.3:2197**.

Presents employment projections for the year 1995, including the economic labor force estimates on which they are based.

1139. **Geographic Profile of Employment and Unemployment, 1984**. Bureau of Labor Statistics. May 1985. 155p. tables. Bulletin 2234. S/N 029-001-02847-4. $6.00. **L2.3/12:984**.

Issued annually. Presents data for regions, states, and selected large metropolitan areas and central cities on average employment and unemployment rates broken down by selected demographic and socioeconomic characteristics.

1140. **Handbook of Labor Statistics**. Bureau of Labor Statistics. June 1985. 464p. tables. Bulletin 2217. S/N 029-001-02846-6. $16.00. **L2.3/5:985**.

Issued annually. This reference book makes available in nearly two hundred tables the major statistical series produced by the Bureau of Labor Statistics including data on the labor force, employment and unemployment, consumer prices, wages and salaries, occupational injuries, and general economic data. References.

1141. **Important Events in American Labor History, 1778-1978**. Department of Labor. 1980. 35p. **L1.2:H62/2/778-978**.

Presents a chronological listing of important events in American labor history from 1778 to 1978.

1142. **Labor Firsts in America**. Department of Labor. 1977. 31p. S/N 029-000-00283-5. $2.75. **L1.2:L11/30**.

Gives dates of important events in the history of labor, including firsts in such areas as labor organizations, pensions, strikes, women's labor, child labor, and more.

1143. **Linking Employment Problems to Economic Status**. Bureau of Labor Statistics. 1985. 51p. tables. Bulletin 2222. S/N 029-001-02838-5. $2.00. **L2.3:2222**.

Contains information on the employment problems faced by American workers in 1983 and the impact of those problems on the economic status of their families and households.

1144. **Major Programs of the Bureau of Labor Statistics**. Rev. June 1983. 52p. BLS Report 693. **L2.71:693**.

Describes BLS programs under the following topics: employment and unemployment, prices and living conditions, wages and industrial relations, productivity and technology, occupational safety and health, and economic growth and employment projections. References.

1145. **Monthly Labor Review**. Bureau of Labor Statistics. Monthly. approx. 100p. tables. S/N 729-007-00000-5. Symbol MLR. $24.00 per year. Single copy $4.00. **L2.6:vol/no**.

This periodical contains scholarly articles on the labor force, wages, prices, productivity, economic growth, and occupational safety and health — usually with statistics. Departments include brief items under the following: Labor Month in Review, Research Summaries, Technical Notes, Major Agreements Expiring Next Month, and Developments in Industrial Relations. The section on current labor statistics presents data in thirty-eight series covering employment and unemployment, wages, prices, productivity, and work stoppages.

1146. **Our Changing Economy: A BLS Centennial Chartbook**. Bureau of Labor Statistics. August 1984. 56p. charts. Bulletin 2211. S/N 029-001-02818-1. $2.75. **L2.3:2211**.

Provides historical data and analyses on the following topics: employment and unemployment, productivity and technology, wages and industrial relations, prices and living conditions, occupational safety and health, and economic growth and employment projections.

1147. **State Workers' Compensation Laws**. Employment Standards Administration. Rev. January 1984. 134p. S/N 029-016-00069-1. $4.75. **L36.2:W89/4/984**.

Presents comparative tables listing under nineteen separate topics the employee benefits which are provided by states under workers' compensation laws.

1148. **200 Years of American Worklife**. Employment and Training Administration. 1977. 192p. ill. S/N 029-000-00293-2. $8.00. **L37.2:W89**.

Consists of thirty-five historical essays by distinguished observers in the fields of labor, employment, and job training to commemorate the American Revolution Bicentennial.

1149. **Unemployment Insurance: Financial Condition and Options for Change**. Congressional Budget Office. July 1983. 77p. tables. S/N 052-070-05854-4. $4.25. **Y10.2:Un2**.

Describes the operation of the present unemployment insurance system, and analyzes its financial history since 1970. Examines options to improve the financial stability of the system and more aggressively to help unemployed workers find jobs.

1150. **Workers without Jobs: A Chartbook on Unemployment**. Bureau of Labor Statistics. July 1984. 64p. charts. Bulletin 2174. S/N 029-001-02759-1. $4.50. **L2.3:2174**.

Presents full-page charts and text on the extent of unemployment in the United States.

See also entry 517.

See also "Careers and Occupations" (entries 305-339), "Equal Employment Opportunity" (entries 583-586), and "Women at Work" (entries 1687-1699).

For additional publications on this topic see Subject Bibliography **SB-064, Labor-Management Relations**.

Land

1151. **Landownership in the United States, 1978**. Economics, Statistics, and Cooperatives Service. April 1980. 100p. charts, maps, tables. Agriculture Information Bulletin 435. S/N 001-000-04139-8. $5.00. **A1.75:435**.

Consists of data collected in 1978 relating to land ownership among farmers, white-collar and blue-collar workers, retired persons, and private and public institutions.

1152. **National Agricultural Lands Study: Final Report**. Department of Agriculture. 1981. 108p. S/N 041-011-00062-9. $5.50. **A1.130:L22/3**.

Presents the findings and recommendations of an interagency study of the availability of the nation's agricultural lands, extent and causes of their conversion to other uses, and ways to retain these lands for agricultural purposes.

1153. **New Tools for Land Protection: An Introductory Handbook**. Department of the Interior. July 1982. 97p. ill. S/N 024-005-00833-1. $5.50. **I1.77/2:L22**.

Discusses methods of land protection alternative to direct acquisition: educational approaches, regulatory approaches, acquisition alternatives, and financing and tax incentives. Provides ten examples where alternative methods were used.

1154. **Zoning to Protect Farming: A Citizen's Guidebook**. National Agricultural Lands Study. 1981. 32p. ill., maps. S/N 041-011-00061-1. $3.75. **A1.130:L22/2**.

Explains the use of zoning tools to protect farming and farmlands. Bibliography.

See also entries 397, 689, 814.

Libraries and
Information Science

1155. **Alliance for Excellence: Librarians Respond to "A Nation at Risk."** Department of Education. July 1984. 69p. S/N 065-000-00207-8. $2.50. **ED1.2:N21/3**.

Presents thirteen recommendations of the library community in response to the critical report of the National Commission on Excellence in Education (entry 596). It was developed by an advisory board of leading librarians which conducted five nation-wide seminars to gain input.

1156. **Bookbinding and the Conservation of Books: A Dictionary of Descriptive Terminology**. Library of Congress. 1982. 306p. ill. S/N 030-000-00126-5. $27.00, cloth. **LC1.2:B64/3**.

Approaches the subjects of bookbinding and conservation of archival materials by examining the meaning and usage of many terms.

1157. **Commercial Library Program Publications List**. Department of State. Rev. August 1983. 51p. Department and Foreign Service Series 230. Department of State Publication 9183. **S1.69:230/2**.

This annotated catalog is designed as a buying guide for Department of State overseas posts which have commercial reference activities. It lists basic business and commercial reference sources and industrial directories. Title index.

1158. **Government Depository Libraries: The Present Law Governing Designated Depository Libraries**. Congress. Joint Committee on Printing. September 1984. 152p. Committee Print, 98th Congress, 2d Session. **Y4.P93/1:D44/984**.

Issued annually. This directory includes two separate lists of federal depository libraries arranged alphabetically by city, and by congressional district in each state. It also includes extracts from current law relating to the depository library program.

1159. **Information for the 1980s: Final Report of the White House Conference on Library and Information Services, 1979**. 1980. 816p. S/N 052-003-00764-9. $16.00, cloth. **Y3.W58/20:2I.61/979/final**.

Includes an overview of the conference, the text of the sixty-four resolutions, and transcripts of proceedings at the nine sessions and three open hearings. References. For a summary report of the conference, see entry 1170.

1160. **Library Statistics of Colleges and Universities, 1982.** National Center for Education Statistics. September 1984. 90p. tables. NCES 84-218. S/N 065-000-00216-7. $3.25. **ED1.122/3:982.**

Data are based on a survey conducted in fall 1982. Some comparisons are provided with the last survey in fall 1979. National summary data are broken down by type of institution, control, and size. Data are not provided for individual libraries or states.

1161. **MEDLARS: The Computerized Literature Retrieval Services of the National Library of Medicine.** Rev. 1982. folder, 8p. map. **HE20.3602:M46/4/982.**

Describes the databases available online through MEDLARS. Includes list of regional medical centers.

1162. **Newspapers Received Currently in the Library of Congress, 1984.** 9th ed. Library of Congress. 1984. 54p. S/N 030-005-00013-9. $2.25. **LC6.7:984.**

Issued biennially. Lists 356 United States and 1,103 foreign newspapers which are received and retained on a permanent basis by the Library of Congress, and an additional 171 U.S. and 62 foreign newspapers retained on a current basis. Title index.

1163. **Procedures for Salvage of Water-Damaged Library Materials.** Library of Congress. 1979. 30p. ill. S/N 030-000-00105-2. $4.50. **LC1.2:Sa3.**

Designed to assist those required to salvage library and archival materials affected by floods or water damage from firefighting, broken water pipes, or other accidents.

1164. **Provision of Federal Government Publications in Electronic Format to Depository Libraries.** Congress. Joint Committee on Printing. 1984. 136p. tables. S.Prt. 98-260. S/N 052-070-05970-2. $5.50. **Y4.P93/1:P96/2.**

The final report of an Ad Hoc Committee on Depository Library Access to Federal Automated Data Bases. Glossary. Bibliography. Index.

1165. **Report of the Task Force on Library and Information Services to Cultural Minorities.** National Commission on Libraries and Information Science. 1983. 106p. S/N 052-003-00927-7. $5.00. **Y3.L61:2L61/4.**

Contains the conclusions and recommendations of a task force appointed by the commission to explore the status of library and information services, programs, and resources for cultural minorities. Footnote references.

1166. **Specifications for Microfilming Manuscripts.** Library of Congress. 1980. 28p. ill. S/N 030-000-00128-1. $3.75. **LC1.6/4:M58/5.**

Describes photoduplication methods at the Library of Congress pertaining to manuscript preparation, filming, processing exposed film, inspection of film, container identification, and storage. Glossary. References.

1167. **Statistics of Public Libraries, 1977-1978.** National Center for Education Statistics. 1982. 143p. tables. S/N 065-000-00136-5. $6.50. **ED1.122/2:977-78.**

Presents detailed statistics on major public library systems in each state. Also includes summary statistics for the United States.

1168.   **Survey of Federal Libraries, Fiscal Year 1978**. National Center for Education Statistics. March 1983. 508p. tables. NCES 83-209. **ED1.115:Su7**.

Presents detailed statistics on the activities, expenditures, resources, functions, and staff of the approximately two thousand libraries serving the federal government worldwide.

1169.   **Toward a Federal Library and Information Services Network: A Proposal**. Library of Congress. 1982. 130p. tables. **LC1.2:F31**.

Analyzes the current situation related to resource sharing among federal and nonfederal libraries and proposes a full-service, multitype network based on a comprehensive federal database. References.

1170.   **The White Conference on Library and Information Services, 1979; Summary**. March 1980. 101p. S/N 040-000-00423-8. $5.50. **Y3.W58/20:2L61/979/sum**.

Includes a summary of the conference, elements of a comprehensive National Library and Information Services (NLIS) program, proposed NLIS Act, and the resolutions of the conferences. For the complete final report of the conference, see entry 1159.

See also entries 709-8, 832, 902, 1614, 1615, 1616, 1617.

For additional publications on this topic see Subject Bibliography **SB-150, Libraries and Library Collections**.

Maps and Mapping

1171. **Coastal Mapping Handbook**. Geological Survey. 1978. 199p. ill., maps. S/N 024-001-03046-2. $11.00. **I19.15/3:C63**.

Provides general information and guidance with regard to coastal mapping needs of state and local coastal zone planners. Describes the types of maps and charts which are available and how they are prepared. References. Index.

1172. **Interpretation of Aerial Photographs**. Bureau of Land Management. 1983. 38p. ill. **I53.2:Ae8**.

Describes how to interpret aerial photographs with specific emphasis on applications to various phases of land management.

1173. **Map Data Catalog: National Mapping Program**. 2d ed. Geological Survey. 1984. 48p. ill., maps. S/N 024-001-03522-7. $4.00. **I19.2:M32/13/984**.

Describes and illustrates the types of cartographic products which are available from the National Cartographic Information Center: topographic map data, other map data, map data in digital form, aerial and space imagery, and geodetic control data. Explains scope of geographic coverage, typical uses of materials, and how to order.

1174. **Map Projections Used by the U.S. Geological Survey**. 2d ed. Geolsogical Survey. May 1983. 326p. ill., maps, tables. Bulletin 1532. S/N 024-001-03497-2. $8.00, cloth. **I19.3:1532/2**.

Describes the sixteen map projections used by the Geological Survey. For each projection a discussion of appearance, use, and history is given together with a technical mathematical presentation. References. Index.

1175. **Map Reading**. Department of the Army. Rev. January 1969 (repr. 1983). 152p. ill., maps. FM 21-26. S/N 008-020-00156-2. $6.50. **D101.20:21-26/4**.

Provides detailed information on the use of maps, aerial photographs, and related cartographic materials, indoors and in the field. Index.

1176. **Maps for America: Cartographic Products of the United States Geological Survey and Others**. 2d ed. Geological Survey. 1981. 279p. ill., maps. S/N 024-001-03449-2. $15.00, cloth. **I19.2:M32/12/981**.

Contains chapters on the development of American mapping; kinds of maps and map data; characteristics of Geological Survey maps; natural and cultural features of maps; boundaries, names, and marginalia; maintenance and cartographic standards; and maps of other agencies. Glossary. References. Index.

1177. **National Mapping Program [leaflets]**. National Cartographic Information Center. **I19.80:ct**.

The National Cartographic Information Center (NCIC) has published a number of educational and information leaflets which provide general information and ordering instructions for cartographic materials available from NCIC. These pamphlets are available free at any NCIC office. A sampling is listed below.

> 1177-1. **. . . Advance Materials**. 1981. folder, 5p. ill. **I19.80:M41**.
> Describes cartographic materials which are available in advance of the final edition of a new or revised topographic map, many of which are available from the orthophotoquad mapping program.

> 1177-2. **. . . America's Place Names**. 1981. folder, 4p. **I19.80:Am3**.
> Describes the *Geographic Names Alphabetical Finding List* which is maintained by the Board on Geographic Names, and copies of which are available on microfiche from the National Cartographic Information Center.

> 1177-3. **. . . Finding Your Way with Map and Compass**. Rev. January 1985. folder, 7p. ill. **I19.80:M32/3/985**.
> Provides brief information on how to determine direction or bearing, and distance using a compass and map.

> 1177-4. **. . . How to Order Maps on Microfilm**. 1981. folder, 5p. ill. **I19.80:M58**.
> Provides brief instructions on ordering microfilm of the over 120,000 topographic maps in the collections of the Geological Survey.

> 1177-5. **. . . Lake Letter**. 1982. folder, 5p. ill. **I19.80:L14**.
> Describes the information on lakes and inland waters which is shown on topographic maps and may be of value to fishermen.

> 1177-6. **. . . Looking for an Old Aerial Photograph**. 1981. folder, 5p. ill. **I19.80:Ol1/2**.
> Provides brief information on the availability of old aerial photographs from the National Archives, Library of Congress, and Geological Survey.

> 1177-7. **. . . Looking for an Old Map**. 1981. folder, 5p. maps. **I19.80:Ol1**.
> Provides brief information on obtaining old maps from the National Archives, Library of Congress, and Geological Survey. Also discusses research on old maps and their uses.

1177-8. . . . **Map Information**. 1984. folder, 7p. ill. **I19.80:In3**.
Briefly describes map information available from the National Cartographic Information Center through its Map and Chart Information System, Cartographic Catalog, Aerial Photography Summary Record System, and the U.S. GeoData program.

1177-9. . . . **Measuring the Nation**. 1981. 4p. ill., maps. **I19.80:N19**.
Describes the National Geodetic Control System which establishes precisely measured control points used to establish veritical and horizontal positions.

1177-10. . . . **National Cartographic Information Center**. Rev. 1984. folder, 7p. ill. **I19.80:C24/984**.
Briefly describes the products and services of the National Cartographic Information Center.

1177-11. . . . **Out-of-Print Maps**. 1981. folder, 5p. ill. **I19.80:M32**.
Provides brief information on how to order reproductions of out-of-print maps from the Geological Survey.

1177-12. . . . **A Selected Bibliography on Maps, Mapping, and Remote Sensing**. 1981. folder, 5p. ill. **I19.80:M32/2**.
A list of basic books on map making, map reading, and use; mental maps; and remote sensing.

1178. **Possible Sources of Wreck Information**. National Ocean Survey. Rev. June 1983. 16p. ill. Educational Pamphlet 8. **C55.431:8/2**.
Describes how shipwrecks are indicated on nautical charts. Lists published materials and organizations which are possible further sources of information on the location of shipwrecks.

See also entries 235, 415, 547-8.

For additional publications on this topic see Subject Bibliographies **SB-102, Maps and Atlases**, and **SB-183, Surveying and Mapping**.

Military Affairs and History

GENERAL

1179. **Defense 85**. American Forces Information Service. Monthly. 24p. ill. S/N 708-017-00000-1. Symbol DEF. $20.00 per yr. Single copy $2.00. **D2.15/3:date**.

This periodical publishes articles intended to provide official and professional information to commanders and key personnel on matters related to defense policies, programs, and interests, and to create understanding and teamwork within the Department of Defense.

1180. **Department of Defense Dictionary of Military and Associated Terms. (Incorporating the NATO and IADB Dictionaries)**. Joint Chiefs of Staff. Rev. April 1984. 413p. JCS Publication 1. S/N 008-004-00020-0. $12.00. **D5.12:1/11**.

Entries in this dictionary indicate approval status for use by "DoD"—all Department of Defense components; "IADB"—member nations of the International American Defense Board; "I"—interdepartmental for national use; and "NATO"—members of the North Atlantic Treaty Organization.

1181. **Manual for Courts-Martial, United States 1984**. Department of Defense. Rev. 1984. 848p. S/N 008-000-00403-0. $13.00. **D1.15:984**.

Contains the rules for court-martial, rules of evidence, punitive articles, and nonjudicial punishment procedures. References. Index.

1182. **Medal of Honor Recipients, 1863-1978**. Congress. Senate. Committee on Veterans' Affairs. Rev. February 1979. 1132p. ill., tables. **Y4.V64/4:M46/3/863-978**.

Contains the citations for all awards of the Medal of Honor since 1863 grouped into twenty-two sections by war, campaign, conflict, or historical era.

1183. **Military Compensation Background Papers**. 2d ed. Department of Defense. July 1982. 414p. tables. S/N 008-000-00396-3. $8.50. **D1.54:C73/982**.

Provides information on the legal authority, purpose, historical background, budget cost for the past ten years, and individual monthly amounts for sixty-five items of military compensation and related manpower costs. Includes tables for basic pay for all grades and steps since 1922.

1184. **Military Leadership**. Department of the Army. Rev. June 1973. 156p. ill. FM 22-100. S/N 008-020-00507-0. $6.50. **D101.20:22-100/5**.

Written for the military commander, this manual deals with basic human needs and behavior, decision making, and requirements for effective leadership.

1185. **Military Manpower Task Force: A Report to the President on the Status and Prospects of the All-Volunteer Force**. November 1982. 103p. charts, tables. **Pr40.8:M59/M59**.

Reviews the current manpower situation in the active and reserve military forces, and examines the prospects for meeting the higher military strength planned through FY 1987 without resorting to conscription.

1186. **Prisoner of War Resistance**. Department of the Army. December 1981. 110p. ill. FM 21-78. **D101.20:21-78**.

Provides guidance for Army personnel in applying techniques of resistance to interrogation, indoctrination, and exploitation and in responding to POW management procedures should they become prisoners of war. References.

1187. **Prisoner of War: Rights and Obligations under the Geneva Convention**. American Forces Information Service. Rev. March 1980. 8p. DoD GEN-35A. **D2.14:GEN-35A**.

Provides brief information on prisoner of war rights and obligations under the 1949 Geneva Convention Relative to the Treatment of Prisoners of War.

1188. **United States Military Posture for Fiscal Year 1986**. Joint Chiefs of Staff. 1985. 109p. ill., charts, tables. S/N 008-004-00022-6. $4.50. **D5.19:986**.

Issued annually. This statement supplements testimony by the chairman of the Joint Chiefs of Staff before congressional appropriations committees. Discusses challenges to America's national security. Compares U.S. and Soviet defense requirements and commitments. Assesses current and projected capability to meet the Soviet threat.

See also entries 317, 370, 1317, 1319, 1323, 1425, 1585, 1586, 1688, 1690.

See also "Arms Control and Disarmament" (entries 1125-1128), "Nuclear Weapons" (entries 1360-1364), and "Veterans and Military Retirement" (entries 1644-1663).

For additional publications on this topic see Subject Bibliographies **SB-098, Military History; SB-131, Armed Forces; SB-153, National Defense and Security;** and **SB-236, United States Naval History.**

MILITARY HISTORY

1189. **American Military History**. Army Center of Military History. 1973 (repr. 1983). 729p. ill., maps. Army Historical Series. S/N 008-029-00089-0. $19.00, cloth. **D114.2:M59/973**.

Provides a historical survey of the organization and accomplishments of the U.S. Army from colonial times to Vietnam. Arranged chronologically by major war or conflict and periods between. References. Bibliography. Index.

1190. **The Defense of the United States**. Air University. Rev. 1982. 111p. ill. **D301.26/6:D36/982**.

A history of U.S. military involvement, with emphasis on the impact of technological and scientific changes, and the effects of wars on military and foreign policy. Used as a textbook for Air Force Junior ROTC.

1191. **Guide to the Study and Use of Military History**. Army Center of Military History. 1979. 523p. S/N 008-029-00105-5. $9.00. **D114.12:St9**.

Topics include the nature and use of military history, army program activities and uses, and historical activities outside the U.S. Army. A bibliographic guide is also included.

1192. **Guide to United States Army Museums and Historic Sites**. Army Center of Military History. 1975. 116p. ill., maps. S/N 008-020-00561-4. $5.50. **D114.2:M97/975**.

Describes the holdings of sixty-four registered museums that comprise the U.S. Army Museum System, as well as historic sites located on Army property. Also describes other Department of Defense museums, and federal, state, and private museums with military collections. Bibliography.

1193. **Historic Ship Exhibits in the United States**. Naval Historical Center. 1969 (repr. 1975). 70p. ill. S/N 008-046-00024-7. $5.00. **D207.10/2:Sh6/3**.

Lists ship exhibits under the following categories: enshrined fighting ships of the Continental, U.S., and Confederate navies; major parts and commemorative displays of fighting ships; foreign warships; and selected merchant ships. Index.

1194. **United States Air Force History: Guide to Documentary Sources**. Office of Air Force History. 1973. 245p. ill. S/N 008-070-00322-8. $6.00. **D301.6/5:H62**.

A listing of public and private depositories containing manuscript collections and private papers which wholly or in part reflect the history of the U.S. Air Force and its predecessors, as well as naval, Marine Corps, and civil aviation.

1195. **U.S. Naval History Sources in the United States**. Naval Historical Center. 1979. 242p. **D207.2:N22**.

Identifies manuscripts, archives, and other special collections deposited in over 250 archives and libraries in the United States. Most of these are the private papers of officers, men, and civilian officials of the U.S. Navy. Includes title of holdings or collection, inclusive dates, and volume.

1196. **Vignettes of Military History**. 2 vols. Army Center of Military History. vol. 1. October 1976. 66p. S/N 008-029-00096-2. $4.50. vol. 2. October 1978. 76p. S/N 008-029-00108-0. $4.75. **D114.2:V68/v.1,2**.

A collection of ancedotes of military history, some serious, many decidedly humorous, but all showing the human side of life in the military.

AIR FORCE

1197. **Air Force Combat Wings: Lineage and Honors Histories, 1947-1977.** Office of Air Force History. 1984. 364p. S/N 008-070-00519-1. $14.00, cloth. **D301.82/5: C71/947-77.**
A compilation of lineage and honors histories of Air Force-controlled combat wings of the post-World War II era. All listings feature numerical designations up to three digits and each wing's history is traced from origin to September 1977.

1198. **Air Force Register, 1984.** Department of the Air Force. 1984. 1076p. AFP 36-28. S/N 008-070-00527-1. $18.00. **D303.7:984.**
Issued annually. Lists the names of officers who were on active duty as of 31 December 1983. Includes the following information; date of birth, competitive category, USAF component, aeronautical rating, source of commission, academic education level, and professional or military schools attended.

1199. **Airman: Official Magazine of the U.S. Air Force.** Department of the Air Force. Monthly. 48p. ill. S/N 708-008-00000-1. Symbol A. $29.00 per yr. Single copy $2.75. **D301.60:vol/no.**
This periodical includes short articles of general interest on Air Force operations and life in the Air Force. Departments provide short news items of interest to Air Force members and their families. Includes regular cartoon page, "Here's Jake."

1200. **Basic Aerospace Doctrine of the United States Air Force.** Department of the Air Force. Rev. March 1984. 63p. charts. AFM 1-1. **D301.7:1-1/3.**
Contains the basic doctrine for preparing and employing the U.S. Air Force as the nation's primary aerospace armed force. Bibliography.

1201. **Encyclopedia of U.S. Aircraft and Missile Systems.** Vol. 1. **Post-World War II Fighters, 1945-1973.** Office of Air Force History. 1978. 371p. ill. S/N 008-070-00411-9. $12.00, cloth. **D301.90:1.**
Covers fighter aircraft from the first jet, the F-80 Shooting Star up to and including the F-5 Freedom Fighter. Describes the development, production, decision dates, program changes, test results, procurement methods, and technical data for each plane.

1202. **Foulois and the U.S. Army Air Corps, 1931-1935.** Office of Air Force History. 1983. 361p. ill. General Histories Series. S/N 008-070-00479-8. $13.00, cloth. **D301.82/3:F82.**
Describes the efforts by the Army Air Corps during the tenure of Major General Benjamin D. Foulois as chief of the Air Corps (1931-1935) to prepare the nation for war; and to gain money, aircraft, and even more, independence. Also describes Foulois's contributions to aviation prior to 1931, and the air mail fiasco during his tenure. Footnote references. Index.

1203. **Planning and Organizing the Postwar Air Force, 1943-1947**. Office of Air Force History. 1984. 378p. ill., charts. General Histories Series. S/N 008-070-00510-7. $12.00, cloth. **D301.82/3:P84**.

An authoritative account of planning and organizing for the U.S. Air Force as an independent military service. Begins with planning directed by General "Hap" Arnold, commanding general, Army Air Forces during World War II, and culminating in the establishment of the U.S. Air Force in 1947. Footnote references. Bibliography. Index.

1204. **United States Air Force Academy Catalog, 1984-1985**. 1984. 144p. ill. **D305.8:984-85**.

Issued annually. Describes the curriculum and courses at the United States Air Force Academy, Colorado Springs, Colorado, for the academic year. Also provides information for the student and prospective candidate on the staff and faculty, facilities, athletic programs, admissions, and cadet life.

1205. **U.S. Air Power: Ascension to Prominence**. Air Training Command. December 1973 (repr. 1984). 172p. ill. **D301.26/12:P87/2**.

A history of the airplane as a weapon of warfare, and of American airpower from 1900-1947. Used as a textbook in Air Force ROTC. Index.

1206. **U.S. Air Power: Key to Deterrence, The U.S. Air Force (1947-1981)**. Air Training Command. April 1981. 255p. ill., maps. **D301.26/12:P87/947-81**.

A history of the U.S. Air Force from its establishment as a separate service in 1947, through the Korean War and Vietnam until 1981. Used as a text for Air Force ROTC. Footnote references. Index.

See also entries 1432, 1433, 1434.

ARMY

1207. **Army Medical Department, 1775-1818**. Army Center of Military History. 1981. 312p. ill., maps. S/N 008-023-00056-5. $12.00. **D114.19:M46/775-818**.

This is the first volume in a history of the Army Medical Department from the start of the American Revolution to World War I. Describes military medicine during the Revolutionary War, and the War of 1812 and the periods between wars until the passage of an act in 1818 which established the Army Medical Department on a permanent basis. Footnote references. Bibliography. Index.

1208. **A City for the Nation: The Army Engineers and the Building of Washington, D.C., 1790-1967**. Army Corps of Engineers. 1979. 81p. ill., maps. EP 870-1-3. S/N 008-022-00132-8. $5.00. **D103.43:870-1-3**.

Discusses the contributions of the Army Corps of Engineers in the building of Washington, D.C., including its famous monuments, buildings, and historic sites.

1209. **Commanding Generals and Chiefs of Staff, 1775-1983: Portraits and Biographical Sketches of the United States Army's Senior Officer**. Army Center of Military History, 1983. 197p. ill. CMH Publication 70-14. S/N 008-029-00125-0. $13.00, cloth. **D114.2:G28**.

Includes portraits and brief biographies of the Army's senior officer who was known as commanding general from 1775 to 1903, and since then as chief of staff. Also includes brief biographies of the artists, and historical background on the role of the senior officer. Bibliography. Index.

1210. **Dictionary of United States Army Terms**. Department of the Army. Rev. October 1983. 283p. AR 310-25. **D101.9:310-25**.

This dictionary is a supplement to the *Department of Defense Dictionary of Military and Associated Terms* (entry 1180). It contains definitions not found in that publication which have specific application to the Department of the Army.

1211. **Guide for New Soldiers**. Department of the Army. January 1985. 31p. ill., map. RPI 925. **D101.43/2:925**.

Provides basic information about the Army of interest to new and prospective recruits and their families.

1212. **Secretaries of War and Secretaries of the Army: Portraits and Biographical Sketches**. Army Center of Military History. 1982. 187p. ill. S/N 008-029-00116-1. $12.00, cloth. **D114.2:Se2**.

Contains a reproduction in color of the official portrait and brief biography of each secretary of war (before 1947) and secretary of the army from Henry Knox of President Washington's first term (1789) to John O. Marsh, Jr., of the Reagan administration. References. Bibliography.

1213. **Soldiers**. Department of the Army. Monthly. 56p. ill. S/N 728-048-00000-3. Symbol SOL. $21.00 per yr. Single copy $2.00. **D101.12:yr/no**.

This official magazine of the U.S. Army contains articles and regular departments which provide timely and authoritative information on the policies, plans, operations, and technical developments of the U.S. Army and reserve components. Includes regular cartoon page ("The Lighter Side") and news items of awards for excellence.

1214. **Twice the Citizen: A History of the United States Army Reserve**. Department of the Army. 1984. 325p. ill. DA Pamphlet 140-14. S/N 008-029-00126-8. $11.00, cloth. **D101.22:140-14**.

The U.S. Army Reserve had its official birth by an act of April 1908. Opening chapters provide historical background on the American tradition of the militia and the volunteer soldier. Subsequent chapters are developed chronologically around the nation's major wars. Extensive footnote references. Index.

1215. **Vanguard of Expansion: Army Engineers in the Trans-Mississippi West, 1819-1879**. Army Corps of Engineers. August 1980. 172p. ill., maps. EP 870-1-4. S/N 008-022-00149-2. $6.00. **D103.43:870-1-4**.

Describes the contribution of Army engineers in the Trans-Mississippi during the years of expansion and settlement. This included geographic surveys and exploration, mapping, road surveys, and river and harbor improvements. Footnote references. Index.

1216. **Weapons Systems, 1985**. Department of the Army. January 1985. 153p. ill. S/N 008-020-01024-3. $8.00. **D101.95:985**.

Issued annually. Describes the latest weapons in use by today's Army. Includes personnel carriers, modular missile systems, howitzers, grenade launchers, communications programs, and more.

See also entries 163, 564, 1424, 1426, 1428.

MARINE CORPS

1217. **A Chronology of the United States Marine Corps, 1935-1946. Volume 2.** Marine Corps. 1965 (repr. 1977). 154p. S/N 008-055-00116-1. $6.50. **D214.13:C46/v.2.**
Cover significant Marine Corps operations and activities during World War II. Bibliography.

1218. **Marines and Helicopters, 1946-1962.** Marine Corps. 1976. 121p. ill. **D214.13: H36/946-62.**
Traces the development of marine helicopters from 1946 to 1962. Contains detailed account of their use in the Korean War. Footnote references. Index.

1219. **Marines and Helicopters, 1962-1973.** Marine Corps. 1978. 271p. ill. S/N 008-055-00112-9. $8.50. **D214.13:H36/962-73.**
Traces the development of helicopters in the Marine Corps from 1962 to 1973. Has a detailed account of helicopter use in Vietnam. Chronology. Footnote references. Index.

1220. **Marines in the Dominican Republic, 1916-1924.** Marine Corps. 1974. 117p. ill., maps. S/N 008-055-00079-3. $5.50. **D214.13:D71.**
Presents the record of the occupation of the Dominican Republic as an example of the active role played by the Marine Corps in the Caribbean region during the first three decades of the twentieth century.

1221. **Marines: The Official Magazine of the U.S. Marine Corps.** Marine Corps. Monthly. approx. 32p. ill. S/N 708-036-00000-5. Symbol MAR. $25.00 per yr. Single copy $3.75. **D214.24:vol/no.**
This periodical contains articles of general interest on individual marines and on Marine Corps activities and programs. Departments include news items from Marine Corps headquarters and Marine Corps posts around the world, Sportsline, and Marine Corps History (a brief article on a significant event or person).

1222. **U.S. Marine Corps Marksmanship Badges from 1912 to the Present.** Marine Corps. 1982. 22p. ill. **D214.13:B14.**
Illustrates and describes marksmanship badges awarded by the Marine Corps during six historical periods since 1912. References. Bibliography.

See also entries 462, 1132, 1435.

NAVY, COAST GUARD

1223. **All Hands: Magazine of the U.S. Navy.** Naval Internal Relations Activity. Monthly. 48p. ill. S/N 708-009-00000-8. Symbol ALLH. $20.00 per yr. Single copy $2.00. **D207.17:no.**

This periodical includes articles of general interest regarding current operations and activities of the U.S. Navy, as well as historical articles. Departments provide brief news items and a list of unit reunions.

1224. **Annapolis: United States Naval Academy Catalog, 1985-86.** 1985. 216p. ill. **D208.109:985-86.**

Issued annually. Describes the curriculum and courses for the academic year at the U.S. Naval Academy, Annapolis, Maryland. Also identifies staff and faculty members, and provides background information for current students and prospective candidates.

1225. **The Battleship in the United States Navy.** Naval History Division. 1970 (repr. 1984). 60p. ill., tables. S/N 008-046-00012-3. $4.75. **D207.10/2:B32.**

Presents a brief history of a century and half of battleships and their development in the U.S. Navy. Includes lists of battleships disposed of before World War II and battleships which saw service in World War II.

1226. **Charting Your Life in the United States Coast Guard.** Coast Guard. 1983. 172p. COMDINST P1750.4. S/N 050-012-00198-7. $4.75. **TD5.2:L62/3.**

Provides a broad range of information and helpful hints for Coast Guard members, and particularly for their families. Index.

1227. **Dictionary of American Naval Fighting Ships.** 8 vols. Naval Historical Center. 1959-1981. 5399p. ill. S/N 008-046-00105-7. $142.00(set), cloth. **D207.10:vol.1-8.**

Provides an alphabetical arrangement by name of the ships of the Continental and U.S. Navies with a historical sketch that contains pertinent information on each ship. Appendices provide lists and data on specific classes of ships. Bibliography. Each volume is sold separately.

> 1227-1. Vol. 1. . . . **A-B.** 1959 (repr. 1983). 367p. S/N 008-046-00041-7. $17.00, cloth.
>
> Appendices include lists of battleships, cruisers, submarines (including tenders and rescue vessels), torpedo boats, destroyers, and escort vessels.

> 1227-2. Vol. 2. . . . **C-F.** 1963 (repr. 1983). 614p. S/N 008-046-00007-7. $18.00, cloth.
>
> Appendices include lists of aircraft carriers, and Confederate forces afloat.

> 1227-3. Vol. 3. . . . **G-K.** 1968 (repr. 1981). 902p. S/N 008-046-00008-5. $32.00, cloth.
>
> Appendices include historic ship exhibits, monitors, Civil War ordnance, and addenda to appendices, vols. 1-2.

> 1227-4. Vol. 4. . . . **L-M.** 1969 (repr. 1981). 771p. S/N 008-046-00009-3. $19.00, cloth.
>
> Appendices include lists of amphibious warfare ships (seventeen classes), aviation auxiliaries (eleven classes), destroyer tenders, and ships of the line.

1227-5. Vol. 5. . . . **N-Q**. 1970 (repr. 1983). 663p. S/N 008-046-00051-4. $18.00, cloth.
Appendices include lists of Union stone fleets of the Civil War (loaded with stone and sunk as obstructions), minecraft, new ships (A-M), and aircraft.

1227-6. Vol. 6. . . . **R-S**. 1976 (repr. 1983). 784p. S/N 008-046-00056-5. $19.00, cloth.
Appendices include lists of submarine chasers, and Eagle-class patrol boats (PE).

1227-7. Vol. 7. . . . **T-V**. 1981. 754p. S/N 008-046-00100-6. $18.00, cloth.
Appendix includes list of tank landing ships (LST).

1227-8. Vol. 8. . . . **W-Z**. 1981. 595p. S/N 008-046-00101-4. $17.00, cloth.

1228. **Naval Aviation, 1911-1984: A Pictorial Study**. Naval Air Systems Command. 1984. 93p. ill. S/N 008-046-00109-0. $3.50. **D202.2:Av5/3/911-84**.
Traces the evolution of naval aviation from its humble beginnings in 1911 to its current role as an essential element of U.S. naval warfare. Photographs are accompanied by short captions, and are grouped under ten historical sections, each of which has short background information.

1229. **Recognition Identification Guide to Ship Associated Flags, Ensigns, and Aircraft Rondel Markings**. Naval Intelligence Support Center. July 1983. 40p. ill. **D201.6/12:R24/983**.
This illustrated recognition guide groups national and naval flags by various appearance categories, such as flags with red fields. Military aircraft markings are also categorized by appearance such as single bull's-eye pattern.

1230. **Register of Commissioned and Warrant Officers of the United States Navy and Reserve Officers on the Active Duty List, 1984**. Bureau of Naval Personnel. 1985. 630p. NAVPERS 15018. S/N 008-047-00373-1. $18.00. **D208.12:984**.
Issued annually. Lists naval officers in lineal order by type of duty (unrestricted line, engineering duty, Medical Corps, etc.) and by grade. Provides following information on each: name, designator code, date of present rank, sex, year of birth, and source code. Index.

1231. **Riverine Warfare: The United States Navy's Operations in Inland Waters**. Naval History Division. 1969. 60p. ill., maps. S/N 008-046-00022-1. $4.75. **D207.10/2: R52/969**.
Discusses riverine warfare operations from the American Revolution to the Vietnam Conflict. Riverine warfare involves use of seapower on inland waters, including rivers that open to the sea.

1232. **Ships, Aircraft, and Weapons of the U.S. Navy**. Department of the Navy. Rev. August 1984. 67p. ill. NAVSO P-3564. S/N 008-047-00362-5. $3.00. **D201.2: Sh6/2/984**.
Presents a series of illustrated fact sheets on significant Navy weapons systems in five general categories: ships, fixed-wing aircraft, helicopters, missiles, torpedoes and guns, and fire control systems.

1233.   **U.S. Coast Guard Academy Bulletin of Information, 1985-1986**. 1985. 124p. ill. **TD5.16/2:985-86**.

Issued annually. Describes the courses and curriculum at the U.S. Coast Guard Academy, New London, Connecticut. Includes information on campus activities and facilities which may be useful to prospective candidates.

1234.   **United States Naval Aviation, 1910-1980**. Naval Air Systems Command. 1982. 561p. ill., maps. NAVAIR 00-80P-1. S/N 008-046-00107-3. $17.00, cloth. **D202.2: Av5/2/910-80**.

Presents a chronology by year, month, and day of significant events in U.S. naval aviation. Appendices provide lists of naval aviators, aviation commands, aviation ships, and aircraft. Indexes by day and by subject.

AMERICAN REVOLUTION
AND COLONIAL WARS

1235.   **A Charming Field for an Encounter: The Story of George Washington's Fort Necessity**. National Park Service. 1975. 63p. ill., maps. S/N 024-005-00580-3. $6.50. **I29.2:C37**.

Discusses the ill-fated campaign of George Washington and two companies of Virginia militia to protect the upper Ohio Valley against French invasion ending in defeat at Fort Necessity, Pennsylvania.

1236.   **The Continental Army**. Army Center of Military History. 1983. 468p. ill. Army Lineage Series. CMH Publication 60-4. S/N 008-029-00122-5. $15.00. **D114.11:C76**.

Traces the development of the Continental Army's tactical doctrine and discusses the influence of eighteenth-century military theorists. It also provides 177 lineages of every permanent unit of the Continental Army. Extensive bibliography. Index.

1237.   **Engineers of Independence: A Documentary History of the Army Engineers in the American Revolution, 1775-1783**. Army Corps of Engineers. October 1983. 417p. EP 870-1-6. S/N 008-022-00166-2. $7.50. **D103.43:870-1-6**.

A collection of original documents, including many previously unpublished which detail the role of Army engineers in the American Revolution. Each is accompanied by historical background information. Glossary. Footnote references. Bibliography. Index.

1238.   **The First Stroke: Lexington, Concord, and the Beginning of the American Revolution**. National Park Service. 1978. 95p. ill., maps. S/N 024-005-00662-1. $7.50. **I29.2:R32/3**.

Describes the battles at Lexington and Concord, Massachusetts, in April 1775 and the events leading up to armed conflict. References.

1239.   **Mud and Guts: A Look at the Common Soldier of the American Revolution**. National Park Service. 1978. 58p. ill. S/N 024-005-00703-2. $4.75. **I29.2:M88**.

To celebrate the two hundredth anniversary of the Valley Forge encampment, the National Park Service commissioned Bill Mauldin, the World War II cartoonist of "GI Joe" to make this informal text-and-cartoon study of the common foot soldier in the Revolutionary War.

1240. **Marines in the Revolution: A History of the Continental Marines in the American Revolution, 1775-1783.** Marine Corps. 1975. 509p. ill., maps. S/N 008-055-00083-1. $18.00. **D214.13:R32/775-83.**

This detailed history prepared for the American Revolution Bicentennial recounts the establishment of the Marine Corps in 1775, and the significant military actions in which marines participated through 1783. References. Bibliography. Index.

1241. **October Nineteenth Seventeen Eighty One: Victory at Yorktown; The Story of the Last Campaign of the American Revolution.** National Park Service. 1976. 35p. ill., maps. S/N 024-005-00660-5. $5.50. **I29.2:Y8/2.**

Describes the military campaign leading up to it, and the seige of Yorktown, Virginia, and the British surrender on 19 October 1781. Bibliography.

1242. **Supplying Washington's Army.** Army Center of Military History. 1981. 484p. ill., maps. Special Studies Series. S/N 008-029-00115-2. $15.00, cloth. **D114.2:W27.**

Describes how the main Continental Army was maintained in the field for eight years. Traces the evolution and contributions of the five supply services: Quartermaster Department, Commissariat, Clothing Department, Ordnance Department, and Hospital Department. Footnote references. Bibliography. Index.

1243. **War of the American Revolution: Narrative, Chronology, and Bibliography.** Army Center of Military History. 1975. 266p. S/N 008-029-00091-1. $7.00. **D114.2:Am3.**

Provides a brief narrative history of the Revolutionary War, a chronology of military events, and a bibliography of over one thousand titles of books, articles, and published source materials on the American Revolution. Index.

1244. **With Fire and Sword: The Battle of Kings Mountain, 1780.** National Park Service. 1978. 82p. ill., maps. S/N 024-005-00710-5. $6.50. **I29.2:K61.**

Describes the campaign and battle at Kings Mountain, South Carolina, which resulted in an American victory on 7 October 1780 and forced British General Cornwallis to make a decisive change in his plans which took him to Yorktown. References.

See also entries 1056, 1059, 1061-18, 1062-20, 1431.

For additional publications on this topic see Subject Bibliography **SB-144, American Revolution.**

CIVIL WAR

1245. **Campaign for Petersburg.** National Park Service. 1970 (repr. 1978). 75p. ill., maps. S/N 024-005-00253-7. $4.50. **I29.58/2:P44.**

Describes the battles around Petersburg, Virginia, from June 1864 to April 1865.

1246. **Civil War Chronology, 1861-1865.** Naval History Division. 1971. 1131p. ill. S/N 008-046-00050-6. $25.00, cloth. **D207.2:C49/comp.**

A superbly detailed book on the activities of the U.S. Navy during the Civil War. Traces naval events chronologically for every day of every month from 1861 to 1865. Includes more than five hundred illustrations.

See also entries 1061-7, 1061-24, 1062-6, 1062-7, 1062-8, 1062-9, 1062-10, 1062-12, 1062-15, 1062-21, 1062-23, 1062-29.

For additional publications on this topic see Subject Bibliography **SB-192, Civil War.**

INDIAN WARS

1247. **Clash of Cultures: Fort Bowie and the Chiricahua Apaches.** National Park Service. 1977. 88p. ill., maps. S/N 024-005-00661-3. $3.00. **I29.2:F77b/2.**
Discusses the role of Fort Bowie in southeastern Arizona in the Indian Wars between the U.S. Army and the Chiricahuas following the Civil War, and ending with the surrender of Geronimo in 1886.

1248. **Fort Huachuca: The Story of a Frontier Post.** Department of the Army. 1981. 433p. ill., maps. S/N 008-020-00872-9. $8.00. **D101.2:F77hu.**
A history of the first one hundred years of Fort Huachuca, Arizona, 1877-1977 from battles with Apaches, through skirmishes with the Mexicans, through two world wars into the electronic age. Footnote references. Bibliography. Index.

See also entries 1061-16, 1062-1, 1062-25.

WORLD WAR I

1249. **Archie in the A.E.F.: The Creation of the Antiaircraft Service of the United States Army, 1917-1918.** Army Air Defense Artillery School. 1984. 204p. ill., charts. **D101.2:Ar2/2.**
Discusses the threat of military aircraft, and the establishment and operations of the U.S. Army antiaircraft service in the American Expeditionary Force (A.E.F.) to combat this threat during World War I. "Archie" was the nickname for antiaircraft artillery. Footnote references. Bibliography.

1250. **U.S. Air Service in World War I.** 4 vols. Office of Air Force History. ill., maps, tables. **D301.82/2:vol.**
This series consists of a selection of documents establishing the military air component of the United States armed forces and tracing its development through World War I experiences of the Air Service. All volumes contain a running editorial commentary.

1250-1. Vol. 1. **The Final Report and a Tactical History.** 1978. 448p. S/N 008-070-00358-9. $15.00, cloth.
Contains two documents. The "Report" is a collection of statistics, data, and charts accompanying the text compiled to depict the progress and achievements of the Air Service. The "Tactical History" summarizes observation,

pursuit aviation, day bombardment, and balloon operations on the various fronts.

1250-2. Vol. 2. **Early Concepts of Military Aviation**. 1978. 475p. S/N 008-00362-7. $15.00, cloth.

A collection of documents reflecting the state of military aviation in the United States from the purchase of the first aircraft from the Wright Brothers through World War I. Reveals the controversy affecting strategic bombardment, differences on the role of military aircraft, and ideas of air superiority. Index.

1250-3. Vol. 3. **The Battle of St. Mihiel**. 1979. 805p. S/N 008-070-00385-6. $19.00, cloth.

A collection of documents regarding the St. Mihiel offensive, September 1918, the first battle in which the U.S. Army fought independently and utilized the largest air force committed to battle during World War I. Index.

1250-4. Vol. 4. **Postwar Review**. 1979. 631p. S/N 008-070-00400-3. $18.00, cloth.

Contains two collections of documents. The first comprises "lesson learned" by officers prior to their return stateside. The second covers an assessment of damage by aerial bombardment by twelve intelligence surveys in 140 towns in France, Germany, and Luxembourg. Index.

WORLD WAR II

1251. **Air Force Combat Units of World War II**. Office of Air Force History. 1961 (repr. 1983). 519p. ill. S/N 008-070-00496-8. $19.00, cloth. **D301.2:C73/3/983**.

Lists combat groups, wings, air divisions, commands, and air forces active during World War II. Lineage is provided for each unit from date of origin to about the mid-fifties; also components of each unit, stations to which assigned, commanders, campaigns, decorations, and officially approved emblem.

1252. **American Forces in Action Series**. War Department. Historical Division. 1943-1947. Reprinted by Army Center for Military History. ill., maps, tables.

This series consists of fourteen volumes depicting military battles and campaigns during World War II. They were prepared from official records and interviews by military historians who accompanied the armies in the field. Most of the volumes are well illustrated with photographs and tactical maps with dispositions often shown down to regimental and battalion level. The following three volumes were reprinted by the Army Center for Military History in view of the interest generated by the fortieth anniversary of the invasion and liberation of Europe.

1252-1. **Omaha Beachhead (6 June-13 June 1944)**. 1945 (repr. 1984). 175p. ill., maps. CMH Publication 100-11. S/N 008-029-00128-4. $8.50. **D114.9:Om1**.

Describes the operations of the U.S. Army V Corps and its first, second, and twenty-ninth divisions in the landings on Omaha Beach on 6 June 1944 and its attacks inland through 13 June to secure the beachhead.

1252-2.   St-Lo (7 July-19 July 1944). 1946 (repr. 1984). 128p. CMH Publication 100-13. S/N 008-029-00127-6. $8.50. **D114.9:Sa2.**

Describes the operations of the XIX Corps, U.S. First Army and its bitter battles around the Vire River leading to capture of St-Lo, France, 7-19 July 1944. This made possible the breakout from the Normandy beachhead.

1252-3.   Utah Beach to Cherbourg (6 June-27 June 1944). 1947 (repr. 1984). 225p. CMH Publication 100-12. S/N 008-029-00129-2. $12.00. **D114.9:Ut1.**

Includes accounts of the landings at Utah Beach at corps level and below. Describes VII Corps combat operations in Normandy which resulted in the capture of the port of Cherbourg on 27 June 1944.

1253.   The Army Air Forces in World War II. 7 vols. Office of Air Force History. 1948-1958 (repr. 1983-1984). ill., maps, tables. Footnote references. Glossary. Index. **D301.82:vol.**

This official history of U.S. Army Air Forces' participation in World War II was edited by Wesley F. Craven and James L. Cate, under contract to the Department of the Air Force and was originally published by the University of Chicago Press. It was reprinted by the Office of Air Force History during 1983-1984, was distributed to depository libraries, and is now available for sale from the Government Printing Office.

1253-1.   Vol. 1.   Plans and Early Operations, January 1939 to August 1942. 1948 (repr. 1983). 819p. S/N 008-070-00497-6. $21.00, cloth.

Documents the plans and preparations prior to Pearl Harbor and offers an intense review of the first months of American involvement in World War II. Traces the strategy the United States adopted for waging war simultaneously against Germany, Italy, and Japan.

1253-2.   Vol. 2.   Europe: Torch to Pointblank, August 1942 to December 1943. 1949 (repr. 1983). 919p. S/N 008-070-00498-4. $22.00, cloth.

Discusses the early phases of the war in Europe and North Africa. Examines the Eighth Air Force and the doctrine of daylight precision strategic bombing, the Twelfth Air Force from Casablanca to Salerno, and the origins of the Fifteenth Air Force. Also reviews the land campaign, planning, and logistics.

1253-3.   Vol. 3.   Europe: Argument to V-E Day: January 1944 to May 1945. 1951 (repr. 1983). 959p. S/N 008-070-00499-2. $22.00, cloth.

Begins with the winter bombardment campaign and ends with Germany's surrender. Describes the drive up the Italian peninsula, the preparation for and tactical support of the Normandy invasion, and the Allied sweep across France and Germany. Also describes the destruction of the Luftwaffe and the German economy by strategic bombing.

1253-4.   Vol. 4.   The Pacific: Guadalcanal to Saipan, August 1942 to July 1944. 1950 (repr. 1983). 857p. S/N 008-070-00500-0. $21.00, cloth.

Highlights differences between the war against Germany and that against Japan. Discusses logistical problems, lack of unity of command, difficulties with communications, supply and maintenance, and close air support.

1253-5. Vol. 5. **The Pacific: Matterhorn to Nagasaki, June 1944 to August 1945**. 1953 (repr. 1983). 916p. S/N 008-070-00501-8. $22.00, cloth.

Details the air offensive against Japan, the action in Burma and China, the return to the Philippines, and the strategic bombardment of Japan from Pacific island bases.

1253-6. Vol. 6. **Men and Planes**. 1955 (repr. 1983). 811p. S/N 008-070-00502-6. $21.00, cloth.

Discusses the origin and mission of the Army Air Forces; reviews the production, distribution, and servicing of equipment; describes U.S. air defense; and traces the development of base facilities.

1253-7. Vol. 7. **Services around the World**. 1958 (repr. 1984). 719p. S/N 008-070-00503-4. $20.00, cloth.

Examines the role of the weather service, communications, medical and air sea rescue, Air Transport Command, aviation engineers, and women in the AAF.

1254. **Army Air Forces in World War II: Combat Chronology, 1941-1945**. Office of Air Force History. 1973. 1000p. S/N 008-070-00334-1. $17.00, cloth. **D301.82: C73/941-45**.

A companion volume to the seven-volume history above (entry 1253). Chronicles combat operations from 7 December 1941 to 15 August 1945. Provides a daily account arranged by events occurring within each numbered Air Force's area of operations. Index.

1255. **Command Decisions**. Army Center of Military History. 1959 (repr. 1984). 573p. maps. S/N 008-029-00071-7. $18.00. **D114.2:D35**.

A collection of twenty-three essays by military historians which analyze significant high-level command decisions critical to the outcome of World War II, such as the German counter-offensive in the Ardennes in December 1944, and the decision to drop the atomic bomb. Footnote references.

1256. **Condensed Analysis of the Ninth Air Force in the European Theater of Operations**. Office of Air Force History. 1946 (repr. 1984). 148p. charts, maps. USAF Warrior Series. S/N 008-070-00513-1. $6.50. **D301.96:Eu7**.

Contains a short history of the Ninth Air Force in World War II from the build-up before the invasion of Europe through subsequent combat operations in 1944 and 1945. Examines problems in conducting joint air-ground operations.

1257. **Pearl Harbor: Why, How, Fleet Salvage and Final Appraisal**. Naval History Division. 1968 (repr. 1982). 392p. ill. S/N 008-046-00020-4. $15.00, cloth. **D207.10/2: P31/2**.

An authoritative historical account of ship salvage operations at Pearl Harbor during 1942 following the Japanese attack by the officer in charge of those operations. Also discusses the events leading up to the attack on 7 December 1941 and the results of the Japanese air raid and offers an appraisal of the attack. Index.

1258. **Strategy for Defeat: The Luftwaffe, 1933-1945**. Office of Air Force History. January 1983. 391p. ill., charts, tables. S/N 008-070-00483-6. $9.50. **D301.26/6: L96/933-45**.

Historical narrative on the German Air Force during World War II from prewar preparations to final defeat. Footnote references. Index.

1259.   **United States Army in World War II**. Army Center of Military History. 1947- . ill., charts, maps, tables. Footnote references. Bibliography. Index. **D114.7:ct.**

This official series includes seventy-eight volumes (three in preparation) which are divided into twelve subseries: *The Army Ground Forces, The Army Service Forces, The China-Burma-India Theater, The European Theater of Operations, The Mediterranean Theater of Operations, The Middle East Theater, Pictorial Record, Special Studies, Technical Services, The War Department, The War in the Pacific,* and *The Western Hemisphere.* The combat volumes which account for about a third of the series are illustrated with action and terrain photographs and military maps. All volumes are in print and for sale by the GPO. They are listed in Subject Bibliography **SB-098, Military History** and the publications catalog of the Army Center of Military History (entry 1710). Samples of interesting volumes from most of the subseries are listed below.

1259-1.   **The Army Ground Forces. The Organization of Ground Combat Troops**. 1947. 558p. S/N 008-029-00064-4. $17.00, cloth. **D114.7:Ar5/v.1.**

Presents six studies dealing with organizational problems of the ground forces.

1259-2.   **The China-Burma-India Theater: Stillwell's Mission to China**. 1953 (repr. 1984). 460p. S/N 008-029-00013-0. $15.00, cloth. **D114.7:C44/v.1.**

Treated at length are the proposals of General Stillwell to the National Government of China in the execution of his orders from the War Department to "support China." Describes the famous march from Burma, and the Stillwell-Chennault controversy.

1259-3.   **The European Theater of Operations. The Ardennes: The Battle of the Bulge**. 1965 (repr. 1972). 742p. S/N 008-029-00069-5. $21.00. **D114.7:Eu7/v.8.**

Relates the German winter counter-offensive from jump-off on 16 December 1944 until the Allied armies were ready to eliminate the bulge in their line in early January 1945. German plans and Allied reaction are described in detail.

1259-4.   **The Mediterranean Theater of Operations. Cassino to the Alps**. 1977 (repr. 1984). 607p. S/N 008-029-00095-4. $19.00, cloth. **D114.7:M46/2/v.4.**

Continues the account of operations in Italy, covering Operation DIADEM, the capture of Rome, the pursuit of the Germans to the Arno River, the Gothic Line battles, the last offensive, the pursuit across the Po Valley, and the negotiations for the surrender of German armies in Italy.

1259-5.   **Pictorial Record. War against Germany, Europe, and Adjacent Areas**. 1951 (repr. 1983). 468p. S/N 008-029-00042-3. $15.00. **D114.7:P58/v.2.**

Illustrates the buildup in the United Kingdom and the Normandy invasion, and the campaigns in northern France, the Rhineland, Ardennes-Alsace, and central Europe.

1259-6.   **Special Studies. The Employment of Negro Troops**. 1966. 740p. S/N 008-029-00028-8. $19.00, cloth. **D114.7:N31.**

Tells in detail how the Army employed Negro troops before and during World War II and describes the combat experiences of Negro units in the Mediterranean, European, and Pacific theaters.

1259-7. **The Technical Services. The Ordnance Department: On Beachhead and Battlefront.** 1968 (repr. 1978). 542p. S/N 008-029-00030-0. $16.00, cloth. **D114.7:Or2/v.3**.

Tells the story of how America's munitions reached U.S. and Allied troops and how Ordnance Department soldiers stored, maintained, supplied, and salvaged materials in the Mediterranean, European, and Pacific theaters.

1259-8. **The War Department: Strategic Planning for Coalition Warfare, 1943-1944**. 1959. 658p. S/N 008-029-00058-0. $17.00, cloth. **D114.7:W19/v.6**.

Discusses the hopes, fears, struggles, frustrations, and triumphs of Army strategic planners coming to grips with the problems of the offensive phase of coalition warfare. The midwar international conferences are covered in detail.

1259-9. **The War in the Pacific. Okinawa, the Last Battle**. 1948. 552p. S/N 008-029-00066-1. $22.00, cloth. **D114.7:P11/v.1**.

Covers the final battle against Japan in the Pacific Theater of Operations, the battle of Okinawa April-June, 1945.

1260. **U.S. Marine Corps Special Units in World War II**. Marine Corps. 1972 (repr. 1977). 115p. ill., maps. S/N 008-055-00113-7. $5.50. **D214.13:Sp3**.

Discusses the development, deployment and eventual demise of five types of special units: raiders, parachutists, glider forces, barrage balloon squadrons, and base defense battalions. Footnote references. Index.

1261. **Vengeance Weapon 2: The V-2 Guided Missile**. National Air and Space Museum. 1983. 87p. ill., maps. **SI9.2:W37**.

Discusses the development and use of the V-2 guided missile by Germany during World War II. Also discusses post-war experiments and tests with the V-2 by the United States. Bibliography.

See also entries 1318, 1427.

KOREAN WAR

1262. **Korea: 1951-1953**. Army Center of Military History. 1956. 328p. ill., maps. S/N 008-029-00117-9. $9.50. **D114.2:K84/951-53**.

Records briefly by text and numerous photographs the Korean War from January 1951 to the cessation of hostilities in July 1953.

1263. **United States Air Force in Korea, 1950-1953**. Office of Air Force History. Rev. 1983. 844p. ill., maps. S/N 008-070-00488-7. $18.00, cloth. **D301.2:K84/2**.

Historical narrative of the Far East Air Force in Korea from 1950 to 1953. Also describes the activities of Marine Corps and Navy as well as other UN air units. Glossary. Bibliography. Index.

1264. **United States Army in the Korean War**. 3 vols. Army Center of Military History. ill., maps.

> 1264-1. **Policy and Direction: The First Year**. 1972 (repr. 1978). 443p. S/N 008-029-00083-1. $18.00, cloth. **D114.2:K84/2/v.3**.
>
> Outlines developments in Korea from August 1945 to the outbreak of war in June 1950. Examines the major policy decisions and planning actions in Washington and Tokyo through June 1951. Includes broad outline of combat operations for orientation. Index.

> 1264-2. **South to the Naktong, North to the Yalu (June-November 1950)**. 1961 (repr. 1981). 839p. S/N 008-029-00079-2. $25.50, cloth. **D114.2:K84/2/v.1**.
>
> Describes early setbacks and withdrawal to the Pusan perimeter, McArthur's landing at Inchon, and the drive north that crushed the North Koreans followed by the ominous stiffening of resistance as UN forces neared the Yalu River and the Manchurian border. Index.

> 1264-3. **Truce Tent and Fighting Front**. 1966 (repr. 1977). 571p. S/N 008-029-00001-6. $20.00, cloth. **D114.2:K84/2/v.2**.
>
> Covers the truce negotiations at Kaesong and Panmunjon from July 1951 to July 1953 between UN forces and the Communist Chinese. Also describes some of the bitter hill fighting and the large-scale prisoner of war riots at Koje-do.

VIETNAM CONFLICT:
AIR FORCE AND AIR WAR

1265. **Aces and Aerial Victories: The United States Air Force in Southeast Asia**. Air University. 1976 (repr. 1978). 188p. ill., maps. S/N 008-070-00365-1. $9.00. **D301.26/6:Ac3/965-73**.

A collection of detailed, first-hand accounts of air battles over North Vietnam. Includes an official listing of credits awarded by the U.S. Air Force (alphabetically and chronologically). Lists the units that participated and describes the weapons that were used on both sides.

1266. **Air Base Defense in the Republic of Vietnam, 1961-1973**. Office of Air Force History. 1979. 287p. ill., tables. S/N 008-070-00436-4. $6.50. **D301.2:Ai7/31/961-73**.

Analyzes the unique problems of defending air bases during the Vietnam Conflict. Centers on the primary efforts of the U.S. Air Force and allied air units to defend ten key air bases in South Vietnam. Footnote references. Index.

1267. **Air Force Heroes in Vietnam**. Air War College. 1979. 100p. ill., maps. USAF Southeast Asia Monograph Series, Vol. 7, Monograph 9. S/N 008-070-00448-8. $4.75. **D301.86:7/9**.

Tells the stories of the twelve Air Force heroes who were awarded the Congressional Medal of Honor for action in the Vietnam Conflict.

1268. **Air Power and the Airlift Evacuation of Kham Duc**. Air War College. 1979. 95p. ill., maps. USAF Southeast Asia Monograph Series, Vol. 5, Monograph 7. S/N 008-070-00434-8. $4.75. **D301.86:5/7**.

Describes the evacuation of over fourteen hundred Americans and Vietnamese from the Kham Duc Special Forces camp in the northern area of South Vietnam near the border of Laos on 12 May 1968. Footnote references.

1269. **Air Power and the Fight for Khe Sanh**. Office of Air Force History. 1973 (repr. 1978). 144p. ill., charts, maps. S/N 008-070-00331-7. $4.75. **D301.2:K52**.
Discusses the contribution of air power, particularly that of the U.S. Air Force to the twenty-sixth Marines' defense of Khe Sanh between January and April 1968. Describes aerial strikes. bombing, and resupply. Footnote references. Index.

1270. **Airpower and the 1972 Spring Invasion**. Department of the Air Force. 1976. 125p. ill., maps. USAF Southeast Asia Monograph Series, Vol. 2, Monograph 3. S/N 008-070-00369-4. $5.00. **D301.86:2/3**.
Describes the 1972 spring offensive by the North Vietnamese Army into South Vietnam, and the contributions of the U.S. Air Force to stopping it. Index.

1271. **Command and Control and Communications Structure in Southeast Asia**. Air University. 1981. 244p. ill. Air War in Indochina. Vol. 1, Monograph 1. S/N 008-070-00468-2. $6.50. **D301.93:1/1**.
Analyzes the development of Southeast Asian command structures and their impact on the control and communications structures, and thus ultimately on the war in Vietnam itself.

1272. **Development and Employment of Fixed-Wing Gunships, 1962-1972**. Office of Air Force History. 1982. 326p. ill., charts, maps, tables. U.S. Air Force in Southeast Asia Series. S/N 008-070-00452-6. $15.00, cloth. **D301.86/2:G99/962-72**.
Traces the fixed-wing gunship's development, deployment and operations from inception in the early 1960s to the end of American involvement in Southeast Asia in early 1973. Footnote references. Index.

1273. **Last Flight from Saigon**. Department of the Air Force. 1978. 151p. ill., maps. USAF Southeast Asia Monograph Series, Vol. 4, Monograph 6. S/N 008-070-00409-7. $5.50. **D301.86:4/6**.
A narrative account of how U.S. armed forces as well as several civilian agencies pulled together to accomplish the largest aerial evacuation in history: the evacuation of Saigon in April 1975. Bibliography.

1274. **Linebacker II: A View from the Rock**. Air War College. 1979. 222p. ill., maps. USAF Southeast Asia Monograph Series, Vol. 6, Monograph 8. S/N 008-070-00433-0. $6.00. **D301.86:6/8**.
Focuses on the involvement of the Strategic Air Command forces stationed at Anderson Air Force Base, Guam, nicknamed "The Rock." Linebacker II was the B-52 bombing of the Hanoi-Haiphong area of North Vietnam in December 1972. Footnote references. Bibliography.

1275. **Operation Ranch Hand: The Air Force and Herbicides in Southeast Asia**. Office of Air Force History. 1982. 253p. ill., maps. S/N 008-070-00466-6. $8.50. **D301.2:R15/961-71**.
Reviews the herbicidal spraying in Southeast Asia, discussing political and environmental problems.

1276. **Search and Rescue in Southeast Asia, 1961-1975**. Office of Air Force History. 1980. 221p. ill., maps. S/N 008-070-00453-4. $7.50. **D301.2:Se1/961-75**.

Tells the story of Air Force efforts to recover air crews downed in combat, focusing on the air war in Southeast Asia. Also discusses the development of search and rescue operations from World War II to 1960. Index.

1277. **Tactical Airlift: The United States Air Force in Southeast Asia**. Office of Air Force History. 1983. 924p. ill., maps, tables. S/N 008-070-00470-4. $14.00. **D301.86/2:Ai7**.

Describes tactical airlift in the changing environment of limited war. Details transportation in the combat zone from the early 1960s to 1975. Featured are the principal aircraft used: C-123 Provider, C-130 Hercules, and the small C-7 Caribou.

1278. **Tale of Two Bridges; and the Battle for the Skies over North Vietnam**. Department of the Air Force. 1976. 204p. ill., maps. USAF Southeast Asia Monograph Series, Vol. 1, Monographs 1 and 2. S/N 008-070-00372-4. $6.00. **D301.86:1/1&2**.

Contains two monographs. The first describes Air Force and navy bombing of two bridges in North Vietnam: the Thanh Hoc rail and highway bridge on the coastal highway and the Paul Doumer bridge outside Hanoi. The second provides a brief history of Air Force operations over North Vietnam from 1964 to 1972. Index.

1279. **United States Air Force in Southeast Asia, 1961-1973: An Illustrated Account**. Office of Air Force History. Rev. 1984. 389p. ill. S/N 008-070-00516-6. $14.00, cloth. **D301.2:Ai7/29/961-73/rev**.

A colorfully illustrated account of U.S. Air Force participation in the Vietnam Conflict, 1961-1973.

1280. **Vietnamese Air Force, 1951-1975: An Analysis of Its Role in Combat; and Fourteen Hours at Koh Tang**. Department of the Air Force. 1977. 175p. ill., maps. USAF Southeast Asia Monograph Series, Vol. 3, Monographs 4 and 5. S/N 008-070-00377-5. $5.50. **D301.86:3/4&5**.

Contains two monographs. The first presents an objective review of the South Vietnamese Air Force and the role the U.S. Air Force played during its short fourteen-year life span. The second is a step-by-step account of the "Mayaguez Affair" during May 1975 and the role of air power. Index.

VIETNAM CONFLICT:
ARMY AND THE GROUND WAR

1281. **Dust Off: Army Aeromedical Evacuation in Vietnam**. Army Center of Military History. 1982. 140p. ill. S/N 008-020-00903-2. $5.50. **D114.2:D94**.

Provides a historical perspective on the use of helicopter ambulances during the Vietnam Conflict.

1282. **Final Collapse**. Army Center of Military History. 1983. 190p. ill., maps. S/N 008-029-00121-7. $5.50. **D114.18:C68**.

An account of the last two years of the Vietnam Conflict, 1973-1975—following the withdrawal of U.S. ground combat forces—and the collapse of the South Vietnamese Army.

1283.   **Seven Firefights in Vietnam**. Army Center of Military History. 1970 (repr. 1984). 159p. ill., maps. CMH Publication 70-4. S/N 008-029-00072-5. $4.25. **D114.2:V67**.

Includes accounts of various small unit combat operations from 1965 through 1968 based on journals, reports, and interviews.

1284.   **Vietnam from Cease-Fire to Capitulation**. Army Center of Military History. 1981. 186p. maps, tables. S/N 008-029-00120-9. $6.50. **D114.2:V67/2**.

Describes the final military operations in South Vietnam following the withdrawal of American ground troops and ending with the capitulation of South Vietnam in 1975.

1285.   **United States Army in Vietnam: Advice and Support: The Early Years, 1941-1960**. Army Center of Military History. 1983. 417p. ill., charts, maps. CMH Publication 91-1. S/N 008-020-00933-4. $11.00. **D114.7/3:Ad9/941-60**.

This is the first volume in a multivolume official history of U.S. Army participation in the Vietnam Conflict, which will provide similar coverage to that of earlier official series on World War II (entry 1259) and Korea (1264). This volume describes the activities of the U.S. Army in Vietnam during World War II, military advice and assistance to the French during the post-war period, and the advisory program that developed after 1954. Footnote references. Index.

1286.   **Vietnam Studies Series**. Department of the Army. 1972-1982. ill., charts, maps, tables. **D101.74:ct**.

The volumes in this series were prepared by senior army commanders and staff officers and their staffs who had served in responsible assignments in the areas covered by their studies.

1286-1.   **Airmobility, 1961-1971**. 1973 (repr. 1982). 318p. S/N 008-020-00479-1. $7.00. **D101.74:Ai7/961-71**.

Traces the evolution of airmobility in the U.S. Army from the post-World War II period to the eventual formation of airmobile divisions used in Vietnam. Describes selected operations in Vietnam from 1961 to 1971 as representative examples of different airmobile tactics. Index.

1286-2.   **Allied Participation in Vietnam, 1965-1970**. 1975. 189p. S/N 008-020-00524-0. $5.50. **D101.74:Al5**.

Describes the participation and contributions by countries allied with the United States and South Vietnam during the Vietnam Conflict, 1965-1970.

1286-3.   **Base Development in South Vietnam, 1965-1970**. 1972. 173p. S/N 008-020-00427-8. $5.50. **D101.74:B29/965-70**.

Describes construction programs by Corps of Engineers units and contractors in South Vietnam from 1965 until disengagement in 1970, embracing ports, airfields, storage areas, ammunition dumps, housing, bridges, roads, and other conventional facilities. Index.

1286-4.   **Cedar Falls-Junction City: Turning Point**. 1974 (repr. 1980). 182p. S/N 008-020-00477-4. $5.50. **D101.74:C32**.

Describes operations "Cedar Falls" and "Junction City" which took place during the first five months of 1967 and were the first multidivisional combat operations in Vietnam to be conducted on a preconceived scale. Index.

1286-5. **Command Control, 1950-1969**. 1974. 114p. S/N 008-020-00500-2. $5.50. **D101.74:C73/2/950-69**.

Describes the development of the U.S. military command and control structure in South Vietnam. The focus is primarily on the Military Assistance Command, Vietnam (MACV) and the U.S. Army in Vietnam (USARV). Divided into four periods: formative years (1950-1962); establishment of MACV (1962-1965); the buildup (1965-1966); and continuing buildup (1966-1969). Index.

1286-6. **Communications-Electronics, 1962-1970**. 1972 (repr. 1980). 195p. S/N 008-020-00425-1. $5.50. **D101.74:C73/962-70**.

Describes the activities and operations of Signal Corps units with respect to providing communications and electronic support in Vietnam from 1966 to 1970.

1286-7. **Development and Training of the South Vietnamese Army, 1950-1972**. 1975. 172p. S/N 008-020-00532-1. $5.50. **D101.74:D49/950-72**.

Describes U.S. Army assistance and participation in the development and training of the South Vietnamese Army during four periods: the formative years (1950-1959); the crucial years (1960-1964); the buildup years (1965-1967); and Vietnamization (1968-1972). Index. Glossary.

1286-8. **Division Level Communications, 1962-1973**. 1982. 119p. S/N 008-020-00884-2. $5.00. **D101.74:C73/5/962-73**.

Describes Signal Corps unit operations and communications experience at division level and lower in Vietnam, 1962-1973. Index.

1286-9. **Field Artillery, 1954-1973**. 1975 (repr. 1980). 253p. S/N 008-020-00556-8. $8.00. **D101.74:F45/954-73**.

Describes the role of U.S. Army field artillery in the Vietnam Conflict.

1286-10. **Financial Management of the Vietnam Conflict, 1962-1972**. 1974. 119p. S/N 008-020-00505-3. $5.50. **D101.74:F49**.

Discusses financial management of the Army operation and maintenance appropriation in the Vietnam Conflict. Includes chapters on planning for financial management of a limited war, budgeting for war, accounting, the reimbursement program, and organization for financial management. Glossary. Index.

1286-11. **Law at War, Vietnam 1964-1973**. 1975. 172p. S/N 008-020-00531-2. $5.50. **D101.74:L41**.

Focuses on the operation and responsibilities of the legal section of MACV primarily during the period 1964-1966. Separate chapters discuss MACV organization for legal services, Vietnamese legal system, prisoners of war and war claims, legal status of forces in Vietnam, and discipline and criminal law. Index.

1286-12. **Logistic Support**. 1974. 289p. S/N 008-020-00473-1. $6.50. **D101.74:L82**.

Describes logistical support of U.S. Army units in Vietnam from 1965 to 1970. Also discusses support to the South Vietnamese Army, allied forces, and the civilian pacification effort; and the effects on the total worldwide logistic effort. Glossary. Index.

1286-13.   **Medical Support of the United States Army in Vietnam, 1965-1970.** 1973. 196p. S/N 008-029-00088-1. $12.00, cloth. **D101.74:M46/965-70.**
Describes the role of the Army Medical Department in providing medical support to Army units in the Vietnam Conflict.

1286-14.   **Mounted Combat in Vietnam.** 1978. 262p. S/N 008-020-00747-1. $7.00. **D101.74:C73/4.**
Provides an account of operations of U.S. Army armored units in Vietnam to include tank and mechanized infantry units, armored cavalry units, and air cavalry units whose primary mode was to fight mounted. Index.

1286-15.   **Riverine Operations, 1966-1969.** 1973 (repr. 1982). 220p. S/N 008-020-00472-3. $5.50. **D101.74:R52/966-69.**
Describes U.S. Army riverine warfare planning and operations in South Vietnam from 1966 to 1969, primarily in the Mekong Delta region. Glossary. Index.

1286-16.   **Role of Military Intelligence, 1965-1967.** 1974 (repr. 1983). 182p. S/N 008-020-00499-5. $5.50. **D101.74:M59/965-67.**
Discusses the role of Army military intelligence in the Vietnam Conflict.

1286-17.   **Sharpening the Edge: The Use of Analysis to Reinforce Military Judgement.** 1974 (repr. 1979). 261p. S/N 008-020-00554-1. $6.50. **D101.74: C73/3.**
Provides a brief treatment of operations research techniques as applied to combat operations in Vietnam primarily in the Ninth Infantry Division and II Field Force Vietnam during the period 1969-1970. Index.

1286-18.   **Tactical and Materiel Innovations.** 1974. 206p. S/N 008-020-00471-5. $6.00. **D101.74:In6.**
Discusses some of the more important tactical and materiel innovations in Vietnam from the viewpoint of the infantry division commander. Uses fifteen battles or operations as case studies to illustrate the use of new weapons or tactics. Glossary. Index.

1286-19.   **United States Army Engineers, 1965-1970.** 1974. 253p. S/N 008-020-00470-7. $6.50. **D101.74:En3/965-70.**
Describes the contributions of Army Engineer units to combat and support operations in Vietnam, 1965-1970. Glossary. Index.

1268-20.   **United States Army Special Forces, 1961-1971.** 1973. 237p. S/N 008-020-00448-1. $6.50. **D101.74:Sp3/961-71.**
Discusses activities and operations of Army special forces units during three periods: 1961-1965, 1966-1968, and 1969-1971. Glossary. Index.

1286-21. **War in the Northern Provinces, 1966-1968.** 1975. 124p. S/N 008-020-00519-3. $5.00. **D101.74:N81p/966-68.**

Describes military operations in the two northernmost provinces of South Vietnam from spring 1966 to spring 1968. Includes descriptions of the battles at Hue and Khe Sanh. Glossary. Index.

VIETNAM CONFLICT: MARINE CORPS AND NAVY

1287.   **The Battle for Khe Sanh.** Marine Corps. 1969 (repr. 1977). 214p. ill., maps. S/N 008-055-00114-5. $7.00. **D214.13:K52.**

Presents a detailed and graphic account of the twenty-sixth Marines' defense of Khe Sanh against North Vietnamese Army assaults, January-April 1968. Footnote references.

1288.   **Marines in Vietnam, 1954-1973: An Anthology and Annotated Bibliography.** 1974 (repr. 1983). 281p. ill., maps. S/N 008-055-00070-0. $7.50. **D214.13:V67/954-73.**

Includes thirteen articles on Marine Corps combat actions in Vietnam arranged chronologically. Also includes articles on aviation logistics and base support.

1289.   **Mobility, Support, Endurance: A Story of Naval Operational Logistics in the Vietnam War, 1965-1968.** Naval History Division. 1972. 296p. ill. S/N 008-046-00057-3. $12.00, cloth. **D207.10/2:L82.**

Discusses underway replenishment; advanced bases, afloat and ashore; the Seabees; sea lines of logistics; shore activities in the western Pacific; repair and supply; and ship salvage and habor clearance. Index.

1290.   **Small Unit Actions in Vietnam, Summer 1966.** Marine Corps. 1967 (repr. 1977). 123p. ill., maps. S/N 008-055-00115-3. $6.50. **D214.13:V67/2/966.**

Describes nine small unit actions by Marine Corps combat units in Vietnam during 1966. Based on interviews in the field and eye-witness accounts.

1291.   **Vietnam Operational History Series.** Marine Corps. 1977- . ill., maps. **D214.13:V67/yrs.**

This is the official history of Marine Corps combat and support operations in the Vietnam Conflict.

1291-1.   **United States Marines in Vietnam, 1954-1964: The Advisory and Combat Assistance Era.** 1977. 190p. S/N 008-055-00094-7. $11.00, cloth. **D214:13V67/954-64.**

Describes advisory and combat assistance to the South Vietnamese during the period 1954-1964 prior to an active combat role by Marine Corps units. Footnote references. Index.

1291-2.   **United States Marines in Vietnam, 1965: The Landing and the Buildup.** 1978. 274p. S/N 008-055-00129-3. $8.00. **D214.13:V67/965.**

Covers the year 1965 when the war in Vietnam escalated, and major American units were committed to combat. Also discusses the activities of Marine Corps advisors. Footnote references. Index.

1291-3.   **United States Marines in Vietnam, 1966: An Expanding War**. 1982. 402p. S/N 008-055-00160-9. $9.00. **D214.13:V67/966**.

Describes the continued military buildup in 1966 of the III Marine Force in South Vietnam's northernmost Corps Area, and the accelerated tempo of combat. Also covers the activities of Marine Corps advisors, the Seventh Fleet Landing Force, and Marines on the staff of the U.S. Military Assistance Command (MACV). Index.

1291-4.   **United States Marines in Vietnam, 1967: Fighting the North Vietnamese**. 1984. 354p. S/N 008-055-00165-0. $10.00. **D214.13:V67/977**.

Focuses on the Third Marine Amphibious Force (III MAF) which fought in the South Vietnamese I Corps area. Emphasis is placed on the ground war of I Corps and III MAF. Also discusses Marine Corps advisors, the two special landing forces of the Seventh Fleet, and logistical support. Index.

VIETNAM CONFLICT: POLITICS AND STRATEGY

1292.   **On Strategy: The Vietnam War in Context**. Army War College. 1981 (repr. 1983). 147p. S/N 008-020-00881-8. $6.00. **D101.2:V67/2/983**.

This book has been adopted as a text at Army, Navy, and Air Force postgraduate schools. Using the theories of Carl von Clausewitz, it attempts to place the Vietnam Conflict in domestic context as well as in the context of war itself. Bibliography. Index.

1293.   **Reorganizing for Pacification Support**. Army Center of Military History. 1982. 99p. ill., charts, maps. S/N 008-020-00883-4. $4.75. **D114.2:P11/2**.

Describes the background and implementation of President Johnson's decision in May 1967 to create a civil/military organization, Civil Operations and Revolutionary Development Support (CORDS) to manage U.S. advice and support to the South Vietnamese government's pacification program. Footnote references.

1294.   **The U.S. Government and the Vietnam War: Executive and Legislative Roles and Relationships**. 2 pts. Congress. Senate. Committee on Foreign Relations. Pt. 1. 1984. 365p. map. S/N 052-070-05915-0. $8.50. Pt. 2. 1985. 434p. S/N 052-070-06002-6. $10.00. Committee Print. **Y4.F76/2:S.prt.98-185/pt.1,2**.

This planned four-part study provides an in-depth analysis of the role of Congress in the Vietnam Conflict, including major decisions of the Executive and the relationships between the two branches. Part 1 covers the period 1945-1961; part 2 covers 1961-1964; and parts 3 and 4 will cover 1965-1969 and 1969-1975. Footnote references. Index.

1295.   **Vietnam: 10 Years Later. What Have We Learned?** Defense Information School. 1984. 112p. ill. S/N 008-020-01023-5. $4.00. **D101.2:V67/3**.

An edited collection of fourteen speeches delivered during a senior public affairs officer course during 1983. Speakers were media correspondents, public affairs officers, and historians.

SOVIET MILITARY AFFAIRS

1296. Dictionary of Basic Military Terms: A Soviet View. Department of the Air Force. 1976 (repr. 1982). 263p. Soviet Military Thought Series No. 9. S/N 008-070-00360-1. $6.50. **D301.79:9**.

Translation of a 1965 Soviet publication. Defines 1,645 Soviet military terms. English index.

1297. The Evolving Soviet Navy. 4th ed. Naval War College. 1978. 116p. tables. S/N 008-047-00258-1. $5.00. **D201.2:So8/3**.

Examines the evolution, mission, and future prospects of the Soviet Navy and provides a chronological listing of Soviet naval ships and weapons, as well as a list of various Soviet military hardware. Footnote references. Bibliography.

1298. NATO and the Warsaw Pact: Force Comparisons. Department of State. Rev. 1984. 52p. charts, maps, tables. **S1.2:N81/984**.

Compares the military forces of the North Atlantic Treaty Organization (NATO) and the Soviet-sponsored Warsaw Pact countries.

1299. Soviet Aerospace Handbook. Department of the Air Force. May 1978. 229p. ill., charts. AFP 200-21. S/N 008-070-00402-0. $6.00. **D301.35:200-21**.

Provides basic information on the Soviet armed forces, and particularly on Soviet aerospace forces.

1300. Soviet Air Power. Air University. 1985. 116p. ill., charts, tables. AU-21. **D301.26/6:So8/3**.

Traces the growth of Soviet air power from its infancy in the early 1900s, through its adolescence, to its present maturity. Footnote references. Bibliography.

1301. The Soviet Armed Forces: A History of Their Organizational Development; A Soviet View. Department of the Air Force. 1984. 516p. ill. Soviet Military Thought Series No. 19. S/N 008-070-00524-7. $14.00. **D301.79:19**.

A translation of a 1978 Soviet history of the Soviet armed forces from their establishment in 1917. Part 1 covers the period 1917-1920; part 2 the period between the two world wars; part 3 the Great Patriotic War (1941-1945); and part 4 the post-World War II period.

1302. Soviet Army Operations. Army Intelligence and Security Command. April 1978. 352p. charts, tables. S/N 008-020-00945-8. $8.00. **D101.2:So8/4**.

Describes the tactics of Soviet ground forces in offensive, defensive, and specialized operations at division level and below. Soviet terminology is used, followed by explanations.

1303. Soviet Military Power, 1985. 4th ed. Department of Defense. April 1985. 143p. ill., charts, tables. S/N 008-000-00410-2. $6.00. **D1.74:985**.

Issued annually. Chapters include Soviet military power, forces for nuclear attack, strategic defense and space programs, ground forces, air forces, naval forces, global ambitions, and U.S. response to the challenge.

1304. **Understanding Soviet Naval Developments**. Office of Chief of Naval Operations. Rev. 1985. 160p. ill. NAVSO P-3560. S/N 008-047-00368-4. $6.50. **D201.2:So8/2/985**.

Issued with separate chart showing Soviet submarine classes, warship classes, warship equipment, and Soviet auxiliary classes.

Mining and Prospecting

1305. **American Coal Miner: A Report on Community and Living Conditions in the Coalfields**. President's Commission on Coal. 1980. 233p. ill. S/N 052-003-00719-3. $8.50. **Pr39.8:C63/C63/3**.

A photographic essay on how coal miners and their families live, and how their lives have changed over the past thirty years, covering housing, health and safety, transportation, lifestyles, women in the coal fields, and Navajo coal miners. References.

1306. **Anatomy of a Mine from Prospect to Production**. Intermountain Forest and Range Experiment Station. Rev. 1983. 69p. ill. General Technical Report INT-35. S/N 001-001-00587-8. $4.00. **A13.88:INT-35/2**.

Describes prospecting, exploration, mine development and operation, and reclamation. Reviews mining laws and regulations and their application to mining in western states.

1307. **Mine Safety and Health**. Mine Safety and Health Administration. Quarterly. approx. 40p. ill. S/N 729-006-00000-9. Symbol MESA. $14.00 per yr. No single copies sold. **L38.9:vol/no**.

This periodical contains articles of general interest on mining, and safety and health related to mining operations. Departments provide brief news items regarding the Mine Safety and Health Administration and the mining industry. "Stamp of Approval" section lists items recently added to the official list of permissible or approved mining equipment.

1308. **Patenting a Mining Claim on Federal Lands**. Bureau of Land Management. January 1980. 20p. IS-4. S/N 024-011-00088-7. $2.50. **I53.26:4-80**.

Provides mining claimants with basic information on how to file an application for a mineral patent and describes the administrative procedures involved.

1309.   **Prospecting for Gold in the United States**. Geological Survey. Rev. 1978 (repr. 1980). 16p. S/N 024-001-02036-0. $2.25. **I19.2:G56/3/978**.

Provides advice on prospecting for gold in placer and lode deposits. Indicates where gold has been found in the past, and lists selected reports regarding those areas.

1310.   **Questions and Answers about Mining the Public Lands**. Bureau of Land Management. 1985. 12p. **I53.2:M66/9/985**.

Provides answers to commonly asked questions about mining on public lands.

1311.   **Staking a Mining Claim on Federal Lands**. Bureau of Land Management. Rev. 1985. 17p. S/N 024-011-00162-0. $1.25. **I53.2:M66/4/984**.

Discusses which federal lands are open and which closed to mining, types of mining claims, and how to record and maintain a mining claim.

See also entry 1353.

For additional publications on this topic see Subject Bibliography **SB-099, Minerals and Mining**.

Minorities and Ethnic Studies

GENERAL

1312. **Characters in Textbooks: A Review of the Literature**. Commission on Civil Rights. May 1980. 19p. Clearinghouse Publication 62. **CR1.10:62**.

Analyzes the portrayal of minorities, older persons, and families in textbooks. Finds that considerable stereotyping remains, although it is diminishing. Footnote references.

1313. **Directory of Minority Arts Organizations**. National Endowment for the Arts. December 1982. 96p. **NF2.2:M66**.

Lists a large number of nonprofit performing groups, presenters, museums, galleries, art centers, and community centers with significant arts programming that have a leadership and constituency that is primarily Asian-American/Pacific Island, black, hispanic, native American, or multiracial.

1314. **A Guide to Minority Aging References**. Federal Council on Aging. 1983. 187p. DHHS Publication No. (OHDS) 83-20194. S/N 017-090-00074-7. $5.50. **HE23.9:M66**.

The citations in this bibliography are arranged under six headings: American Indian/Alaska native, Pacific/Asian, hispanic, black, multiethnic, and uncodified.

1315. **Minorities and Women in the Health Fields**. Bureau of Health Professions. 1984. 191p. charts, tables. S/N 017-022-00856-4. $7.00. **HE20.9302:M66**.

This statistical report updates the 1974 edition. It includes separate racial/ethnic and male/female sections with analyses and data on a number of medical and health fields and professions. Most sections present historical data and trends from 1971.

1316. **The Minority Elderly in America: An Annotated Bibliography**. Administration on Aging. May 1980. 46p. DHHS Publication No. (OHDS) 80-20071. **HE23.3011:M66**.

An annotated list of books and journal articles relating to American Indians, blacks, hispanics, Pacific/Asian, and cross-cultural groups, and general topics on minorities.

See also 547-1, 1165, 1461.

See also "Discrimination, Civil Rights, and Equal Opportunity" (entries 570-586).

For additional publications on this topic see Subject Bibliography **SB-006, Minorities**.

BLACKS

1317. **Black Americans in Defense of Our Nation**. Department of Defense. Rev. 1985. 189p. ill. S/N 008-000-00413-7. $5.50. **D1.2:B56/985**.
Provides a historical overview of the contributions of black Americans in conflicts, large and small, from colonial times to Vietnam. Also contains separate chapters on black recipients of the Medal of Honor, black women in the military services, black general and flag officers, blacks at the military academies, and black civilians in the Defense Department.

1318. **Blacks in the Army Air Forces during World War II: The Problem of Race Relations**. Office of Air Force History. 1977. 227p. ill., charts, maps. S/N 008-070-00378-3. $6.00. **D301.2:B56**.
Discusses how the leadership of the War Department and the army air force tried to deal with the problem of race and the prejudices of American society, and black racial protests and riots which that discrimination provoked. Bibliography. Index.

1319. **Integration of the Armed Forces, 1940-1965**. Army Center of Military History. 1981. 667p. ill. Defense Studies Series. S/N 008-029-00113-6. $19.00, cloth. **D114.2:In8/940-65**.
Essentially an administrative history that attempts to measure the influence of several forces, most notably the civil rights movement, and the tradition of segregated service in development of racial policies of the armed forces. Footnote references.

1320. **Social and Economic Status of the Black Population in the United States: An Historical View, 1790-1978**. Bureau of the Census. 1979. 277p. charts, tables. Current Population Reports, Series P-23, No. 80. S/N 003-024-01659-1. $8.00. **C3.186:P-23/80**.
Presents a historical view of the changes in the demographic, social, and economic characteristics of the black population in the United States.

See also entries 612, 615, 962, 1054, 1259-6.

HISPANICS

1321. **Condition of Education for Hispanic Americans**. National Center for Education Statistics. 1980. 286p. charts, tables. NCES 80-303X. S/N 065-000-00023-7. $8.00. **ED1.102:H62**.

Presents data and analyses of Hispanic participation in education at the elementary and secondary school levels, and in higher education. Also provides information on the sociological, demographic, and employment characteristics of Hispanic Americans and how these relate to their educational attainments.

1322. **Condition of Hispanics in America Today**. Bureau of the Census. 1984. 28p. charts. S/N 003-024-05700-0. $1.75. **C3.2:H62**.

This chart book contains summary demographic, economic, and social data from the 1980 Census of Population and Housing on the status of Hispanic Americans. References.

1323. **Hispanics in America's Defense**. Department of Defense. 1982. 156p. ill. **D1.2:H62/2**.

Provides summary information on the contribution of Hispanic Americans during all major wars and military conflicts of the United States.

AMERICAN INDIANS

1324. **American Indians**. Bureau of Indian Affairs. 1984. 44p. ill. S/N 024-002-00083-7. $2.50. **I20.2:Am3**.

Provides a brief review of federal policy regarding American Indians from colonial times to the present. Discusses the role of the Bureau of Indian Affairs yesterday and today, tribes and reservations, and economic development programs among native Americans.

1325. **Brief History of the Federal Responsibility to the American Indian**. Office of Education. 1979. 35p. ill. DHHS Publication No. (OE) 79-02404. S/N 017-080-02033-5. $4.50. **HE19.102:In2/6**.

Reviews treaty guarantees made by the federal government, and the educational services to be provided under those guarantees. Summarizes congressional intent from the end of the treaty period (1871) to the present in assigning responsibilities to federal agencies for American Indian affairs. Also examines judicial history.

1326. **Federal Programs of Assistance to American Indians**. Congress. Senate. Select Committee on Indian Affairs. December 1982. 288p. ill. Committee Print, 97th Congress, 2d Session. **Y4.In2/11:As7/982**.

Describes federal programs designed specifically to benefit American tribes and individuals as well as other programs which are of special interest to American Indians. Index.

1327. **Guide to Records in the National Archives of the United States relating to American Indians**. National Archives and Records Service. 1981. 480p. ill. **GS1.6/6:Am3/3**.

Entries are arranged by agency, mainly the Bureau of Indian Affairs and War Department, but also by many other agencies which had relations with native Americans. Also includes nonfederal, prefederal, and foreign records and private papers in the National Archives.

1328. **Handbook of American Indians**. Smithsonian Institution. ill., maps, tables. References. Bibliography. Index. **SI1.20/2:vol**.

This planned twenty-volume set provides an encyclopedic summary of what is known about the prehistory, history, and culture of the aboriginal peoples of North America who lived north of the urban civilization of central Mexico.

> 1328-1.   Vol. 5.   **Arctic**. 1984. 845p. S/N 047-000-00398-9. $29.00, cloth.
> Covers the Eskimo people of North America who lived in the Arctic area.

> 1328-2.   Vol. 6.   **Subarctic**. 1981. 853p. S/N 047-000-00374-1. $25.00, cloth.
> Covers an area of approximately two million square miles which extends from the coast of Labrador on the Atlantic coast to Cook Inlet, Alaska, and beyond into the Pacific Ocean.

> 1328-3.   Vol. 8.   **California**. 1978. 815p. S/N 047-000-00347-4. $25.00, cloth.
> Covers about sixty tribes who lived in the present state of California.

> 1328-4.   Vol. 9.   **Southwest**. 1979. 717p. S/N 047-000-00361-0. $23.00, cloth.
> The area covered includes Arizona, New Mexico, and North Mexico to about 23 degrees latitude. Covers the prehistory, general history, and language of the entire Southwest, and the culture and history of the Pueblo peoples.

> 1328-5.   Vol. 10.   **Southwest**. 1983. 884p. S/N 047-000-00390-3. $25.00, cloth.
> Covers the culture and history of the non-Pueblo people of the Southwest, and some surveys of topics germane to the entire Southwest area.

> 1328-6.   Vol. 15.   **Northeast**. 1978. 940p. S/N 047-000-00351-2. $27.00, cloth.
> Covers the area from Maine south to Virginia and Kentucky, and west to Wisconsin and Illinois including southeastern Canada.

1329.   **Sacred Articles of the Yaqui Indians**. Customs Service. 1979. 12p. ill. Customs Publication No. 505. **T17.2:Y1**.

Intended to assist Customs officers in identifying various religious articles which the Yaqui of Arizona import from Mexico for use in their religious ceremonies.

1330.   **USDA Programs of Interest to American Indians**. Department of Agriculture. August 1983. 79p. **A107.2:Am3**.

Describes federal assistance, grant, and loan programs administered by the Department of Agriculture which are available to American Indians.

See also entries 570, 1061-19, 1062-13, 1062-14, 1062-17, 1062-26.

ETHNIC STUDIES

1331. **Blue Ridge Harvest: A Region's Folklife in Photographs**. American Folklife Center. 1981. 116p. ill. Publication 7. S/N 030-000-00127-3. $6.00. **LC39.9:7**.

A photographic essay of the cultural life and traditions along a one hundred mile stretch of the Blue Ridge Parkway in Virginia and North Carolina. References.

1332. **Cultural Conservation: The Protection of Cultural Heritage in the United States**. American Folklife Center. 1983. 131p. ill. Publication 10. S/N 030-000-00148-6. $4.50. **LC39.9:10**.

This report directed by Congress includes findings and recommendations on preserving, conserving, and encouraging the continuation of tangible elements of our cultural heritage such as arts, skills, folklife, and folkways. Bibliography.

1333. **Ethnic Recordings in America: A Neglected Heritage**. American Folklife Center. 1982. 269p. Studies in American Folklife No. 1. S/N 030-001-00098-2. $13.00, cloth. **LC39.11:1**.

A collection of nine papers prepared for a conference on ethnic recordings in America which was held at the Library of Congress. Index.

1334. **Highland People: The People of the Great Smokies**. National Park Service. 1978. 189p. ill., maps. **I29.58/2:H53**.

Describes the life of the highland people of the Great Smoky Mountains from colonial times to the present. Bibliography.

National Parks,
Forests, and Recreation Areas

GENERAL

1335. **Camping and Picnicking Guide**. Forest Service. Intermountain Region. 1983. 78p. maps, tables. **A13.36/2:C15/2**.

Provides detailed information on camping, picnicking, and recreation sites and facilities in the national forests of the Intermountain Region (Idaho, Nevada, and Utah).

1336. **Golden Eagle, Golden Age, Golden Access Passports: Federal Recreation Fee Program**. National Park Service. Rev. 1984. folder, 9p. **I29.2:G56e/984**.

Describes three passports for entrance to federal parks and recreational areas that charge user fees: the Golden Eagle annual passport for persons under 62; Golden Age free lifetime passport for senior citizens; and Golden Access free lifetime passport for the blind and disabled.

1337. **National Forest Vacations**. Forest Service. Rev. September 1979. 55p. ill., map. PA 1037. **A1.68:1037/2**.

A brief guide to the national forests with information for selected areas on attractions and facilities for camping, hiking, fishing, skiing, and other outdoor recreation.

1338. **Recreation Areas. . . .** Bureau of Reclamation. 1980. folder. ill., map, tables. **I27.7/4:R24/map[no]**.

These maps describe and list the recreation activities and facilities that are available to the public at federal water and power projects in the states listed.

1338-1. Map 1. **Idaho, Oregon, Washington**.

1338-2. Map 2. **Montana, Nebraska, North Dakota, South Dakota, Wyoming**.

1338-3.   Map 3.   **Arizona, California, Nevada, Utah.**

1338-4.   Map 4.   **Colorado, Kansas, Oklahoma, New Mexico, Texas.**

1339.   **Recreation Sites in Southwestern National Forests.** Forest Service. Southwestern Region. Rev. August 1984. 69p. ill., maps, tables. **A13.2:R24/28/984.**

Describes recreation activities and facilities available at the twelve national forests located in Arizona and New Mexico, and the three national grasslands in New Mexico, Oklahoma, and Texas.

1340.   **Recreational Opportunities at Hydroelectric Projects Licensed by the Federal Energy Regulatory Commission, 1978.** Federal Energy Regulatory Commission. 1979. 70p. ill., maps, tables. DOE/FERC-0025. S/N 061 002 00014-6. $5.00. **E2.12:0025.**

Lists over four hundred major hydroelectric projects under license to the Federal Energy Regulatory Commission in forty-one states. Indicates in tabular format the recreational activities available at each including swimming, boating, hiking, camping, picnicking, fishing, hunting, and skiing.

1341.   **Visitors Guide to the National Wildlife Refuges.** Fish and Wildlife Service. Rev. 1985. folder. ill., maps, tables. S/N 024-010-00660-9. **I49.44/2:guide.**

Consists of a map of the United States which includes locations of all national wildlife refuges and a list of their names and addresses and a description of available recreational facilities.

See also entry 196.

NATIONAL PARKS

1342.   **Access National Parks: A Guide for Handicapped Visitors.** National Park Service. 1978. 197p. ill. S/N 024-005-00691-5. $6.50. **I29.9/2:H19/2.**

Provides information about the accessibility of facilities, services, and interpretative programs in almost three hundred areas of the National Park System. Includes addresses and telephone numbers, average elevation where it is a consideration, availability of first aid and medical facilities, and more.

1343.   **Guide and Map: National Parks of the United States.** National Park Service. 1984. map, 20x26". S/N 024-005-00852-7. $34.00 per 100 copies. No single copies sold. **I29.8:G94.**

Features a map of the United States locating all national parks, and on the verso a table listing services and facilities at each.

1344.   **Index: National Park System and Related Areas as of June 1, 1982.** National Park Service. Rev. 1982. 94p. ill., tables. S/N 024-005-00829-2. $4.75. **I29.103:982.**

Lists the name and mailing address of the 333 parks and other areas in the National Park System. Also includes a list of affiliated areas, wild and scenic rivers system, and the national trail system. Alphabetical index.

1345.   **Lesser-Known Areas of the National Park System**. National Park Service. Rev. 1985. 48p. S/N 024-005-00911-6. $1.50. **I29.9/2:P21/985**.

A state-by-state listing of lesser-known parks, including forested areas, desert canyons, seashores, native American ruins, and numerous historical sites. Includes information on location, attractions, facilities, and accommodations.

1346.   **Mountains and Meadowlands along the Blue Ridge Parkway**. National Park Service. 1975. 46p. ill. S/N 024-005-00598-6. $5.50. **I29.2:B62**.

Describes and illustrates the scenic beauty available to travelers along the Blue Ridge Parkway through the Great Smoky Mountains of Virginia and North Carolina.

1347.   **Place Where Hell Bubbled Up: History of the First National Park**. 1972. 68p. ill., maps. S/N 024-005-00486-6. $5.25. **I29.2:H36**.

Provides a history of Yellowstone National Park from its discovery and establishment as the first national park into the twentieth century.

1348.   **Stehekin: A Wilderness Journey into the North Cascades**. National Park Service. 1977. 43p. ill., map. S/N 024-005-00658-3. $5.00. **I29.2:St3**.

Describes and illustrates a trip upstream on Lake Chelan from Chelan to Stehekin in the North Cascades National Park, Washington.

See also entries 202, 203, 206, 1052, 1056, 1060, 1369.

Nuclear Energy

NUCLEAR POWER

1349. Commercial Nuclear Power 1984: Prospects for the United States and the World. Energy Information Administration. 1984. 126p. charts, tables. DOE/EIA-0438(84). S/N 061-003-00412-1. $4.75. **E3.2:N88/3/984.**

Presents historical data on commercial nuclear power in the United States, projections of domestic nuclear capacity and generation through the year 2000, and projections of nuclear capacity through the year 2000 for thirty foreign countries.

1350. Investor Perceptions of Nuclear Power. Energy Information Administration. 1984. 116p. charts, tables. DOE/EIA-0046. S/N 061-003-00382-6. $4.25. **E3.2:In8/6.**

Attempts to determine whether investors perceive the securities of utilities with nuclear facilities to be more or less risky than those with non-nuclear facilities, and to quantify any relative risk premium. Footnote references.

1351. Nuclear Plant Cancellations: Causes, Costs, Consequences. Energy Information Administration. April 1983. 122p. charts, tables. DOE/EIA-0392. S/N 061-003-00308-7. $5.50. **E3.2:N88/2.**

Presents a historical overview of nuclear plant cancellations through 1982, the cost associated with those cancellations, and the reasons the projects were terminated. Also identifies other nuclear plants which may be cancelled in the future.

1352. Nuclear Power in an Age of Uncertainty. Congress. Office of Technology Assessment. February 1984. 293p. ill., charts, tables. OTA-E-216. S/N 052-003-00941-2. $10.00. **Y3.T22/2:2N88/4.**

Discusses the future of nuclear power in the light of uncertain financial, economic, social, and political factors. Concludes that no additional reactors will be completed in this country by the year 2000 beyond those already under construction. Index.

1353. **World Uranium Supply and Demand: Impact of Federal Policies**. Energy Information Administration. March 1983. 231p. charts, tables. DOE/EIA-0387. S/N 061-003-00302-8. $7.50. **E3.2:Ur1**.

Describes the federal government's role in the uranium industry, and reviews the current status of the domestic industry.

For additional publications on this topic see Subject Bibliography **SB-200, Atomic and Nuclear Power**.

NUCLEAR ACCIDENTS

1354. **Accident at the Three Mile Island Nuclear Powerplant**. 2 pts. Congress. House. Committee on Interior and Insular Affairs. 1979. 674p. **Y4.In8/14:96-8/pt.1,2**.

Transcript of hearings held during May 1979 on the accident on 28 March 1979 at the Three Mile Island Nuclear Powerplant, Middletown, Pennsylvania. Includes testimony of participants, witnesses, and responsible industry and government officials.

1355. **Crisis Contained: The Department of Energy at Three Mile Island; A History**. Department of Energy. December 1980. 217p. ill. DOE/EV-10278-T1. **E1.28: DOE/EV-10278-T1**.

This history of the Department of Energy's response to the accident at the Three Mile Island nuclear power plant was prepared by an outside historical consultant. Footnote references. Index.

1356. **The Need for Change: The Legacy of Three Mile Island. Report of the President's Commission on the Accident at Three Mile Island**. October 1979. 201p. ill. S/N 052-003-00718-5. $7.00. **Pr39.8:T41/T41**.

This is the final report of the President's commission to investigate the accident at Three Mile Island. It includes an account of the accident, and the conclusions of the commission which was chaired by John G. Kemeny. Glossary. Separate reports by the various task forces of the commission were also published.

1357. **Nuclear Powerplant Safety after Three Mile Island**. Congress. House. Committee on Science and Technology. March 1980. 74p. Committee Print, 96th Congress, 2d Session. **Y4.Sci2:96/JJ**.

Summarizes and analyzes hearings held in 1979 on nuclear power safety following the accident at Three Mile Island. Also considers the results of investigations by the President's Commission and the Nuclear Regulatory Commission.

1358. **Three Mile Island: A Report to the Commissioners and to the Public**. Nuclear Regulatory Commission. 1980. ill., charts, maps, tables. NUREG/CR-1250. **Y3.N88:1250/vol/pt**.

    1358-1. **Vol. 1**. 193p.

    Contains a narrative description of the accident at the Three Mile Island (TMI) nuclear power plant on 28 March 1979 and a discussion of the major conclusions and recommendation of a commission chaired by Mitchell Rogovin to investigate the accident.

1358-2. **Vol. 2. Part 1**. 318p.
Focuses on the pre-accident licensing and regulatory background. Includes an examination of overall licensing and regulatory systems for nuclear power plants from different perspectives. Includes licensing, operating, and inspection history of TMI.

1358-3. **Vol. 2. Part 2**. 509p.
Provides a technical description of the accident. Includes time line chronology discussion of radioactive release and radioactive protection at TMI, and an assessment of plant behavior, of core demage, of alternative accident scenarios, and of human factors.

1358-4. **Vol. 2. Part 3**. 479p.
Contains a description and assessment of responses to the accident by the utility, the Nuclear Regulatory Commission, and state and federal agencies. Analyzes information provided to the media. Includes study of management factors related to the accident. Footnote references.

NUCLEAR WEAPONS

1359. **Defense against Ballistic Missiles: An Assessment of Technologies and Policy Implications**. Department of Defense. April 1984. 31p. ill. S/N 008-047-00358-7. $1.50. **D1.2:M69**.
Discusses advances in five technology areas which offer the greatest promise for an effective defense against ballistic missiles.

1360. **The Effects of Nuclear War**. Congress. Office of Technology Assessment. May 1979. 151p. ill., charts, maps, tables. OTA-NS-89. S/N 052-003-00668-5. $6.50. **Y3.T22/2:2N88/2**.
Examines the social, economic, political, and health effects of various levels of nuclear attacks on the United States and the Soviet Union. Identifies the large areas of uncertainty regarding those effects. Footnote references.

1361. **Effects of Nuclear Weapons**. 3d ed. Department of Defense. 1977 (repr. 1983). 653p. ill. S/N 008-046-00093-0. $17.00, cloth. **D1.2:N88/2**.
Discusses the effects of various nuclear explosions. Includes photographs taken at Hiroshima and Nagasaki, Japan, and at test sites. Dial in pocket has title "Nuclear Blast Effects Computer."

1362. **MX Missile Basing**. Congress. Office of Technology Assessment. September 1981. 342p. ill., charts, maps, tables. OTA-ISC-140. S/N 052-003-00849-1. $9.00. **Y3.T22/2:2M69**.
Reviews five ways in which the MX missile could be based, and assesses the technical feasibility, strategic utility, cost, impact on the region, and future consequences of each. Footnote references.

1363. **Nuclear Proliferation Factbook**. Congress. Senate. Committee on Governmental Affairs. September 1980. 542p. charts, tables. Committee Print, 96th Congress, 2d Session. S/N 052-070-05419-1. $8.50. **Y4.G74/9:N88/12**.

Provides a wide selection of basic documents and international statistical data pertinent to the spread, or proliferation, of the ability to make nuclear weapons. References.

1364.   **Nuclear Safeguards: A Reader**. Congress. House. Committee on Science and Technology. December 1983. 1017p. charts, tables. Committee Print, 97th Congress, 1st Session. S/N 052-070-05891-9. $17.00. **Y4.Sci2:98/T**.
A compilation of excerpts from public laws, treaties, and official reports, together with related statements, articles, and other writings dealing with nuclear safeguards such as record keeping to account for nuclear materials, verification by inspection, and other measures.

See also entries 566, 567, 569.

Oceans

1365. **Our Living Oceans: Secrets of the Sea**. National Marine Fisheries Service. 1980. 8p. ill. S/N 003-017-00486-4. $1.75. **C55.302:Oc2/970-80**.
Discusses ways of studying the sea, sea life, and mineral resources.

1366. **Questions about the Oceans**. Naval Oceanographic Office. 1968 (repr. 1985). 121p. ill. S/N 008-042-00032-2. $5.00. **D203.24:G-13/paper**.
Includes one hundred questions and answers about the oceans. Provides guide to further reading for each question.

1367. **Why Is the Ocean Salty?** Geological Survey. 1980. 15p. **I19.2:Oc2**.
Explains how the ocean becomes salty from the gradual concentration of dissolved chemicals eroded from the Earth's crust and washed into the sea.

For additional publications on this topic see Subject Bibliography **SB-032, Oceanography**.

Outdoor Recreation

1368. **Backpacking**. Forest Service. Rev. July 1981. 52p. ill. PA 1239. S/N 001-000-04247-5. $3.50. **A1.68:1239/2**.

Discusses general safety and emergency procedures, and special precautions for hiking and camping in bear country.

1369. **Camping in the National Park System**. National Park Service. Rev. 1985. 26p. ill., tables. S/N 024-005-00875-6. $1.50. **I29.71:985**.

Contains basic information about the facilities and recreational opportunities available to users of the National Park System camping areas.

1370. **Camping on Public Lands**. Bureau of Land Management. Rev. 1983. folder, 16p. ill., map, tables. S/N 024-011-00155-7. $2.00. **I53.11:C15/983**.

Provides information on facilities and camping and outdoor recreation activities available on federal public lands in the western states and Alaska.

1371. **Snow Avalanche: General Rules for Avoiding and Surviving Snow Avalanches**. Forest Service. Pacific Northwest Region. 1982. folder, 8p. ill. **A13.2:Sn6/8**.

A guide to avoiding and surviving snow avalanches in mountain areas.

1372. **Survival in Antarctica**. National Science Foundation. 1984. 106p. ill. NSF 84-55. S/N 038-000-00549-9. $4.00. **NS1.2:Su7**.

Discusses survival problems in Antarctica, clothing, shelters, overland travel, crevass detection, animal life, emergency landing on the continent, survival on sea ice and at sea, and fire. Bibliography.

1373. **Winter Recreation: Safety and Health Guidelines**. Centers for Disease Control. April 1981. 14p. ill. DHHS Publication No. (CDC) 81-8389. **HE20.7008:W73**.

Describes winter hazards for campers, and discusses precautionary measures and first aid treatment. References.

1374.   **Winter Recreation Safety Guide**. Forest Service. Rev. 1978. 38p. PA 1140. S/N 001-000-03856-7. $2.00. **A1.68:1140/2**.

Discusses hazards of winter recreation (snow avalanches, frostbite, altitude sickness, becoming lost or injured) and provides precautions necessary for safe recreational activity in forest and mountain areas.

See also "National Parks, Forests, and Recreation Areas" (entries 1335-1348).

For additional publications on this topic see Subject Bibliography **SB-017, Recreation and Outdoor Activities**.

Pests and Pest Control

1375. **Ants in the Home and Garden: How to Control Them**. Department of Agriculture. Rev. December 1978. 11p. Home and Garden Bulletin 28. S/N 001-000-03840-1. $1.00. **A1.77:28/11**.

Provides advice on finding ant nests both outdoors and indoors, and controlling ants in the home and garden.

1376. **Be Safe from Insects in Recreation Areas**. Department of Agriculture. Rev. August 1978. 7p. Home and Garden Bulletin 200. S/N 001-000-03802-8. $2.00. **A1.77:200/3**.

Provides advice on the use of repellents and space sprays and other methods to prevent insect annoyance.

1377. **Cabbage Insects: How to Control Them in the Home Garden**. Department of Agriculture. Rev. July 1978. folder, 8p. ill., tables. Home and Garden Bulletin 44. **A1.77:44/9**.

Provides advice on the types of pesticide to use to control cabbage insects.

1378. **Cockroaches: How to Control Them**. Department of Agriculture. Rev. April 1980. 10p. Leaflet 430. S/N 001-000-04226-2. $2.25. **A1.35:430/10**.

Describes cockroaches which are troublesome in buildings. Describes chemical methods, as well as other methods to control them.

1379. **Common Poisonous and Injurious Plants**. Food and Drug Administration. 1981. 28p. ill. DHHS Publication No. (FDA) 81-7006. S/N 017-012-00296-0. $3.25. **HE20.4002:P69**.

Illustrates each of twenty-six species of common poisonous and injurious plants, and discusses emergency treatment.

1380. **Control of Caterpillars on Cabbage and Other Cole Crops.** Department of Agriculture. October 1980. 24p. ill., tables. Farmers' Bulletin 2271. **A1.9:2271.**
Describes the different types of caterpillars that damage cole crops. Provides advice on selecting and applying pesticides to control them, and on natural and cultural methods of control.

1381. **Control of Insects on Deciduous Fruits and Tree Nuts in the Home Garden.** Department of Agriculture. Rev. May 1981. 36p. ill. Home and Garden Bulletin 211. S/N 001-000-04231-9. $2.00. **A1.77:211/3.**
Tells home gardeners how to control insect and mite pests of deciduous fruits and tree nuts in widespread areas of the United States through methods that exclude use of pesticides or minimize their use.

1382. **Controlling Clover Mites around the Home.** Department of Agriculture. Rev. February 1979. 4p. ill. Home and Garden Bulletin 134. **A1.77:134/2.**
Provides brief advice on controlling mites indoors and outdoors.

1383. **Controlling Head Lice.** 2d ed. Centers for Disease Control. September 1984. 18p. ill. DHHS Publication No. (CDC) 84-8397. **HE20.7002:L61/2.**
Describes the biology, diagnosis, and treatment of head lice. Discusses control of head lice in schools and other institutions. References.

1384. **Controlling Household Pests.** Department of Agriculture. Rev. July 1979. 31p. ill. Home and Garden Bulletin 96. S/N 001-000-03927-0. $1.50. **A1.77:96/7.**
Describes twenty-one varieties of household pests including ants, flies, mice, termites, and wasps and provides advice on how to control them.

1385. **Controlling the Japanese Beetle.** Agricultural Research Service. Rev. January 1982. 14p. ill. Home and Garden Bulletin 159. **A1.77:159/5.**
Discusses natural as well as chemical control of the Japanese beetle.

1386. **Controlling Wasps.** Agricultural Research Service. Rev. February 1978. 8p. ill. Home and Garden Bulletin 122. S/N 001-000-03757-9. $1.75. **A1.77:122/5.**
Describes the development of wasps and their nests, and discusses how to control them.

1387. **Douglas-Fir Tussock Moth Handbook: Protecting Ornamental and Shade Trees.** Forest Service. 1982. 11p. Agriculture Handbook 604. S/N 001-001-00583-5. $1.50. **A1.76:604.**
Describes the detection and removal of Douglas fir tussock moth from ornamental and shade trees, as well as from forest trees in western North America.

1388. **Gypsy Moth Handbook: Homeowner and the Gypsy Moth; Guidelines for Control.** Department of Agriculture. August 1979. 34p. ill. Home and Garden Bulletin 227. S/N 001-000-03950-4. $2.00. **A1.77:227.**
The gypsy moth is the most important defoliating insect of hardwood trees in the eastern United States. This guide tells the homeowner how to detect and control this insect. References.

1389.   **House Bat Management**. Fish and Wildlife Service. 1982. 37p. ill. Resource Publication 143. S/N 024-010-00606-4. $4.50. **I49.66:143**.

Provides numerous acceptable alternatives to lethal chemicals and poisons for dealing with bat problems and hazards.

1390.   **Insects and Related Pests of House Plants: How to Control Them**. Department of Agriculture. Rev. November 1978. 14p. ill. Home and Garden Bulletin 67. S/N 001-000-03498-7. $2.00. **A1.77:67/9**.

Tells how to recognize and control most common insects and selected pests that attack plants in houses and home greenhouses.

1391.   **Insects on Trees and Shrubs around the Home**. Department of Agriculture. Rev. June 1980. 51p. ill. Home and Garden Bulletin 214. S/N 001-000-04029-4. $4.25. **A1.77:214/2**.

Tells homeowners how to recognize and control the more common insects and mites that attack trees and shrubs in widespread areas of the United States. Also tells how to recognize beneficial insects. Index.

1392.   **Lawn Insects: How to Control Them**. Department of Agriculture. Rev. July 1980. 20p. ill. Home and Garden Bulletin 53. S/N 001-000-04142-8. $2.75. **A1.77:53/8**.

Describes how to control pests that infest soil and roots, that feed on leaf stems, that suck plant juice, and that inhabit but do not damage lawns.

1393.   **Pesticide Safety Guidelines for Personnel Protection**. Forest Service. October 1982. 45p. ill. **A13.36/2:P36/2**.

Provides instructions for the safe use of pesticides while they are being handled, stored, and applied in the field. Bibliography. Index.

1394.   **Poison Ivy, Poison Oak, and Poison Sumac: Identification, Precautions, Eradication**. Department of Agriculture. Rev. December 1978. 16p. ill., maps. Farmers' Bulletin 1972. **A1.9:1972/10**.

Describes different types of poison ivy, poison oak, and poison sumac. Discusses poisoning to man and animals, precautions, and control of plants by mechanical and chemical means.

1395.   **Protecting Home Cured Meat from Insects**. Department of Agriculture. Rev. March 1980. 6p. ill. Home and Garden Bulletin 109. **A1.77:109/5**.

Describes the pests which damage home-cured meat, and provides advice on how to protect against them.

1396.   **Southern Pine Beetle Handbook: Southern Pine Beetles Can Kill Your Ornamental Pine**. Department of Agriculture. October 1978. 15p. ill. Home and Garden Bulletin 226. **A1.77:226**.

Provides advice for the homeowner on how to detect and control the spread of the southern pine beetle.

1397.   **Subterranean Termites: Their Prevention and Control in Buildings**. Forest Service. Rev. October 1983. 36p. ill. Home and Garden Bulletin 64. S/N 001-000-04341-2. $2.50. **A1.77:64/8**.

Discusses biological considerations regarding termites, prevention of subterranean termite attack during construction, and control of termites in existing buildings.

1398.   **You Can Protect Your Home from Termites**. Forest Service. 1977. 12p. ill. S/N
001-001-00420-1. $1.00. **A13.2:T27**.
    Provides a pictorial background on the types of termites and their living and eating
habits, illustrates obvious signs of termite infestations, and shows which structural
situations attract termites.

    See also entry 104.

    For additional publications on this topic see Subject Bibliographies **SB-034, Insects**
and **SB-227, Pesticides, Insecticides, Fungicides, and Rodenticides**.

Pets and Animal Care

1399. **Animal Health, Livestock and Pets**. Department of Agriculture. 1984. 687p. ill. Yearbook of Agriculture 1984. S/N 001-000-04434-6. $10.00, cloth. **A1.10:984**.

Includes ninety-three articles which provide helpful information to both pet owners and those who have livestock in their charge under the following sections: backyard poultry and pet birds, dairy and beef cattle, sheep and goats, swine, keeping fish healthy, dogs and cats, rabbits and other small animals, and horses.

1400. **Getting Acquainted**. Bureau of Land Management. 1983. 28p. ill. **I53.2:Ac7**.

Intended to assist participants in the bureau's Adopt-a-Horse Program in caring for their new wild horse or burro during the first month or two, when the needs of wild horses or burros vary from those of their domestic counterparts.

1401. **Man Made Mobile: Early Saddles of Western North America**. Smithsonian Institution. 1980. 157p. ill. Smithsonian Studies in History and Technology No. 39. S/N 047-000-00359-8. $5.50. **SI1.28:39**.

Discusses appearances of prototypes of western saddles from the sixteenth to the nineteenth century, Mexican origins, developments among U.S. riders before the professional cowboy era, and developments among the native Americans of the Plains. Glossary. References.

1402. **So You'd Like to Adopt a Wild Horse or Burro?** Bureau of Land Management. Rev. 1983. 14p. ill. **I53.2:H78/2/983**.

Excess wild horses or burros that roam the public lands of the western states are placed for adoption in sixteen centers in ten western states, and one each in Pennsylvania and Tennessee. Participants may request ownership one year after adoption.

See also entry 528.

Physical Fitness

1403. Aqua Dynamics: Physical Conditioning through Water Exercises. President's Council on Physical Fitness and Sports. 1977 (repr. 1981). 32p. ill. S/N 040-000-00360-6. $3.75. **HE20.102:Aq3**.

An illustrated guide to over seventy conditioning exercises that can be done in a swimming pool.

1404. Children and Youth in Action: Physical Activities and Sports. Administration for Children, Youth and Families. November 1980. 57p. DHHS Publication No. (OHDS) 80-30182. **HE23.1002:C43/2**.

Gives parents suggestions for fostering their children's physical, social, and mental development by careful selection of physical activities and sports throughout the growing years from birth to the teen years.

1405. Fitness Fundamentals: Guidelines for Personal Exercise Programs. President's Council on Physical Fitness and Sports. 1985. folder, 8p. **HE20.108:F96**.

Provides advice on beginning or continuing an individual physical fitness program.

1406. Fitness Trail: Building, Signing, and Using the Trail. Forest Service. August 1984. 32p. ill. S/N 001-001-00599-1. $1.75. **A13.2:F55/2**.

Describes the "fitness trail," and provides plans for building the trail, construction guidelines, materials lists, and information on signs.

1407. The Individual's Handbook on Physical Fitness. Department of the Army. May 1983. 88p. ill. DA Pamphlet 350-18. **D101.22:350-18**.

Provides guidelines on designing an exercise program, diet and nutrition, weight control, and managing stress.

1408. **Introduction to Physical Fitness**. President's Council on Physical Fitness and Sports. 1980 (repr. 1984). 25p. ill. DHHS Publication No. (OS) 84-50068. S/N 017-002-00144-5. $2.75. **HE20.108:P56/2**.

Includes self-testing activities, graded exercises, and a jogging program.

1409. **An Introduction to Running: One Step at a Time**. President's Council on Physical Fitness and Sports. 1980. 16p. ill. S/N 017-001-000425-1. $2.75. **HE20.102:St4**.

Includes suggestions for developing a comfortable and economical running style, and on what to wear. Describes six stretching exercises.

1410. **Physical Readiness Training**. Department of the Army. Rev. October 1980. 257p. ill. FM 21-20. **D101.21:21-20/3**.

Intended for army leaders to establish and conduct physical readiness training programs. Includes a number of individual exercises and group games.

1411. **Suggestions for School Programs: Youth Physical Fitness**. President's Council on Physical Fitness and Sports. Rev. September 1980. 98p. ill. S/N 017-001-00432-4. $4.75. **HE20.108:Y8/980**.

Includes a number of individual exercise and physical fitness programs which are suitable for elementary and secondary schools.

1412. **Walking for Exercise and Pleasure**. President's Council on Physical Fitness and Sports. 1984. 13p. ill. S/N 017-001-00447-2. $1.00. **HE20.102:W15**.

Provides information on the importance of walking as a form of exercise. Explains how walking provides exercise to people of all ages, how walking contributes to fitness, and what to wear. Includes warmup exercises.

See also entry 975.

For additional publications on this topic see Subject Bibliography **SB-239, Physical Fitness**.

Postal Service

GENERAL

1413. At the Crossroads: An Inquiry into Rural Post Offices and the Communities They Serve. Postal Rate Commission. 1980. 65p. tables. **Y3/P84/4:2C88**.

Reviews the history and development of postal delivery and the Postal Service as it affects rural areas, and develops a profile of the communities and rural population served. Bibliography.

1414. A Consumer's Directory of Postal Services and Products. Postal Service. Rev. November 1983. 18p. ill. Publication 201. **P1.2:C76/2/983**.

Provides basic information on the products and services provided by the post office.

1415. Express Mail: Shipment Claim Locations, Post to Post Office. Postal Service. April 1983. 193p. Publication 272. **P1.2:Sh6**.

Lists all of the facilities at which Express Mail Post Office to Post Office Service shipments may be claimed.

1416. How to Prepare and Wrap Packages. Postal Service. August 1982. 7p. ill. Publication 227. **P1.2:P12/2**.

Provides advice on how to select the proper container, cushion the contents, use proper wrapping and closures, and correctly address and mark the package.

1417. National Five Digit ZIP Code and Post Office Directory. Postal Service. 1985. 2214p. Publication 65. S/N 039-000-00270-1. $9.00. **P1.10/8:985**.

Issued annually. Lists the current five-digit zip codes for states and territories of the United States. Each state usually has two sections: a list of post offices arranged alphabetically and a detailed breakdown for large cities and metropolitan areas. It also includes an alphabetical list and a numerical list of post offices.

1418. Postal Bulletin. Postal Service. Weekly. paging varies. ill., tables. S/N 739-001-00000-5. Symbol POB. $71.00 per year. Single copy $1.50. **P1.3:no**.

This periodical is primarily intended to forward changes in postal rules and regulations to postal officials and employees. Includes stamp posters with information regarding new stamps that was previously published separately. Contains notices of new issues which are of interest to philatelists.

1419.   Zip +4 State Directory. . . . Postal Service. October 1984. Publication 66-no. $9.00 per volume from: St. Louis PDC, ZIP +4 State Directory Orders. P.O. Box 14921, St. Louis, MO 63180-9988. Make checks payable to "U.S. Postal Service." **P1.10/9:66-no/985**.

Provides detailed lists of areas by street numbers, buildings, businesses and institutions to indicate nine-digit zip code numbers. The first two digits of the "+4" denote a delivery "sector," which may be several blocks, a group of streets, several office buildings, or a small geographic area. The last two digits denote a delivery "segment" which might be one floor of an office building, one side of a street, a firm, a suite, a post office box or group of boxes, or other specific geographic locations.

> 1419-1.   **Alaska, Oregon**. 736p. Publication 66-33.

> 1419-2.   **Alabama, Mississippi**. 1099p. Publication 66-18.

> 1419-3.   **Arizona, New Mexico**. 799p. Publication 66-30.

> 1419-4.   **Arkansas, Louisiana**. 1161p. Publication 66-24.

> 1419-5.   **California**. 4 vols. vol. 1. **Acampo thru Hayfork**. 1198p. vol. 2. **Hayward thru Oakhurst**. 1174p. vol. 3. **Oakland thru San Joaquin**. 1170p. vol. 4. **San Jose thru Zenia**. 1123p. Publication 66-32/v.1-4.

> 1419-6.   **Colorado**. 693p. Publication 66-29.

> 1419-7.   **Connecticut, Rhode Island**. 832p. Publication 66-03.

> 1419-8.   **Delaware, District of Columbia, Maryland**. 1033p. Publication 66-07.

> 1419-9.   **District of Columbia, Virginia**. 1174p. Publication 66-08.

> 1419-10.   **Florida**. 2 vols. vol. 1. **Alachua thru Merritt Island**. 1205p. vol. 2. **Miami thru Zolfo Springs**. 1291p. Publication 66-12/v.1,2.

> 1419-11.   **Georgia**. 1105p. Publication 66-11.

> 1419-12.   **Hawaii and Caribbean and Pacific Locations**. 441p. Publication 66-35.

> 1419-13.   **Illinois**. 2 vols. vol. 1. **Abingdon thru Johnston City**. 1092p. vol. 2. **Joliet thru Zion**. 939p. Publication 66-20/v.1,2.

> 1419-14.   **Indiana**. 1062p. Publication 66-15.

> 1419-15.   **Iowa**. 660p. Publication 66-22.

> 1419-16.   **Kansas, Nebraska**. 948p. Publication 66-26.

> 1419-17.   **Kentucky, West Virginia**. 989p. Publication 66-16.

> 1419-18.   **Maine, New Hampshire, Vermont**. 475p. Publication 66-01.

1419-19.   **Massachusetts.** 1192p. Publication 66-02.

1419-20.   **Michigan.** 2 vols. vol. 1. **Acme thru L'Anse.** 804p. vol. 2. **Lansing thru Zeeland.** 675p. Publication 66-13/v.1,2.

1419-21.   **Minnesota.** 937p. Publication 66-21.

1419-22.   **Missouri.** 986p. Publication 66-23.

1419-23.   **Nevada, Utah.** 553p. Publication 66-31.

1419-24.   **New Jersey.** 1307p. Publication 66-06.

1419-25.   **New York.** 3 vols. vol. 1. **Accord thru Florida.** 757p. vol. 2. **Flushing thru New Woodstock.** 780p. vol. 3. **New York thru Yulan.** 1091p. Publication 66-04/v.1-3.

1419-26.   **North Carolina.** 972p. Publication 66-09.

1419-27.   **North Dakota, South Dakota, Montana, Wyoming.** 831p. Publication 66-25.

1419-28.   **Ohio.** 2 vols. vol. 1. **Aberdeen thru Danville.** 885p. vol. 2. **Dayton thru Zoar.** 1097p. Publication 66-14/v.1,2.

1419-29.   **Oklahoma.** 664p. Publication 66-27.

1419-30.   **Pennsylvania.** 2 vols. vol. 1. **Aaronsburg thru Petrolia.** 1118p. vol. 2. **Philadelphia thru Zullinger.** 776p. Publication 66-05/v.1,2.

1419-31.   **South Carolina.** 528p. Publication 66-10.

1419-32.   **Tennessee.** 792p. Publication 66-17.

1419-33.   **Texas.** 3 vols. vol. 1. **Abbott thru Fort Stockton.** 1025p. vol. 2. **Fort Worth thru Lozano.** 871p. vol. 3. **Lubbock thru Zephyr.** 930p. Publication 66-28/v.1-3.

1419-34.   **Washington.** 975p. Publication 66-34.

1419-35.   **Wisconsin.** 1009p. Publication 66-19.

STAMP COLLECTING

1420.   **Exploring the World of Stamps in Your Classroom: A Teacher's Guide to Stamp Collecting.** Postal Service. 1982. 103p. ill. **P1.31/4:St2/teacher.**
Includes classroom lesson plans and suggested games and activities to incorporate stamps into the elementary and secondary school curriculum. Includes background information on stamps. References.

1421.   **For the Fun of It: A Helpful Guide for New Stamp Collectors.** Postal Service. October 1978. 31p. ill. **P1.31/4:F96.**
Provides advice on starting a stamp collection. Glossary.

1422. **Postage Stamps of the United States.** Postal Service. 1974-1981. 570p. ill. Publication 9. S/N 039-000-00267-1. $24.00. **P4.10:970/trans. 1-7.**

An illustrated description of all U.S. postage and special service stamps issued from 1 July 1847 through 1980. Tables containing detailed statistics on postage stamps issued since 1933 appear in appendix. Updated by annual looseleaf supplements, which are sold separately.

See also entries 211, 212.

For additional publications on this topic see Subject Bibliography **SB-011, U.S. Postage Stamps.**

Posters

1423. **America the Beautiful**. Soil Conservation Service. 1966 (repr. 1976). 52 posters, 20x24" ea. S/N 001-007-00045-9. $20.00. **A57.8/2:set.**
  Set of fifty-two colored lithographics representing each state plus Puerto Rico and the Virgin Islands.

1424. **American Soldier**. Department of the Army. posters. 9x13" ea.
  This series of colored posters is intended to show uniforms of the American soldier during various wars or intervening historical periods.

> 1424-1. **Set Number 1**. 1964 (repr. 1975). 10 posters. S/N 008-020-00226-7. $6.00. **D101.35:So4/set 1.**
>   Covers the period 1781-1855.

> 1424-2. **Set Number 2**. 1965 (repr. 1975). 10 posters. S/N 008-020-00227-5. $6.00. **D101.35:So4/set 2.**
>   Covers the period 1863-1963.

> 1424-3. **Set Number 3**. 1969 (repr. 1975). 10 posters. S/N 008-020-00225-9. $6.00. **D101.35:So4/set 3.**
>   Covers the period 1775-1965.

> 1424-4. **Set Number 4**. 1980. 10 posters. S/N 008-020-00760-9. $6.00. **D114.13: So4/2/set 4.**
>   Covers the period 1776-1975.

> 1424-5. **Set Number 5**. 1982. 10 posters. S/N 008-020-00886-9. $6.00. **D114.13: So4/2/set 5.**
>   Covers the period 1780-1966.

1425.   **Armed Forces Decorations and Awards**. American Forces Information Service. 1984. poster, 28x42". S/N 008-001-00140-1. $4.00. **D2.9:17-D**.
    This color poster depicts various medals, ribbons, and clasps awarded to members of the Army, Navy, Air Force, Marine Corps, and Coast Guard.

1426.   **Army Art: The Revolution to Vietnam**. Department of the Army. 1975. 12 posters, 17x22" ea. S/N 008-020-00902-4. $8.00. **D101.35:So4/2/no.1**.
    Reproductions of color paintings showing Army military actions in the Revolutionary War, Mexican War, Civil War, Indian Wars, Spanish American War, World War I, World War II, Korean War, and Vietnam Conflict.

1427.   **Army Engineers at War: Combat Art of the War in Europe, 1943-1945**. Army Corps of Engineers. 1981. 12 posters, 16x20" ea. S/N 008-022-00154-9. $8.00. **D103.49/3:Ar5**.
    Reproductions of color paintings which depict Army Engineer combat and construction operations during the liberation of Western Europe in World War II.

1428.   **Eastman Forts**. Army Center of Military History. 1979. 10 posters, 16x20" ea. and pamphlet. S/N 008-029-00112-8. $7.50. **D114.13:Ea7**.
    Reproductions of paintings by Seth Eastman, an Army engineer during the period 1850-1875. Illustrates Army forts located in Connecticut, New York, Pennsylvania, South Carolina, Florida, Michigan, Minnesota, Arizona Territory, and Dakota Territory.

1429.   **Portfolio of American Agriculture**. Department of Agriculture. 1981. 20 posters, 20x24" and folder. S/N 001-000-04236-0. $11.00. **A1.32:Am3**.
    Color photographs and paintings of various agricultural scenes and landscapes in America. Folder describes the posters and provides credits.

1430.   **Snakes: Poisonous and Nonpoisonous Species**. Army Corps of Engineers. 1981. poster, 28x37". S/N 008-022-00153-1. $4.75. **D103.49/3:Sn1**.
    Illustrates eighteen species of snakes including the northern copperhead, timber rattlesnake, black king snake, and black rat snake.

1431.   **Soldiers of the American Revolution**. Army Center of Military History. 1974. 10 posters, 17x22" ea. S/N 008-020-00534-7. $7.00. **D114.13:So4**.
    These full-color prints depict famous battles of the Revolutionary War, from Montreal to Charleston.

1432.   **United States Air Force Composite**. Department of the Air Force. 1981. poster, 17x23". S/N 008-070-00464-0. $4.25. **D301.76/5:Un3/2**.
    Illustrates and identifies about thirty different military aircraft of the U.S. Air Force.

1433.   **United States Air Force Fine Art Series**. Department of Air Force. poster, 17x23" ea. **D301.76/4:no**.
    Reproductions of color paintings from the U.S. Air Force Art Collection depicting scenes relating to military aviation from the Wright brothers to the present.

1433-1.   **Set 2.** 1980. 12 posters. S/N 008-070-00424-1. $8.50.

1433-2.   **Set 3.** 1980. 12 posters. S/N 008-070-00450-0. $8.00.

1433-3.   **Set 4.** 1982. 12 posters. S/N 008-070-00469-1. $8.50.

1433-4.   **Set 5.** 1982. 12 posters. S/N 008-070-00477-1. $8.00.

1433-5.   **Set 6.** 1984. 12 posters. S/N 008-070-00518-2. $16.00.

1434.   **United States Air Force Lithographic Series.** Department of Air Force. posters, 17x23". **D301.76:no.**

Reproductions of color photographs of U.S. Air Force military aircraft and missiles, or typical operations.

1434-1.   **Set No. 31.** 1981. 12 posters. S/N 008-070-00455-1. $8.50.

1434-2.   **Set No. 32.** 1981. 12 posters. S/N 008-070-00467-4. $8.00.

1434-3.   **Set No. 33.** 1983. 11 posters. S/N 008-070-00473-9. $8.00.

1434-4.   **Set No. 34.** 1982. 12 posters. S/N 008-070-00476-3. $8.50.

1434-5.   **Set No. 35.** 1984. 12 posters. S/N 008-070-00491-7. $8.00.

1435.   **United States Marine Corps Uniforms, 1983.** Marine Corps. 12 posters, 16x21" and booklet. S/N 008-055-00162-5. $14.00. **D214.16/4:Un3/983.**

Reproductions of paintings of various uniforms and insignia worn by Marine Corps officer and enlisted personnel. Includes booklet with description of each poster.

1436.   **Wildlife Portrait Series.** Fish and Wildlife Service. posters, size varies. **I49.71:no.**

Reproductions of color photographs or paintings of fish and wildlife in their natural habitat. The sets below include a booklet or sheet which describes each poster.

1436-1.   **No. 1. Birds and Mammals.** 1969 (repr. 1976). 10 posters, 14x17" ea. and booklet. S/N 024-010-00190-9. $6.50.

1436-2.   **No. 2. Sports Fish.** 1971. 10 posters, 14x17" ea. and booklet. S/N 024-010-00277-8. $6.00.

1436-3.   **No. 4. Host of Sea Birds, Alaska.** 1980. 6 posters, 16x24" ea. and booklet. S/N 024-010-00530-1. $6.00.

1436-4.   **No. 5. Birds and Mammals.** 1980. 10 posters, 16x20" ea. and sheet. S/N 024-010-00528-9. $7.50.

See also entries 458, 459, 461.

For additional publications on this topic see Subject Bibliography **SB-057, Posters, Charts, Picture Sets, and Decals.**

Public Assistance
Programs, Poverty

1437. **Background on Poverty**. Congress. House. Committee on Ways and Means. October 1983. 171p. charts, tables. Committee Print, 98th Congress, 1st Session. **Y4.W36:WMCP 98-15**.

Analyzes trends in poverty since 1960. Examines reasons for changes in the rate of poverty, and discusses demographic characteristics of the poverty population. Analyzes techniques used to measure the number of poor Americans. Footnote references.

1438. **Characteristics of State Plans for Aid to Families with Dependent Children under the Social Security Act, Title IV-A: Eligibility, Assistance, Administration**. Social Security Administration. 1984. 355p. tables. SSA Publication No. 80-21235. **HE3.65/2:984**.

Summarizes characteristics of plans of each state in a four-part format; administration, eligibility, assistance, and optional extension of assistance.

1439. **Characteristics of the Population below the Poverty Level: 1983**. Bureau of the Census. 1985. 218p. tables. Current Population Reports, Series P-60, No. 147. S/N 003-001-91653-3. $7.00. **C3.186:P-60/147**.

Issued annually. Poverty statistics are cross-tabulated by such characteristics as race, family relationship, type of residence, education, work experience, and type of income received.

1440. **Do Food Stamp and Other Customers Buy the Same Products in Supermarkets?** Economics, Statistics and Cooperatives Service. March 1979. 21p. tables. Agricultural Economics Report 421. **A1.107:421**.

This study, based on a 1976 survey analyzes and compares the supermarket purchases of people receiving food stamps and all other customers. Intended as a first step to determine if food stamp users are buying foods required for satisfactory nutrition. References.

1441. **Expenditures for Public Assistance Programs (Approved under Titles I, IV-A, IV-B, X, XIV, XVI, XIX, and XX of the Social Security Act), Fiscal Year 1979**. Social Security Administration. June 1979. 22p. tables. SSA Publication No. 13-11951. **HE3.70:979**.

Provides summary data on expenditures by states for the following five programs: Aid to Families with Dependent Children, Supplementary Security Income, Medicaid, Social Services under Title XX, and Child Welfare Services under Title IV-B.

1442. **Facts about the Food Stamp Program**. Food and Nutrition Service. April 1984. 10p. PA 1340. **A1.68:1340**.

Provides brief information on eligibility requirements, applications, and receiving and using food stamps.

1443. **Helping the Homeless: A Resource Guide**. Department of Health and Human Services. 1984. 213p. S/N 017-000-00247-3. $7.00. **HE1.6/3:H75**.

Provides information on effective ways to establish and operate local projects to feed, shelter, and in other ways care for homeless persons.

1444. **Program and Demographic Characteristics of Supplemental Security Income Beneficiaries, December 1982**. Social Security Administration. December 1983. 51p. SSA Publication No. 13-11977. S/N 017-070-00403-2. $2.00. **HE3.71/2:982**.

Presents summary data by state on the 3.8 million aged, blind, and disabled persons who received federally administrated supplementary security income (SSI) payments in December 1982.

1445. **Public Assistance Recipients in Standard Metropolitan Statistical Areas: February 1982**. Social Security Administration. April 1983. 34p. tables. SSA Publication No. 13-11921. S/N 017-070-00396-6. $3.75. **HE3.61/2:982**.

Presents caseload data for standard metropolitan statistical areas (SMSAs) under the program of Aid to Families with Dependent Children and General Assistance.

1446. **Research Tables Based on Characteristics of State Plans for Aid to Families with Dependent Children: Administration, Eligibility, Assistance Payments in Effect October 1, 1983**. Social Security Administration. 1984. 92p. tables. **HE3.65/2:984/ tables**.

Presents analyses of thirty-eight items in state plans for Aid to Families with Dependent Children and compares variations among the fifty states, the District of Columbia, Guam, Puerto Rico, and the Virgin Islands.

1447. **Supplemental Security Income Program for the Aged, Blind, and Disabled: Selected Characteristics of State Supplementation Programs as of January 1, 1984**. Social Security Administration. December 1984. 101p. tables. SSA Publication No. 13-11975. S/N 017-070-00410-5. $4.50. **HE3.2:Su7/3**.

Focuses on eligibility provisions and basic levels of assistance payments for persons receiving supplementary payments in various states and the District of Columbia.

For additional publications on this topic see Subject Bibliography **SB-030, Social Welfare and Services**.

Public Lands

1448. **Are There Any Public Lands for Sale?** Bureau of Land Management. September 1983. 11p. **I53.2:P96/15**.
Provides information about the sale of public lands which have been declared excess.

1449. **50 Years of Public Land Management, 1934-1984**. Bureau of Land Management. 1984. 27p. ill. **I53.2:P96/934-84**.
Provides a history of the Taylor Grazing Act of 1934 which ended the previously free and unregulated grazing on public lands and introduced federal protection and management of public lands and their resources.

1450. **Promise of the Land**. Bureau of Land Management. 1980. 40p. ill., charts. **I53.2:L22/10**.
Designed to acquaint the general public with the bountiful assets of the public lands and the promise they hold for Americans today and in the future.

1451. **Public Land Statistics, 1983**. Bureau of Land Management. 1984. 237p. map, tables. S/N 024-011-00158-1. $6.50. **I53.1/2:983**.
Issued annually. Provides a wide variety of statistics relating to the public lands of the United States. Subject index.

1452. **Surveying Our Public Lands**. Bureau of Land Management. Rev. 1980. 17p. ill., maps. S/N 024-011-00125-5. $3.50. **I53.2:P76/7/980**.
Provides a brief history and description of how the public lands are surveyed.

1453. **Your Public Lands**. Bureau of Land Management. Quarterly. 24p. ill. **I53.12:vol/no**.
This periodical includes articles of general interest on the public lands in the American West and Alaska, including Bureau of Land Management administration of the public lands, and recreational activities and opportunities.

See also entries 1308, 1310, 1311.

Science, Engineering, and Technology

1454. **Brief History of Measurement Systems with a Chart of the Modernized Metric System**. National Bureau of Standards. Rev. August 1981. 4p. chart. Special Publication 304A. S/N 003-003-02366-3. $1.75. **C13.10:304A/7**.

Provides a brief history of measurement systems, and includes a chart of the seven base units in the metric system.

1455. **Characteristics of Recent Science/Engineering Graduates, 1982**. National Science Foundation. 1984. 114p. tables. NSF 84-318. **NS1.22:En3/982**.

Presents detailed data on demographic and employment characteristics of men and women who received a bachelor's or master's degree in science and engineering during the 1979/1980 and 1980/1981 academic years. Data reflect status as of spring 1982.

1456. **Mathematics**. 3 vols. Bureau of Naval Personnel. **D208.11:M42/2/vol/yr**.

1456-1. **Vol. 1**. 1966 (repr. 1980). 233p. NAVPERS 10069-C. S/N 008-047-00082-1. $7.50.

Covers number systems, fractions, exponents, radicals, common logarithms, algebraic fundamentals, plane and solid geometry, and trigonometry. Index.

1456-2. **Vol. 2**. 1968 (repr. 1981). 273p. NAVPERS 10071-B. S/N 008-047-00083-9. $8.00.

Covers mathematics from quadratic equations through the first principles of differential calculus at the college level. Index.

1456-3. **Vol. 3**. 1969. 187p. NAVPERS 10073-A. S/N 008-047-00084-7. $7.00.

Covers descriptive statistics and statistical inferences, number systems, sets and subsets, boolean algebra, and matrices and determinants. Index.

1457.   **National Science Foundation Guide to Programs, Fiscal Year 1985**. 1984. 90p. NSF 84-40. S/N 038-000-00550-2. $3.50. **NS1.20:P94/985.**

Describes under seven categories or disciplines the research programs of the National Science Foundation for which grants and awards will be made during FY 1985. Provides information on submitting requests for prospective applicants.

1458.   **Science and Engineering Education for the 1980s and Beyond**. National Science Foundation. October 1980. 88p. tables. NSF 80-78. S/N 038-000-00467-1. $5.50. **NS1.2:Ed8/20.**

Examines basic scientific and technological education of all citizens, and analyzes science and mathematics education at the high school level. Discusses the supply and demand for scientific and engineering personnel, and analyzes professional education for engineers, scientists, and technicians. Footnote references. Bibliography.

1459.   **Science and Engineering Employment, 1970-1980**. National Science Foundation. 1981. 25p. charts, tables. NSF 81-310. S/N 038-000-00495-6. $3.25. **NS1.2:Em7/3.**

Presents data on employment growth in the 1970s; occupational trends for scientists, computer specialists, and engineers; sectoral employment in business/industry, educational institutions, and federal government.

1460.   **Science Indicators, 1982**. National Science Board. 1983. 344p. charts, tables. NSB 83-1. S/N 038-000-00538-3. $9.50. **NS1.28:83-1.**

Issued biennially. Presents a quantitative assessment of the status of science and technology in the United States. References. Subject index.

1461.   **Women and Minorities in Science and Engineering**. National Science Foundation. January 1982. 124p. charts, tables. NSF 82-302. S/N 038-000-00498-1. $7.00. **NS1.2:W84/2/982.**

Most of the data in this series of biennial statistical reports are for the 1978-1979 period. Most of the data on minorities are focused on blacks and Asian-Americans.

See also entries 488, 490, 492, 712.

Smoking and Health

1462.   **Become an Ex-Smoker. How a Non-Smoker Can Help a Smoker.** Public Health Service. 1983. folder, 3p. DHHS Publication No. (PHS) 83-50200. **HE20.8:Sm7/3.**
Intended to help the nonsmoker understand why it is difficult for a smoker to quit.

1463.   **Calling It Quits: The Latest Advice on How to Give Up Cigarettes.** National Cancer Institute. February 1980. 37p. ill., tables. NIH Publication No. 80-1824-A. **HE20.3152:Q4/2.**
Provides advice on quitting smoking. Includes lists of formal programs available to stop smoking.

1464.   **For Good: A Guide to Living as a Nonsmoker.** National Cancer Institute. August 1983. 20p. ill. NIH Publication No. 83-2494. **HE20.3158:N73.**
Provides advice for the former smoker who has quit.

1465.   **A Guide to Smoking and Your Health: What You Don't Know Will Hurt You.** Public Health Service. 1983. folder, 3p. DHHS Publication No. (PHS) 83-50197. **HE20.8:Sm7.**
Provides answers to frequently asked questions about the risks from smoking.

1466.   **The Health Consequences of Smoking: Cancer; A Report of the Surgeon General.** Office on Smoking and Health. 1982. 322p. charts, tables. DHHS Publication No. (PHS) 82-50179. S/N 017-001-00441-3. $6.50. **HE20.25/2:982.**
Issued annually. In contrast with the fourteen previous reports in this annual series, the 1982 report examines the relationship between smoking and a single category of disease—cancer. References. Index.

1467.   **The Health Consequences of Smoking: Cardiovascular Disease; A Report of the Surgeon General, 1983.** Office on Smoking and Health. 1984. 384p. charts, tables. DHHS Publication No. (PHS) 84-50204. S/N 017-001-00448-1. $9.00. **HE20.25/2:983.**

The 1983 annual report is the second volume in the series to focus on a specific category of disease. This report finds that the number of deaths from coronary diseases caused by smoking significantly exceeds those from cancer. Extensive footnote references. Index.

1468. **Health Consequences of Smoking for Women: A Report of the Surgeon General**. Office on Smoking and Health. 1980. 375p. charts, tables. S/N 017-001-00430-8. $9.50. **HE20.2:Sm7/5**.

This twelfth annual report on the health consequences of smoking focuses on risks to women from lung cancer, heart disease, and other consequences as well as the harm which smoking causes to the unborn babies and infants of smoking mothers. References.

1469. **Health Consequence of Smoking: The Changing Cigarette; A Report of the Surgeon General**. Office on Smoking and Health. 1981. 269p. charts, tables. DHHS Publication No. (PHS) 81-50156. S/N 017-002-00149-6. $7.00. **HE20.2:Sm7/7**.

This fourteenth annual report on the health consequences of smoking considers the relative health effects of cigarettes with varying levels of tar and nicotine, and the relative health effects of cigarette additives. References. Index.

1470. **A Parent's Guide to Smoking and Teenagers. If Your Kids Think Everybody Smokes, They Don't Know Everybody**. Public Health Service. 1983. folder, 3p. DHHS Publication No. (PHS) 83-50201. **HE20.8:Sm7/2**.

Provides answers to frequently asked questions about teenage smoking.

1471. **Quit It: A Guide to Help You Stop Smoking**. National Cancer Institute. Rev. August 1983. 12p. ill. NIH Publication No. 83-1824. **HE20.3158:Q4/983**.

Provides tips to help the smoker quit his habit.

1472. **Smoking, Tobacco, and Health: A Fact Book**. Office on Smoking and Health. 1981. 36p. charts, tables. DHHS Publication No. (PHS) 80-50150. S/N 017-001-00431-6. $4.75. **HE20.2:Sm7/6**.

Presents economic, social, and medical information on the extent of smoking and on tobacco and its effects on health.

1473. **Teenage Smoking: Immediate and Long Term Patterns**. National Institute of Education. November 1979. 268p. tables. **HE19.202:Sm7**.

Presents detailed statistics from a 1979 survey of teenagers (twelve to eighteen years) regarding their smoking behavior and related attitudes and demographics, and from a follow-up survey of a sample surveyed in 1974 when they were teenagers to trace their smoking practices into young adulthood (seventeen to twenty-three years).

1474. **Why Do You Smoke?** National Cancer Institute. Rev. August 1984. folder, 6p. NIH Publication No. 84-1822. **HE20.3152:Sm7/5/984**.

Includes a self-test which measures six factors that describe one's smoking behavior.

For additional publications on this topic see Subject Bibliography **SB-015, Smoking**.

Social and Ethical Issues

1475. **Deciding to Forego Life-Sustaining Treatment: A Report on the Ethical, Medical and Legal Issues in Treatment Decisions**. President's Commission for the Study of Ethical Problems in Medicine and Biomedical and Behavioral Research. March 1983. 554p. S/N 040-000-00470-0. $8.00. **Pr40.8:Et3/L62/2**.

Part 1 examines considerations common to all decision making on life-sustaining therapy. Part 2 examines particular groups which raise special concerns: incapacitated, unconscious, infants, and heart-stopped patients. Footnote references.

1476. **Defining Death: Medical, Legal and Ethical Issues in the Determination of Death**. President's Commission for the Study of Ethical Problems in Medicine and Biomedical and Behavioral Research. July 1981. 166p. ill., charts, tables. S/N 040-000-00451-3. $6.50. **Pr40.8:Et3/D34**.

Discusses the need to redefine the meaning of death, who ought to redefine death, and what definition ought to be adopted. Footnote references.

1477. **Making Health Care Decisions: The Ethical and Legal Implications of Informed Consent in the Patient-Practitioner Relationship. Vol. 1. Report**. President's Commission for the Study of Ethical Problems in Medicine and Biomedical and Behavioral Research. October 1982. 196p. tables. S/N 040-000-00459-9. $6.00. **Pr40.8:Et3/H34/v.1**.

This study traces the history of informed consent in the law and in medical practice and discusses current issues including making health care decisions for patients who lack a decision-making capacity. Footnote references.

1478. **National Agenda for the Eighties: Report of the President's Commission for a National Agenda for the Eighties**. 1980. 214p. S/N 040-001-00227-8. $7.50. **Pr39.8:Ag3/Ag3**.

This is the report of a commission appointed by President Carter to conduct an objective study of problems facing the nation in the 1980s. Discusses the demographic background, restoring economic growth, the social agenda, democracy and politics, and foreign policy. Includes summaries of the nine panel reports on these topics, which were published separately and are available from the GPO.

1479.   **Securing Access to Health Care: The Ethical Implications of Differences in the Availability of Health Services. Vol. 1. Report.** President's Commission for a Study of Ethical Problems in Medicine and Biomedical and Behavioral Research. March 1983. 223p. charts, tables. S/N 040-000-00472-6. $6.00. **Pr40.8:Et3/H34/2/v.1.**

Examines the effects of differences in ability to pay and distribution of health care services; impact of existing government policies and programs on access to health care; and problems of achieving equitable access in a time of rising health care costs. Footnote references. Index.

1480.   **Summing Up: Final Report on Studies of the Ethical and Legal Problems in Medicine and Biomedical and Behavioral Research.** President's Commission for the Study of Ethical Problems in Medicine and Biomedical and Behavioral Research. March 1983. 137p. S/N 040-000-00475-1. $5.50. **Pr40.8:Et3/Su6.**

Presents an overview of the work of the commission since January 1980. Provides summaries of its six studies on health care and six studies on biomedical and behavioral research. The final chapter discusses recurrent themes. Bibliography.

Social Security

GENERAL

1481.   Annotated Readings in Social Security. Social Security Administration. October 1982. 600p. SSA Publication No. 13-11754. S/N 017-070-00386-9. $12.00. **HE3.38: R22/2**.

This annotated bibliography contains 2,593 entries for books, journal articles, and government documents pertaining to social security programs. Entries are grouped under twelve broad topics. Author and subject indexes.

1482.   Compilation of Social Security Laws. Congress. House. Committee on Ways and Means. Rev. 1985. 1009p. Committee Print, 99th Congress, 1st Session. **Y4.W36:WMCP 99-7**.

Includes the full text of the Social Security Act in effect as of 1 January 1985 including all amendments. Also includes selected provisions of the Internal Revenue Code of 1954, as amended dealing with social security taxes. Index.

1483.   Report of the National Commission on Social Security Reform. January 1983. 276p. charts, tables. S/N 040-000-00463-7. $7.50. **Pr40.8:So1/So1**.

Contains the findings and recommendations of the commission concerning the financial condition of the Old-Age, Survivors, and Disability Insurance Trust funds in both the short range (1983-1989) and the long range (1983-2056).

1484.   Social Security Beneficiaries by State and County: December 1983. Social Security Administration. 1984. 231p. SSA Publication No. 13-11954. S/N 017-070-00409-1. $7.00. **HE3.73/2:983**.

Provides data by state and county on the number of persons receiving social security benefits, and the monthly amount being paid.

1485. **Social Security Bulletin**. Social Security Administration. Monthly, and annual statistical supplement. approx. 60p. tables. S/N 717-026-00000-4. Symbol SSB. $23.00 per yr. Single monthly copy $2.50. **HE3.3:vol/no. Annual Statistical Supplement**. approx. 280p. tables. $6.50. **HE3.3/3:yr.**

This periodical includes articles of general interest on social security and related topics. Regular department on current operating statistics presents detailed data in forty-two series under the following topics; income maintenance programs, social security trust funds, OASI cash benefits, supplemental security income, public assistance, black lung benefits, unemployment insurance, and economic indicators. *Annual Statistical Supplement* contains detailed current and historical statistics on these programs. Introductory section contains detailed historical description on these programs, and how benefits are determined.

1486. **Social Security Handbook**. 8th ed. Social Security Administration. 1984. 441p. tables. SSA Publication No. 05-10135. S/N 017-070-00406-7. $9.00. **HE3.6/2: So1/3/984.**

Presents detailed information on federal programs covered in the Social Security Act, including retirement insurance, survivors' insurance, disability insurance, health insurance, supplemental security income, and black lung benefits. Index.

1487. **Social Security Programs throughout the World, 1983**. Social Security Administration. Rev. 1984. 307p. tables. Research Report 59. SSA Publication No. 13-11805. S/N 017-070-00408-3. $9.00. **HE3.49:59.**

Highlights the principal features of the social security systems of 140 countries and territories around the world. Information is presented in the form of a two-page chart for each country.

For additional publications on this topic see Subject Bibliography **SB-165, Social Security**.

SOCIAL SECURITY ADMINISTRATION PAMPHLETS

The following pamphlets describing social security eligibility and benefits are available free at Social Security Administration local offices throughout the country.

1488. **Estimating Your Social Security Retirement Check: For Workers Who Reach 62 in 1979-83**. Rev. January 1983. folder, 11p. tables. SSA Publication No. 05-10088. **HE3.2:R31/5/985.**

Provides step-by-step instructions for retired workers who reach sixty-two in 1979 or later to estimate their social security benefits. A 1979 amendment to the Social Security Act changed the method for determining benefits.

1489. **Estimating Your Social Security Retirement Check: For Workers Who Reached 62 before 1979**. Rev. January 1985. folder, 9p. tables. SSA Publication No. 05-10047. **HE3.2:R31/11/985.**

Provides step-by-step instructions and tables for retired workers who reached sixty-two before 1979 to estimate their social security benefits.

1490. **Estimating Your Social Security Retirement Check: Using the "Indexing" Method.** Rev. 1984. folder, 14p. SSA Publication No. 05-10070. **HE3.2:R31/12/984.**

Provides an alternate, and more accurate method for workers who reached sixty-two in 1979 and later to estimate their social security benefits than the publication described in entry 1488. The 1979 amendment inaugurated a procedure for indexing each year's earnings.

1491. **Farmers: How to Report Your Income for Social Security.** Rev. January 1985. folder, 8p. SSA Publication No. 05-10025. **HE3.2:F22/4/985.**

Provides information to farmers on what income is creditable for social security benefits, and how to report that income.

1492. **Government Pension Offset: How It May Affect You.** Rev. January 1985. folder, 7p. SSA Publication No. 05-10007. **HE3.2:P38/985.**

Provides a brief explanation on how the government pension offset may reduce the amount of benefits for a spouse or surviving spouse.

1493. **How Work Affects Your Social Security Checks.** Rev. January 1985. folder, 12p. SSA Publication No. 05-10069. **HE3.2:W89/5/985.**

Explains the "earnings test" regarding the maximum amount of earnings a retired worker is allowed to earn without sacrificing social security benefits.

1494. **If You Become Disabled.** Rev. January 1985. 31p. SSA Publication No. 05-10029. **HE3.2:D63/6/985.**

Explains the requirements for disability benefits under social security, how to apply, and how a decision is made on eligibility and amount of benefits.

1495. **If You're Self Employed: Reporting Your Income for Social Security.** Rev. January 1985. folder, 8p. SSA Publication No. 05-10022. **HE3.2:Se4/985.**

Provides information on how self-employed persons should report their earnings to obtain social security benefits.

1496. **Social Security and Your Household Employee.** Rev. January 1985. folder, 6p. SSA Publication No. 05-10021. **HE3.2:H81/3/985.**

Provides brief information on who is covered, which wages must be reported, and when to report wages of household employees.

1497. **Social Security Checks for Students.** Rev. January 1985. folder, 6p. SSA Publication No. 05-10048. **HE3.2:St9/985.**

Provides information for students who receive benefits based on their parents' eligibility.

1498. **Thinking about Retiring?** Rev. January 1985. folder, 12p. SSA Publication No. 05-10055. **HE3.2:R31/7/985.**

Provides information for prospective retirees on how to apply for social security benefits.

1499. **A Woman's Guide to Social Security.** Rev. June 1983. 15p. SSA Publication No. 05-10127. **HE3.6/3:W84/983.**

Provides advice on what a woman worker, a wife, and every woman should know about social security.

1500.   **Your Disability Claim**. Rev. March 1985. folder, 7p. SSA Publication No. 05-10052. **HE3.2:D63/14/985**.

Explains how a claim for disability benefits is handled, responsibility of the applicant to furnish additional information if required, and how the applicant is notified of the decision on the claim.

1501.   **Your Social Security**. Rev. January 1985. 35p. tables. SSA Publication No. 05-10035. **HE3.2:So13/25/985**.

Provides an overview of social security benefits, including Medicare.

1502.   **Your Social Security Checks While You Are Outside the United States**. Rev. March 1985. 24p. SSA Publication No. 05-10137. **HE3.2:C41/985**.

Explains how being outside the United States may affect your social security checks, and what information must be reported to insure that checks will be received.

1503.   **Your Social Security Rights and Responsibilities: Disability Benefits**. Rev. January 1985. 23p. SSA Publication No. 05-10153. **HE3.2:D63/3/985**.

Explains a disabled person's rights to social security benefits, and his or her responsibilities for reporting any change in status which affects those benefits.

1504.   **Your Social Security Rights and Responsibilities: Retirement and Survivors Benefits**. Rev. January 1985. 23p. SSA Publication No. 05-10077. **HE3.2:R44/985**.

Provides basic information to social security beneficiaries on what changes must be reported, and how to obtain assistance to resolve problems.

Taxes and Taxation

GENERAL

1505. **Cumulative List of Organizations Described in Section 170(c) of the Internal Revenue Code of 1954 (revised to October 31, 1984)**. Internal Revenue Service. Rev. 1984. 1068p. S/N 948-005-00000-0. Symbol Cl. $29.00 (subscription includes 3 quarterly supplements). **T22.2:Or3/984**.

Issued annually. Lists alphabetically organizations which have received outstanding rulings from the Internal Revenue Service that contributions to them are deductible under federal income tax laws and regulations.

1506. **1985 Federal Income Tax Guide for Older Americans: Information for Filing 1984 Returns**. Congress. House. Select Committee on Aging. December 1984. 25p. Committee Publication No. 98-473. **Y4.Ag4/2:In2/6/985**.

Intended to assist older Americans of moderate incomes in preparing their 1984 federal income tax returns.

1507. **Package X: Informational Copies of Federal Tax Forms, 1984**. Internal Revenue Service. Rev. 1984. 354p. S/N 048-004-01874-8. $7.50. **T22.2:P12/984**.

Issued annually. Contains full-sized copies of federal income tax forms used to prepare 1984 returns. These forms may be copied and used instead of the official forms.

1508. **Protecting Older Americans against Overpayment of Income Taxes (a Checklist of Deductions and Credits for Use in Taxable Year 1984)**. Congress. Senate. Special Committee on Aging. Rev. December 1984. 22p. tables. Committee Print 98th Congress, 2d Session. S/N 052-070-05984-2. $1.25. **Y4.Ag4:S.prt.98-256**.

Discusses common income tax deductions and credits which are most applicable to older Americans.

1509. A Selection of 1984 Internal Revenue Tax Information Publications. 4 vols. Internal Revenue Service. Rev. 1984. 1104p. Publication 1194. S/N 048-004-01880-2. $10.00(set). **T22.44/2:1194/2/v.1-2.**

Issued annually. This four-volume compilation includes the most frequently used of the IRS tax information publications which are revised annually to assist taxpayers in preparation of their returns. For a complete list of these publications see entry 1513.

1510. Statistics of Income, 1982: Individual Income Tax Returns. Internal Revenue Service. 1984. 192p. tables. Publication 79. S/N 048-004-01875-6. $5.50. **T22.35/2:In2/982.**

Issued annually. Presents data on individual taxpayer's income, exemptions, deductions, credits, and tax. The classifications used include size of adjusted gross income, marital status, and state of residence.

1511. Tax Guide for Small Business for Use in Preparing 1984 Returns. Internal Revenue Service. November 1984. 184p. Publication 334. **T22.19/2:Sm1/984.**

Issued annually. Contains basic information about federal income tax laws that the following types of small business need in preparing their annual tax returns: sole proprietorship, partnership, corporation, and Subchapter S corporation.

1512. Your Federal Income Tax for Individuals for Use in Preparing 1984 Returns. Internal Revenue Service. November 1984. 184p. Publication No. 17. **T22.44:984.**

Issued annually. Provides detailed instructions for individuals on preparing their federal income tax returns. Index.

For additional publications on this topic see Subject Bibliography **SB-195, Taxes and Taxation**.

INTERNAL REVENUE SERVICE
TAX INFORMATION PUBLICATIONS

1513. Tax Information Publications. Internal Revenue. Revised annually. Publication No. **T22.44/2:no.**

Most of the publications in this series are revised annually and are devoted to a specific topic to provide information for use in preparing annual income tax returns. Most of them are available free from regional IRS offices at tax preparation time. They are listed numerically by publication number with title, date of latest revision, and pagination.

1513-1.　　54.　**Tax Guide for U.S. Citizens and Resident Aliens Abroad.** November 1984. 32p.

1513-2.　　378.　**Fuel Tax Credits.** February 1983. 8p.

1513-3.　　448.　**Federal Estate and Gift Taxes.** September 1984. 55p.

1513-4.　　463.　**Travel Entertainment and Gift Expenses.** November 1984. 20p.

1513-5.　　501.　**Exemptions.** November 1984. 12p.

1513-6.　　502.　**Medical and Dental Expenses.** November 1984. 15p.

1513-7. 503. **Child and Dependent Care Credit, and Employment Taxes for Household Employees.** November 1984. 12p.

1513-8. 504. **Tax Information for Divorced or Separated Individuals.** November 1984. 20p.

1513-9. 505. **Tax Withholding and Estimated Tax.** November 1984. 30p.

1513-10. 506. **Income Averaging.** November 1984. 8p.

1513-11. 508. **Educational Expenses.** November 1984. 4p.

1513-12. 509. **Tax Calendars for 1985.** October 1984. 12p.

1513-13. 510. **Excise Taxes.** October 1984. 16p.

1513-14. 513. **Tax Information for Visitors to the United States.** November 1984. 8p.

1513-15. 514. **Foreign Tax Credits for U.S. Citizens and Resident Aliens.** November 1983. 20p.

1513-16. 515. **Withholding of Tax on Nonresident Aliens and Foreign Corporations.** November 1984. 26p.

1513-17. 516. **Tax Information for U.S. Government Civilian Employees Stationed Abroad.** November 1984. 4p.

1513-18. 517. **Social Security for Members of the Clergy and Religious Workers.** November 1984. 11p.

1513-19. 518. **Foreign Workers, Scholars and Exchange Visitors.** November 1984. 27p.

1513-20. 519. **U.S. Tax Guide for Aliens.** November 1984. 33p.

1513-21. 520. **Scholarships and Fellowships.** November 1984. 8p.

1513-22. 521. **Moving Expenses.** November 1984. 12p.

1513-23. 523. **Tax Information on Selling Your Home.** November 1984. 12p.

1513-24. 524. **Credit for the Elderly and the Permanently and Totally Disabled.** November 1984. 8p.

1513-25. 525. **Taxable and Nontaxable Income.** November 1983. 20p.

1513-26. 526. **Charitable Contributions.** November 1984. 8p.

1513-27. 527. **Rental Property.** November 1984. 16p.

1513-28. 529. **Miscellaneous Deductions.** November 1984. 4p.

1513-29. 530. **Tax Information for Owners of Homes, Condominiums, and Cooperative Apartments.** November 1984. 8p.

1513-30. 531. **Reporting Income from Tips.** November 1984. 4p.

1513-31. 533. **Self-Employment Tax.** November 1984. 8p.

1513-32. 534. **Depreciation.** December 1984. 44p.

1513-33.   535.   **Business Expenses.** November 1984. 36p.

1513-34.   536.   **Net Operating Losses and the At-Risk Limits.** November 1983. 12p.

1513-35.   537.   **Installment Sales.** November 1984. 20p.

1513-36.   538.   **Accounting Periods and Methods.** November 1984. 20p.

1513-37.   539.   **Employment Taxes.** November 1983. 24p.

1513-38.   541.   **Tax Information on Partnerships.** November 1980. 24p.

1513-39.   542.   **Tax Information on Corporations.** November 1984. 28p.

1513-40.   544.   **Sales and Other Disposition of Assets.** November 1984. 32p.

1513-41.   545.   **Interest Expense.** November 1984. 8p.

1513-42.   547.   **Nonbusiness Disasters, Casualties and Thefts.** November 1984. 12p.

1513-43.   548.   **Deductions for Bad Debts.** November 1984. 8p.

1513-44.   549.   **Condemnations and Business Casualties and Thefts.** November 1984. 16p.

1513-45.   550.   **Investment Income and Expenses.** November 1984. 32p.

1513-46.   551.   **Basis of Assets.** November 1984. 8p.

1513-47.   552.   **Recordkeeping for Individuals and a List of Tax Publications.** November 1984. 4p.

1513-48.   553.   **Highlights of 1984 Tax Changes.** November 1984. 22p.

1513-49.   554.   **Tax Benefits for Older Americans.** November 1984. 52p.

1513-50.   555.   **Community Property and the Federal Income Tax.** September 1984. 4p.

1513-51.   556.   **Examination of Returns, Appeal Rights, and Claims for Refund.** November 1984. 8p.

1513-52.   557.   **How to Apply and Retain Tax-Exempt Status for Your Organization.** February 1980. 78p.

1513-53.   558.   **Tax Information for Sponsors of Contests and Sporting Events.** November 1984. 2p.

1513-54.   559.   **Tax Information for Survivors, Executors, and Administrators.** November 1984. 28p.

1513-55.   560.   **Self-Employed Retirement Plans.** April 1984. 16p.

1513-56.   561.   **Determining the Value of Donated Property.** November 1983. 11p.

1513-57.   564.   **Mutual Fund Distributions.** November 1984. 12p.

1513-58.   567.   **U.S. Civil Service Retirement and Disability.** November 1984. 8p.

1513-59.   570.   **Tax Guide to U.S. Citizens Employed in U.S. Possessions.** November 1984. 12p.

1513-60.   571.   **Tax-Sheltered Annuity Programs for Employees of Public Schools and Certain Tax-Exempt Organizations.** March 1983. 19p.

1513-61.   572.   **Investment Credit.** November 1984. 23p.

1513-62.   575.   **Pension and Annuity Income.** November 1984. 32p.

1513-63.   578.   **Tax Information for Private Foundations and Foundation Managers.** November 1984. 40p.

1513-64.   583.   **Information for Business Taxpayers: Business Taxes, Identification Numbers, Recordkeeping.** November 1984. 20p.

1513-65.   584.   **Disaster and Casualty Loss [Workbook].** November 1984. 24p.

1513-66.   585.   **Voluntary Tax Methods to Help Finance Political Campaigns.** November 1980. 4p.

1513-67.   586A.   **The Collection Process (Income Tax Accounts).** April 1983. 8p.

1513-68.   587.   **Business Use of Your Home.** November 1984. 12p.

1513-69.   588.   **Tax Information for Homeowners Associations.** November 1984. 23p.

1513-70.   589.   **Tax Information on S Corporations.** December 1984. 23p.

1513-71.   590.   **Individual Retirement Arrangements (IRA's).** November 1984. 16p.

1513-72.   593.   **Income Tax Benefits to U.S. Citizens Who Go Overseas.** December 1984. 8p.

1513-73.   594.   **The Collection Process (Employment Tax Accounts).** April 1983. 8p.

1513-74.   595.   **Tax Guide for Commercial Fishermen.** October 1984. 52p.

1513-75.   596.   **Earned Income Credit.** November 1984. 8p.

1513-76.   597.   **Information on United States-Canada Income Tax Treaty.** January 1983. 8p.

1513-77.   721.   **Comprehensive Tax Guide to U.S. Civil Service Benefits.** September 1983. 54p.

1513-78.   850.   **English-Spanish Glossary of Words and Phrases Used in Publications Issued by the Internal Revenue Service.** April 1985. 36p.

1513-79.   901.   **U.S. Tax Treaties.** November 1984. 12p.

1513-80.   903.   **Energy Credits for Individuals.** November 1984. 4p.

1513-81.   904.   **Interrelated Computations for Estate and Gift Taxes**. June 1982. 28p.

1513-82.   905.   **Tax Information on Unemployment Compensation**. November 1984. 6p.

1513-83.   906.   **Jobs and Research Credits**. November 1984. 12p.

1513-84.   907.   **Tax Information for Handicapped and Disabled Individuals**. November 1984. 36p.

1513-85.   908.   **Bankruptcy**. November 1982. 8p.

1513-86.   909.   **Alternative Minimum Tax**. November 1984. 8p.

1513-87.   910.   **Taxpayer Guide to IRS Information, Assistance and Publications**. October 1984. 27p.

1513-88.   911.   **Tax Information for Direct Sellers**. November 1984. 20p.

1513-89.   915.   **Tax Information on Social Security Benefits (and Tier 1 Railroad Retirement Benefits)**. November 1984. 15p.

1513-90.   1167.   **Substitute Printed, Computer-Prepared and Computer-Generated Tax Forms and Schedules**. February 1984. 30p.

1513-91.   1183.   **Rules for Tax Return Preparers**. May 1985. 8p.

Television and Radio

1514. **FTC Staff Report on Television Advertising to Children**. Federal Trade Commission. February 1978. 365p. **FT1.2:T23/2**.

Discusses petitions requesting a trade rule regulating television advertising of candy and other sugared products for children.

1515. **How to Identify and Resolve Radio-TV Interference Problems**. 2d ed. Federal Communications Commission. Rev. September 1982. 36p. ill. S/N 004-000-00398-5. $5.00. **CC1.7/4:In8/982**.

Describes procedures to identify and resolve problems of interference to television and other home electronic entertainment equipment. Describes FCC complaint procedures, and lists other sources of assistance.

1516. **Radio and Television Handbook**. Defense Information School. August 1981. 114p. ill. S/N 008-020-00880-0. $5.50. **D1.6/2:R11**.

Provides information on broadcasting techniques, audio and television production, television scripting, lighting and graphics for television, film and videotape, and performing for radio and TV.

1517. **Research on the Effects of Television Advertising on Children: A Review of the Literature and Recommendations for Future Research**. National Science Foundation. 1977. 237p. charts, tables. NSA/RA 77015. S/N 038-000-00336-4. $7.50. **NS1.2:T23/4**.

Identifies major policy issues of current interest and reviews existing research related to violence and unsafe acts in TV commercials, premium offers, food advertising, and proprietary medicines. References.

1518. **Television and Behavior: Ten Years of Scientific Progress and Implications for the Eighties**. 2 vols. National Institute of Mental Health. 1982. Vol. 1. **Summary Report**. 102p. DHHS Publication No. (ADM) 82-1195. S/N 017-024-01129-1. $5.00. Vol. 2. **Technical Reviews**. 368p. charts, tables. DHHS Publication No. (ADM) 82-1196. S/N 017-024-01141-0. $9.00. **HE20.8102:T23/2/v.1,2**.

Surveys the public issues related to television viewing including violence and aggression, cognitive and emotional functions, socialization, family and interpersonal relationships, educational programming, and health. Volume 2 includes edited reviews of the scientific literature since 1972. References.

See also entries 234, 411, 629.

Transformation

Transportation

1519. **Moving People: An Introduction to Public Transportation**. Department of Transportation. January 1981. 46p. ill. charts, DOT-I-81-8. S/N 050-000-00193-8. $4.75. **TD1.20/8:81-8**.

Discusses how public transportation is planned, how citizens can make their views known, why subsidies are necessary, how much value the public gets for its tax dollars, and what is being done to improve public transportation.

1520. **A Nation in Motion: Historic Transportation Sites**. Department of Transportation. August 1976. 133p. ill. S/N 050-000-00127-0. $6.00. **TD1.2:N21/6**.

Lists and describes extant historic transportation sites under four categories: waterways, roads, railroads, and aeronautics. Each category is arranged by states and then chronologically.

1521. **National Transportation Statistics, 1984**. Department of Transportation. 1984. 250p. ill. DOT-TSC-RSPA-84-3. S/N 050-000-00497 0. $7.50. **TD10.9:984**.

Issued annually. Provides a summary of selected national transportation statistics from a wide variety of government and private sources regarding air carriers and general aviation, automobiles, bus and truck transportation, local transit, railroads, water transportation, and oil and gas pipelines for the period since 1972.

See also entries 547-13, 1062-30.

See also "Air Transportation" (entries 35-50) and "Highways" (entries 188-195).

Travel

DIRECTORIES

1522. **Federal Hotel/Motel Discount Directory, 1985**. General Services Administration. Rev. 1985. 107p. S/N 022-003-01113-7. $3.00. **GS2.21/2:985**.

Lists lodging establishments throughout the world which have agreed to provide rooms on a space-available basis at discount rates to federal employees traveling on official business.

1523. **Federal Travel Directory**. General Services Administration and Military Traffic Management Command. Monthly. approx. 108p. tables. S/N 722-006-00000-3. Symbol FTD. $28.00 per yr. Single copy $4.00. **GS1.29:no**.

Contains schedules and discount fares for air transportation which have been contracted by GSA and MTMC for federal employees and military personnel traveling on official business. Also includes AMTRAK city-pairs. Provides information on ground transportation at airports, reservation telephone numbers, and guidelines for use of AMTRAK and the contracted airlines.

1524. **USA Plant Visits, 1977-1978**. Travel Service. 1978. 153p. ill. S/N 003-012-00041-7. $6.50. **C47.2:P69/977-78**.

Contains a list of industrial plant tours that welcome visitors and offer various programs and plant tours. Arranged by state and city and cross-referenced by industries. Entries include times of tours, tour restrictions and more.

INTERNATIONAL TRAVEL

1525. **Electric Current Abroad, 1984**. Bureau of Industrial Economics. Rev. January 1984. 88p. tables. S/N 003-008-00193-9. $2.50. **C62.2:El2/984**.

Lists the characteristics of electric current type, number of phases, frequency, and voltage found in major foreign cities around the world.

1526.   **Health Information for International Travel. Supplement to** *Morbidity and Mortality Weekly Report*, **Vol. 33**. Centers for Disease Control. 1984. 129p. maps, tables. DHHS Publication No. (CDC) 84-8280. $4.25. **HE20.7009:33/supp**.

Issued annually. Presents a country-by-country list of vaccinations required by travelers, and information on malaria risk. Presents recommendations of the Public Health Service for vaccinations and prophylaxis against specific quarantinable and nonquarantinable diseases. Index by country. Subject index.

1527.   **Tips for Travelers to Cuba: A U.S. Government Warning**. Department of State. Rev. May 1983. folder, 7p. Department and Foreign Service Series 274. Department of State Publication 9232. **S1.69:274/2**.

Provides brief information on visas and passports, customs and currency regulations, photographs and drugs. Includes warning that travelers may buy neither goods nor services, and dual nationals must have Cuban passports.

1528.   **Tips for Travelers to Eastern Europe and Yugoslavia**. Department of State. November 1982. 13p. European and British Commonwealth Series 84. Department of State Publication 9329. **S1.74:84**.

Provides general advice on customs, currency, driving, photography, and police registration. Provides advice on specific Eastern European countries.

1529.   **Tips for Travelers to Mexico**. Department of State. Rev. December 1984. folder, 7p. Inter-American Series 115. Department of State Publication 9308. **S1.26:115/4**.

Provides advice on visas and passports, customs, currency, health, driving safety, nationality, operation of CB equipment, and embassies.

1530.   **Tips for Travelers to Saudi Arabia**. Department of State. September 1983. folder, 8p. Department and Foreign Service Series 372. Department of State Publication 9369. **S1.69:372**.

Provides advice on Saudi culture and customs, visas and passports, alcohol and drugs, commercial/business disputes, customs, and U.S. embassies.

1531.   **Tips for Travelers to the Caribbean**. Department of State. Rev. September 1983. folder, 7p. Department and Foreign Service Series 299. Department of State Publication 9261. **S1.69:299/2**.

Provides advice on visas, currency and customs regulations, travel by private boat or plane, and location of embassies.

1532.   **Tips for Travelers to the Middle East**. Department of State. May 1984. folder, 8p. Department and Foreign Service Series 386. Department of State Publication 9395. **S1.69:386**.

Provides advice on dual nationality and visa requirements and specific tips for travel to Egypt, Iran, Iraq, Israel, Israeli Occupied Territories, Jerusalem, Jordan, Lebanon, and Syria.

1533.   **Tips for Travelers to the People's Republic of China**. Department of State. Rev. August 1984. folder, 6p. Department and Foreign Service Series 246. Department of State Publication 9199. **S1.69:246/3**.

Provides advice on visas, customs, currency regulations, health, dual nationality, and U.S. embassies.

1534. **Tips for Travelers to the USSR**. Department of State. September 1982. folder, 7p. Department and Foreign Service Series 329. Department of State Publication 9301. **S1.69:329**.

Provides advice on visas and passports, customs and currency regulations, photography, restricted areas, and U.S. embassies.

1535. **Trademark Information for Travelers**. Customs Service. Rev. October 1983. 21p. tables. Customs Publication 508. **T17.2:T67/983**.

Lists registered trademarks of the following goods which protect against unauthorized importation of foreign-made merchandise bearing that trademark: cameras and photo equipment, musical instruments and tape recorders, jewelry, perfumes, and watches.

1536. **Travel Tips for Senior Citizens**. Department of State. Rev. September 1983. folder, 7p. Department and Foreign Service Series 168. Department of State Publication 8970. S/N 044-000-01986-8. $2.00. **S1.69:168/2**.

Provides advice on visa and passports, clothing, money, health, and assistance from U.S. embassies.

1537. **Traveler's Tips on Bringing Food, Plant, and Animal Products into the United States**. Animal and Plant Health Inspection Service. Rev. October 1980. 17p. tables. PA 1083. **A1.68:1083/7**.

Discusses customs and insepction procedures, and import restrictions. Includes list showing entry status for a variety of products from overseas locations.

1538. **Visa Requirements of Foreign Governments**. Department of State. Rev. April 1984. 8p. M-264. **S1.2:V82/2/984**.

Present brief information on passport and visa requirements of foreign governments which are applicable to U.S. citizens traveling abroad as tourists.

1539. **You and the Law Overseas**. American Forces Information Service. Rev. 1981. 36p. DoD GEN-37A. S/N 008-001-00120-7. $2.00. **D2.14:GEN-37A**.

Intended to provide armed forces personnel and their families with information on how the law in foreign countries may affect them.

1540. **Your Trip Abroad**. Department of State. Rev. 1983. 32p. Department and Foreign Service Series 155. Department of State Publication 8872. S/N 044-000-01990-6. $1.00. **S1.69:155/7**.

Provides basic information to help the traveler prepare for a less troublesome trip abroad.

See also entries 524, 526, 529.

For additional publications on this topic see Subject Bibliography **SB-302, Travel and Tourism**.

GUIDES

1541. **Pocket Guide to [the].** . . . American Forces Information Service. ill., maps. DoD PG-no. **D2.14:PG-no.**

This series was developed for the use of U.S. armed forces personnel and their dependents serving or visiting abroad. It provides basic information about various countries and regions of the world. Each guide provides a brief review of the country's social customs, history, geography, language, currency, weights and measures, and the like. A glossary of useful words and phrases in the native language is usually included.

1541-1. . . . **Arabian Peninsula.** August 1981. 66p. S/N 008-001-00123-1. $4.50. **D2.14:PG-1.**

1541-2. . . . **Egypt.** Rev. June 1981. 31p. S/N 008-001-00115-1. $3.75. **D2.14:PG-10B.**

1541-3. . . . **Germany.** Rev. October 1981. 62p. S/N 008-001-00125-8. $4.25. **D2.14:PG-3A.**

1541-4. . . . **Greece.** Rev. January 1982. 58p. S/N 008-001-00126-6. $4.50. **D2.14:PG-5B.**

1541-5. . . . **Horn of Africa.** January 1982. 46p. S/N 008-001-00124-0. $4.25. **D2.14:PG-12.**

1541-6. . . . **Iceland.** April 1983. 62p. S/N 008-001-00139-8. $4.00. **D2.14: PG-13.**

1541-7. . . . **Israel.** November 1981. 51p. S/N 008-001-00127-4. $4.25. **D2.14:PG-11.**

1541-8. . . . **Italy.** Rev. July 1981. 48p. S/N 008-001-00117-7. $4.50. **D2.14: PG-6A.**

1541-9. . . . **Japan.** Rev. February 1982. 67p. S/N 008-001-00130-4. $4.50. **D2.14:PG-7B.**

1541-10. . . . **Korea, Republic of.** Rev. January 1982. 58p. S/N 008-001-00129-1. $4.50. **D2.14:PG-8B.**

1541-11. . . . **Low Countries: Belgium, Luxembourg, the Netherlands.** Rev. 1983. 99p. S/N 008-001-00138-0. $4.25. **D2.14:PG-9/2.**

1541-12. . . . **NATO.** August 1981. 13p. S/N 008-001-00119-3. $2.75. **D2.14: PG-30.**

1541-13. . . . **Panama.** September 1981. 52p. S/N 008-001-00118-5. $4.50. **D2.14:PG-2.**

1541-14. . . . **Philippines.** Rev. 1982. 58p. S/N 008-001-00132-1. $4.50. **D2.14:PG-14B.**

1541-15. . . . **Portugal and the Portuguese Azores.** Rev. June 1982. 79p. S/N 008-001-00136-3. $4.50. **D2.14:PG-20A.**

1541-16. . . . **Puerto Rico.** July 1983. 48p. S/N 008-001-00141-0. $3.50. **D2.14:PG-24.**

1541-17. . . . **Spain**. Rev. September 1981. 56p. S/N 008-001-00121-5. $4.50. **D2.14:PG-16B**.

1541-18. . . . **Turkey**. Rev. August 1981. 52p. S/N 008-001-00122-3. $4.50. **D2.14:PG-18A**.

1541-19. . . . **United Kingdom**. Rev. February 1982. 85p. S/N 008-001-00133-9. $4.75. **D2.14:PG-4B**.

1542. **Port Guide** series. Naval Military Personnel Command. ill., maps. **D208.6/4:ct**.
    These guides are intended for the use of naval personnel who are either stationed or on liberty in the port or country indicated. They provide much   useful tourist information for the international traveler.

1542-1. **Africa/Mideast Safari**. April 1977. 62p. NAVPERS 15288. **D208.6/4:Af8**.

1542-2. **Arabian Peninsula [Bahrain, Kuwait, Oman, Qatar, Saudi Arabia, United Arab Emirates, North and South Yemen]**. March 1981. 174p. NAVPERS 15391. **D208.6/4:Ar1**.

1542-3. **Athens**. Rev. September 1982. 47p. NAVPERS 15282. **D208.6/4: At4/982**.

1542-4. **Barcelona, Spain**. Rev. September 1983. 69p. NAVPERS 15284. **D208.6/4:B23/983**.

1542-5. **Belgium**. September 1979. 48p. NAVPERS 15386. **D208.6/4:B41**.

1542-6. **Bermuda**. July 1979. 39p. NAVPERS 15381. **D208.6/4:B45**.

1542-7. **East Africa**. September 1980. 58p. **D208.6/4:Af8/2**.

1542-8. **Germany**. December 1977. 75p. NAVPERS 15296. **D208.6/4:G31**.

1542-9. **Great Britain (London, Plymouth, Portsmouth)**. December 1977. 74p. **D208.6/4:G79**.

1542-10. **Italian Port Guide (Bari, Brindisi, Taronto)**. July 1979. 41p. NAVPERS 15383. **D208.6/4:It1**.

1542-11. **Italian Riveria (Liguria)**. July 1979. 74p. NAVPERS 15377. **D208.6/4:It1/2**.

1542-12. **Kenya**. October 1984. 31p. NAVPERS 15394. **D208.6/4:K42**.

1542-13. **Livorno**. July 1979. 48p. NAVPERS 15378. **D208.6/4:L76**.

1542-14. **Napoli**. Rev. June 1982. 63p. NAVPERS 15283. **D208.6/4:N16/982**.

1542-15. **Netherlands**. June 1978. 41p. **D208.6/4:N38**.

1542-16. **Northern Brazil**. October 1979. 84p. NAVPERS 15384. **D208.6/4: B73/2**.

1542-17. **Norway**. January 1978. 73p. NAVPERS 15297. **D208.6/4:N83**.

1542-18. **Palma de Mallorca, Spain**. Rev. September 1982. 55p. NAVPERS 15286. **D208.6/4:P18/982**.

1542-19.   **Puerto Rico and the Virgin Islands.** July 1979. 54p. NAVPERS 15380. **D208.6/4:P96.**

1542-20.   **Riviera Cote d'Azur, France.** April 1977. 100p. NAVPERS 15285. **D208.6/4:R52.**

1542-21.   **Rota, Spain.** Rev. June 1982. 53p. NAVPERS 15293. **D208.6/4: R74/982.**

1542-22.   **Senegal, Republic of.** June 1984. 36p. NAVPERS 15393. **D208.6/4: Se5.**

1542-23.   **Sicily.** June 1978. 85p. **D208.6/4:Si1.**

1542-24.   **Southern Brazil.** Rev. September 1982. 70p. NAVPERS 15376. **D208.6/4:B73/982.**

1542-25.   **Valencia.** September 1978. 61p. **D208.6/4:V23.**

1543.   **Post Report** series. Department of State. ill., maps. Department and Foreign Service Series (DFSS) [no]. Department of State Publication [no]. **S1.127:ct.**
This series is designed to acquaint new foreign service personnel with important information about the host country and the city in which they will be serving. Topics covered include: area, geography, and climate; population; transportation; communications; health and medicine; employment opportunities for spouses and dependents; life at the post in specific cities; customs, duties, and passage; firearms and ammunition; banking and currency; weights and measures; taxes; and national and local holidays. Each volume also includes a list of references for additional information about the country, as well as a street map of the area in which the U.S. embassy or chancery is located.

1543-1.   **Algeria.** Rev. April 1984. 16p. DFSS 256. Department of State Publication 9209. S/N 044-000-02015-7. $1.00. **S1.127:Al3/984.**

1543-2.   **Argentina.** Rev. May 1982. 20p. DFSS 296. Department of State Publication 9258. S/N 044-000-01906-0. $3.25. **S1.127:Ar3/982.**

1543-3.   **Australia.** Rev. March 1982. 32p. DFSS 287. Department of State Publication 9248. S/N 044-000-01907-8. $4.50. **S1.127:Au7/982.**

1543-4.   **Austria.** Rev. July 1981. 16p. DFSS 243. Department of State Publication 9196. S/N 044-000-01861-6. $2.50. **S1.127:Au7/2/981.**

1543-5.   **Bahamas.** Rev. August 1980. 16p. DFSS 192. Department of State Publication 9134. S/N 044-000-01803-9. $3.00. **S1.127:B14/2/980.**

1543-6.   **Bahrain.** Rev. May 1983. 12p. DFSS 341. Department of State Publication 9323. S/N 044-000-01970-1. $2.50. **S1.127:B14/983.**

1543-7.   **Bangladesh.** Rev. June 1981. 16p. DFSS 239. Department of State Publication 9192. S/N 044-000-01860-8. $2.75. **S1.127:B22/981.**

1543-8.   **Barbados.** Rev. November 1983. 16p. DFSS 210. Department of State Publication 9156. S/N 044-000-01998-1. $1.25. **S1.127:B23/983.**

1543-9. **Belgium**. Rev. August 1983. 28p. DFSS 186. Department of State Publication 9125. S/N 044-000-01987-6. $3.50. **S1.127:B41/3/983**.

1543-10. **Belize**. Rev. March 1983. 16p. DFSS 352. Department of State Publication 9337. S/N 044-000-01958-2. $2.75. **S1.127:B41/983**.

1543-11. **Benin**. Rev. February 1984. 12p. DFSS 183. Department of State Publication 9122. S/N 044-000-02009-2. $1.00. **S1.127:B43/984**.

1543-12. **Bermuda**. Rev. June 1981. 20p. DFSS 238. Department of State Publication 9191. S/N 044-000-01858-6. $3.00. **S1.127:B45/981**.

1543-13. **Botswana**. Rev. September 1980. 16p. DFSS 189. Department of State Publication 9130. S/N 044-000-01807-1. $2.75. **S1.127:B65/980**.

1543-14. **Brazil**. Rev. June 1982. 52p. DFSS 301. Department of State Publication 9263. S/N 044-000-01919-1. $4.75. **S1.127:B73/982**.

1543-15. **Bulgaria**. Rev. March 1982. 16p. DFSS 292. Department of State Publication 9524. S/N 044-000-01895-1. $2.75. **S1.127:B87**.

1543-16. **Burkina Faso**. October 1984. 16p. DFSS 255. Department of State Publication 9208. S/N 044-000-02033-5. $1.50. **S1.127:B91**.

1543-17. **Burma**. Rev. February 1982. 16p. DFSS 285. Department of State Publication 9246. S/N 044-000-01889-6. $2.75. **S1.127:B92/982**.

1543-18. **Burundi**. Rev. February 1983. 16p. DFSS 334. Department of State Publication 9306. S/N 044-000-01953-1. $3.00. **S1.127:B95/983**.

1543-19. **Cameroon**. Rev. April 1983. 20p. DFSS 338. Department of State Publication 9310. S/N 044-000-01959-1. $3.00. **S1.127:C14/983**.

1543-20. **Canada**. Rev. March 1981. 56p. DFSS 224. Department of State Publication 9175. S/N 044-000-01845-4. $4.75. **S1.127:C16/981**.

1543-21. **Cape Verde**. April 1982. 18p. DFSS 297. Department of State Publication 9259. S/N 044-000-01909-4. $2.75. **S1.127:C17**.

1543-22. **Central African Republic**. Rev. February 1983. 15p. DFSS 302. Department of State Publication 9264. S/N 044-000-01949-3. $3.00. **S1.127: Af8/983**.

1543-23. **Chad**. September 1982. 16p. DFSS 315. Department of State Publication 9282. S/N 044-000-01930-2. $3.00. **S1.127:C34**.

1543-24. **Chile**. Rev. March 1981. 19p. DFSS 284. Department of State Publication 9244. S/N 044-000-01900-1. $3.25. **S1.127:C43/981**.

1543-25. **Colombia**. Rev. April 1981. 36p. DFSS 225. Department of State Publication 9176. S/N 044-000-01848-9. $4.50. **S1.127:C72/981**.

1543-26. **Congo**. June 1982. 12p. DFSS 298. Department of State Publication 9260. S/N 044-000-01911-6. $2.75. **S1.127:C76**.

1543-27. **Costa Rica**. Rev. January 1984. 19p. DFSS 369. Department of State Publication 9363. S/N 044-000-02004-1. $1.75. **S1.127:C82/984**.

1543-28. **Cuba**. July 1983. 12p. DFSS 363. Department of State Publication 9356. S/N 044-000-01984-1. $3.00. **S1.127:C89**.

1543-29. **Czechoslovakia**. Rev. May 1980. 20p. DFSS 182. Department of State Publication 9120. S/N 044-000-01784-9. $3.00. **S1.127:C99/980**.

1543-30. **Denmark**. Rev. May 1984. 16p. DFSS 375. Department of State Publication 9372. S/N 044-000-02017-3. $1.50. **S1.127:D41/984**.

1543-31. **Djibouti**. January 1981. 12p. DFSS 215. Department of State Publication 9163. S/N 044-000-01831-4. $2.50. **S1.127:D64**.

1543-32. **Dominican Republic**. June 1983. 24p. DFSS 353. Department of State Publication 9339. S/N 044-000-01977-9. $3.25. **S1.127:D71**.

1543-33. **Ecuador**. Rev. October 1982. 28p. DFSS 322. Department of State Publication 9293. S/N 044-000-01933-7. $3.50. **S1.127:Ec9/982**.

1543-34. **Egypt**. Rev. December 1982. 24p. DFSS 335. Department of State Publication 9307. S/N 044-000-01940-0. $3.50. **S1.127:Eg9/982**.

1543-35. **El Salvador**. Rev. February 1983. 24p. DFSS 330. Department of State Publication 9302. S/N 044-000-01956-6. $3.50. **S1.127:El7/983**.

1543-36. **Ethiopia**. Rev. August 1983. 15p. DFSS 265. Department of State Publication 9221. S/N 044-000-01985-0. $3.50. **S1.127:Et3/983**.

1543-37. **Federal Republic of Germany**. Rev. July 1982. 48p. DFSS 304. Department of State Publication 9266. S/N 044-000-01923-0. $4.75. **S1.127: G31/2/982**.

1543-38. **Finland**. Rev. November 1982. 24p. DFSS 336. Department of State Publication 9308. S/N 044-000-01934-5. $3.50. **S1.27:F49/982**.

1543-39. **Gabon**. Rev. June 1980. 12p. DFSS 188. Department of State Publication 9129. S/N 044-000-01795-4. $2.75. **S1.127:G11/980**.

1543-40. **Gambia**. Rev. November 1984. 12p. DFSS 389. Department of State Publication 9399. S/N 044-000-02036-0. $1.25. **S1.127:G14/984**.

1543-41. **Geneva**. Rev. June 1981. 12p. DFSS 241. Department of State Publication 9194. S/N 044-000-01856-0. $2.75. **S1.127:G28/9891**.

1543-42. **German Democratic Republic [East Germany]**. Rev. December 1981. 15p. DFSS 269. Department of State Publication 9227. S/N 044-000-01885-3. $3.00. **S1.127:G31/981**.

1543-43. **Ghana**. Rev. August 1982. 20p. DFSS 313. Department of State Publication 9278. S/N 044-000-01916-7. $3.25. **S1.127:G34/982**.

1543-44. **Greece**. Rev. November 1981. 35p. DFSS 267. Department of State Publication 9224. S/N 044-000-01877-2. $4.50. **S1.127:G81/981**.

1543-45. **Grenada**. February 1985. 16p. DFSS 391. Department of State Publication 9401. S/N 044-000-02042-4. $1.50. **S1.127:G86**.

1543-46. **Guinea**. Rev. August 1981. 16p. DFSS 209. Department of State Publication 9154. S/N 044-000-01868-3. $2.75. **S1.127:G94/981**.

1543-47.   **Guinea-Bissau**. Rev. March 1982. 8p. DFSS 286. Department of State Publication 9247. S/N 044-000-01890-0. $2.25. **S1.127:G94/2/982**.

1543-48.   **Guyana**. Rev. February 1983. 19p. DFSS 349. Department of State Publication 9333. S/N 044-000-01955-8. $3.25. **S1.127:G99/983**.

1543-49.   **Haiti**. Rev. April 1983. 16p. DFSS 347. Department of State Publication 9331. S/N 044-000-01960-4. $2.75. **S1.127:H12/983**.

1543-50.   **Honduras**. Rev. July 1983. 24p. DFSS 213. Department of State Publication 9160. S/N 044-000-01980-9. $3.25. **S1.127:H75/2/983**.

1543-51.   **Hungary**. Rev. February 1984. 24p. DFSS 367. Department of State Publication 9361. S/N 044-000-02007-6. $1.50. **S1.127:H89/984**.

1543-52.   **Iceland**. Rev. May 1983. 16p. DFSS 344. Department of State Publication 9329. S/N 044-000-01971-0. $2.75. **S1.127:Ic2/983**.

1543-53.   **India**. Rev. January 1984. 51p. DFSS 362. Department of State Publication 9355. S/N 044-000-02003-3. $2.00. **S1.127:In2/2/984**.

1543-54.   **Indonesia**. Rev. October 1981. 36p. DFSS 248. Department of State Publication 9201. S/N 044-000-01880-2. $4.50. **S1.127:In2/981**.

1543-55.   **Iraq**. Rev. January 1981. 12p. DFSS 205. Department of State Publication 9150. S/N 044-000-01839-0. $2.75. **S1.127:Ir1/981**.

1543-56.   **Ireland**. Rev. September 1982. 16p. DFSS 317. Department of State Publication 9284. S/N 044-000-01927-2. $3.00. **S1.127:Ir2/982**.

1543-57.   **Israel**. Rev. December 1982. 20p. DFSS 323. Department of State Publication 9294. S/N 044-000-01943-4. $3.25. **S1.127:Is7/982**.

1543-58.   **Italy**. April 1983. 48p. DFSS 342. Department of State Publication 9324. S/N 044-000-01969-8. $4.00. **S1.127:It1**.

1543-59.   **Ivory Coast**. Rev. November 1981. 24p. DFSS 260. Department of State Publication 9215. S/N 044-000-01876-4. $3.25. **S1.127:Iv7/981**.

1543-60.   **Jamaica**. Rev. April 1981. 28p. DFSS 228. Department of State Publication 9180. S/N 044-000-01851-9. $3.50. **S1.127:J22/981**.

1543-61.   **Jerusalem**. October 1983. 11p. DFSS 358. Department of State Publication 9346. S/N 044-000-01995-7. $1.00. **S1.127:J48**.

1543-62.   **Jordan**. Rev. May 1981. 16p. DFSS 229. Department of State Publication 9182. S/N 044-000-01852-7. $2.75. **S1.127:J76/981**.

1543-63.   **Kenya**. Rev. October 1981. 16p. DFSS 263. Department of State Publication 9219. S/N 044-000-01871-3. $2.75. **S1.127:K42/981**.

1543-64.   **Korea**. Rev. August 1982. 28p. DFSS 314. Department of State Publication 9279. S/N 044-000-01926-4. $3.75. **S1.127:K84/982**.

1543-65.   **Kuwait**. Rev. February 1984. 19p. DFSS 199. Department of State Publication 9144. S/N 044-000-02008-4. $1.50. **S1.127:K96/984**.

1543-66.   **Laos**. Rev. January 1984. 12p. DFSS 206. Department of State Publication 9151. S/N 044-000-02002-5. $1.25. **S1.127:L29/984**.

1543-67.   **Lesotho**. Rev. July 1981. 12p. DFSS 237. Department of State Publication 9190. S/N 044-000-01864-1. $2.75. **S1.127:L56/981**.

1543-68.   **Liberia**. Rev. December 1984. 16p. DFSS 232. Department of State Publication 9185. S/N 044-000-02037-8. $1.50. **S1.127:L61/984**.

1543-69.   **Luxembourg**. Rev. July 1980. 15p. DFSS 181. Department of State Publication 9119. S/N 044-000-01797-1. $3.00. **S1.127:L97/980**.

1543-70.   **Madagascar**. Rev. April 1982. 16p. DFSS 295. Department of State Publication 9257. S/N 044-000-01908-6. $3.00. **S1.127:M26/982**.

1543-71.   **Malawi**. Rev. October 1984. 16p. DFSS 177. Department of State Publication 9111. S/N 044-000-02032-7. $1.50. **S1.127:M29/2/984**.

1543-72.   **Malaysia**. Rev. May 1983. 20p. DFSS 337. Department of State Publication 9328. S/N 044-000-01961-2. $3.00. **S1.127:M29/3/983**.

1543-73.   **Mali**. Rev. October 1981. 16p. DFSS 257. Department of State Publication 9212. S/N 044-000-01873-0. $2.75. **S1.127:M29/981**.

1543 74.   **Malta**. February 1982. 19p. DFSS 283. Department of State Publication 9243. S/N 044-000-01893-4. $3.00. **S1.127:M29/4**.

1543-75.   **Martinique**. Rev. April 1984. 11p. DFSS 371. Department of State Publication 9365. S/N 044-000-02013-1. $1.00. **S1.127:M36/984**.

1543-76.   **Mauritius**. Rev. November 1984. 16p. DFSS 207. Department of State Publication 9152. S/N 044-000-02031-9. $1.50. **S1.127:M44/2/984**.

1543-77.   **Mexico**. Rev. June 1984. 59p. DFSS 187. Department of State Publication 9128. S/N 044-000-02021-1. $2.50. **S1.127:M57/984**.

1543-78.   **Morocco**. Rev. July 1981. 28p. DFSS 245. Department of State Publication 9198. S/N 044-000-01862-4. $3.75. **S1.127:M82/981**.

1543-79.   **Mozambique**. June 1982. 16p. DFSS 293. Department of State Publication 9255. S/N 044-000-01910-8. $3.00. **S1.127:M87**.

1543-80.   **Nepal**. Rev. December 1984. 27p. DFSS 218. Department of State Publication 9169. S/N 044-000-02040-8. $1.75. **S1.127:N35/984**.

1543-81.   **Netherlands Antilles**. Rev. April 1983. 12p. DFSS 339. Department of State Publication 9311. S/N 044-000-01957-4. $2.75. **S1.127:N38/2/983**.

1543-82.   **New Zealand**. Rev. February 1982. 23p. DFSS 278. Department of State Publication 9238. S/N 044-000-01892-6. $3.25. **S1.127:N42/982**.

1543-83.   **Nicaragua**. Rev. November 1983. 16p. DFSS 361. Department of State Publication 9353. S/N 044-000-01993-1. $1.50. **S1.127:N51/983**.

1543-84.   **Niger**. Rev. October 1980. 12p. DFSS 201. Department of State Publication 9147. S/N 044-000-01813-6. $2.50. **S1.127:N56/2/980**.

1543-85.   **Nigeria**. Rev. August 1984. 28p. DFSS 382. Department of State Publication 9387. S/N 044-000-02023-8. $1.75. **S1.127:N56/984**.

1543-86.   **Norway**. Rev. April 1981. 20p. DFSS 227. Department of State Publication 9178. S/N 044-000-01846-2. $3.25. **S1.127:N83/981**.

1543-87. **Oman**. Rev. July 1982. 12p. DFSS 309. Department of State Publication 9273. S/N 044-000-01925-6. $2.75. **S1.127:Om1/982**.

1543-88. **Pakistan**. October 1983. 36p. DFSS 365. Department of State Publication 9358. S/N 044-000-01992-2. $2.00. **S1.127:P17**.

1543-89. **Panama**. Rev. September 1984. 19p. DFSS 214. Department of State Publication 9161. S/N 044-000-02028-9. $1.50. **S1.127:P19/984**.

1543-90. **Papua New Guinea**. Rev. July 1981. 16p. DFSS 244. Department of State Publication 9197. S/N 044-000-01859-4. $3.75. **S1.127:P19/2/981**.

1543-91. **Paraguay**. Rev. March 1981. 23p. DFSS 219. Department of State Publication 9170. S/N 044-000-01841-1. $3.25. **S1.127:P21/981**.

1543-92. **People's Republic of China**. Rev. January 1983. 28p. DFSS 223. Department of State Publication 9174. S/N 044-000-01947-7. $3.75. **S1.127: C44/983**.

1543-93. **Peru**. Rev. November 1981. 16p. DFSS 276. Department of State Publication 9236. S/N 044-000-01875-6. $3.00. **S1.127:P43/981**.

1543-94. **Poland**. Rev. June 1983. 28p. DFSS 350. Department of State Publication 9334. S/N 044-000-01976-1. $3.50. **S1.127:P75/983**.

1543-95. **Portugal**. Rev. August 1982. 32p. DFSS 310. Department of State Publication 9274. S/N 044-000-01932-9. $4.50. **S1.127:P83/982**.

1543-96. **Qatar**. Rev. October 1983. 16p. DFSS 360. Department of State Publication 9352. S/N 044-000-01994-9. $1.50. **S1.127:Q1/983**.

1543-97. **Romania**. Rev. June 1983. 23p. DFSS 180. Department of State Publication 9006. S/N 044-000-01974-4. $3.25. **S1.127:R66/983**.

1543-98. **Rwanda**. Rev. February 1980. 12p. DFSS 172. Department of State Publication 8998. S/N 044-000-01779-2. $2.75. **S1.127:R94/980**.

1543-99. **Saudi Arabia**. Rev. July 1983. 28p. DFSS 175. Department of State Publication 9009. S/N 044-000-01983-3. $3.50. **S1.127:Sa8/983**.

1543-100. **Senegal**. Rev. November 1981. 20p. DFSS 273. Department of State Publication 9231. S/N 044-000-01882-9. $3.00. **S1.127:Se5/981**.

1543-101. **Seychelles**. Rev. February 1983. 12p. DFSS 328. Department of State Publication 9300. S/N 044-000-01946-9. $2.75. **S1.127:Se9/983**.

1543-102. **Sierra Leone**. Rev. July 1980. 16p. DFSS 185. Department of State Publication 9124. S/N 044-000-01800-4. $3.00. **S1.127:Si1/980**.

1543-103. **Singapore**. Rev. May 1983. 23p. DFSS 343. Department of State Publication 9325. S/N 044-000-01962-1. $3.25. **S1.127:Si6/983**.

1543-104. **Somalia**. Rev. November 1982. 12p. DFSS 324. Department of State Publication 9295. S/N 044-000-01944-2. $2.75. **S1.127:So5/982**.

1543-105. **South Africa**. Rev. August 1982. 28p. DFSS 315. Department of State Publication 9282. S/N 044-000-01924-8. $4.50. **S1.127:So8af/982**.

1543-106. **Spain**. Rev. December 1983. 32p. DFSS 366. Department of State Publication 9359. S/N 044-000-02001-7. $2.00. **S1.127:Sp1/983**.

1543-107. **Sri Lanka and Republic of Maldives**. Rev. August 1983. 24p. DFSS 364. Department of State Publication 9357. S/N 044-000-01988-4. $3.00. **S1.127:Sr3/983**.

1543-108. **Sudan**. Rev. April 1983. 16p. DFSS 357. Department of State Publication 9344. S/N 044-000-01964-7. $2.75. **S1.127:Su2/983**.

1543-109. **Suriname**. Rev. December 1981. 12p. DFSS 279. Department of State Publication 9239. S/N 044-000-01887-0. $2.50. **S1.127:Su7/981**.

1543-110. **Swaziland**. Rev. December 1981. 16p. DFSS 253. Department of State Publication 9206. S/N 044-000-01881-1. $2.75. **S1.127:Sw2/981**.

1543-111. **Sweden**. Rev. December 1983. 16p. DFSS 170. Department of State Publication 9000. S/N 044-000-01999-0. $1.75. **S1.127:Sw3/983**.

1543-112. **Switzerland**. Rev. March 1980. 16p. DFSS 176. Department of State Publication 9110. S/N 044-000-01787-3. $2.75. **S1.127:Sw6/980**.

1543-113. **Syria**. Rev. August 1982. 16p. DFSS 307. Department of State Publication 9269. S/N 044-000-01917-5. $2.75. **S1.127:Sy8/982**.

1543-114. **Tanzania**. Rev. March 1984. 16p. DFSS 211. Department of State Publication 9158. S/N 044-000-02016-5. $1.00. **S1.127:T15/984**.

1543-115. **Thailand**. Rev. February 1984. 24p. DFSS 174. Department of State Publication 9008. S/N 044-000-02011-4. $1.75. **S1.127:T32/984**.

1543-116. **Togo**. Rev. March 1981. 16p. DFSS 220. Department of State Publication 9171. S/N 044-000-01843-8. $3.00. **S1.127:T57/981**.

1543-117. **Trinidad and Tobago**. Rev. April 1983. 24p. DFSS 345. Department of State Publication 9327. S/N 044-000-01963-9. $3.25. **S1.127:T73/983**.

1543-118. **Tunisia**. Rev. May 1981. 20p. DFSS 234. Department of State Publication 9187. S/N 044-000-01855-1. $3.25. **S1.127:T83/981**.

1543-119. **Turkey**. Rev. October 1982. 36p. DFSS 318. Department of State Publication 9286. S/N 044-000-01938-8. $4.50. **S1.127:T84/982**.

1543-120. **Uganda**. Rev. August 1981. 12p. DFSS 242. Department of State Publication 9195. S/N 044-000-01863-2. $2.75. **S1.127:Ug1/981**.

1543-121. **United Arab Emirates**. Rev. December 1981. 16p. DFSS 275. Department of State Publication 9233. S/N 044-000-01886-1. $2.75. **S1.127: Un3a/981**.

1543-122. **United Kingdom**. Rev. November 1982. 36p. DFSS 171. Department of State Publication 9004. S/N 044-000-01941-8. $4.50. **S1.127:Un3/3/982**.

1543-123. **U.S. Mission to the United Nations**. Rev. June 1984. 8p. DFSS 240. Department of State Publication 9193. S/N 044-000-02020-3. $1.00. **S1.127: Un3/4/984**.

1543-124. **USSR**. Rev. July 1983. 32p. DFSS 173. Department of State Publication 9007. S/N 044-000-01979-5. $3.75. **S1.127:Un3/5/983**.

1543-125. **Uruguay**. Rev. November 1982. 23p. DFSS 326. Department of State Publication 9298. S/N 044-000-01935-3. $3.50. **S1.127:Ur8/982**.

1543-126. **Venezuela**. Rev. August 1984. 30p. DFSS 208. Department of State Publication 9153. S/N 044-000-02030-1. $1.75. **S1.127:V55/984**.

1543-127. **Yemen Arab Republic**. Rev. July 1982. 12p. DFSS 303. Department of State Publication 9265. S/N 044-000-01920-5. $2.75. **S1.127:Y3/982**.

1543-128. **Yugoslavia**. Rev. October 1981. 32p. DFSS 259. Department of State Publication 9214. S/N 044-000-01874-8. $3.75. **S1.127:Y9/981**.

1543-129. **Zaire**. Rev. July 1983. 28p. DFSS 179. Department of State Publication 9116. S/N 044-000-01981-7. $3.50. **S1.127:Z1/2/983**.

1543-130. **Zambia**. Rev. 1982. 16p. DFSS 316. Department of State Publication 9283. S/N 044-000-01929-9. $3.00. **S1.127:Z1/982**.

1543-131. **Zimbabwe**. August 1981. 12p. DFSS 258. Department of State Publication 9213. S/N 044-000-01872-1. $2.50. **S1.127:Z6**.

1544. **A Walker's Guide to Pennsylvania Avenue**. Pennsylvania Avenue Development Corporation. 1983. folder, 14p. ill. **Y3.P38:8W15**.

Includes a bird's eye view of the buildings on Pennsylvania Avenue, the parade route of the nation's capital, and adjacent Constitution Avenue.

1545. **Washington, Past and Present: A Guide to the Nation's Capital**. United States Capitol Historic Society. 1983. 143p. ill. S/N 066-001-00003-2. $6.00. **Y3.H62/2:8W27**.

This colorfully illustrated guidebook describes significant historical landmarks in Washington, D.C., and the surrounding area.

United States Government

GENERAL

1546. **Analysis of the Grace Commission's Major Proposals for Cost Control.** Congressional Budget Office and General Accounting Office. February 1984. 410p. tables. S/N 052-070-05908-7. $10.00. **Y10.2:C75.**

Analyzes the major proposals of the President's Private Sector Survey on Cost Control, known as the "Grace Commission" after its chair, J. Peter Grace. References.

1547. **Current Salary Schedules of Federal Officers and Employees together with a History of Salary and Retirement Annuity Amendments.** Congress. House. Committee on Post Office and Civil Service. Rev. July 1984. 48p. tables. Committee Print 98-15. **Y4.P84/10:Sa3/16/984-2.**

Contains current salary tables for federal employees. It also includes a history of salary and annuity adjustments for federal employees and for the President, cabinet officers, members of Congress, and federal judges.

1548. **Equal Justice under Law: The Supreme Court in American Life.** 4th ed. Supreme Court Historical Society. 1982. 159p. ill. S/N 066-002-00001-2. $8.50. **Y3.H62/3:2J98.**

This richly illustrated book describes the work of the Supreme Court and high-lights events, trends, and significant decisions throughout its history. Endpapers include pictures of the 102 justices who have served on the Supreme Court as of 1982.

1549. **Federal Expenditures by State for Fiscal Year 1984.** Bureau of the Census. 1985. 73p. tables. S/N 003-024-06199-6. $3.00. **C3.266:984.**

Issued annually. Includes data on federal government expenditures for grants to state and local governments, salaries and wages, procurement, direct payments to individuals, and other selected major programs. Data are presented by federal agency and program.

1550.   **The Great Seal of the United States**. Department of State. Rev. July 1980. 16p. ill. S/N 044-000-01796-2. $3.00. **S1.2:Se1/5/980**.

Discusses the design of the seal in the 1780s, the meaning of the seal, the first die cut in 1792, and the four replacement dies cut since then.

1551.   **Management**. Office of Personnel Management. Quarterly. approx. 34p. ill. S/N 706-006-00000-1. Symbol CSJ. $13.00 per yr. Single copy $3.50. **PM1.11/2: vol/no**.

This periodical provides articles related to federal management, as well as general management techniques and procedures. Departments include news items on management activities in the federal government and foreign governments, book reviews, an advice column (Ms Management), and a profile of an outstanding civil servant.

1552.   **Our American Government: What Is It? How Does It Function? 150 Questions and Answers**. Congress. Rev. 1981. 75p. tables. House Document 96-351. S/N 052-071-00627-3. $4.50. **X96-2:H.doc.351**.

Provides answers to questions most frequently asked of federal legislators regarding the U.S. government. Index.

1553.   **President's Private Sector Survey on Cost Control: A Report to the President**. 2 vols. 1984. 751p. charts, tables. S/N 003-000-00616-6. $19.00. **Pr40.8:C82/P92/v.1,2**.

This final report of the survey, also known as the "Grace Commission" after its chair, J. Peter Grace, summarizes and highlights the major findings, conclusions, and recommendations of the survey's thirty-seven task forces. The task forces made 2,478 specific recommendations on 784 different issues which the survey claimed would result in net savings of $424.5 billion over three years if implemented. The reports of the task forces were also published, and are available from the GPO.

1554.   **The United States Government Manual, 1984/85**. Office of the Federal Register. 1984. 918p. charts. S/N 022-003-01109-9. $12.00. **GS4.109:984-85**.

Issued annually. This official handbook of the federal government provides comprehensive information on the agencies of the legislative, judicial, and executive branches.

1555.   **United States Government Policy and Supporting Positions**. Congress. Senate. Committee on Governmental Affairs. 1984. 270p. tables. Committee Print, 98th Congress, 2d Session. S/N 052-070-05960-5. $9.00. **Y4.G74/9:S.prt.98-286**.

Issued every four years, following presidential elections. Lists selected Schedule A and B positions, appointments under Schedule C, and selected positions in the Senior Executive Service. Called the "Plum Book," since it identifies positions subject to political appointments by a new administration.

CONGRESS

1556. **Biographical Directory of the American Congress, 1774-1971**. Congress. 1971 (repr. 1977). 1972p. Senate Document 92-8. S/N 052-071-00249-9. $40.00, cloth. **X92-1:S.doc.8**.

Includes brief biographies of persons who have served in the Continental and U.S. Congress from 1774 to 1971, and of Presidents who were not members of Congress. Lists cabinet officers of each administration, and state delegations for each Congress with a list of officers and dates for each session.

1557. **The Capitol: A Pictorial History of the Capitol and of the Congress**. 8th ed. Congress. 1981. 192p. ill. House Document 96-374. S/N 052-071-00621-4. $6.50. **X96-2:II.doc.374**.

Discusses the history of the Capitol building and its architecture. Provides a history of Congress as an institution, and describes the work of the Congress today.

1558. **Congressional District Atlas: Districts of the 99th Congress**. Bureau of the Census. January 1985. 588p. maps, tables. S/N 003-024-06132-5. $15.00. **C3.62/5:985**.

Presents maps showing boundaries of the congressional districts for the Ninety-ninth Congress of the fifty states, District of Columbia, Puerto Rico, and outlying areas. Also includes listings of the congressional districts in which counties and incorporated municipalities are located.

1559. **Congressional Pictorial Directory, 99th Congress**. Congress. Joint Committee on Printing. January 1985. 209p. ill. S/N 052-070-05992-3. $6.00, paper. S/N 052-070-05993-1. $10.00, cloth. **Y3.P93/1:1p/99**.

Issued biennially for each Congress. Contains photographs of members of the Ninety-ninth Congress arranged by state and congressional district. Name index.

1560. **Congressional Record (including Index Issues)**. Congress. daily while Congress is in session. paging varies. S/N 752-002-00000-2. Symbol CR. $218.00 per yr. Single copy $1.00. **X/a.Cong.-sess.:vol/no**.

Contains a verbatim official account of the debates and other proceedings on the floor of the House of Representatives and Senate during open sessions of the Congress. Also includes considerable material on a variety of topics submitted for the record, or as an extension of remarks.

1561. **Guide to Research Collections of Former U.S. Senators, 1789-1982**. Congress. Senate. Historical Office. 1983. 362p. ill. Senate Bicentennial Publication No. 1. Senate Document 97-41. **Y1.1/3:97-41**.

Provides information on the location of former Senators' manuscript collections, oral history interview transcripts, photographs and portraits, and memorabilia. Index.

1562. **Official Congressional Directory, 99th Congress, 1985-1986**. Congress. Joint Committee on Printing. 1985. 1200p. S/N 052-070-05994-0. $13.00, paper. S/N 052-070-05995-8. $17.00, cloth. **Y4.P93/1:1/99-1**.

Issued biennially for each Congress. Includes brief biographies of members of Congress, a list of state delegations, tables showing terms of service. lists of congressional committees including staff members, and maps of congressional districts.

Also includes directories of principal executive and judicial agencies and officials. Name index.

1563. **Requirements for Recurring Reports to the Congress: A Directory**. General Accounting Office. Rev. 1982. 945p. 1982 Congressional Sourcebook Series. GAO/PAD-82-28. S/N 020-000-00212-3. $15.00. **GA1.22:R29/982**.

Describes approximately 3,250 requirements for recurring and one-time reports to Congress from the executive, legislative, and judicial branches and from independent and federally chartered corporations.

1564. **We the People: The Story of the United States Capitol, Its Past and Its Promise**. 12th ed. United States Capitol Historical Society. 1981. 144p. ill. S/N 022-002-00085-6. $7.50. **Y3.H62/2:2P39/981**.

A colorfully illustrated guidebook with the history of the Capitol building and Congress, and the work of the Congress today in this historic building.

See also entries 157, 632.

PRESIDENT

1565. **Collection of White Books**. 4 books. White House Historical Association. 1981-1982. 490p. ill. S/N 066-000-00005-2. $19.00, paper. S/N 066-000-00010-9. $25.00, cloth. **Y3.H62/4:F51/set**.

This set includes copies of publications described in entries 1566, 1568, 1570, and 1573 below.

1566. **The First Ladies**. 3d ed. White House Historical Association. 1981. 91p. ill. S/N 066-000-00004-4. $6.50, paper. S/N 066-000-00009-5. $8.00, cloth. **Y3.H62/4:2F51**.

Contains a portrait and a brief biography of each First Lady of the White House from Martha Washington to Nancy Reagan.

1567. **List of Visits of United States Presidents to Foreign Countries**. Department of State. September 1983. 41p. S/N 044-000-01991-4. $3.75. **S1.2:V82/4**.

Provides a chronological list of visits by Presidents and Presidents-elect to foreign countries, and an alphabetical list of the countries visited.

1568. **The Living House**. 17th ed. White House Historical Association. 1982. 151p. ill. S/N 066-000-00003-6. $7.50, paper. S/N 066-000-00008-7. $9.00, cloth. **Y3.H62/4: 2W58**.

This colorfully illustrated guide of the White House emphasizes the residence as the place where the President and family live and entertain. Index.

1569. **The President's House**. President. 1984. 28p. ill. **Pr40.2:H81**.

Describes the public rooms in the White House, and a typical day in the life of the President and First Lady. Includes highlights in the life of President Reagan and portraits of the forty Presidents.

1570.   **The Presidents of the United States of America.** 9th ed. White House Historical Association. 1982. 87p. ill. S/N 066-000-00002-8. $6.50, paper. S/N 066-000-00007-9. $8.00, cloth. **Y3.H62/4:2P92**.

Includes a color portrait or photograph and a brief biography of the Presidents of the United States from George Washington to Ronald Reagan. Index.

1571.   **Public Papers of the Presidents of the United States. Ronald Reagan.** Office of the Federal Register. ill. **GS4.113:yr/bk**.

This series contains the papers and speeches of the President as issued by the White House Press Office for the years indicated. Documents are published in chronological order. Volumes were also published for the administrations of Presidents Hoover, Truman, Eisenhower, Kennedy, Johnson, Nixon, Ford, and Carter. For a list of in-print volumes see Subject Bibliography **SB-106, Presidents of the United States**.

    1571-1.   **1981.** 1374p. S/N 022-003-01081-5. $25.00, cloth.

    1571-2.   **1982. Book 1. January 1 to July 2, 1982.** 1983. 920p. S/N 022-003-01098-0. $19.00, cloth.

    1571-3.   **1982. Book 2. July 3 to December 31, 1982.** 1984. 817p. S/N 022-003-01107-2. $25.00, cloth.

    1571-4.   **1983. Book 1. January 1 to July 1, 1983.** 1984. 1040p. S/N 022-003-01111-1. $31.00, cloth.

1572.   **Weekly Compilation of Presidential Documents.** Office of the Federal Register. Weekly. paging varies. S/N 722-007-00000-0. Symbol PD. $60.00 per yr. Single copy $1.75. **AE2.109:vol/no**.

Includes transcripts of the President's news conferences, and texts of messages to Congress, public speeches and statements, and other materials released by the White House. Includes lists of public laws approved, nominations sent to the Senate, and a checklist of White House releases. Index in each issue, as well as quarterly indexes, and a cumulative annual index.

1573.   **The White House: An Historic Guide.** 15th ed. White House Historical Association. 1982. 159p. ill. S/N 066-000-00001-0. $7.50, paper. S/N 066-000-00006-1. $9.50, cloth. **Y3.H62/4:8W58**.

This colorfully illustrated guide describes the various rooms in the White House and their furnishings. Also describes architectural changes made in the White House since 1800.

See also entries 630, 631, 1062-2, 1062-16.

For additional publications on this topic see Subject Bibliography **SB-106, Presidents of the United States**.

FOREIGN AFFAIRS

1574.   Atlas of U.S. Foreign Relations: Development Assistance. Department of State. March 1982. 13p. charts, maps. S/N 044-000-01894-2. $2.50. **S1.3/a:At6/assistance**.

Illustrates with charts, maps, and text the history and achievements of foreign aid after World War II. Reprinted from the *Department of State Bulletin*, December 1981.

1575.   Department of State Bulletin: The Official Record of United States Foreign Policy. Department of State. Monthly, and annual index. approx. 80p. ill. S/N 744-002-00000-1. Symbol DSB. $25.00 per yr. Single copy $2.75. **S1.3:no**.

Intended to provide information on developments in U.S. foreign relations and the work of the Department of State and of the Foreign Service. Includes the texts of major addresses and news conferences of the President and the secretary of state, and other official documents. Includes lists of press releases, Department of State publications, and *Background Notes*.

1576.   Diplomatic List. Department of State. Quarterly. 90p. Department and Foreign Service Series 202. Department of State Publication 7894. S/N 744-004-00000-4. Symbol DIPL. $14.00 per yr. Single copy $3.75. **S1.8:yr/no**.

Contains the names, titles, addresses, and telephone numbers of the members of the diplomatic staff of all foreign missions in the United States. Also includes the address and telephone number of the country's embassy or chancery located in Washington, D.C.

1577.   Foreign Consular Offices in the United States, 1984. Department of State. 1985. 100p. Department and Foreign Service Series 128. Department of State Publication 7846. S/N 044-000-02045-9. $3.50. **S1.69/2:984**.

Issued annually. Contains a complete and official list of the consular offices of foreign countries located in the United States, together with their jurisdictions and a list of recognized consular officers with their titles and dates of recognition.

1578.   Key Officers of Foreign Service Posts: Guide for Business Representatives. Department of State. Three times a year. 82p. Department of State Publication 7877. S/N 744-006-00000-7. Symbol KOFS. $10.00 per yr. Single copy $3.75. **S1.40/5:yr-no**.

Lists key officers at U.S. foreign service posts. Also lists all U.S. embassies, legations, and consulates general. Geographic index.

1579.   Report of the National Bipartisan Commission on Central America. January 1984. 132p. S/N 040-000-00477-7. $4.75. **Pr40.8:B52/C33**.

Provides an analysis of economic, social, and democratic development in Central America. Proposes that significant attention should be devoted to this previously neglected area of the hemisphere through concrete policy recommendations. Also known as the "Kissinger Report" after its chair, Henry Kissinger.

1580.   The Senate Role in Foreign Affairs Appointments. Congress. Committee on Foreign Relations. July 1982. 127p. charts, tables. Committee Print, 97th Congress, 2d Session. **Y4.F76/2:F76/29/982**.

Discusses constitutional background for Senate confirmation of appointments, practice and procedures in the executive and legislative branch, problems of volume, appointments made without Senate confirmation, and statistical data. Footnote references. Bibliography.

1581. **Treaties in Force: A List of Treaties and Other International Agreements of the United States in Force on January 1, 1985**. Department of State. 1985. 346p. Department of State Publication 9433. **S9.14:985**.

Issued annually. Contains a list of treaties and other international agreements to which the United States has become a party and which are still in force. The first part includes bilateral treaties arranged by country. The second part includes multilateral treaties arranged by subject.

1582. **United States Chiefs of Mission, 1778-1982**. Department of State. Rev. August 1982. 394p. tables. Department and Foreign Service Series 147. Department of State Publication 8738. **S1.69:147/2**.

Lists alphabetically by country, then chronologically United States chiefs of mission to foreign countries and to international organizations from 1778 to 1982. Also lists all secretaries of state, and deputy undersecretaries and assistant secretaries. Personal name index.

1583. **United States Contributions to International Organizations: 32nd Annual Report to the Congress for Fiscal Year 1983**. Department of State. October 1984. 123p. tables. International Organization and Conference Series 164. Department of State Publication 9404. **S1.70:164**.

Issued annually. For each international organization supported by the United States information is provided on the executive director, origin and development, purpose, structure, initial date of U.S. participation, and amount and percent of contribution of each member.

1584. **United States Participation in the United Nations: Report by the President to the Congress for the Year 1983**. Department of State. 1984. 383p. International Organization and Conference Series 165. Department of State Publication 9406. S/N 044-000-02026-2. $8.50. **S1.70:165**.

Issued annually. Describes significant activities of the United Nations and its specialized agencies under broad topics, and reports U.S. participation and policy under each.

1585. **The War Powers Resolution**. Congress. House. Committee on Foreign Affairs. 1982. 307p. Committee Print, 97th Congress, 2d Session. S/N 052-070-05725-4. $7.00. **Y4.F76/1:W19/11**.

Discusses why the War Powers Resolution of 1973 was enacted beginning with a discussion of the Tonkin Gulf incidents of 1964, and giving a history of the resolution's implementation since 1973.

1586. **The War Powers Resolution: Relevant Documents, Correspondence, Reports**. Congress. House. Committee on Foreign Affairs. December 1983. 92p. Committee Print, 98th Congress, 1st Session. **Y4.F76/1:W19/10/983**.

Includes the text of the War Powers Resolution of 1973, committee reports, legislative history, reports submitted by the President in compliance with the resolution, and related correspondence.

See also "International Social and Political Problems" (entries 1117-1132).

LAWS AND REGULATIONS

1587. **Enactment of a Law: Procedural Steps in the Legislative Process.** Congress. Senate. 1982. 44p. Senate Document 97-20. **Y1.1/3:97-20.**

Describes procedural steps in the legislative process with emphasis on actions in the Senate. Includes sample cover pages from bills, reports, and slip laws.

1588. **Federal Register.** Office of the Federal Register. Daily, except weekends and legal holidays. paging varies. S/N 722-004-00000-1 (paper). Symbol FR. $300.00 per yr. Single copy $1.50. S/N 722-003-00000-4 (microfiche). $145.00 per yr. Single copy $1.50. Subscription includes **Index** (monthly) and **List of CFR Sections Affected** (monthly). **AE2.106:vol/no.**

Includes proposed rules and final rules published by federal agencies to implement the general provisions of laws passed by Congress. Also includes legal notices of public interest, presidential proclamations, and executive orders.

1589. **Federal Register: What It Is and How to Use It: A Guide for the User of the Federal Register, Code of Federal Regulations System.** Office of the Federal Register. Rev. 1980. 136p. ill. **GS4.6/2:F31/980.**

Describes the types of documents published in the *Federal Register* and their relationship to the *Code of Federal Regulations.* Index.

1590. **Finding the Law: A Workbook on Legal Research for Laypersons.** Bureau of Land Management. 1982. 283p. ill. S/N 024-011-00148-4. $8.50. **I53.2:L41.**

This guidebook on finding federal statute law and case law includes many sample pages from the legal finding tools which it describes. Intended to serve as a workbook, it includes review exercises at the end of each section. Index.

1591. **How Our Laws Are Made.** Congress. House. Rev. 1981. 79p. ill. House Document 97-120. S/N 052-071-00617-6. $4.50. **Y1.1/7:97-120.**

Provides a nontechnical outline of the background and the numerous steps of our federal lawmaking process from the origin of an idea through its publication as a law.

1592. **Senate Legislative Procedural Flow (and Related House Actions): Bills, Resolutions, Nominations, and Treaties.** Congress. Senate. Rev. November 1978. 103p. ill. S/N 052-002-00033-8. $4.75. **Y1.3:L52/978.**

Traces the path of a bill from its introduction to its publication as a law through the Senate, House, and President. Also traces treaties and presidential nominations.

BUDGET OF THE
UNITED STATES GOVERNMENT

1593. **Budget of the United States Government, Fiscal Year 1986.** Office of Management and Budget. 1984. 619p. S/N 041-001-00282-1. $13.00. **PrEx2.8:986.**

Issued annually. Contains the budget message of the President and presents an overview of the president's budget proposals.

1594. **Budget of the United States Government, Fiscal Year 1986; Appendix.** Office of Management and Budget. 1984. 927p. tables. S/N 041-001-00283-9. $19.00. **PrEx2.8:986/app.**

Issued annually. Contains more detailed information than any of the other budget documents. Includes for each agency the proposed text of appropriation language, budget schedules for each account, explanations of work to be performed and funds needed, and schedules for permanent positions.

1595. **Budget of the United States Government, Fiscal Year 1986. Special Analysis.** Office of Management and Budget. 1985. 421p. S/N 041-001-00285-5. $8.00. **PrEx2.8/5:986**.

Issued annually. Contains analyses that are designed to highlight specific program areas, or provide other significant presentations of federal budget data that are of current interest.

1596. **Historical Tables [Budget of the United States Government, Fiscal Year 1986].** Office of Management and Budget. 1985. 322p. charts, tables. S/N 041-001-00288-0. $9.00. **PrEx2.8/8:986**.

Provides budget data on receipts, outlays, surpluses or deficits, and federal debt covering extended periods (1940-1990). Data are expressed in current prices, constant prices, and as percentages by budget totals of the Gross National Product.

1597. **Management of the United States Government, Fiscal Year 1986.** Office of Management and Budget. 1985. 110p. tables. S/N 041-001-00287-1. $3.75. **PrEx2.8/9:986**.

Issued as part of the FY 1986 Budget documents. Discusses the President's management improvement program, "Reform '88"; the congressional role; management improvements targeted by Congress; and the status of the recommendations of the Grace Commission.

1598. **The United States Budget in Brief, Fiscal Year 1986.** Office of Management and Budget. 1985. 82p. S/N 041-001-00284-7. $2.50. **PrEx2.8/2:986**.

Issued annually. This version of the budget is designed for use by the general public. It provides a more concise, less technical overview of the budget than the other volumes.

For additional publications on this topic see Subject Bibliography **SB-204, Budget of the U.S. Government and Economic Report of the President.**

GOVERNMENT PROGRAMS

1599. **Catalog of Federal Domestic Assistance.** Office of Management and Budget. Rev. 1984. looseleaf. 1281p. S/N 941-001-00000-9. Symbol COFA. $36.00 (includes basic manual and supplements). **PrEx2.20:984**.

Designed to assist in identifying the type of federal assistance available, and by describing eligibility requirements and applications procedures.

1600. **Catalog of Federal Loan Guarantee Programs.** Congress. House. Committee on Banking, Finance and Urban Affairs. Rev. January 1982. 235p. Committee Print, 97th Congress, 2d Session. S/N 052-070-05673-8. $5.50. **Y4.B22/1:L78/17/982.**

Provides a listing and description of federal loan guarantee programs arranged by agency.

1601. **Summary of SBA Programs**. Congress. House. Committee on Small Business. Rev. February 1983. 29p. Committee Print, 98th Congress, 1st Session. **Y4.Sm1: P94/16/983**.

Presents summaries of Small Business Administration (SBA) programs outlining their principal purposes, terms, and eligibility requirements.

See also entries 36, 283, 296, 343, 417, 895, 1144, 1158, 1326, 1330, 1442, 1457.

FEDERAL AGENCIES: HISTORY, ORGANIZATION, SERVICES

1602. Central Intelligence Agency. **Donovan and the CIA: A History of the Establishment of the Central Intelligence Agency**. 1981. 606p. ill., charts. **PrEx3.10:D71**.

The overriding thesis of this history is that Major General William J. Donovan, wartime chief of the Office of Strategic Services (OSS) was the factual and spiritual father of the Central Intelligence Agency. Traces the history of American intelligence efforts from the 1920s to the establishment of the CIA by the National Security Act of 1947. Footnote references. Bibliography. Index.

1603. Coast Guard. **Missions of the United States Coast Guard**. Rev. 1984. folder, 8p. ill. **TD5.8:M69/984**.

Provides a brief description of the missions of the Coast Guard including boating safety, search and rescue, aids to navigation, maritime safety, and maritime law enforcement.

1604. Commission on Civil Rights. **United States Commission on Civil Rights**. Rev. 1984. 15p. ill. **CR1.2:C49/984**.

Provides brief information on the duties, powers, organization, members, staff, and regional offices of the Commission on Civil Rights.

1605. Department of Agriculture. **How to Get Information from the United States Department of Agriculture**. Rev. September 1984. 12p. **A107.2:In3/984**.

Lists sources of information in the Department of Agriculture and its various bureaus and agencies, primarily public information offices and Freedom of Information officers.

1606. Department of Agriculture. **Services Available through the U.S. Department of Agriculture**. February 1984. 23p. PA 1336. **A1.68:1336**.

Describes services available under the following categories: farms, forests, markets, communities, consumers, business and industry, and natural resources.

1607. Department of Agriculture. **Your United States Department of Agriculture: How It Serves People on the Farm, and in the Community, Nation, and the World**. Rev. November 1982. 31p. ill. PA 824. **A1.68:824**.

Describes the activities and programs of the Department of Agriculture and the agencies which administer these programs.

1608. Department of Energy. **A History of the Atomic Energy Commission**. August 1982. 26p. charts, maps, tables. DOE/ES-0003. **E1.102:0003**.

A brief history of the Atomic Energy Commission, 1947-1977. Includes lists of AEC commissioners, laboratories and production facilities, and nuclear detonations as well as organizational charts and maps showing AEC facilities. References.

1609.   Department of Energy. **The United States Department of Energy: A History.** November 1982. 25p. charts, maps, tables. DOE/ES-0004. **E1.102:0004.**
A brief history of the Department of Energy from its establishment in 1977. Includes organization chart and map of DOE facilities. References.

1610.   Department of Justice. **Attorneys General of the United States, 1789-1985.** 1985. 156p. ill. S/N 027-000-01217-5. $5.50. **J1.2:At8/6/789-985.**
Includes black-and-white reproductions of the official portraits of the attorneys general from the first, Edmund Jennings Randolph (1789-1794) to the seventy-fourth, William French Smith, who resigned in 1985. Includes brief biography of each attorney general as well as each artist.

1611.   Department of State. **The Secretaries of State: Portraits and Biographical Sketches.** November 1978. 125p. ill. Department and Foreign Service Series 162. Department of State Publication 8921. **S1.69:162.**
Includes black-and-white reproductions of the official portraits of the secretaries of state from Washington's administration (Robert R. Livingston) to Carter's (Cyrus R. Vance). Includes brief biography of each secretary as well as each artist.

1612.   Farmers Home Administration. **A Brief History of the Farmers Home Administration.** Rev. February 1983. 51p. charts, tables. **A84.2:H62/983.**
Presents a brief history of the Farmers Home Administration and its predecessor agencies, including relevant enabling legislation. Provides descriptions with current and historical statistical data on FHA major loan programs.

1613.   Federal Trade Commission. **A Guide to the Federal Trade Commission.** May 1984. 20p. **FT1.8/2:F31.**
Includes a short history of the Federal Trade Administration, descriptions of its three main operating bureaus, and a list of where to get more information about the FTC. References.

1614.   Library of Congress. **For Congress and the Nation: A Chronological History of the Library of Congress.** 1979. 209p. ill. S/N 033-003-00018-7. $12.00, cloth. **LC1.2:C76/6.**
A chronology of significant events in Library of Congress history from 1774 to 1975. Index.

1615.   Library of Congress. **Librarians of Congress, 1802-1974.** 1977. 273p. ill. S/N 030-001-00080-0. $13.00, cloth. **LC1.2:L61/16/802-974.**
Discusses the contributions of the twelve persons who have been Librarians of Congress from 1802 to 1974.

1616.   Library of Congress. **Ten First Street, Southeast: Congress Builds a Library, 1886-1897.** 1980. 105p. ill. S/N 030-000-00122-2. $5.50. **LC1.2:C76/9.**
Provides a historical account of the construction of the Library of Congress Main Building, and a chronology from original proposals (1871) to the present. The second half is a catalog of a 1980 exhibition on this topic. References.

1617. National Library of Medicine. **A History of the National Library of Medicine: The Nation's Treasury of Medical Knowledge**. July 1982. 531p. ill. NIH Publication 82-1904. S/N 017-052-00224-4. $14.00, cloth. **HE20.3602:H62**.

Traces the history of the National Library of Medicine from its beginnings in 1818 as the Library in the Army Office of the Surgeon through the legislation which created it in 1956 and the move to the present facility in 1962, into the 1980s. Footnote references. Index.

1618. National Oceanic and Atmospheric Administration. **NOAA: A Young Agency with an Historic Tradition of Service to the Nation**. October 1980. 40p. ill. NOAA/PA 80002. S/N 003-017-00491-1. $2.75. **C55.2:H62**.

Discusses the history, organization, and services of the National Oceanic and Atmospheric Administration from its creation in 1970.

1619. National Weather Service. **National Weather Service Offices and Stations**. 23d ed. March 1985. 52p. tables. **C55.102:Of2/985**.

Lists all first- and second-order offices and stations operated by, or under the supervision of the National Weather Service, and shows the type and location of each station, and the nature of its weather observation program.

1620. Patent and Trademark Office. **The Story of the United States Patent and Trademark Office**. Rev. July 1981. 49p. tables. S/N 003-004-00579-3. $3.50. **C21.2:P27/3/981**.

Provides a chronicle of major events regarding the Patent and Trademark Office and of American patent and trademark policy from the enactment of the first patent act in 1790 to 1981.

1621. Postal Service. **History of the United States Postal Service, 1775-1982**. Rev. 1983. 27p. charts, tables. **P1.2:H62/775-982**.

Presents a brief history of the American postal system from colonial times to the present.

1622. Secret Service. **The Secret Service Story**. Rev. 1983. folder, 7p. ill. **T34.2: Se2/2/983**.

A brief history of the Secret Service, and a description of its missions.

1623. Small Business Administration. **Your Business and the SBA**. Rev. May 1983. 23p. **SBA1.2:B96/5/983**.

Describes the assistance available to small businesses, and how to get help from the Small Business Administration. Includes lists of SBA field offices.

1624. Veterans Administration. **VA History in Brief: What It Is, Was, and Does**. April 1983. 20p. ill. VA Pamphlet 06-83-1. **VA1.19:06-83-1**.

Provides a brief history of federal programs to assist military veterans before and after the establishment of the Veterans Administration in 1930. Includes list of VA facilities.

See also entries 21, 26, 38, 39, 40, 158, 160, 302, 411, 412, 413, 468, 542, 568, 1168, 1486, 1703.

GOVERNMENT PROPERTY:
PURCHASE AND SALES

1625. Defense Logistics Agency. **How to Buy Surplus Personal Property from the United States Government**. Rev. July 1981. 23p. maps. S/N 008-007-03269-1. $1.50. **D7.2:P94/4/981**.

Discusses types of property sold, methods of sale, and conditions of sale. Does not apply to real estate or military weapons.

1626. Department of Agriculture. **Selling to the USDA**. Rev. May 1983. 16p. tables. **A1.2:Se4/983**.

Includes directory of Department of Agriculture purchasing offices.

1627. Department of Commerce. **Commerce Business Daily**. Daily (except weekends and holidays). paging varies. S/N 703-013-00000-7. Symbol COBD. $81.00 per yr. No single copies sold. **C1.76:date**.

Provides a synopsis of U.S. government-proposed procurement for services and supplies, equipment, and materials. Provides list of unclassified contract awards exceeding $25,000 also broken down under services and supplies, equipment, and materials and under each category by a number of subclassifications. Also includes notices of surplus property sales, proposed foreign government standards which could affect U.S. exports, and search for research and development sources.

1628. Department of Commerce. **How to Sell to the United States Department of Commerce**. September 1984. 19p. S/N 003-000-00634-4. $1.50. **C1.2:Se4/2**.

Intended primarily for small, women-owned and minority-owned businesses.

1629. Department of Defense. **Selling to the Military: Army, Navy, Air Force, Defense Logistics Agency**. Rev. 1983. 141p. tables. S/N 008-000-00392-1. $6.00. **D1.2:Se4/983**.

Intended for businesses that have little or no experience in selling their products and services to the Department of Defense.

1630. Department of Energy. **Doing Business with the Department of Energy**. October 1984. 198p. ill., charts. DOE/MA-0164. **E1.35/2:0164**.

Intended primarily for small business, minority- and women-owned business, and labor surplus areas. References.

1631. Department of Justice. **Doing Business with the Department of Justice**. 1984. 36p. **J1.2:B96/2**.

Describes the organization and functions of major bureaus of the Department of Justice, lists what they buy, and provides contact points.

1632. Department of Labor. **What the U.S. Department of Labor Buys**. 1983. 31p. **L.12:B98/3**.

Provides basic information to prospective contractors on what and how the Department of Labor buy supplies and services and which offices are responsible for making purchases. References.

1633.   Department of State. **A Guide to Doing Business with the Department of State**. Rev. March 1985. 52p. Department and Foreign Service Series 351. Department of State Publication 9335. **S1.69:351/5**.

Designed to familiarize small, minority-, and female-owned businesses with the Department of State procurement program for various categories of supplies and services.

1634.   Department of the Interior. **This Is Interior: Contracting Guide**. 1982. 49p. **I1.77/2:In8**.

Identifies major Department of the Interior procurement offices, and some of the primary supplies and services purchased by each.

1635.   Department of the Treasury. **Selling to the Department of the Treasury**. Rev. April 1985. 30p. ill. **T1.2:Se4/985**.

Designed to provide information to small and minority-owned businesses on selling products and services to the Treasury Department.

1636.   Department of Transportation. **Contracting with the Department of Transportation**. Rev. November 1984. 43p. charts, tables. **TD1.2:C76/984-2**.

Describes major organizations within the Department of Transportation, their functions, what they buy, and their procurement offices.

1637.   General Services Administration. **Doing Business with the Federal Government**. Rev. October 1981. 42p. ill. S/N 022-000-00186-8. $4.50. **GS1.2:B96/2/981**.

Provides basic information on selling products and services to the civilian and military agencies of the U.S. government.

1638.   General Services Administration. **Guide to Specifications, Standards, and Commercial Item Descriptions of the Federal Government**. Rev. February 1984. 24p. ill. **GS2.6/3:Sp3/984**.

Intended primarily for small businesses to provide basic information on federal specifications, standards, and commercial item descriptions, their purposes, and uses.

1639.   General Services Administration. **How to Acquire Federal Real Property: A Guide for the Public's Use**. 1981. 63p. ill., charts. **GS1.6/6:P94/2**.

Describes the duties and responsibilities of the General Services Administration in the transfer and disposal of excess federal real property, and the steps that must be taken to acquire such property.

1640.   National Aeronautics and Space Administration. **Selling to NASA**. Rev. December 1984. 44p. ill. S/N 033-000-00925-9. $2.50. **NAS1.2:Se4/984**.

Designed to assist the prospective contractor in doing business with NASA. Describes major NASA field installations, the procurement process, and what NASA buys.

1641.   Naval Sea Systems Command. **Contracting Opportunities**. 3d ed. 1984. 172p. tables. **D211.2:C76/984**.

Includes guidelines for preparing more effective proposals; a listing of commodities and services which are contracted; and a qualified products list for military and federal specifications. References.

1642. Small Business Administration. **Small Business Subcontracting Directory**. 1984. 78p. **SBA1.2:Sm1/10**.

Provides a list of major prime contractors to the federal government arranged alphabetically within each of the ten SBA regions that offer the greatest potential for subcontracting to small businesses.

1643. Small Business Administration. **Women Business Owners: Selling to the Federal Government**. October 1984. 72p. **SBA1.2:W84/4**.

Describes how the federal government buys goods and services, and provides advice to women business owners on how to sell to the government. Includes samples of standard bid and procurement forms.

For additional publications on this topic see Subject Bibliography **SB-171, How to Sell to Government Agencies**.

Veterans and
Military Retirement

VETERANS

1644. Caring for the Older Veteran. Veterans Administration. July 1984. 125p. charts, tables. S/N 051-000-00168-1. $5.00. **VA1.2:V64/7**.

Profiles the aging issue, both in the population at large and in veterans. Highlights VA's existing capabilities, pilot programs, and research efforts directed at the aging issue. References.

1645. Data on Female Veterans, Fiscal Year 1983. Veterans Administration. July 1984. 54p. charts, tables. **VA1.2:F34/2**.

Presents national and state data on female veterans covering the following topics: population, health care, compensation and pensions, and education benefits.

1646. Directory of Veterans Administration Facilities. Veterans Administration. March 1983. 50p. tables. **VA1.2:D62**.

Contains a consolidated list of VA facilities by state. Also contains separate lists broken down by type of facility.

1647. Directory of Veterans Organizations, 1984. Veterans Administration. June 1984. 104p. **VA1.62:984**.

Includes lists of national veterans' service organizations, and of state departments of veterans affairs which are recognized by the VA.

1648. Federal Benefits for Veterans and Dependents. Veterans Administration. Rev. January 1985. 84p. tables. IS-1 Fact Sheet. S/N 051-000-00162-1. $2.25. **VA1.34: IS-1/28**.

Describes benefits available to veterans from the Veterans Administration and from other federal agencies. Includes directory of VA facilities. Index.

1649. **Interments in National Cemeteries**. Veterans Administration. Rev. December 1984. 8p. VA-DMA-IS-1. **VA1.53:1/6**.

Provides general information on eligibility and application for burial in national cemeteries administered by the Veterans Administration. Includes lists of cemeteries with information on availability of grave sites.

1650. **Myths and Realities: A Study of Attitudes toward Vietnam Era Veterans**. Congress. Senate. Committee on Veterans Affairs. July 1980. 529p. Committee Print No. 29. **Y4.V64/4:V67/10**.

Presents the results of a comprehensive survey of Vietnam veterans, the general public, employers, and educators regarding attitudes and problems for Vietnam veterans in adjusting to civilian life.

1651. **National Survey of Veterans: Summary Report**. Veterans Administration. January 1980. 142p. tables. **VA1.2:Su7/4**.

Summarizes the results of a 1977 mail survey covering the following: veterans' beneficiaries, medical care, compensation and pensions, GI insurance, education and rehabilitation, loan guaranty, and burial benefits.

1652. **Once a Veteran: Benefits, Rights, Obligations**. American Forces Information Service. Rev. 1984. 43p. DoD PA-5E. S/N 008-001-00144-4. $2.00. **D2.14:PA-5E/2**.

Provides information on eligibility, rights, and benefits for major veterans' programs. Includes directory of VA installations, state agencies, and places to get assistance.

1653. **Service Organizations' Representatives Currently Recognized in the Presentation of Claims before the Veterans Administration**. Veterans Administration. Rev. January 1983. 39p. tables. IB-2-151. **VA1.22:2-151/5**.

Provides a complete list of the name of accredited representatives of organizations recognized by the VA for the presentation of claims.

1654. **State Veterans' Laws**. Congress. House. Committee on Veterans' Affairs. Rev. 1984. 319p. Committee Print, 98th Congress, 2d Session. S/N 052-070-05914-1. $8.00. **Y4.V64/3:L41/2/984**.

Presents digests of state laws regarding the rights, benefits, and privileges of veterans and their dependents in effect as of February 1984.

1655. **Survey of Aging Veterans: A Study of the Means, Resources, and Future Expectations of Veterans Aged 55 and Over**. Veterans Administration. March 1984. 343p. tables. **VA1.2:Ag4/5**.

Presents the results of a national sample survey of older veterans covering socio-demographic characteristics, health status, economic resources, health insurance and medical services utilization, use of VA hospitals and services, and future expectations of veterans.

1656. **Veterans Day Ceremonies**. Veterans Administration. Rev. 1984. 13p. ill. **VA1.2:V64/4/984**.

Includes suggested community programs and classroom activities for celebration of Veterans Day, plus instructions on the correct display of the American flag.

1657. **Veterans in the United States: A Statistical Portrait from the 1980 Census**. Veterans Administration. July 1984. 54p. tables. **VA1.2:V64/8**.

Provides national data on the demographic and socioeconomic characteristics of veterans including age, period of service, marital status, education, employment and unemployment, and income.

For additional publications on this topic see Subject Bibliography **SB-080, Veterans Affairs and Benefits**.

MILITARY RETIREMENT
AND SURVIVORS' BENEFITS

1658. **A Complete Guide to the Survivor Benefit Plan for Military Retirees and Their Survivors**. Department of the Army. August 1983. 22p. ill., tables. DA Pamphlet 608-23. **D101.22:608-23**.

Provides a summary of benefits available to current and future military retirees under the Survivor Benefit Plan which was enacted in 1972.

1659. **A Guide to the Survivors of Deceased Army Members**. Department of the Army. Rev. July 1984. 60p. DA Pamphlet 608-4. **D101.22:608-4**.

Provides information on the rights and benefits available to the survivors of deceased military personnel.

1660. **Handbook on Retirement Services for Army Personnel and Their Families**. Department of the Army. Rev. 1982. 143p. DA Pamphlet 600-5. S/N 008-020-00912-1. $5.50. **D101.22:600-5/5**.

Provides information on the benefits, privileges, and responsibilities of military personnel entitled to retired pay.

1661. **Help Your Widow While She's Still Your Wife: A Guide to the Rights and Benefits for Widows of Retired Servicemembers**. Department of the Army. May 1983. 28p. ill., tables. DA Pamphlet 608-22. **D101.22:608-22**.

Provides information on the rights and benefits of spouses of deceased retired military personnel. Includes checklists and forms to enable retired members to place their personal affairs in order.

1662. **Marine Corps Retirement Guide**. Rev. September 1983. 121p. NAVMC 2642. **D214.9/2:R31/983**.

Describes the rights, benefits, and privileges available to retired Marine Corps military personnel. Provides advice on personal affairs, action required upon the death of a retired member, and employment of retired personnel.

1663. **Navy Guide for Retired Personnel and Their Families**. Bureau of Naval Personnel. Rev. March 1979. 158p. NAVPERS 15891E. S/N 008-047-00268-8. $6.50. **D208.6/3:R31/979**.

Provides comprehensive information on the rights, benefits, privileges, and responsibilities of retired naval personnel and their families.

Water

1664. **Clean Lakes and Us**. Environmental Protection Agency. March 1979. 37p. ill. EPA-440/5-79-021. S/N 055-001-01085-1. $4.50. **EP1.2:L14/5**.

Explains the geological and man-induced processes that form lakes, as well as the physical and biological principles that affect their quality. References.

1665. **Guidance Manual for Sewerless Sanitary Devices and Recycling Methods**. Department of Housing and Urban Development. July 1983. 189p. ill., charts, tables. HUD-PDR-738. **HH1.6/3:Se8**.

Provides technical information and criteria for selecting practical, effective, and affordable on-site wastewater treatment and disposal systems in rural and semirural communities. References.

1666. **Manual of Individual Water Supply Systems**. Environmental Protection Agency. Rev. October 1982. 163p. ill., tables. EPA-570/9-82-004. S/N 055-000-00229-1. $6.00. **EP2.8:In2/983**.

Intended for the individual or institution unable to obtain water from a community or public water system, and needing to choose and install an alternative water supply. Bibliography. Index.

1667. **Principal Rivers and Lakes of the World**. National Ocean Survey. July 1982. 56p. ill., maps, tables. Educational Pamphlet 10. **C55.431:10**.

Provides general information on the formation and importance of rivers and lakes. Includes tables which contain brief data on the principal rivers and lakes of the world.

1668. **Our Nation's Lakes**. Environmental Protection Agency. July 1980. 69p. ill. EPA-440/5-80-009. S/N 055-000-00197-9. $6.00. **EP1.2:L14/10**.

This colorfully illustrated booklet explains the many dynamic interactions that create a lake and keep it healthy. Describes ways in which lakes change and how carelessness can destroy them. Glossary. Reference.

1669. **Water in America, 1983**. Geological Survey. November 1983. 18p. ill., maps. S/N 024-000-00883-5. $1.75. **I19.2:W29/39**.

Looks at some of the policy issues in the Geological Survey's *National Water Summary, 1983*, including resolving interstate water conflicts, acid rain, salinity, and water claims of native Americans.

1670. **Water in the Urban Environment: Erosion and Sediment**. Geological Survey. 1981. 11p. ill. **I19.2:Er6/3**.

Discusses problems of erosion and sediment, methods of control, and local responsibility for preventing erosion.

1671. **Water Supply Sources for the Farmstead and Rural Home**. Department of Agriculture. Rev. November 1978. 18p. ill., tables. Farmers' Bulletin 2237. **A1.9:2237/4**.

Describes ground and surface water sources and how to develop them for the farmstead and rural home.

1672. **Water Wise: A Conservation Handbook**. Bureau of Reclamation. 1979. 20p. ill. **I27.19/2:W29/4**.

Discusses uses for water for cities and towns, farms, recreation, energy, fish, and wildlife. Suggests classroom activities for elementary and secondary schools.

1673. **Where to Get Information about Soil and Water Conservation**. Soil Conservation Service. Rev. September 1983. 16p. **A57.2:In3/2/983**.

Lists the names and telephone numbers of public information officers and conservation specialists at the headquarters of the Soil Conservation Service and its field offices.

Wetlands

1674. My Wetland Coloring Book. Environmental Protection Agency. 1980. 28p. ill. S/N 055-000-00187-1. $4.00. **EP1.2:W53**.

A coloring book designed to give children a better understanding of our wetlands and a growing concern for the fragile nature of the world around them.

1675. Our Nation's Wetlands: An Interagency Task Force Report. Council on Environmental Quality. 1978. 75p. ill. S/N 041-011-00045-9. **PrEx14.2:W53**.

Many full-color illustrations help to tell the story of America's wetlands. Describes the ways a wetland functions and how alterations can affect its natural balance. Footnote references.

1676. Wetlands of the United States: Current Status and Recent Trends. Fish and Wildlife Service. March 1984. 66p. ill., charts, maps. S/N 024-010-00656-1. $3.00. **I49.2:W53/8**.

Identifies the current status of U.S. wetlands and major areas where wetlands are in greatest jeopardy. Describes the major types of wetlands, and why they are important. References.

1677. Wetlands: Their Use and Regulation. Congress. Office of Technology Assessment. March 1984. 208p. ill., charts, maps, tables. OTA-O-206. S/N 052-003-00944-7. $8.00. **Y3.T22/2:2W53**.

Describes the ecological value of wetlands, trends in wetland use, and the effect of federal and state programs on wetlands. It discusses the current controversy between those who want to convert them to economic use and conservationists. Footnote references. Index.

Women

GENERAL

1678. **American Women: Three Decades of Change**. Bureau of the Census. 1983. 43p. ill. CDS 80-8. S/N 003-024-05743-3. $3.50. **C3.261:80-8**.

This demographic essay on women covers trends in marriage, divorce, widowhood, childbearing, education, earnings, and labor force participation from 1950 to 1980.

1679. **Report on Women in America**. Department of State. November 1977. 61p. ill. International Organization and Conference Series 132. Department of State Publication 8923. S/N 044-000-01670-2. $4.75. **S1.70:132**.

Prepared for International Women's Year. Provides brief summaries on women in American history, women's movement, combating discrimination, women and education and work, and economic and social agenda for women. References.

1680. **The Spirit of Houston: The First National Conference; An Official Report to the President, the Congress, and the People of the United States**. National Commission on the Observance of International Women's Year, 1978. 1978. 308p. ill. S/N 052-003-00505-1. $6.00. **Y3.W84:1/978**.

Contains the final report of the conference held in Houston on 18-21 November 1977.

1681. **A Statistical Portrait of Women in the United States: 1978**. Bureau of the Census. February 1980. 176p. charts, tables. Current Population Reports, Series P-23, No. 100. **C3.186:P-23/100**.

Provides a statistical overview on the changing status of women in American society during the 1970s.

1682. **Voices for Women, 1980: Report of the President's Advisory Committee for Women**. December 1980. 192p. ill., charts. S/N 029-002-00061-4. $7.00. **Pr39.8: W84/2/V87/980**.

Report of the ninth body appointed by the President since 1961 to study the status of women in the United States.

1683. **We, the American Women**. Bureau of the Census. Rev. November 1984. 16p. ill., charts, tables. S/N 003-024-05694-1. $1.00. **C3.2:Am3/6/no.2/984-2**.
Presents statistical highlights from the 1980 Census of Population and Housing on the status of American women.

1684. **Women of the World: Latin America and the Caribbean**. Bureau of the Census. 1984. 173p. charts, maps, tables. WID-1. S/N 003-024-05667-4. $5.50. **C3.2:W84/4**.
Presents detailed statistics and analyzes the condition of women in twenty-one countries of Latin America and the Caribbean region. Latin America consists of countries of Spanish, Portuguese, and French language and heritage.

1685. **Women of the World: Sub-Saharan Africa**. Bureau of the Census. 1984. 200p. charts, tables. WID-2. **C3.2:W84/5**.
Presents detailed statistics and analyzes the condition of women of over forty developing countries in the Sub-Saharan region of Africa.

1686. **Women's Rights in the United States of America**. Commission on Civil Rights. March 1979. 18p. Clearinghouse Publication 57. **CR1.10:57**.
This report was prepared for the Inter-American Commission on Women, Organization of American States. Footnote references.

See also entries 1061-8, 1645.

See also "Discrimination, Civil Rights, and Equal Opportunity" (entries 570-586).

For additional publications on this topic see Subject Bibliography **SB-111, Women**.

WOMEN AT WORK

1687. **Disabled Women in America: A Statistical Report Drawn from Census Bureau Data**. President's Committee on Employment of the Handicapped. 1984. 33p. charts. **PrEx1.10:D63/7**.
Presents data on the disability status of working women in America.

1688. **Going Strong! Women in Defense**. Department of Defense. 1984. 28p. ill. S/N 008-001-00146-1. $1.75. **D1.2:W84/5**.
Highlights contributions made by women in the Department of Defense, including enlisted and officer military personnel, civilian employees, and military wives.

1689. **Job Options for Women in the 80s**. Women's Bureau. 1980. 28p. ill., tables. Pamphlet 18. S/N 029-002-00059-2. $3.50. **L36.112:18**.
Discusses the status of women in the work force, the employment outlook for some jobs that may be in demand in the 1980s, and job hunting techniques.

1690.   **Military Women in the Department of Defense**. Department of Defense. April 1983. 48p. charts. S/N 008-000-00395-5. $4.00. **D1.2:W84/4**.

Contains three sections: a statistical look at women and men officers by grade, occupation, branch, experience, and education; similiar information for enlisted men and women; and a graph portrayal of advancement of women and men during the past decade.

1691.   **Perspectives on Working Women: A Databook**. Bureau of Labor Statistics. October 1980. 116p. tables. Bulletin 2080. S/N 029-001-02527-1. $5.50. **L2.3:2080**.

Presents a wide array of information on the characteristics of working women in the United States and their changing socioeconomic status, especially during the 1970s.

1692.   **The Relationship between Women's Studies, Career Development, and Vocational Choice**. National Institute of Education. February 1980. 70p. Women's Studies Monograph Series. **HE19.220:C18**.

Reviews and analyzes the literature on the relationship between women's studies, career development, and vocational choices. References. Bibliography.

1693.   **Time of Change: 1983 Handbook on Women Workers**. Women's Bureau. 1984. 192p. charts, tables. Bulletin 298. S/N 029-002-00065-7. $6.50. **L36.103:298**.

This update of the 1975 handbook through statistical data and accounts of legal developments documents the significant changes in the role of women in the labor force. Footnote references.

1694.   **United States Women in Aviation, 1919-1929**. Smithsonian Institution. 1983. 60p. Smithsonian Studies in Air and Space No. 5. S/N 047-002-00027-3. $2.75. **SI1.42:5**.

Discusses the activities and accomplishments of women pilots from 1919 to 1929. References.

1695.   **United States Women in Aviation through World War I**. Smithsonian Institution. 1978. 47p. ill. Smithsonian Studies in Air and Space No. 2. S/N 047-002-00023-1. $5.50. **SI1.42:2**.

Highlights the activities of women passengers, promoters, participants, pilots, and premier performers in aviation through World War I. References.

1696.   **Women at Work: A Chartbook**. Bureau of Labor Statistics. April 1983. 35p. charts. Bulletin 2168. S/N 029-001-02750-8. $4.00. **L2.3:2168**.

Focuses on women's economic activity: labor force trends, occupational and industrial employment patterns, unemployment, and market worth of women in a family context.

1697.   **Women in the Department of State: Their Role in American Foreign Affairs**. Department of State. September 1978. 329p. charts, tables. Department and Foreign Service Series 169. Department of State Publication 8951. **S1.69:169**.

Provides a broad historical account of the nearly two hundred years during which women have been striving to achieve a greater place in the Department of State and the Foreign Service. Does not discuss in depth policy matters or provide biographies, or include contributions of wives of Foreign Service personnel. Footnote references. Index.

1698. **Women's Guide to Apprenticeship**. Women's Bureau. 1980. 36p. ill. Pamphlet 17. S/N 029-002-00058-4. $3.00. **L36.112:17**.

Discusses problems that women encounter in seeking apprenticeship opportunities, and describes how the apprenticeship system operates.

1699. **A Working Woman's Guide to Her Job Rights**. Women's Bureau. Rev. 1984. 60p. Leaflet 55. S/N 029-002-00069-0. $2.25. **L36.112:55/5**.

Outlines women's legal rights related to promotion, training, and maternity leave, and defines the protection and services afforded under federal law.

See also entries 1315, 1461, 1499.

WOMEN IN BUSINESS

1700. **Ask US: U.S. Department of Commerce Programs to Aid Women Business Owners**. Department of Commerce. February 1984. 42p. **C3.2:W84/3**.

Provides a list of Commerce Department units and description of assistance they offer and the products they purchase; a primer on selling to the U.S. government; and a list of regional and district offices of Women in Business representatives throughout federal government agencies.

1701. **The Bottom Line: Equal Enterprise in America; Report of the President's Interagency Task Force on Women Business Owners**. June 1978. 242p. S/N 052-003-00550-6. $7.50. **Pr39.8:W84/En8**.

Includes the findings and recommendations of an interagency task force directed to identify the practices or conditions which discourage women from becoming entrepreneurs or have the effect of discriminating or placing them at a competitive disadvantage. References. Bibliography.

1702. **For Women: Managing Your Own Business: A Resource and Information Handbook**. Small Business Administration. March 1983. 232p. S/N 045-000-00217-9. $6.50. **SBA1.2:W84/2**.

Intended for the woman who is thinking of starting a business, or is already an owner. Glossary.

1703. **Women's Handbook: How SBA Can Help You Go into Business**. Small Business Administration. Rev. April 1983. 16p. **SBA1.2:W84/983**.

Provides information on the management, technical, and financial assistance available from or through the SBA to women entrepreneurs. References.

WOMEN: MEDICAL AND SOCIAL ISSUES

1704. **Childspacing among Birth Cohorts of American Women: 1905 to 1959**. Bureau of the Census. 1984. 119p. tables. Current Population Reports, Series P-20, No. 385. S/N 003-001-90784-4. $4.75. **C3.186:P20/385**.

Provides national data on the interval between first marriage and first birth, and the interval from second to fifth order births of American women born between 1905 and 1959.

1705. **Fertility of American Women: June 1983**. Bureau of the Census. 1984. 68p. tables. Current Population Reports, Series P-20, No. 395. S/N 003-001-90794-1. $2.75. **C3.186:P-20/395**.

Issued annually. Presents national data on the birth expectations of American women, and the number of children ever born by race, age, marital status, and selected socioeconomic characteristics. References.

1706. **The Menopause Time of Life**. National Institutes of Health. September 1983. 20p. NIH Publication No. 83-2461. **HE20.3002:M52/2**.

Discusses the natural process of menopause in women, and conditions which may require medical treatment. Provides advice on staying healthy following menopause.

1707. **Rape and Older Women**. National Institute of Mental Health. 1979. 180p. charts. DHHS Publication No. (ADM) 78-734. S/N 017-024-00849-4. $5.50. **HE20.8108:R18**.

Discusses the vulnerability of older women, the extent of victimization, special problems of rape, and avoidance of rape. Glossary. Bibliography.

1708. **Toxic Shock Syndrome and Tampons**. Food and Drug Administration. Rev. 1983. folder, 6p. DHHS Publication (FDA) 83-4169. **HE20.4002:T66/3/983**.

Provides answers to commonly asked questions about the causes, symptoms, treatment, and prevention of toxic shock syndrome.

1709. **Victims of Rape**. National Institute of Mental Health. 1977. 30p. DHEW Publication No. (ADM) 77-485. S/N 017-024-00683-1. $2.75. **HE20.8102:R18/2**.

Based on a Philadelphia study of rape victims, it describes the type of people raped, their reactions to the crime, reactions of society, and medical and criminal justice responses. References.

See also entries 117, 126, 506-10, 1468.

See also "Birth Control" (entries 216-230), and "Breast Cancer" (entries 935-944).

Appendix
Publications Catalogs

This list of catalogs provides references to aditional government publications of general interest. Many of these catalogs are serials which are published frequently at regular intervals, or are catalogs which are frequently revised. They thus provide information on revisions or later editions of titles listed in this guide, as well as on new titles.

1710.   Army Center of Military History. **Publications, Fall/Winter 1984-85**. 1984. 32p. ill. CMH Publication 105-1. **D114.10:984-85**.

Lists the in-print publications of the Army Center of Military History and its predecessor, the Office of the Chief of Military History. Many entries are annotated. Most titles are GPO sales publications, and stock numbers and prices are included.

1711.   **Bureau of the Census Catalog, 1984**. 1984. 268p. S/N 003 024 05668 2. $7.00. **C3.163/3:984**.

Issued annually. This catalog provides information about reports, machine-readable data files, microfiche, and maps which have been issued by the Bureau of the Census during the year. Includes abstracts, prices, and ordering information. Index.

1712.   Commission on Civil Rights. **Catalog of Publications**. Rev. May 1984. 26p. **CR1.9:C28/984**.

This annotated catalog lists in-print publications of the Commission on Civil Rights. Arrangement is by type of publication.

1713.   Congress. Office of Technology Assessment. **List of Publications**. Rev. December 1984. 61p. OTA-P-58. **Y3.T22/2:9P96/984-2**.

An annotated catalog of publications of the Office of Technology Assessment arranged by program area. Includes stock numbers, prices, and ordering information for sale and free publications.

1714. Congressional Budget Office. **List of Publications**. 1984. 90p. **Y10.14:984**.
Issued annually. This catalog includes a cumulative chronological as well as a topical listing of Congressional Budget Office publications.

1715. Congressional Research Service. **CRS Studies in the Public Domain**. Semi-annual. 15p. S/N 730-011-00000-8. Symbol CRSSC. $4.25. Single copy $2.50. **LC14.20:date**.
Lists studies and reports by CRS which have been printed in some form by the Government Printing Office. Most of these were part of committee prints or separate committee prints. Others were included in congressional hearings, reports, and documents and in the *Congressional Record*. Cumulative editions are published irregularly.

1716. Consumer Information Center. **Consumer Information Catalog**. Quarterly. 16p. **GS11.9:date**.
An annotated catalog of free and inexpensive popular U.S. government publications distributed by the Consumer Information Center, Pueblo, Colorado. Entries are organized under topics such as careers and education, federal benefits, food, gardening, health, housing, small business, travel and hobbies, and miscellaneous.

1717. Copyright Office. **Publications on Copyright**. Rev. August 1983. 11p. Circular R2. **LC3.4/2:2/14**.
Lists current publications of the Copyright Office which are available to the public. Publications are grouped according to the source providing them.

1718. Defense Logistics Agency. **Federal Supply Classification Listing of Department of Defense Standardization Documents**. July 1984. 809p. S/N 908-006-00000-3. Symbol FSCL. $37.00 per yr. (subscription includes basic catalog plus bimonthly supplements). **D7.14/2:984**.
Issued annually. A cumulative listing of current documents arranged alphabetically within a numerical listing by federal supply classification (FSC) code.

1719. Department of Defense. **Index of Specifications and Standards**. 2 pts. July 1984. Pt. 1. **Alphabetical Listing**. Pt. 2. **Numerical Listing**. 1392p. S/N 908-004-00000-1. Symbol DIS. $68.00 per yr. (includes basic catalog plus bimonthly supplements). **D7.14:984/pt.1,2**.
Issued annually. Lists unclassified federal, military and departmental specifications, standards, and related standardization documents, and those industry documents which have been coordinated for Department of Defense use.

1720. **Department of Health and Human Services Publications Catalog, 1983**. 1983. 388p. **HE1.18/3:983**.
Issued annually. This catalog contains the entries for Department of Health and Human Services publications (author symbol "HE") which were listed in the *Monthly Catalog of U.S. Government Publications* during the year. It also includes the seven indexes available in the *Monthly Catalog*.

1721. Federal Aviation Administration. **Guide to Federal Aviation Administration Publications**. Rev. June 1983. 57p. FAA-APA-PG-6. **TD4.17/6:6**.
Lists current and in-print publications of the Federal Aviation Administration. Includes availability and ordering information.

1722. **Federal Election Commission Free Publications.** Rev. December 1984. folder, 7p. **Y3.El2/3:2P96/2/984.**
An annotated list of free FEC publications. Includes order form.

1723. General Accounting Office. **Publications List.** Semiannual. 74p. **GA1.16/2: yr/no.**
Lists reports of GAO audits and surveys of federal government activities as well as miscellaneous GAO publications issued during the period. Arrangement is by broad government functions.

1724. General Services Administration. **Index of Federal Specifications, Standards, and Commercial Item Descriptions.** Rev. April 1984. 399p. tables. FPMR 101-29.1. S/N 022-001-00122-8. $13.00. **GS2.8/2:984.**
Issued annually. Includes alphabetical title and numerical document lists of current federal specifications and commercial items descriptions, and of current federal standards.

1725. Geological Survey. **Guide to Obtaining USGS Information.** Rev. 1985. 35p. tables. Circular 900. **I19.4/2:900.**
Descriptions of information sources are arranged by subject (product type, office function, or field of earth science) with USGS sources preceding other federal, state, or private organizations.

1726. Geological Survey. **Publications of the Geological Survey, 1984.** 1985. 330p. **I19.14:984.**
Issued annually. Lists publications and maps (except topographic quadrangle maps) that were issued by the Geological Survey during the year, plus articles by USGS personnel published in outside journals and books. Subject and geographic index, and author index.

1727. Government Printing Office. **Government Periodicals and Subscription Services.** Quarterly. 65p. Price List No. 36. **GP3.9:36/no.**
This annotated catalog lists periodicals and subscriptions which are available on annual subscription from the Superintendent of Documents. Price and order information are provided. Agency index.

1728. Government Printing Office. **GPO Sales Publications Reference File.** Bimonthly. approx. 240 fiche. S/N 721-002-00000-4. Symbol PRF. $142 per yr. Single copy $26.00. **GP3.22/3:yr/no.**
A microfiche catalog of in-print publications offered for sale by the Superintendent of Documents. Arranged in three sequences: GPO stock number; Superintendent of Documents classification number; and alphabetical arrangement of subjects, titles, agencies series and report numbers, key words and phrases, and personal authors. Entries in each sequence provide the full record with bibliographic and order information. A complete file is mailed in odd numbered months; a one fiche supplement, *GPO New Sales Publications*, which lists new publications in a single title listing is mailed separately in even numbered months.

1729. Government Printing Office. **List of Classes of United States Government Publications Available for Selection by Depository Libraries.** Quarterly. 150p. S/N 721-007-00000-6. $24.00 per yr. Single copy $6.00. **GP3.24:yr/no.**

Lists the U.S. government publications series which are available for selection by federal depository libraries. Entries are arranged by Superintendent of Documents (SuDocs) alphanumeric class stem, and include the title of the series, depository item number, and code to designate whether distributed in paper or microform format.

1730. Government Printing Office. **Monthly Catalog of United States Government Publications.** Monthly, plus **Periodicals Supplement** and biennial and annual cumulative indexes. Symbol MCM. S/N 721-003-00000-1 (paper). $217.00 per yr. Single monthly copy $17.00. Semiannual index (January-June), $46.00. Annual index, $75.00. *Periodicals Supplement*, $17.00. S/N 721-005-00000-3 (microfiche). $59.00 per yr. Single monthly copy, $3.75. Semiannual index, $5.50. Annual index, $10.00. *Periodicals Supplement* $3.50. **GP3.8:yr/mo.**

This is the "comprehensive index" of publications issued by U.S. government agencies. Arranged by Superintendent of Documents (SuDocs) classification number, or agency. Entries provide the complete catalog record according to AACR2 standards which has been entered into the OCLC database. Each monthly issue has six indexes: author, title, subject, series/report, stock number, and title keyword. The semiannual and annual indexes have a seventh index by SuDocs classification number.

1731. Government Printing Office. **New Books.** Bimonthly. approx. 18p. **GP3.17/6: vol/no.**

Provides a complete list of items which have been added to the GPO sales publications program during the period. Entries are arranged by broad topics, and include title, date, pagination, Superintendent of Documents number, stock number, and price.

1732. Government Printing Office. **Subject Bibliography** series. SB-no. **GP3.22/2:no.**

Subject Bibliographies provide a list of in-print publications for sale by the Superintendent of Documents on a wide variety of topics. They are available free from the Superintendent of Documents, U.S. Government Printing Office, Washington, DC 20402. An Index issue **(SB-599)** includes an order form for the Subject Bibliographies and is also available free on request. The approximately 250 current Subject Bibliographies (SBs) are listed below alphabetically by title.

Accidents and Accident Prevention. SB-229.

Accounting and Auditing. SB-042.

Adult Education. SB-214.

Africa. SB-284.

Aging. SB-39.

Agricultural Research, Statistics, Economic Reports. SB-162.

Agricultural Yearbooks. SB-031.

Air Force Manuals. SB-182.

Air Pollution. SB-46.

Aircraft, Airports, and Airways. SB-013.

Airman's Information Manual. SB-014.

Alcohol, Tobacco and Firearms. SB-246.

Alcoholism. SB-175.

American Revolution. SB-144.

Annual Reports. SB-118.

Anthropology and Archeology. SB-205.

Architecture. SB-215.

Armed Forces. SB-131.

Army Corps of Engineers. SB-261.

Army Technical and Field Manuals. SB-158.

Art and Artists. SB-107.

Asia and Oceania. SB-288.

Astronomy and Astrophysics. SB-115.

Atomic Energy and Nuclear Power. SB-200.

Aviation Information and Training Materials. SB-018.

Background Notes. SB-093.

Banks and Banking. SB-128.

Birds. SB-177.

Board of Tax Appeals and Tax Court Reports. SB-067.

Budget of the United States Government and Economic Report of the President.
SB-204.

Building Science Series. SB-138.

Bureau of Land Management Publications. SB-256.

Bureau of Reclamation Publications. SB-249.

Business and Business Management. SB-004.

Canada. SB-278.

Canning, Freezing, and Storage of Foods. SB-005.

Care and Disorders of the Eyes. SB-028.

Census of Agriculture. SB-277.

Census of Business. SB-152.

Census of Construction. SB-157.

Dentisty. SB-022.

Digest of U.S. Practice in International Law and Digest of International Law. SB-185.

Directories and Lists of Persons and Organizations. SB-114.

Disarmament and Arms Control. SB-127.

Disaster Preparedness and Civil Defense. SB-241.

Diseases in Humans. SB-008.

Drug Education. SB-163.

Earth Sciences. SB-160.

Educational Statistics. SB-083.

Electricity and Electronics. SB-053.

Elementary Education. SB-096.

Employment and Occupations. SB-044.

Energy Conservation and Research Technology. SB-306.

Energy Management for Consumers and Business. SB-303.

Energy Policy, Issues and Programs. SB-305.

Energy Supplies, Prices and Consumption. SB-304.

Engineering other than Civil. SB-132.

Environmental Education and Protection. SB-088.

Europe (including the United Kingdom). SB-289.

Family Planning. SB-292.

Farms and Farming. SB-161.

Federal Aviation Regulations. SB-012.

Federal Communications Commission Publications. SB-281.

Federal Government. SB-141.

Federal Government Forms. SB-090.

Federal Maritime Commission Publications. SB-190.

Federal Trade Commission Publications. SB-100.

Financial Aid to Students. SB-085.

Firefighting, Prevention, and Forest Fires. SB-076.

Fish and Marine Life. SB-209.

Food, Diet and Nutrition. SB-291.

Foreign Affairs of the United States. SB-075.

Foreign Area Studies. SB-166.

Foreign Education. SB-235.

Foreign Investments. SB-275.

Foreign Languages. SB-082.

Foreign Relations of the United States. SB-210.

Foreign Trade and Tariff. SB-123.

Fossils. SB-143.

Gardening. SB-301.

General Accounting Office Publications. SB-250.

General Services Administration Publications. SB-247.

Government Printing Office Publications. SB-244.

Government Specifications and Standards. SB-231.

Grants and Awards. SB-258.

The Handicapped. SB-037.

Hearing and Hearing Disability. SB-023.

Heart and Circulatory System. SB-104.

High School Debate Topic, Publications Relating to. SB-043.

Higher Education. SB-217.

Highway Construction, Safety, and Traffic. SB-003.

Historical Handbook Series. SB-016.

The Home. SB-041.

Home Economics. SB-276.

Hospitals. SB-119.

Housing, Urban and Rural Development. SB-280.

How to Sell to Government Agencies. SB-171.

Immigration, Naturalization, and Citizenship. SB-069.

Insects. SB-034.

Insurance. SB-294.

Intergovernmental Relations. SB-211.

Internal Revenue Service Cumulative Bulletins. SB-066.

Interstate Commerce Commission Publications. SB-187.

Irrigation and Drainage. SB-094.

Juvenile Delidnquency. SB-074.

Labor-Management Relations. SB-064.

Latin America and the Caribbean. SB-287.

Law Enforcement. SB-117.

Libraries and Library Collections. SB-150.

Livestock and Poultry. SB-010.

Mammals and Reptiles. SB-070.

Maps and Atlases (U.S. and Foreign). SB-102.

Marine Corps Publications. SB-237.

Marketing Research. SB-125.

Mass Transit. SB-055.

Mathematics. SB-024.

Medicine and Medical Science. SB-154.

Mental Health. SB-167.

Middle East. SB-286.

Military History. SB-098.

Minerals and Mining. SB-151.

Minerals Yearbook. SB-099.

Minorities. SB-006.

Motion Pictures, Films, and Audiovisual Information. SB-073.

Motor Vehicles. SB-049.

Music. SB-221.

NASA Educational Publications. SB-222.

NASA Scientific and Technical Publications. SB-257.

National and World Economy. SB-097.

National Bureau of Standards Handbooks and Monographs. SB-133.

National Bureau of Standards Special Publications. SB-271.

National Bureau of Standards Technical Notes. SB-148.

National Credit Union Administration Publications. SB-267.

National Defense and Security. SB-153.

National Ocean Survey Publications. SB-260.

National Park Service Folders. SB-170.

National Science Foundation Publications. SB-220.

National Standard Reference Data Series. SB-139.

Naval Facilities Engineering Command Publications. SB-219.

Naval History. SB-236.

Naval Personnel Bureau and Naval Education and Training Command Publications. SB-173.

Navigation. SB-029.

Noise Abatement. SB-063.

Nurses and Nursing Care. SB-019.

Occupational Outlook Handbook. SB-270.

Occupational Safety and Health. SB-213.

Oceanography. SB-032.

Office of Personnel Management Publications. SB-300.

Patents and Trademarks. SB-021.

Personnel Management, Guidance, and Counseling. SB-202.

Pesticides, Insecticides, Fungicides, and Rodenticides. SB-227.

Photography. SB-072.

Physical Fitness. SB-239.

Poetry and Literature. SB-142.

Postal Service. SB-169.

Posters, Charts, Picture Sets, and Decals. SB-057.

Presidents of the United States. SB-106.

Prices, Wages, and Cost of Living. SB-226.

Printing and Graphic Arts. SB-077.

Procurement, Supply Cataloging, and Classification. SB-129.

Public and Private Utilities. SB-298.

Public Buildings, Landmarks, and Historical Sites of the United States. SB-140.

Public Health. SB-122.

Radiation and Radioactivity. SB-048.

Railroads. SB-218.

Reading. SB-164.

Recreational and Outdoor Activities. SB-017.

Rehabilitation. SB-081.

Retirement. SB-285.

Revenue Sharing. SB-059.

Rural Electrification Administration (REA) Forms and Bulletins. SB-168.

School Administration, Buildings, and Equipment. SB-223.

Science Experiments and Projects. SB-243.

Secondary Education. SB-068.

Securities and Investments. SB-295.

Shipping and Transportation. SB-040.

Ships, Shipping, and Shipbuilding. SB-225.

Small Business. SB-307.

Smithsonian Institution Popular Publications. SB-252.

Smoking. SB-015.

Social Security. SB-165.

Social Welfare and Services. SB-030.

Soil and Soils Management. SB-007.

Solar Energy. SB-009.

Soviet Union. SB-279.

Space, Rockets, and Satellites. SB-297.

Spanish Publications. SB-130.

Statistical Publications. SB-273.

Stenography, Typing, and Writing. SB-087.

Subversive Activities. SB-259.

Surveying and Mapping. SB-183.

Taxes and Taxation. SB-195.

Teachers and Teaching Methods. SB-137.

Telecommunications. SB-296.

Travel and Tourism. SB-302.

Treaties and Other International Agreements of the United States. SB-191.

Trees, Forest Products, and Forest Management. SB-086.

United States Code. SB-197.

United States Intelligence Activities. SB-272.

United States Postage Stamps. SB-011.

United States Reports. SB-025.

Veterans Affairs and Benefits. SB-080.

Vital and Health Statistics. SB-121.

Vocational and Career Education. SB-245.

Waste Management. SB-095.

Water Pollution and Water Resources. SB-050.

Weather. SB-234.

Weights and Measures. SB-109.

Wildlife Management. SB-116.

Women. SB-111.

1733. Government Printing Office. **U.S. Government Books**. Quarterly. 56p. ill. **GP3.17/5:vol/no.**

An annotated and illustrated catalog of approximately one thousand U.S. government publications of broad general interest which are in print and sold by the Superintendent of Documents. The initial section includes "New Releases." Following sections are arranged by broad topics from "Agriculture" to "Vacation and Travel." Order forms are included.

1734. Internal Revenue Service. **Publications Catalog**. Rev. August 1984. 57p. Publication 987. **T22.44/2:987/2.**

Lists numerically, alphabetically by title, and functionally all IRS publications and documents issued by the National Office. Also includes list of titles which are new, revised, or obsolete since the last edition.

1735. Internal Revenue Service. **Reference Listing of Federal Tax Forms and Publications**. December 1984. 44p. Publication 1200. **T22.44/2:1200.**

Includes annotated numerical lists of IRS forms and IRS publications, and a separate subject index to each list.

1736. **Library of Congress Publications in Print, 1983**. Rev. 1983. 105p. **LC1.12/2: P96/983.**

Issued biennially. An annotated listing of in-print books, pamphlets, and serials published by the Library of Congress. Entries are arranged alphabetically by title. Includes price and order information. Index.

1737. **Library of Congress Selected Publications, 1984**. 1984. 27p. ill. **LC1.12/2: P96/2/984.**

Issued annually. Provides detailed abstracts of significant publications which were issued during the year. Order information is provided.

1738. Library of Congress. **Popular Names of U.S. Government Reports: A Catalog**. 4th ed. 1984. 272p. S/N 030-005-00012-1. $12.00. **LC6.2:G74/984.**

Lists over fifteen hundred government reports by their popular names, usually the name of the person, subject matter, or geographical descriptor associated with the report. Index.

1739.   National Aeronautics and Space Administration. **Records of Achievement: NASA Special Publications**. 1983. 146p. ill. NASA SP-470. **NAS1.21:470**.
This annotated catalog lists all numbered publications issued in the NASA Special Publications (SP) series. Also includes selected list of numbered reports in the Conference Publication (NASA CP) and Reference Publication (NASA RP) series which were intended primarily for the general public.

1740.   National Archives and Records Service. **Select List of Publications of the National Archives and Records Service**. Rev. 1982. 67p. General Information Leaflet 6. **GS4.22:3/6**.
Lists current publications of the National Archives and Records Service.

1741.   National Cancer Institute. **Publications List for the Public and Patients**. Rev. March 1985. 9p. **HE20.3183:985/1**.
An annotated list of free National Cancer Institute publications.

1742.   National Center for Health Statistics. **Catalog of Publications of the National Center for Health Statistics, 1979-1983**. Rev. June 1984. 29p. **HE20.6216:C28/979-83**.
Issued annually. Presents a numerical list of reports published during the latest five-year period. Index.

1743.   National Technical Information Service. **General Catalog of Information Services. No. 8a**. Rev. 1983. 40p. **C51.11/4:8a**.
Describes the major products and services of the National Technical Information Service (NTIS).

1744.   Naval Historical Center. **Naval Historical Publications in Print**. Rev. August 1981. 21p. **D207.11:H62/3/981**.
Lists and describes current publications of the Naval Historical Center and its predecessor organizations known as the Naval History Division, and Office of Naval Records and Library. Many entries are annotated. Includes stock number for GPO sales publications.

1745.   **Office of Air Force History Publications**. 1984. 22p. **D301.62/2:9P96**.
An annotated list of Office of Air Force History publications. Includes out-of-print titles, and stock number and price for in-print titles.

1746.   Small Business Administration. **For Sale Management Assistance Publications**. Rev. June 1984. folder, 5p. **SBA1.2:M31/16/984**.
Includes titles, stock numbers, and prices of SBA management assistance publications which are sold by the Superintendent of Documents.

1747.   Small Business Administration. **Free Management Assistance Publications**. Rev. May 1984. folder, 5p. **SBA1.18:984**.
Lists the titles and series of SBA management assistance publications which are available free from the Small Business Administration.

1748.   Soil Conservation Service. **List of Published Soil Surveys: January 1985**. 1985. 29p. **A57.38:list/985**.
Lists the most recently published soil survey for counties (or areas) in the United States. Arranged alphabetically by state, then by county or area.

Title Index

Citations refer to entry numbers.

Subject Index

Subjects shown in bold type are the topics and subtopics under which publications are arranged within this book. For citations to publications on individual countries, refer to the title index under the name of the country. Citations refer to entry numbers.

Accidents, accident prevention, and safety, 1-16. *See also* 73, 83, 174, 185, 238, 242, 369, 443, 708, 731, 733, 1104, 1106, 1373, 1374, 1535
Accounting, 292
Acid rain, 691, 692
Ada programming language, 456
Adams National Historical Site, 1052
Adolescence and youth, 361-367. *See also* 118, 121, 123, 124, 129, 130, 135, 136, 140, 141, 142, 145, 146, 216-223, 349, 508, 955, 974, 987, 1404, 1470, 1473
Aerial bombing, 1250-4, 1274, 1278
Aerial photographs, 1171, 1177-7
Aeromedical evacuation, 1281
Aeronautics and aviation, 28-34. *See also* 324, 406, 412, 525, 709-4, 1062-24, 1694, 1695
Aeronautics and space sciences, 17-62. *See also* 710, 711
Aerospace doctrine, 1200
Affirmative action, 583
Africa, Sub-Saharan, 1685
Agate Fossil Beds National Monument, 1061-5
Agent Orange, 1275

Aging and Problems of the Elderly, 63-82. *See also* 506-12, 931, 932, 989, 1045, 1049, 1312, 1314, 1315, 1336, 1506, 1508, 1535, 1644, 1655; **Medicare and medical insurance; Social security; Veterans and military retirement**
Agriculture and farming, 89-110. *See also* 449, 506-7, 547-3, 1152, 1154, 1399, 1413, 1423, 1429, 1671, 1707
Aid to families with dependent children (AFDC), 1438, 1446
Air base defense, 1266
Air force, 1197-1216. *See also* 1194, 1432-1434; Department of the Air Force; United States Air Force
Air pollution, 691-696. *See also* 182
Air transportation, 35-40. *See also* 324, 898
Aircraft carriers, 1227-2
Airmobility, 1286-1
Alabama, 1419-2
Alaska, 1061-21, 1419-1
Alcohol abuse and alcoholism, 112-122. *See also* 184
Allergies, 923-930

Families, 697-704. *See also* 81, 127, 128, 247, 257, 365, 366, 500, 961, 1068, 1071, 1312
Farmers Home Administration, 1612
Farming. *See* **Agriculture and farming**
Federal agencies: History, organization, services, 1602-1624. *See also* 21, 26, 38, 39, 40, 158, 160, 302, 411, 412, 413, 468, 542, 568, 1168, 1486, 1703
Federal Aviation Administration, 37, 38, 39, 1721
Federal Communications Commission, 467
Federal Election Commission, 1722
Federal Energy Regulatory Commission, 1340
Federal information centers, 827
Federal Textbook on Citizenship, 387, 388
Federal Trade Commission, 465, 1613
Feet, 989
Fertility, 1705
Field artillery, 1286-9
Films and audiovisual materials, 705-712. *See also* 987
Finance. *See* **Banking, finance, and investment**
Fingerprints, 513
Fire Island, 202
Firearms, explosives, and gun control, 713-726
Fireplaces, 1098, 1107
Fires, fire prevention and safety, 727-733. *See also* 506-1, 567, 709-3, 824
First aid and emergency treatment, 734-738. *See also* 11, 13, 1379
First Ladies, 1566
Fishing, 209, 210, 213, 233, 1177-5
Fixed-wing gunships, 1272
Flags, 462, 464, 1229
Floods, 414-418. *See also* 567
Florida, 203, 1419-10
Flowering crabapples, 841
Flowering perennials, 842
Flowers, 837-845
Fluoride, 982
Food and nutrition, 739-799. *See also* 74, 85, 97, 110, 247, 680, 689, 1440
Food buying guides, 753-763. *See also* 244
Food preservation and storage, 764-773
Food stamps, 1440, 1442

Ford's Theatre and the house where Lincoln died, 1062-2
Foreign affairs, 1574-1586. *See also* 326, 531, 533, 536, 539
Foreign area studies, 800-813. *See also* *individual countries in the* Title Index
Foreign consular offices, 1577
Foreign education. *See* **Education in foreign countries**
Foreign languages, 809-813. *See also* 604, 709-5
Forensic science, 510, 511, 512
Forests and forestry, 814-824. *See also* 689
Fort Bowie, 1247
Fort Davis National Historic Site, 1062-28
Fort Huachuca, 1248
Fort Laramie National Historic Site, 1061-16, 1062-11
Fort McHenry National Monument, 1062-3
Fort Necessity, 1235
Fort Pulaski National Monument, 1062-10
Fort Sumter National Monument, 1061-24, 1062-8
Fort Union National Monument, 1062-25
Fort Vancouver National Historic Site, 1061-11
FORTRAN, 452
Forts, 1428
Foulois, Benjamin D., 1202
Franchising, 294, 295
Franklin, Benjamin, 1061-12
Frauds, 67, 506-3
Fredericksburg (battle), 1062-29
Freedom of information, privacy, and information policy, 825-833. *See also* 457, 1164, 1169
Freer Gallery of Art, 158
Freezing foods, 764, 767
French (language), 809, 810, 813-5
Fruits, 746-5, 756, 757, 765, 767, 773, 846-850
Funerals, 474, 478, 1649

Gardens and gardening, 834-873
Gas utilities. *See* **Electric and natural gas utilities**
Gaslighting, 1063
Geese, 106

Livestock, 1399
Logistics, 1242, 1286-12, 1289
Lou Gehrig's disease, 1006
Louisiana, 1062-19, 1419-4
Luftwaffe, 1258
Lungs, 966-8, 1041

Mail order, 465
Maine, 1419-18
Mainstreaming preschoolers series, 383
Management audit, 297, 298
Manassas (Bull Run) National Battle-
    field Park, 1062-9
Manufactures, 292, 547-15
Maps and mapping, 1171-1178. *See*
    also 235, 408, 415, 547-8, 1452
Marijuana, 132, 133, 138
Marine Corps, 1217-1222. *See also*
    462, 1132, 1240, 1435, 1662;
    United States Marine Corps
Marketing in [foreign countries] series,
    285. *See also individual coun-*
    tries in the Title Index.
Marksmanship, 1222
Mars, 52, 60
Maryland, 1061-4, 1061-8, 1062-21,
    1419-8
Masks, respiratory, 16
Massachusetts, 585, 1052, 1419-19
Mastectomy, 941
Mathematics, 357-2, 1456
Mayaguez Affair, 1280
Mcat, 754, 759, 760, 761, 766
Meat and poultry, 779-783
Medal of Honor, 1182, 1267, 1317
Medals, 440, 441
Medicaid, 1048
Medical care. *See* **Health and medical**
    care
Medicare and medical insurance,
    1046-1051
Medicines, 88, 917, 919
Mediterranean theater of operations,
    1259-4
MEDLARS, 1161
Melanoma, 969
Menopause, 1706
Mental health and mental disorders,
    1000-1015. *See also* 383-5
Mercury spacecraft, 59
Metric system, 286, 1454
Mexico, 1529
Michigan, 1419-20
Middle East, 1532

Mildew, 434
Military affairs and history, 1179-1304
Military aircraft, 1201, 1430, 1433, 1434
Military history, 1189-1196. *See also*
    1744, 1745
Military intelligence, 1286-16
Military leadership, 1184
Military pay, 1183
Military retirement and survivor's
    benefits, 1658-1663. *See also* 338
Military uniforms, 1424, 1435
Military weapons, 1216
Mining and prospecting, 1305-1311. *See*
    also 547-16, 1353
Minnesota, 1419-21
Minorities and ethnic studies, 1312-1334.
    See also 302, 547-1, 579, 1165,
    1461
Miscellaneous health and medical prob-
    lems, 1031-1045. *See also* 363,
    383-2, 472, 1383
Missiles, 1201, 1362
Mississippi, 1062-12, 1419-2
Missouri, 1419-22
Mites, 1382
Mold allergy, 929
Money. *See* Currency
Montana, 1062-1, 1338-2, 1419-27
Moon exploration. *See* Apollo
    spacecraft
Morristown National Historical Park,
    1061-18
Mortages, 1112
Motels, 1522
Moths, 1387, 1388
Mount St. Helens, 883, 884, 886
Movers, 477
Multiple sclerosis, 1023
Museums, 305, 1192
Music, 162
MX missile, 1362
Myeloma, 970

Napoli translation card, 813-8
Narcotics, 134
National Aeronautics and Space Admin-
    istration, 21-27, 710, 711, 1640,
    1739
National Agricultural Lands Study,
    1152, 1154
National Archives and Records Service,
    148, 149, 150, 153, 1740
National Bipartisan Commission on
    Central America, 1579

Okinawa (battle), 1259-9
Oklahoma, 1338-4, 1419-29
Omaha beachhead, 1252-1
Operations research, 1286-17
Ordnance Department, 1259-7
Oregon, 1061-3, 1338-1, 1419-1
Orthopedic handicaps, 383-6
Outdoor recreation, 1368-1374

Pacific Ocean, 210, 1419-12
Pacific theater of operations, 1259-9
Paget's disease, 1045
Painting, 1086
Parachute units, 1260
Parkinson's disease, 1025
Patent and Trademark Office, 485,
    486, 1620
Patents, 488, 490, 491, 492
Pearl Harbor, 1257
Pennsylvania, 1062-6, 1419-30
Peonies, 843
People's Republic of China, 1533
Peptic ulcer, 1039
Periodicals, 1727
Pests and pest control, 1375-1398. *See
    also* 104, 862, 863, 885
Petersburg (battle), 1245
Pets and animal care, 1399-1402. *See
    also* 528
Physical fitness, 1403-1412. *See also* 975
Pickles, 770
Pilots, 31, 32, 33, 34, 525
Pioneer spacecraft, 53, 62
Pistols. *See* Revolvers and pistols
Plant tours, 1524
Plantings, 199, 200
Play, 357-3, 377, 378
Pocket guide to [foreign countries]
    series, 1541. *See also individual
    countries in the* Title Index
Poetry, 166
Poison ivy, 930, 1394
Poison oak, 1394
Poison sumac, 1394
Poisons, 3, 8, 910
Police and law enforcement, 515-518.
    See also 709-3
Polygraphs, 514
Population, 545, 546, 547-7, 551, 552,
    553, 560, 805
Pork, 105, 746-7, 781
Porpoises, 204, 205
Port guide series, 1542
Portuguese (language), 811, 813-10

Post report series, 1543. *See also
    individual countries in the* Title
    Index
Postal service, 1413-1422
Posters, 1423-1436. *See also* 458, 459,
    461
Poultry, 746-8, 760, 761, 766, 782
Poverty, 541, 1437, 1439
Prenatal and infant care, 344-353. *See
    also* 113, 243, 1035, 1039
President, 1565-1573. *See also* 630, 631,
    1062-2, 1062-16
Presidential Commission on Drunk
    Driving, 122
Presidential Commission on World
    Hunger, 1122
President's Advisory Committee for
    Women, 1682
President's Commission for a National
    Agenda for the Eighties, 1478
President's Commission for the Study
    of Ethical Problems in Medicine
    and Biomedical and Behavioral
    Research, 1475
President's Commission on Foreign
    Language Instruction and Inter-
    national Studies, 604
President's Commission on Housing,
    1072
President's Commission on the Holo-
    caust, 1123
President's Interagency Task Force on
    Women Business Owners, 1701
President's Private Sector Survey on
    Cost Control, 1546, 1553, 1597
President's Task Force on Victims of
    Crime, 501
Prisoners of war, 1186, 1187
Privacy, 457, 828, 833
Prospecting, 1309
Puberty, 363
Public assistance programs, poverty,
    1437-1447. *See also* 530
Public lands, 1448-1453. *See also* 1308,
    1310, 1311, 1370
Public transportation, 1519
Publications catalogs, 1710-1748
Publications reference file, 1728
Pulmonary disease, 1034
Purchasing, 301

Radiation therapy, 943, 956, 957
Radioactive materials, 13
Radishes, 857